Living with Florida's Atlantic Beaches

Living with the Shore

Series editors, Orrin H. Pilkey and William J. Neal

Living with Florida's Atlantic Beaches

Coastal Hazards from Amelia Island to Key West

David M. Bush   William J. Neal   Norma J. Longo

Kenyon C. Lindeman   Deborah F. Pilkey   Luciana Slomp Esteves

John D. Congleton   Orrin H. Pilkey

DUKE UNIVERSITY PRESS   Durham and London 2004

Living with the Shore Series

Publication of 22 volumes in the Living with the Shore series has been funded by the Federal Emergency Management Agency.

Publication has been greatly assisted by the following individuals and organizations: the American Conservation Association, an anonymous Texas foundation, the Charleston Natural History Society, the Office of Coastal Zone Management (NOAA), the Geraldine R. Dodge Foundation, the William H. Donner Foundation, Inc., the George Gund Foundation, the Mobil Oil Corporation, Elizabeth O'Connor, the Sapelo Island Research Foundation, the Sea Grant programs in New Jersey, North Carolina, Florida, Mississippi/ Alabama, and New York, The Fund for New Jersey, M. Harvey Weil, Patrick H. Welder Jr., and the Water Resources Institute of Grand Valley State University. The Living with the Shore series is a product of the Duke University Program for the Study of Developed Shorelines, which was initially funded by the Donner Foundation.

Contents

List of Figures, Tables, and Risk Maps

Figures

Tables

Risk Maps

Preface

In 1984 we produced *Living with the East Florida Shore*, which summarized coastal hazards and the human response to such hazards, and provided citizens with guidelines to reduce the vulnerability of their property to coastal processes. The East Florida and West Florida volumes were two of the more popular of the twenty-plus volumes in the Living with the Shore series and went out of print.

Much has changed along this coast since 1984, not the least being the impact of Hurricane Andrew in 1992, the costliest natural disaster in U.S. history, and the massive evacuation problems caused by the threat of Hurricane Floyd in 1999. Development has greatly increased, beach erosion is perceived as a greater problem, the response to dredge-and-fill beaches is more widespread and costly, regulations have changed (e.g., the 2001 Florida Building Code), and risk mapping has improved. As a result, we decided the time was right to produce new volumes for both East and West Florida.

During the past eighteen years, East Florida experienced huge property losses in Hurricane Andrew and several lesser storms, and residents learned valuable lessons from storm losses in other areas, particularly from Hurricanes Hugo, Opal, and Fran. These disasters provided new insights into how construction techniques and coastal regulations could be improved to reduce property losses, how to better manage protective beaches and dunes, and the need for new approaches to property damage mitigation. During the same period, our knowledge of coastal evolution, especially of barrier island dynamics, has grown. Our approach to evaluating coastal development risk has progressed and expanded as a result. Risk-mapping techniques have grown from a focus only on the shoreline and the obvious property at risk to a whole-island or "coastal zone" approach. Even the philosophy of shoreline stabilization has changed from an emphasis on engineering structures such as seawalls and groins to beach dredge-and-fill and the ultimate mitigation option of choice: relocation. Some coastal regulations have changed, moving in the direction of resource management and risk reduction.

Unfortunately, not all of the changes have been positive. The population concentrated in the coastal zone continues to increase. More people and property are at risk, and the majority of these coastal dwellers are unaware, inexperienced, or complacent about the dangers they face in living on the coast. The recovery period after storms has not been a time of prudent corrections of past mistakes; rather, the reconstruction has replaced beach cottages with beach mansions and single-family dwellings with condominiums, all following the "bigger is better" philosophy. The result is more property and related infrastructure at risk than before the storm loss. Development has spread from the barrier islands and sandy beaches to mainland shores that a generation or two ago were considered less attractive. Much of this development, old and new, is in flood-prone areas where each disaster places a growing burden on taxpayers at large, many living far from the ocean, who must pick up tabs that have grown from millions to billions of dollars. In addition, shallow coastal ecosystems already degraded by habitat loss, nutrient pollution, overfishing, sea-level rise, and other impacts are being subjected to large and increasingly common dredge-and-fill projects ("beach renourishment"). Generations of shore-hardening structures are still contributing to beach degradation and downdrift erosion problems. And people are still asking the universal question, "When is someone going to do something about my eroding beach?" A week rarely goes by without some media story about coastal issues. And the sea level continues to rise! It seems appropriate to take all of these factors into consideration and reexamine *Living with the East Florida Shore.*

Like the other volumes in the Living with the Shore series, this volume is the result of a team effort. The series coeditors and contributing authors— Orrin Pilkey Jr. of Duke University and William Neal of Grand Valley State University—are joined by several coastal experts who are concerned with the quality of coastal living.

Dave Bush is an associate professor at the University of West Georgia in Carrollton, Georgia, and an authority on coastal hazards, risk assessment mapping, and property damage mitigation. Dr. Bush has experience with the U.S. Atlantic, Caribbean, and Gulf coasts, and was part of the National Academy of Sciences postdisaster field study teams after Hurricanes Gilbert and Hugo. He was involved with planning the U.S. Decade for Natural Hazard Reduction and is the senior author of *Living with the Puerto Rico Shore, Living by the Rules of the Sea,* and *Living on the Edge of the Gulf.* At West Georgia Dr. Bush teaches courses in risk assessment, geomorphology, and oceanography; he has published numerous peer-reviewed papers on hurricane impacts, coastal hazard assessment, and mitigation.

William Neal, a professor of geology at Grand Valley State University in Allendale, Michigan, has coauthored numerous volumes of the Living with the Shore series. He has conducted coastal studies with Drs. Bush and Pilkey in the United States, the Caribbean, South America, and Europe.

Norma Longo, an avid naturalist, traveler, and beach lover, is a graduate of Duke University who has worked in the Program for the Study of Developed Shorelines for several years. Her field analyses and video/photo documentation of the Florida shoreline provided a continuous coastal overview and summaries of armoring and development. Most of the uncredited photos are hers.

Ken Lindeman, formerly at the University of Miami and National Marine Fisheries Service and now senior scientist with Environmental Defense, a 35-year-old nonprofit organization, brings a new element to the volume: an independent biologist's perspective on the environmental impacts of dredging and beach filling. Dr. Lindeman has published dozens of research articles on coastal biology and applied management in Florida and the northern Caribbean and is a coeditor of *Ecology of the Marine Fishes of Cuba*, published by the Smithsonian Institution Press. His chapter and other contributions throughout the book are an important addition to this volume.

The late Orrin Pilkey Sr. contributed a construction chapter to each of the earlier Living with the Shore books. His granddaughter, Deborah Pilkey, maintains the family tradition by authoring the construction chapter in this volume, including concepts and design recommendations based on the lessons learned from Hurricanes Andrew, Fran, Hugo, Iniki, and Opal. Dr. Pilkey received her Ph.D. in engineering from Virginia Polytechnic Institute and State University in 1998.

Luciana Esteves's 1997 master's thesis at Florida Atlantic University, "Evaluation of Shore Protection Measures Applied to Eroding Beaches in Florida," updated our knowledge of the sandy shorelines of East Florida. Luciana was our most distant author, providing her input all the way from the Department of Geosciences at the Fundaçao Universidade Federal do Rio Grande, Brazil, where she teaches courses on shore erosion and protection, marine sediments, and depositional environments. She is a consultant on coastal problems in Brazil.

John Congleton is currently supervisor of the Geospatial Analysis Laboratory in the Department of Geosciences at the State University of West Georgia. He has a master's degree in geology from Southern Methodist University and has mapped diverse areas from sub-Saharan Africa and the Middle East to eastern North America. He brings the technical expertise to make high-quality digital maps and the geology background to understand the natural physical processes represented in the maps.

Orrin Pilkey Jr. is James B. Duke Professor of Geology, emeritus, at Duke University. Dr. Pilkey is renowned as an authority on coastal geology, particularly barrier islands. He is a coeditor of the Living with the Shore series and a contributing author to most of the series' volumes. He has authored numerous peer-reviewed papers on coastal problems.

The Living with the Shore series has been supported in the past by the Federal Emergency Management Agency. The conclusions of this book, however, are those of the authors, based on reviews of published reports and studies of record, and are not meant to reflect the views of FEMA or any other agency. The Program for the Study of Developed Shorelines of Duke University is the activity center for the series, and we invite readers to visit the website—http://www.env.duke.edu/psds/—for further information, updates, and links to relevant sites.

We are indebted to the positive feedback and support of many individuals, without whom this book would not have been completed. Special thanks are due to our FEMA colleagues, especially Jane Bullock, Dick Krimm, and Gary Johnson. Thanks also are due to professionals in various offices and departments involved with Florida's coast and environmental protection for providing assistance and materials over the years, especially Mike McDonald, Michael Loehr, Frank Koutnik, Don Collins, Heidi Recksiek, Paden Woodruff, Jim Balsillie, Ralph Clark, Virginia Baker, Mark Leadon, Tom Waters, and Phil Flood. Several students at our respective institutions helped with fieldwork, map preparation, typing, and countless other thankless tasks. Thanks especially to Chester Jackson and Amy Green at West Georgia. Jocelyn Karazsia and Joe Roumelis helped immensely with last-minute checking of facts for several of the chapters and provided valuable assistance during final manuscript preparation.

We also thank the authors of the previous East Florida book for laying the groundwork, namely Dinesh Sharma, Harold Wanless, Larry Doyle, and Barbara Gruver. And, as for so many years, a special thanks to Amber Taylor for drafting all the line drawings. Finally, we thank all of the coastal residents who shared their knowledge, experiences, and concerns from living on the coast. We hope this book serves you and others who want to live with the shore.

William J. Neal and Orrin H. Pilkey
Series Editors, December 2002

1 From Fort Clinch to Fort Taylor: East Florida's Dynamic Coast

Vocabulary reflects attitude, and the words used in discussing the coast are often military in tone. We *armor* the shore and draw a *line of defense* in our *battle* with the sea. Some regard *retreat* in the face of sea-level rise as unacceptable. Appropriately in this context, the primary federal agency with authority over coastal activities is the U.S. Army Corps of Engineers; and among the oldest man-made structures along Florida's coast are military forts. Fort Clinch and Fort Taylor not only mark the northern and southern extremities of Florida's east coast (figs. 1.1 and 1.2), they also reflect the extremes of coastal dynamic settings from erosion to accretion, from a foundation of loose sand to solid reef rock, and from temperate climate to tropical climate. Even the way we choose to defend structures from shoreline retreat is mirrored in the history of the armoring of the shores in front of these historic forts.

Florida's oldest fort is the Castillo de San Marcos. Completed in the late 1600s, it was located on the mainland with command of St. Augustine Inlet. Early settlements commonly located on the naturally protected mainland rather than on the open-ocean shore. But by the 1800s, forts as well as settlements were being constructed on the seaward side of Florida's barrier islands. Fort Clinch, on Amelia Island at the mouth of the St. Marys River, was begun in 1847 and, although never completed, has stood as a fixed reference point next to the changing shoreline (fig. 1.1). Long threatened by shoreline erosion, the fort illustrates how reliance on shore-hardening engineering requires additional projects to hold the shore in place. Groins were constructed seaward of the fort in 1886 and again in the 1930s, about the same time the Civilian Conservation Corps restored the fort and it became a park.

The U.S. Army Corps of Engineers built a new set of rock groins at Fort Clinch in 1992, but the erosion problem persisted. Yet another set of groins, this one utilizing the T-head design and rock-filled mattresses, was em-

1.1 Fort Clinch, Amelia Island, has been a shoreline reference point since 1847. The battle with coastal erosion has gone on for well over 100 years at this location. These T-groins, constructed in 2000, are the fourth generation of shoreline defenses. Photo courtesy of Olsen Associates, Inc., Jacksonville, Fla.

placed in 2000, and the cells between the groins were filled with dredged sand in 2001 (fig. 1.1). North Florida is subject to hurricanes and northeasters, large winter storms with associated wave erosion. Fort Clinch's battle with the sea is not over.

Construction of Fort Taylor on Key West began in 1845 but was not completed until 1866. Hurricanes, the bane of South Florida, were among the reasons for the delay. The fort was constructed 1,000 feet offshore, on the bedrock of a key, with walls 5 feet thick to withstand both cannonballs and waves. In 1976 the fort became the property of the Florida Park Service, and in 1985 it was opened to the public. Visitors to the park will notice that the fort is now landlocked because sedimentation has gradually filled the shallow water around the fort, aided by some dredge fill (fig. 1.2). The fresh water supply was a problem, as it is for the Keys in general, and the fort had one of the earliest desalinization plants.

Houses, hotels, and high-rises may not be looked on as forts, but if your home is your castle, and a castle is a fortress, the analogy may fit—especially if the building is sitting on the shoreline! Every building on the shoreline is subject to the same problems that beset Florida's old forts. And East Flor-

I.2 Fort Taylor, Key West, in the late nineteenth century. In 1871 the fort was surrounded by water, but by the 1890s combined accretion and filling were moving the shoreline beyond the fort. Later photographs show dune growth after this embayment became a sand flat. Photo from the Photographic Collection of the Florida State Archives.

ida's shoreline is crowded with buildings that house both year-round residents and visitors by the millions.

Coastal Images

Name a community along the coast of East Florida. What image do you associate with that community? Each community may conjure up a unique image: Ocean Drive on Miami Beach, spring break in Fort Lauderdale, beach traffic on Daytona Beach, elegant homes on Palm Beach, Cocoa Beach in the shadow of Cape Canaveral, Amelia Island's golf greens, or laidback Key West at the end of the road. Perhaps your image of choice is a glimpse of what Florida's shores looked like before wholesale development occurred: the dunes on Talbot Island, the wetlands behind Apollo State Park, the natural ecosystem of one of the national wildlife preserves, or an unbroken view of sea and beach as seen from an open stretch of Highway A1A. Collectively, Florida's shorelines are its greatest asset.

And all along the east coast, from Fort Clinch to Fort Taylor, these communities, parks, and preserves share a common trait: they are part of Nature's most dynamic system at the interface between the land and the sea. Our focus will be on this dynamism—the constant and endless change that takes place at the shore—and the consequences we face if we choose to live in conflict with such change. The coastal zone is even more dangerous today after the boom in coastal populations that has taken place over the past few decades.

The history of Florida's development and economy is usually described in terms of "boom" and "bust," and is always closely tied to tourism. The formula of recent and continued change includes the resounding boom of the population bomb! And along with the spiraling population come ever-increasing real estate values and all types of development to serve the growing demand.

To live *with* the coast rather than simply *at* the coast, we must understand the geology and climate as well as coastal processes and how humans interact with each factor. Knowledge is the basis of survival, and mitigating (reducing) the impact of storms and shoreline erosion is essential to reducing economic losses at the shore. What lessons can we learn from both natural history and human history?

Geology: The Basis of Environment

The great peninsula of Florida illustrates the principles that geology is a fundamental component of our environment and that all things change. Although the great age of the Earth might lead us to believe that natural change is gradual and not of concern on the human time scale, the geologic record suggests that rapid change is often the rule. The longer history of change also provides the answers to some simple questions. For example, why is Florida a relatively low-lying peninsula?

Figure 1.3 lists events pertinent to Florida through geologic history. Far back in time, the rocks deep beneath the state were once part of a much larger continent that included Africa. That ancient continental mass collided and merged with North America and other land masses to form a supercontinent, Pangea, which subsequently broke up into the present continents. A fragment of ancient Africa remained attached to North America and became the base on which the Florida Platform grew. The distinct Florida peninsular outline is the emergent portion of this much larger Florida Platform (fig. 1.4), a mass of buried limestones (carbonates) that formed in persistent shallow marine environments like those found today in the Bahama Banks and the Florida reef tract. These limestones began forming as much as 145 million years ago, and continued into Pleistocene time in South Florida.

The great carbonate bank was separated from North America by a trough, the Suwannee Channel, which effectively kept the sands and muds

	Holocene	0.01 Ma	−Modern sea-level rise −Modern barriers form
Quaternary	Pleistocene	2 Ma	−Ice Age sea-level changes −Pleistocene barrier islands form

Tertiary	Pliocene	5 Ma	−Terrigenous sediments from
			  Appalachians move along
			  emergent platform

	Miocene	25 Ma	

	Oligocene	38 Ma	−Suwannee Trough fills
			−Limestones accumulate
			  over the area of the Florida
			  Platform

	Eocene	55 Ma	
	Paleocene	65 Ma	
Cretaceous		140 Ma	Florida Platform
Jurassic			Opening of Atlantic

Ma: Million years before present

1.3 Geologic time scale with selected events for Florida. Note that the scale begins with the Jurassic and does not include much of geologic time.

eroded off the Appalachian Mountains from reaching Florida (fig. 1.4). Later in time, the trough filled with sediment and the platform became attached to the mainland, allowing quartz-rich sands to move south along both the Atlantic and Gulf of Mexico shores. During the Pleistocene Ice Age the sea level fell during the times of glaciation and rose during the warmer interglacial episodes. When the sea level was lower, one can imagine that more sand was carried down the rivers from the Appalachian Mountains, and then along the coast from north to south, supplying Florida's ancestral beaches with sand. The abundant shells of marine animals also were broken up by waves to become beach sand. These two sources account for differences in Florida's natural beaches. Beaches rich in quartz sand tend to be whiter, finer grained, and firmer, like Daytona Beach in the days of beach racing (fig. 1.5). Shelly sand beaches are less firm, slightly coarser, and brownish tan. Today's beaches often don't have the same character as the original beaches because many are now artificially maintained with sands that are dredged from offshore.

During times when the sea level was rising, conditions were favorable for the formation of barrier islands—emergent sand bodies that paralleled the coast, separated from the mainland by a lagoon, marsh, or mangrove swamp. Some of these barriers migrated landward as the sea level rose, and their migration rates are well within the time frame by which we measure human history. The story of these continuing changes does not bode well for the future of coastal development.

Some of the earlier Pleistocene barrier islands welded onto the mainland

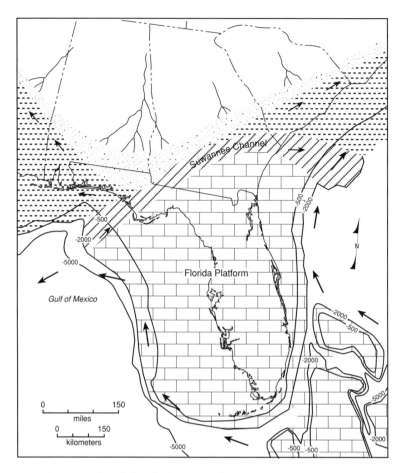

1.4 The geography of Florida about 45 million years ago. The Suwannee Channel separated quartz sand–dominated deposition to the north from carbonate bank deposition to the south (block pattern). The channel was an active marine seaway that prevented quartz-rich sediments from reaching the carbonate bank. Arrows indicate directions of current flow at the time the Suwannee Channel existed. When the channel closed, land-derived sand was moved to the south by longshore currents. From R. A. Davis and A. C. Hine, *Quaternary Geology and Sedimentology of the Barrier Island and Marshy Coast, West-Central Florida, U.S.A.,* 1989, Field Trip Guidebook T375, American Geophysical Union, Washington D.C.

or were left high and dry when the sea level fell during the next cold-climate episode. The most recent low stand of sea level was about 18,000 to 15,000 years ago at the end of the Pleistocene, when the sea level was 300 to 400 feet below its present elevation and the shoreline was out at the edge of the continental shelf. Large amounts of water were tied up in the massive glacial ice sheets (like present Antarctica and Greenland) that covered parts of North America, Europe, and Asia. The great sea-level rise that followed,

known as the Holocene transgression, was one of the most significant pre-
determining events relative to the origin of the present shorelines. As the ice
caps melted, the postglacial sea-level rise (fig. 1.6) caused the shorelines to
migrate across Florida's continental shelf as much as 130 miles to their present positions.

Climatic warming and melting of those icecaps was well under way by
10,000 years ago, and the sea level was rising at a rate of 3 to 4 feet per century
until 5,000 to 4,000 years ago when the rate decreased (fig. 1.6). Although
scholars disagree on the details, the sea level has continued to rise since then,
although at a much slower rate, perhaps on the order of 4 to 8 inches per century. This slower rate of sea-level rise across the low coastal plain favored the
formation and development of new barrier islands. Most of these barriers
welded onto older Pleistocene islands or the mainland shore, sometimes
forming spits. The northernmost two islands of East Florida, Amelia and
Little Talbot Islands, are like the Sea Islands of Georgia—composites of
modern islands that have merged with Ice Age (Pleistocene) islands. Although much of the remaining coast has an artificial aspect and a different
origin, the principles that control shoreline erosion, storm response, and
how engineering structures impact the shore are the same all along the East
Florida shore.

A hundred years ago, there were 11 natural inlets along the approximately
365-mile East Florida coast between the Georgia state line and Key Biscayne.
Today, the same reach has 21 active inlets, although only 5 (Nassau Sound,
Boca Chica, Matanzas, Norris Cut, and Bear Cut) are natural, unjettied in-
lets (figs. 1.7, 1.8, and 1.9). Inlets are more common south of Cape Canav-
eral, with 14 of the state's 21, including what were once natural inlets at
Jupiter, Boca Raton, and Hillsboro (these were later jettied; figs. 1.8 and 1.9).
The other inlets were dredged or in many cases blasted through rock,

1.5 The firm beach at Daytona has attracted automobile traffic as well as race cars
for a century. Scenes like this one suggest that automobile access was important in
drawing tourists to the beach in the 1920s and 1930s. Photo from the Photographic
Collection of the Florida State Archives.

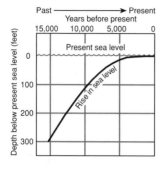

1.6 Sea-level rise off the U.S. East Coast from 15,000 years ago to present. Melting of the continental ice caps caused the sea to rise and the shoreline to migrate landward.

mostly in the 1920s. Almost all are now routinely dredged to maintain artificial channels. A century ago, before these artificial inlets were cut, the equivalent of a 150-mile-long barrier island extended on either side of Cape Canaveral, from Ponce de Leon Inlet south of Daytona Beach to Jupiter Inlet near Palm Beach. This barrier island was the longest in the world, longer than 135-mile-long Padre Island in South Texas.

Palm Beach, the "wealthiest barrier island in America," once sat in front of a freshwater body called Lake Worth. In 1917, Lake Worth Inlet was opened by mule, drag pan, and dynamite. When South Lake Worth Inlet was opened in 1927, Palm Beach became an island.

Lagoons of several origins back the East Florida islands. Behind some islands are freshwater marshes. At one time it was possible to wade through the marshes to get to the islands, albeit with some difficulty. Other open-water lagoons have river or lake names, reflecting their origins. Examples include the Halifax River behind Daytona Beach, the Indian River behind Melbourne Beach, Lake Worth behind Palm Beach, and Lake Mable, which became the Port Everglades turning basin near Fort Lauderdale. Today the Intracoastal Waterway is behind the entire coast and sometimes constitutes the only reason for the designation "island."

Most people would not call the southeastern Florida shore a rocky coast, but in fact, this coast has a foundation of rock covered with a thin layer of sand (see appendix C, ref. 56). Underlying many of the barrier islands and most of the beaches is coquina rock or limestone, hard Pleistocene rock (Anastasia Formation) originally deposited as barrier islands or coral reefs and believed to have formed during the 120,000-year sea-level high. So the current barrier island chain coincides with the ancient barrier island chain. Due to the shallow rocky substrate, the Intracoastal Waterway behind the islands was blasted rather than dredged for much of its length. According to Florida coastal geologist Charles Finkl, the typical thickness of sand over the rock is only 3 to 6 feet. Hutchinson Island, Singer Island, Hillsboro Beach, Fort Lauderdale Beach, Dania Beach, and Miami Beach are examples of rock-cored islands. On Palm Beach a ridge of coral reef

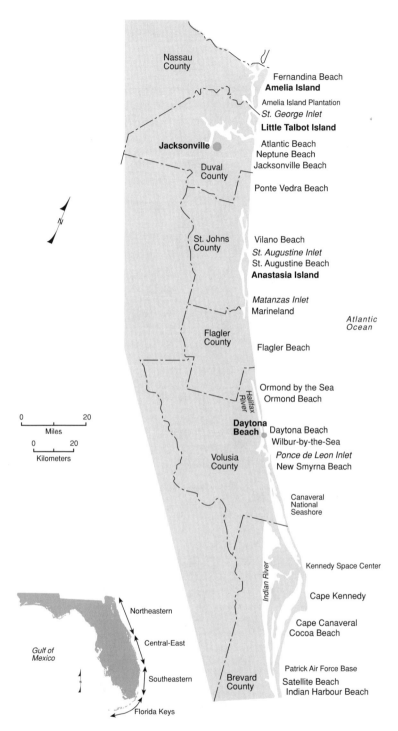

1.7 Index map of northeastern Florida coastal counties: Nassau, Duval, St. Johns, Flagler, Volusia, and Brevard counties.

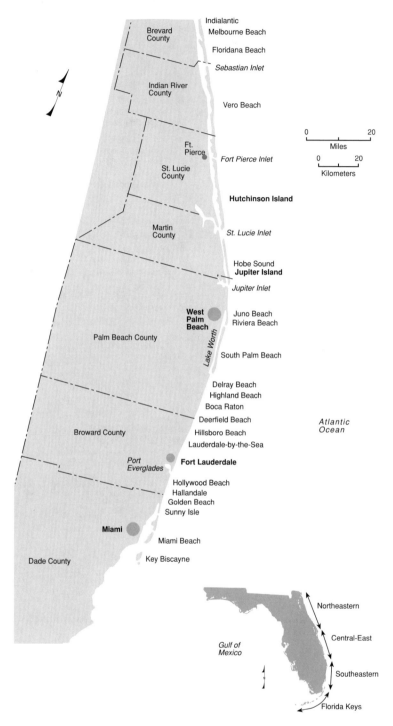

1.8 Index map of East Florida coastal counties: Brevard, Indian River, St. Lucie, Martin, Palm Beach, Broward, and Dade counties.

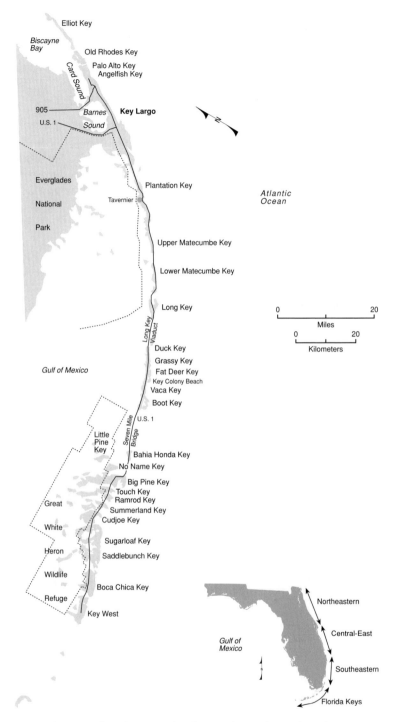

1.9 Index map of southeastern Florida coastal counties: Dade and Monroe counties and the Florida Keys.

limestone forms the spine of the island; it can be seen in a local road cut on the island.

The facts that the post-Pleistocene sea-level rise probably reduced sand delivery from the more northerly sources and that Florida's rivers neither drain high uplands nor carry sand to the coast have serious coastal management implications. Given that the continental shelf has very limited sand reserves, the barrier islands depend largely on the reworking of their own sands, and to a lesser degree on the erosion of shelly sands from coquina rock units such as the Anastasia Formation. Because there are relatively few inlets along the East Florida coast, sands derived from inlet-associated tidal deltas are of only local importance. In effect, the existence of East Florida's beaches depends on limited sand resources of ancient origin—that is, fossil

1.10 Future coastal changes in Florida for two different sea-level rise scenarios. Even a lesser sea-level rise than shown here would not bode well for South Florida or most of the development along the East Florida coast. Adapted from *Florida's Geological History and Geological Resources,* 1994 (appendix C, ref. 3).

Under water after 15-foot rise in sea level

Under water after 25-foot rise in sea level

High ground

1.11 House destroyed in the Miami area in the hurricane of September 1926. Photo from the Photographic Collection of the Florida State Archives.

sand. The Atlantic's waves and currents are reworking deposits from earlier times. This geology dictates prudent sand management.

The geologic record illustrates that climate and sea level are in a constant state of flux, and whether one accepts the premise of the greenhouse effect or not, the climate and the level of the sea are changing over both the short and long terms. We need to go back only to previous interglacial warm periods to find that the sea level was 150 feet higher than at present, inundating well over half of the present land area of Florida—an inundation likely to be repeated in Florida's not-so-distant future (fig. 1.10). The geologic lesson is that sea level falls and rises, sediment supplies change, and we should not expect the shorelines to remain as they are today.

Short-term events can have effects just as important as long-term events. Hurricanes and smaller storms, and even the day-to-day wind and waves, reshape beaches, dunes, shorelines, and inlets, obliterating buildings that have their foundations in such mobile features (fig. 1.11). Repeated storms leave platted lots behind in the surf while accreting new ephemeral shores in your former fishing spot!

Coastal Landforms

The long, straight stretches of East Florida's coast illustrate Nature's rule of equilibrium: the tendency of landforms to adjust to a shape that is stable under the dominant conditions. If a coast could think, it would want to be straight. When natural processes or human structures create irregularities in the coastline, Nature will work to restraighten the shore. The present condition of the coast is part of a continuum of such change, and the coastal variations we see today are the result of the differences in geology, oceanography, and climate of the various reaches. Understanding the different coastal types and how they function is fundamental to understanding and mitigating coastal hazards. In the broadest view, the East Florida shore can be subdivided into four reaches (figs. 1.7–1.9): the slightly arcuate northeastern reach extending from the Sea Islands of Georgia to Cape Canaveral; the central-east reach, which includes the line of barriers from Cape Canaveral to the change in the coastal orientation near the line between Martin and Palm Beach Counties; the southeastern reach, which includes the counties of Palm Beach, Broward, and northern Dade; and the chain of limestone islands that make up the Florida Keys. Each of these areas is discussed in detail in chapter 7.

Coastal barriers, whether they are islands, spits, capes, or beaches, have several characteristics, as recognized by the U.S. Fish and Wildlife Service:

They are subject to the impacts of coastal storms and sea-level rise and are hazardous for human occupation.

They buffer the mainland from the impact of storms.

Usually they protect and maintain productive estuarine and wetland systems that are vital to the fishing and shellfishing industries as well as landward aquatic habitats.

Most consist primarily of unconsolidated sediments (and even a rock core will not prevent sand from being moved).

They are subject to wind, wave, and tidal energies.

Barrier islands also are magnets for coastal development. The beauty of their beaches, the serenity—even starkness—of their sand and water, and the many recreational opportunities they offer are prime attractions. Although coastal development and population growth are controlled in part by landforms, human nature seems to dictate that we try to out-engineer Nature. The result is increasing property losses and more people at risk. If we are to live successfully with the coast, coastal management should be structured on the basis of such landform differences.

Coastal Processes and the Importance of Sand

Living with the shore requires an appreciation of physical processes—the ways in which energy flows—and how they shape sediments and create

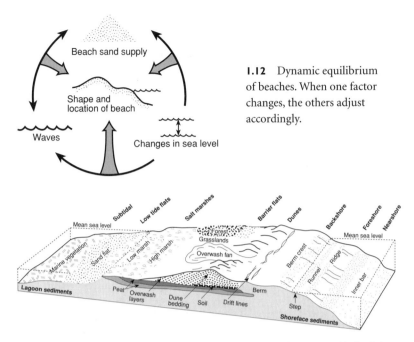

1.12 Dynamic equilibrium of beaches. When one factor changes, the others adjust accordingly.

1.13 Typical barrier island cross section. Environments change quickly both laterally and across the barrier, and storm impacts vary by environment. Adapted from work by Paul Godfrey.

unique environments. Beaches, for example, attain a shape in response to the sea level, wave energy, and sediment supply; they are another example of a landform approaching an equilibrium or natural balance (fig. 1.12). As the sea level rises, wave conditions change, or sediment supply fluctuates, the beach shifts, flattens, steepens, narrows, or widens. Nature does not remain the same long enough to allow the beach any permanence in terms of being a suitable footing for a hotdog stand, cottage, or condominium. The same can be said for dunes, overwash fans, tidal deltas, and most landforms associated with barrier systems.

The physical rhythm of the shore is one of wind, waves, currents, tides, and the associated sand flow. Storms are the acme of such processes. In the case of barrier islands, the entire island system behaves much like the beach, moving to reach equilibrium with the same controls over longer time scales. As the sea level rises, the barrier must adjust by building its elevation and shifting landward. Dunes and overwash are examples of both cross-island sediment transport and mechanisms by which the island builds its elevation. All of these processes control the environments and landforms that we commonly associate with the coast (fig. 1.13).

Of these equilibrium factors, sand supply is the most critical. The sheer extent of the Atlantic coast beaches and dunes gives the impression of an unending sand supply, but we now know that sand is a limited resource to conserve. Legally, issues of sand rights are taking on the same character as water rights: Does a community, property owner, or other political entity have the right to cut off or reduce the sand supply to downdrift beaches, thereby causing beach loss and potential property loss? Variations on this question are now litigated with some frequency in Florida.

Referring to the economic importance of Florida's beaches, W. B. Stronge stated in a 1994 issue of *Shore and Beach* magazine: "These beaches are important economic assets, and their maintenance is necessary to preserve the economic health of one of Florida's most important industries. . . . An important part of tourist development is maintenance of the state's barrier island beaches." By the state's own estimates, however, approximately 560 miles of Florida's sandy coasts are eroding or critically eroded!

Climate: A Fundamental Component of Environment

Hurricanes bear the names of people (e.g., Andrew, Floyd, Georges, Irene, Opal) as if they are living beings. Of course, storms cannot think, but each has an origin, evolution or development, and ultimately a unique history. On a larger and longer scale, climate changes through time, altering the land and the ocean as well as life in those environments. Climate is a fundamental component of the human environment, a fact that coastal residents sometimes forget or ignore. The coastal zone is dynamic, subject to almost constant natural change. This change does not recognize static buildings or structures placed in the paths of storms, waves, currents, or the resulting shoreline retreat! Hurricanes, tropical storms, northeasters, droughts, El Niño and La Niña effects, and changing weather in general provide frequent reminders that the Florida coast spans 7 to 8 degrees of latitude across three climatic belts between two oceans; in other words, it is prime real estate in the middle of an energy combat zone! These climatic zones create living conditions that range from temperate to tropical in diverse environments. But the most significant climatic factor is that this coast is in a zone of ocean storms: hurricanes, tropical storms, and northeasters.

Animals and Plants: The Health of the Coast

The different climatic zones, coastal types, and geological settings and processes of East Florida create a great diversity of environments within the coastal zone. Reefs, salt marshes, and mangrove wetlands are among the most productive ecosystems on Earth. They are nursery areas for both sea and land, and the loss of marshes, mangroves, or reefs can affect fisheries that are found far beyond these key environments. The river estuaries and offshore shelf areas are just as important. In Florida, manatees and turtles get much of the media coverage, but the biota of the ocean are impacted by shoreline activities as well (see chapter 5). Some of these species are like the miners' canaries of old—they are the indicators of the health of the environment in which we all live, and impacts to one population can negatively cascade through others in unanticipated ways. Some species have already gone extinct along the Florida coast; many other important populations have been greatly reduced by centuries of human coastal activity (appendix C, ref. 50).

Plants also play a major role in the coastal barrier system—onshore, offshore, and in intertidal areas. Two major intertidal plant communities—mangroves and salt marshes—exist behind the barriers. Cape Canaveral is the approximate boundary between the two on the East Florida coast. Mangroves predominate to the south, and salt marshes dominate to the north. Salt marshes are thick mats of salt-tolerant grasses that grow in strips on the intertidal flats, where they are subject to periodic flooding by salt water. Mangroves also occur as strips or patches of intertidal vegetation. Both types of wetlands play an important role in barrier island evolution by stabilizing lagoon shorelines and preventing their erosion. At the same time, mangroves and salt marshes are land builders. The plant communities are effective at dampening waves and currents, which in turn causes sediment to accumulate, raising the elevation of the intertidal surface to the point that it eventually adds to the land area of the barrier system. This back-side growth is an important part of the island migration process that allows a barrier to move landward in response to the sea-level rise.

Mangroves and salt marshes also support the coastal food webs that include fishes, birds, and numerous invertebrates. They act as nursery areas for many marine organisms and provide vast amounts of nutrients to the surrounding waters. Yet, mangroves and salt marshes are still cleared and filled in for development projects large and small. Those who do so may pay a price beyond a fine. Individual property owners have cleared mangroves for a better view or for waterfront access, only to see their property erode after this protection was removed.

Coastal beaches and dunes, maritime thickets and forests, coastal grasslands, high marshes, tidal flats, shallow sea-grass beds, and reefs each have their own flora and fauna, but all are interconnected parts of the whole coastal system (fig. 1.14). From microscopic organisms that live between sand grains in the beach, to coquina clams and beach burrowers, to wading birds, nesting turtles, and the diverse coastal flora, the shore's organisms are living in a balance with the physical environment. This diversity of life in the onshore and offshore environments is one of the coastal zone's main at-

1.14 A number of ecosystems may exist on a barrier island, depending on barrier width, elevation, sediment supply, climate, and vegetation types. From *Purchasing Paradise: Things to Know and Questions to Ask When Buying Coastal Property in Florida*, Florida Department of Community Affairs, Florida Coastal Management brochure, June 1997.

tractions, one of the golden eggs that Nature's goose has provided to the Florida coast. We must learn to live with, enjoy, and sustainably manage these living resources.

Prehistoric Life: Early Humans

Ten thousand years ago, or perhaps earlier, when the first humans ventured into Florida, they found an environment far different from the one we know today. The sea level was 100 feet lower, and the shores were far seaward of the present coastline. The inner continental shelf was dry land and the climate was temperate. Fresh water was probably more restricted, limited to rivers and deep sinkholes that intersected a deeper water table. Animals were abundant, as the Florida peninsula was a refuge for animals that migrated south during the severe climate of the Pleistocene Ice Age. The fossil record in the region's Pleistocene and younger sediments includes a wide range of marine and nonmarine animals and plants. The vertebrate animal record includes an impressive list of now-extinct animals and species that are now rare or absent from the region. Mammoths and mastodons, giant sloths, bears, beavers, camels, saber-toothed cats, horses, lemmings, llamas, tapirs, dire wolves, and others may have greeted the early hunters who ventured into the Southeast.

The record of early humans in North America is sparse, but over the generations these early inhabitants witnessed the retreating shoreline and climatic change that brought subtropical to tropical conditions to Florida's coasts. Kitchen middens, shell heaps left by people who took advantage of the coastal food resources, provide evidence of human presence in the coastal zone at least as far back as 3,500 years. By that time, the climate was approaching conditions more like the present and humans were well established in the area, leaving as their record fired-clay pottery and stone tools. No doubt the elements sometimes treated these people harshly, but no evidence exists that they tried to build and maintain villages at the edge of the rising sea or to hold back the inundation. They had no need to be taught to utilize and enjoy resources while minimizing environmental risk.

Access: The Key to Development

Juan Ponce de León, famous for his unsuccessful search for a fountain of youth, completed the first recorded cruise along Florida's east coast in the spring of 1513, a mere 21 years after the discovery of the New World. Some years later, in 1565, Pedro Menéndez de Avilés established a Spanish settlement at St. Augustine, and the development of Florida's east coast began in earnest, albeit slowly. By 1599 the population of St. Augustine had survived Indian warfare, attacks by the British, and a hurricane; those early residents probably did not consider Florida a subtropical paradise.

Even in these early times the sea threatened the coastal trappings of humans, and a shoreline milestone was achieved with the completion of the St. Augustine seawalls, Florida's first, in 1690. By 1761 the English had pushed the Spanish out of Florida. During the next few years, settlers dribbled in from several directions. By the time the Revolutionary War broke out, 100 plantations had been established along the east coast. But the political instability continued as the British gave Florida back to Spain when they lost their American colonies. Florida finally became U.S. territory in 1821 under the terms of the Adams-Onis Treaty. Development proceeded slowly in the early 1800s because the land was in the hands of people without much money; and few wanted to buy land in Florida after the Seminoles went on the warpath in 1836.

In the mid-1800s settlement along the east coast began to increase. The site of Miami was picked in 1843. By 1854 Volusia County had a population of "300, plus 318 slaves" (in the language of the day). In 1865 the first land rush by northerners began. In 1868 Ormond (later called Ormond Beach) was founded, and in 1871 Mathias Day began to develop a tract of land that would someday be called Daytona. By 1875 Daytona's population had shot up to 70, but only two houses had been built on the adjacent island. In 1882 Henry M. Flagler, one of Florida's most colorful developers, appeared on the scene with the purchase of a large portion of Miami Beach. In 1885 Flagler began buying marsh land near St. Augustine, which he filled in for development. He built the 450-room Ponce de Leon Hotel, among others, at a cost of $250,000. Flagler also was responsible for building the East Coast Railway to Miami; the first train arrived in April 1896. Although packet boats had generated tourism early in Florida's history, the railroads fueled the first real tourism boom. Access spurred development. In 1895 construction began on the original Breakers Hotel in Palm Beach (it was subsequently replaced after fires in 1903 and 1925). The twentieth century brought an expanding system of roads, and the improved access brought even more development.

Florida quickly tapped into Americans' love affair with the new automobile, and in 1902 James Hathaway, trying out his Stanley Steamer on the beach, "discovered" the great Ormond-Daytona racecourse. In 1903 Ransom E. Olds and his "Pirate" hit speeds in excess of 57 mph on the beach, but beach racing received a black eye when F. Marriott totaled his car "Rocket" on an uneven stretch of sand. Car racing recommenced in 1927, at Ormond Beach, and eventually, speeds reached 200 mph. The big annual races continued until World War II.

By 1913 Miami Beach was connected to the mainland by the Collins Bridge, and three developers (Messrs. Fisher, Lummus, and Collins) began to build what would soon be regarded as the world's most famous beach resort. By 1920 the Florida frontier was conquered, and the land boom of the 1920s brought a surge of tourism and coastal development. Miami Beach had a population of 644 in 1920, and mainland Miami was home to more than 110,000 souls. A brand-new smuggling industry sprang up overnight with the passage of Prohibition, and Florida soon proved to be one of the "leakiest" states with regard to illicit booze.

The 1926 and 1928 hurricanes (see chapter 2), followed shortly afterward by the Depression and the terrible 1935 hurricane, almost burst East Florida's real estate boom bubble. During the 1930s Floridians began to realize that they had to attract people 12 months a year, not just in winter, and they were eventually successful. In spite of the hurricane history, the population nearly doubled between 1920 and 1940, and tourism stimulated the coastal economy. The World War II years introduced new generations to Florida who would return again and again in the years to come. By the early 1940s, approximately 2.6 million tourists per year were visiting Florida. At the same time, a shift from rural to urban living was occurring. The 1950s saw a postwar building boom, and in 1953, 5.1 million tourists spent an estimated $930 million—one-third of Florida's total income! During the remainder of the twentieth century "bigger was better," and Nature cooperated in promoting the boom by sending only one great hurricane. Big government cooperated by providing more and more money to underwrite bigger coastal engineering projects to repair the growing problems of beach loss and soaring property damage from the storms that hit the state at the end of the century and the increasingly crowded development that all the funding creates. The results are there to see today, from Amelia Island all the way to Key West.

Hurricanes have always played an important role in determining the success or failure of development schemes on Florida's east coast. In fact, the names *Florida* and *hurricane* became almost synonymous, helped along by Hollywood movies such as *Key Largo*. But the hurricane association is based on fact, not fiction. In a ranking of areas of the United States, the Caribbean, and Mexico where hurricanes and tropical storms came within 60 miles of a given locale between 1871 and 2000, East Florida has 7 of the top 15 locations. Significant storms occur here every 2.7 to 2.9 years. Delray

Beach is number 5 overall in storm frequency, and number 1 in the continental United States! This is somewhat surprising because more hurricanes have struck the Gulf coast; however, many tropical storms and hurricanes track up the Atlantic east of Florida. These storms are less threatening than those that make landfall, but they induce wind and wave damage, including incessant shoreline erosion. The fact that 11 great hurricanes have struck southeast Florida in this time span is historical evidence that a great hurricane is always on the horizon, especially for South Florida, and when the next one hits, the property losses will dwarf the Andrew statistics!

One of the authors of this book visited the Florida Keys a few days after Hurricane Donna struck in 1960. The sight of the destruction was awe-inspiring, but even more striking was the widespread pessimism of the survivors. Everyone seemed to feel that Donna, following on the heels of so many storms that had hit the Keys, had struck a fatal blow to future development. But these same survivors and their predecessors had reoccupied the Keys after the horrific 1935 hurricane. They should have anticipated the cavalier attitude of the developers who came after Donna's destruction and the generations of property buyers who would follow, ignorant of Nature's warning signals or arrogant in the face of past storm history.

Many thousands of new inhabitants now live on sites once covered by Donna's debris, and it is doubtful that the Keys can be effectively and safely evacuated in a hurricane emergency situation. The maximum estimated evacuation clearance time of the Keys was estimated to be more than 36 hours in 1992! Population growth, particularly in the Metropolitan Miami area into which evacuation must take place, has no doubt added to that time in subsequent years. Even with improved prediction technology, forecasters may not be able to accurately predict a hurricane's path 36 hours in advance. And even if they could, a large percentage of the populace would not perceive the danger that far in advance and would delay in evacuating.

Mainland coastal communities may be no better off in terms of evacuation. Florida's low-lying interior and the cumulative effects of adjacent communities required to evacuate for the same storm may make evacuation times even greater. The West Palm Beach area may need a maximum clearance time greater than that for the Keys, and all East Florida communities should plan on evacuation clearance times in excess of the estimates.

Lighthouse Lessons

Along with forts, lighthouses are among the oldest survivors of coastal development, and several nineteenth-century lighthouses grace the East Florida coast. These structures offer some important lessons about how buildings hold up to the forces of coastal processes and the best solutions for dealing with coastal erosion.

Lighthouses by their very nature must be located near shorelines subjected to waves and storm impacts. They are designed and built to resist such forces. Nevertheless, history tells us that lighthouses can eventually fail. The relentless shoreline retreat ultimately brings the lighthouse to the water's edge and out of service, or a single storm takes the structure down.

The encroaching sea claimed the St. Augustine lighthouse in 1880. The Ponce de Leon Inlet (originally called Mosquito Inlet) lighthouse was undermined and tilted by a storm in October 1835, and two months later it fell into the sea. Construction of the Rebecca Shoal lighthouse began in the 1850s but was delayed by storms, particularly an 1858 storm that tore out some of the construction. Completed in 1886, the structure did not last a hundred years as its destruction came with a 1953 hurricane. Lighthouses in the Keys have a record of high loss to hurricanes: the first Garden Key lighthouse suffered damage in 1873; the Dry Tortugas lighthouse fell in an 1856 hurricane, and its replacement was damaged in the hurricanes of 1873 and 1875; and the first Key West lighthouse was destroyed by an 1846 hurricane that devastated Key West.

Our ancestors were sometimes more insightful with respect to hazards than we are today. After the 1846 loss, the replacement lighthouse on Key West was located farther inland. In fact, when lighthouses were threatened by erosion in the 1800s, a common solution was to move the lighthouse out of harm's way. The Amelia Island lighthouse was originally on the south end of Cumberland Island, Georgia, but was dismantled in 1838 and reassembled on Amelia Island. The St. Johns River lighthouse was moved inland in 1835 (just six years after its construction) when it was threatened by the retreating shoreline. Ironically, this lighthouse had the opposite problem by 1853; sand dunes had built up to a level that blocked the light's visibility. The Cape Canaveral lighthouse was moved in 1893 after the shore had moved progressively closer to the base of the lighthouse through the 1880s (fig. 1.15). By this time, some lighthouses were designed to be dismantled because moving the structure was recognized as the best alternative for structures built on a retreating shoreline.

This lesson of relocation seems to have been lost over the last century. People have even resisted the idea that a lighthouse can be moved using modern technology, as was the case with the famous Cape Hatteras lighthouse in North Carolina, which was successfully moved back from the eroding shore in 1999 to a distance equal to its original setback. The point is that if a substantial, tall structure like a lighthouse can be moved, then this approach can be considered first as a solution to the erosion "problem" for other structures.

In short, history tells us that the word *dynamic* is just as appropriate for coastal development by humans as it is for natural processes. And human dynamics in altering the coast is contributing to Nature's reshaping of

1.15 The Cape Canaveral lighthouse has a history of response to coastal change. The first tower (left) was lit in 1848. The second tower was designed to be moved if necessary. Constructed of curved iron-plate sections, the tapering structure went into operation in 1867. The builders' foresight paid off. When coastal retreat threatened the lighthouse in 1893, it was disassembled and moved 1 mile west, and was back in operation by 1894. Photo from the Photographic Collection of the Florida State Archives.

Florida's beaches. This formula of change is being multiplied by the effects of burgeoning coastal population growth.

Population Explosion in the Coastal Zone

The population growth rate in Florida's coastal counties reflects the national trend of the post–World War II population shift into the nation's coastal zones; however, Florida's growth rates are phenomenal. Fewer than 600,000 people lived in all of Florida's coastal counties in 1920. By 1950 the number was over 2 million, and the population had doubled again by the 1960s. The rate of population growth peaked in 1960 and has since declined, but in terms of absolute numbers the population continues to increase and is alarmingly high because much of this growth is in areas vulnerable to coastal hazards. Between 1960 and 1988, eastern Florida's population increased by 152 percent. From 1980 to 1990, the state's population grew by nearly 33 percent, far higher than the national average. By 1988 four out of five people living in the coastal southeastern United States were in eastern Florida. By 1995, 7.8 million people, more than 60 percent of Florida's entire population, were living in the coastal zone. East Florida's coastal urban corridor reflects continuous development from Greater Miami through Hollywood and Fort Lauderdale to North Palm Beach.

Another way to look at population pressure is to examine the ratio of population to shoreline mile, which is projected to be 2,689 people per mile by 2010 for East Florida. This number is not the population density at the beachfront, but it reflects the potential for conflicting land uses and emergency management issues. The increasing population requires more infrastructure, including beach maintenance, that residents must pay for and will suffer from in the future, whether it is shrinking recreation space on the beach, lack of berths for your boat, or more people fleeing with you in the face of a hurricane than the roads can accommodate. Even more frightening, these numbers reflect only residents; they do not include the thousands of tourists who add to the population on any given day.

Much of East Florida's coastal population is concentrated on or behind the sandy barrier island coasts—the same areas in which tourists concentrate—swelling the number of people at risk from coastal hazards. Again, maximum clearance times needed to evacuate such populations in the face of a hurricane now exceed 30 to 40 hours in some areas, well in excess of the maximum warning time the Weather Service may be able to give for some storms.

Florida's economy continues to attract increasing numbers of people to the coastal zone. The coastal counties with sandy shores generate about 50 percent of the state's income. By the 1990s nearly 40 million tourists per year were visiting Florida—with the beaches the number one draw—pumping close to $17 billion per year into the economy.

The loss of beaches to erosion and the increasing property losses associated with even low-rank hurricanes have led to increased pressure to build coastal stabilization structures (fig. 1.16). Shoreline engineering, particularly shore-hardening structures, offers short- to intermediate-term protection of property, but it accelerates beach loss. Unless the state, coastal communities, and individual property owners conserve beaches and take measures to mitigate storm impacts, the future of the beach-based economy is in question.

More people and property are being put at risk daily, so the price of each successive storm has been and will be greater. Given the rapid population growth both past and present, the collective memory of Florida's population is less than a generation, and probably less than a decade. The lessons

1.16 A 1955 view of Miami Beach. Hotel Row's growth was spurred by the tourist economy. The barrier island's beach had all but disappeared, destroyed by seawalls and groins. These structures, constructed to combat erosion, were part of the problem. Even as the beaches were disappearing, new construction continued right on the shore (lower left). With the loss of the beach, the local economy waned, leading to the $68 million beach fill project of approximately 15 million cubic yards of sand, completed in 1981. Photo from the Photographic Collection of the Florida State Archives.

of Hurricanes Andrew (1992), which demonstrated wind power, and Opal (1995), a Gulf coast storm that demonstrated how devastating storm surge can be, are already fading from memory. In this great age of communication we seem to be ignoring knowledge from the past; development in high-risk zones continues.

Opal's severest damage occurred within 200 to 300 feet of the shoreline, coinciding closely with the zone defined by Florida's Coastal Construction Control Line (CCCL). Nearly half of the non-permitted structures under the CCCL program were seriously damaged or destroyed, while only two permitted structures were seriously damaged. In Andrew, the wind damage extended well beyond the shoreline, demonstrating that the entire coastal zone is a hazard area. The houses that survived with minimal damage were structures built to code, with no shortcuts taken in materials or building inspections. These two experiences suggest that storm damage can be mitigated (but not eliminated) through the use of setback controls and building codes.

That is the point of this book—to consider how to live *with* the coast as opposed to living *at* the coast and being potential victims of its natural

1.17   Part of Miami Beach after the 1926 hurricane. Compare with figure 1.16. Development was relatively light in 1926. Imagine the difference in losses were the same storm to hit today. Note also that a beach existed in 1926, even after the storm, although it had moved landward. Photo from the Photographic Collection of the Florida State Archives.

hazards. The aftermath of Andrew and more recent small storms such as Floyd and Irene, along with the history of previous major hurricanes (fig. 1.17) and giant northeasters, and storms yet to come send an age-old message: "Better safe than sorry." If we are to live with the coast, we must understand and plan for its dynamics, for it has a will of its own.

Prospects for the Future

We would like to state that the phenomenal population growth in the coastal zone will not continue, but that is not the case. By the year 2020, the population of Florida's coastal counties is projected to be over 15 million, twice the 1980 population. Even under the best management, this level of growth and the momentum of development to support it will disrupt physical processes, degrade coastal ecosystems, and increase vulnerability to natural and human-induced hazards.

Future storm damages will routinely be in the billions of dollars, matching and possibly dwarfing losses associated with hurricanes such as Andrew and Opal. Loss of lives in major storms will increase as the population density exceeds the capability to warn and evacuate large numbers of people in a relatively short time, reversing a long trend of declining fatalities in storms. The sea level will continue to rise, and for the low, sloping areas of the east coast, this spells a long-term pattern of impact on all coastal development (see fig. 1.10).

The immediate lesson is that coastal carrying capacity has been exceeded. If we cannot collectively make prudent decisions on how to live with the coast, then individual property owners and coastal dwellers must make informed choices. The overall goal of this book is to provide guidance in making such choices, particularly on barrier islands and sandy shores.

2 The Vulnerable Coast: Living with Storms

When discussing hurricanes or other coastal storms, it can be difficult to separate activity along Florida's east coast from that on the west (Gulf) coast (appendix C, ref. 54). Owing to the narrowness of the Florida peninsula, many storms can impact both coasts (fig. 2.1). Regardless of the setting, hurricanes are a fact of coastal life, but time often blurs our perception of reality when recalling recent storms. The names of recent hurricanes may be familiar (e.g., Floyd, Irene, Georges, Andrew), but their impacts are either forgotten or remembered incorrectly. East Florida also experiences significant erosion—and sometimes flooding—from northeasters and winter waves.

Figure 2.2 puts the Florida peninsula in perspective with regard to the size of a hurricane. Size isn't the only property of a hurricane to consider, however; the storm's strength and direction also determine the extent of property damage. One of the strongest hurricanes to hit the East Florida coast in recent times was Hurricane Andrew (1992), a category 4 storm at landfall although it was small in area (fig. 2.2). Andrew came in straight and hard like a fastball. In September 1999, Hurricane Floyd bore down on the east coast of Florida, also as a strong category 4 hurricane (see "Ranking Hurricane Intensities," below). Floyd threatened to wreak major havoc (fig. 2.2) but then turned and paralleled the coast, passing about 95 miles east of Cape Canaveral. In our baseball analogy, Floyd was a curveball that missed the peninsula. The storm diminished in strength while still off Florida, and finally made landfall near Cape Fear, North Carolina, in the early morning of September 16 as a category 2 hurricane. Later that same year, Hurricane Irene passed northward over the Florida Keys and off the east coast, but its sustained winds earned it only a category 1 ranking. Irene did bring 10–20 inches of rain, similar to several hurricanes in the 1930s and 1940s. When Hurricane Georges passed the Florida Keys in 1998, its highest sustained winds were 91 mph (category 1), with gusts to 107 mph.

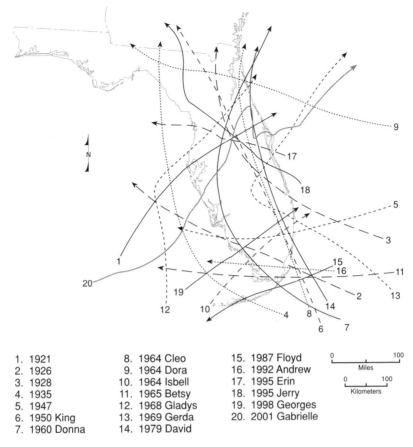

1. 1921	8. 1964 Cleo	15. 1987 Floyd
2. 1926	9. 1964 Dora	16. 1992 Andrew
3. 1928	10. 1964 Isbell	17. 1995 Erin
4. 1935	11. 1965 Betsy	18. 1995 Jerry
5. 1947	12. 1968 Gladys	19. 1998 Georges
6. 1950 King	13. 1969 Gerda	20. 2001 Gabrielle
7. 1960 Donna	14. 1979 David	

2.1 Storm tracks of landfalling and other hurricanes to affect East Florida, 1921–1999. The National Hurricane Center's website (see appendix B for address) has tracks of more recent hurricanes. Various types of arrows are for clarity only.

Stories of "living through" these hurricanes abound, but not one of the three actually made landfall with hurricane-force winds! Not a single person in Florida who felt the impacts of Georges or Irene or Floyd can accurately say they have "survived a hurricane"—at least not in reference to those three storms.

Even the devastating Hurricane Andrew of 1992, the costliest natural disaster in U.S. history, with more than $25 billion in damages, has already begun to fade from memory. People have forgotten that although Andrew was an extremely powerful storm (category 4), it was also a relatively small storm. The storm surge in excess of 6 feet spread along the coast for only about 25 miles, compared with more than 80 miles for Hugo.

It is often useful to think of individual storms in terms of "lessons learned." Ideally, as we recover and rebuild after a hurricane—or any natu-

2.2 Satellite photo comparison of Hurricanes Floyd (1999) and Andrew (1992). Andrew, which tracked east to west across South Florida, was a tight but powerful storm that affected a relatively small swath. Floyd passed offshore, sparing Florida the great damage this large storm would have reaped over a larger coastal and land area. Even Floyd's offshore passage caused considerable coastal erosion damage. From NOAA satellite image archives.

ral disaster—we should learn from the experience and not make the same mistakes again. Sadly, the lessons from Hurricane Andrew indicate that we still have much to learn. The lessons learned from Andrew should include the following:

1. You should not rely on elected or appointed officials to create a low-risk coastal environment.

2. Building codes are a minimal mitigation technique, and even less so when they are not enforced (do not rely on codes or building inspectors).

3. The choice to spend a few hundred extra dollars to improve the integrity of your house or building may be the difference between survival and loss.

4. Don't become complacent! You lack storm experience (even if you think you have been through a hurricane).

5. You cannot out-engineer Nature.

6. Development will never be discouraged by a hurricane.

Hurricanes and tropical storms have always been an intimate part of the Florida experience (fig. 2.1), and the danger posed by these massive storms cannot be overstated. Tables 2.1 and 2.2 give information, respectively, on the costliest and deadliest hurricanes to hit the United States. Unfortunately, growth rates in the coastal zone constantly renew the population with generations of inexperienced coastal dwellers. Andrew and its cousins should not just shake our memories of the past; they should also provide us with a glimpse of the future.

Table 2.1 The Costliest Hurricanes in the United States, 1900–1996

Ranking	Hurricane	Year	Category	Damage (u.s.)[a]
1	Andrew (s.e. fl/s.e. la)	1992	4	$30,475,000,000
2	Hugo (sc)	1989	4	$8,491,561,181
3	Agnes (n.e. u.s.)	1972	1	$7,500,000,000
4	Betsy (fl/la)	1965	3	$7,425,340,909
5	Camille (ms/al)	1969	5	$6,096,287,313
6	Diane (n.e. us)	1955	1	$4,830,580,808
7	Frederic (al/ms)	1979	3	$4,328,968,903
8	New England	1938	3[b]	$4,140,000,000
9	Fran (nc)	1996	3	$3,200,000,000
10	Opal (n.w. fl/al)	1995	3[b]	$3,069,395,018
11	Alicia (n. tx)	1983	3	$2,983,138,781
12	Carol (n.e. u.s.)	1954	3[b]	$2,732,731,959
13	Carla (tx)	1961	4	$2,223,696,682
14	Juan (la)	1985	1	$2,108,801,956
15	Donna (fl/e. u.s.)	1960	4	$2,099,292,453
16	Celia (s. tx)	1970	3	$1,834,330,986
17	Elena (ms/al/n.w. fl)	1985	3	$1,757,334,963
18	Bob (nc and n.e. u.s.)	1991	2	$1,747,720,365
19	Hazel (sc/nc)	1954	4[b]	$1,665,721,649
20	fl (Miami)	1926	4	$1,515,294,118
21	n. tx (Galveston)	1915	4	$1,346,341,463[c]
22	Dora (n.e. fl)	1964	2	$1,343,457,944
23	Eloise (n.w. fl)	1975	3	$1,298,387,097
24	Gloria (e. u.s.)	1985	3[b]	$1,265,281,174
25	n.e. u.s.	1944	3[d]	$1,064,814,815
26	Beulah (s. tx)	1967	3	$970,464,135
27	s.e. fl/la/ms	1947	4	$810,897,436
28	n. tx (Galveston)	1900	4	$809,207,317[e]
29	Audrey (la/n. tx)	1957	4	$802,325,581
30	Claudette (n. tx)	1979	t.s.[f]	$752,864,157

Note: The top 30 cyclones with more than $400 million damage on the u.s. mainland are listed.

[a] Adjusted to 1996 dollars on basis of u.s. Department of Commerce Implicit Price Deflator for Construction.

[b] Moving more than 30 mph.

[c] Damage estimate was considered too high in 1915 reference.

[d] Probably higher.

[e] Using 1915 cost adjustment base; none available prior to 1915.

[f] Only of tropical storm intensity but included because of high damage.

Source: The Deadliest, Costliest, and Most Intense United States Hurricanes of This Century (and Other Frequently Requested Hurricane Facts) (appendix C, ref. 9).

Table 2.2 The Deadliest Hurricanes in the United States 1900–1996

Ranking	Hurricane	Year	Category	Deaths
1	TX (Galveston)	1900	4	8,000[a]
2	FL (Lake Okeechobee)	1928	4	1,836
3	FL (Keys)/S. TX	1919	4	600[b]
4	New England	1938	3[c]	600
5	FL (Keys)	1935	5	408
6	Audrey (S.W. LA/N. TX)	1957	4	390
7	N.E. U.S.	1944	3[c]	390[d]
8	LA (Grand Isle)	1909	4	350
9	LA (New Orleans)	1915	4	275
10	TX (Galveston)	1915	4	275
11	Camille (MS/LA)	1969	5	256
12	FL (Miami)/MS/AL/Pensacola	1926	4	243
13	Diane (N.E. U.S.)	1955	1	184
14	S.E. FL	1906	2	164
15	MS/AL/Pensacola	1906	3	134
16	Agnes (N.E. U.S.)	1972	1	122
17	Donna (St. Thomas, VI)	1960	4	107
18	Hazel (SC/NC)	1954	4[c]	95
19	Betsy (S.E. FL/S.E. LA)	1965	3	75
20	Carol (N.E. U.S.)	1954	3[c]	60
21	S.E. FL/LA/MS	1947	4	51
22	Donna (FL/E. U.S.)	1960	4	50
23	GA/SC/NC	1940	2	50
24	Carla (TX)	1961	4	46
25	S. CA	1939	T.S.[e]	45
26	Eloise (Puerto Rico)	1975	T.S.[e]	44
27	TX (Velasco)	1909	3	41
28	TX (Freeport)	1932	3	40
29	S. TX	1933	3	40
30	Hilda (LA)	1964	3	38

Note: The top 30 cyclones for the U.S. mainland and Caribbean are listed.
[a] May actually have been as high as 10,000 to 12,000.
[b] Over 500 of these lost on ships at sea; 600–900 estimated deaths.
[c] Moving more than 30 mph.
[d] Some 344 of these lost on ships at sea.
[e] Only of tropical storm intensity.
Source: The Deadliest, Costliest, and Most Intense United States Hurricanes of This Century (and Other Frequently Requested Hurricane Facts) (appendix C, ref. 9).

Hurricanes are responsible for most of the storm-related coastal property damage in the United States. However, other types of storms, particularly northeasters along the U.S. Atlantic coast, are very important as well. Properly referred to by meteorologists as extratropical cyclones, or cyclones that form outside the tropics, these storms are associated with large, intense low-pressure systems that move offshore along the coast and are accompa-

Table 2.3 Atlantic/Caribbean/Gulf of Mexico Cities or Islands Ranked in Terms of Hurricane and Tropical Storm Activity, 1871–2001

Ranking	Location	Average Years Between Storms	Total Number of Storm Passages
1	Cayman Islands	2.22	59
2	Andros Island, Bahamas	2.42	54
7	Florida City, FL	2.67	49
8	Hollywood, FL	2.67	49
10	Miami, FL	2.73	48
11	Cancun, Mexico	2.73	48
12	Delray Beach, FL	2.73	48
13	Boca Raton, FL	2.73	48
15	Key West, FL	2.79	47
16	Isle of Youth, Cuba	2.79	47
17	Fort Pierce, FL	2.79	47
19	Cape Hatteras, NC	2.85	46
20	Fort Lauderdale, FL	2.85	46
21	Stuart, FL	2.91	44
23	Deerfield Beach, FL	2.91	45
25	Key Largo, FL	2.98	44
26	Jupiter, FL	2.98	44
27	Nassau, Bahamas	2.98	44
28	Lake Worth, FL	2.98	44
45	Vero Beach, FL	3.19	41
46	Palm Beach, FL	3.19	41
47	Marathon, FL	3.27	40

Note: Based on all hurricanes and tropical storms moving within 60 miles of the city. Listed are Florida east coast cities, plus other selected cities for comparison. Note that this is a ranking that changes annually, and it reflects the passage of storms within 60 miles of a given locale, not direct hits.
Source: From http://www.hurricanecity.com.

nied by winds and waves out of the southwest. Such storms are frequent enough and severe enough to cause significant coastal damage along the shoreline (tables 2.1 and 2.3). Rarely a year goes by without a hurricane or northeaster eroding some part of the Florida shore.

Hurricanes

The actual processes that affect the coastal zone are similar in all storms, but they are most intense in hurricanes. During the relatively hurricane-free period from the 1960s to 1992, the majority of Florida's coastal residents and property owners had never experienced the full force of such storms. Even though some significant hurricanes hit during this period, including Donna in 1960, Dora and Isbell in 1964, and Betsy in 1965, these years can be thought of as a time of relative quiescence. The quiet ended with Andrew in 1992. There have been some close calls, but no major hurricane has made landfall on the Florida east coast since then. Even the near-record Atlantic Basin activity year of 1995 (19 named storms, 11 hurricanes) brought no major activity to the east coast of the Sunshine State.

This lull has led to an apathetic disregard for the hurricane menace and increased development in high-hazard zones. Times of recovery from large storms, such as Andrew, were looked on as opportunities to come back "bigger and better" rather than as times to plan new development better able to weather the next storm. You never see a poststorm slogan that says "We'll come back smaller and safer." The odds are evening out. The big one will hit, and likely sooner rather than later (tables 2.1, 2.2, and 2.3). Time is not on the side of coastal development.

Each year on June 1 the official hurricane season begins. For the next five or six months, conditions favorable to hurricane formation can develop over the tropical to subtropical waters of the Western Hemisphere. Early-season tropical cyclones form mostly in the Gulf of Mexico or Caribbean Sea where the waters can heat up faster than the Atlantic Ocean. The monster hurricanes that strike the U.S. east and Gulf of Mexico coasts usually originate later in the season (August, September, and October) in the eastern North Atlantic and intensify on their long, slow trek across the ocean. Of the 11 most severe hurricanes that hit the Florida east coast between 1900 and 1996, 7 hit in September.

The classic "Cape Verde" hurricane begins as clusters of thundershowers moving off the west coast of Africa. The rotating winds create airflow in, up, and out. With increased organization of wind rotation, a tropical depression is formed. A tropical depression evolves into a tropical storm when the wind speed reaches 39 mph. Once formed, the storm mass begins to track westward and into higher latitudes and may continue to grow in size and strength, attaining hurricane status when wind velocities reach 74 mph or greater. The velocity of the storm's tracking movement can vary from nearly stationary to greater than 60 mph. When a hurricane makes landfall, the destructive forces are at their maximum in the area to the right of the forward motion of the eye (fig. 2.3). The entire landfall area, however, will experience the severity of the storm, and even storms that pass offshore can generate significant destruction. You should not feel any security in the knowledge that you are to the left of the eye or that the eye is passing offshore! Even in areas where the tidal range is small, if the hurricane strikes during a high tide, especially a spring high tide (the highest high tide), the effects of storm-surge flooding, waves, and overwash will be magnified. And Florida's coastal residents face a double whammy because hurricanes can strike and cross the state from both the Atlantic Ocean and the Gulf of Mexico.

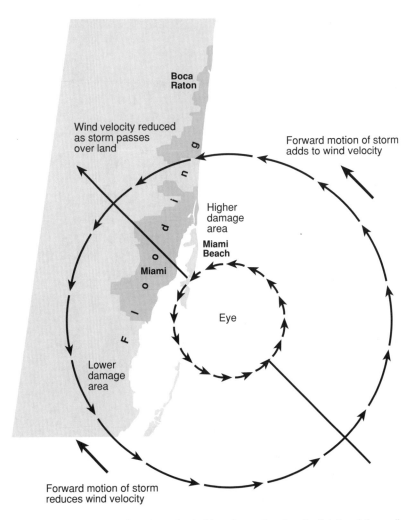

Boca
Raton

Wind velocity reduced
as storm passes
over land

Forward motion of storm
adds to wind velocity

Landing

Higher
damage
area

Miami
Beach

Miami

Eye

Florida

Lower
damage
area

Forward motion of storm
reduces wind velocity

2.3 Wind distribution for a hypothetical hurricane showing the "right of the eye" effect. The path shown here is probably the one of greatest potential destruction to the reach from Miami Beach to Fort Lauderdale.

Hurricane Probability

The probability that a hurricane will make landfall at any given point along the coast in any one year is low, and the probability that it will be a great hurricane is even lower (fig. 2.4). But low probabilities stated for any given year give a false sense of security. The lesson of hurricane history tells us that such a storm is likely in the lifetime of a coastal structure. For example, a study by James Balsillie suggests that a house with a 50-year planned life has a 40 percent chance of experiencing the 100-year erosional event (1 percent annual probability) in the course of its planned life (appendix C, ref.

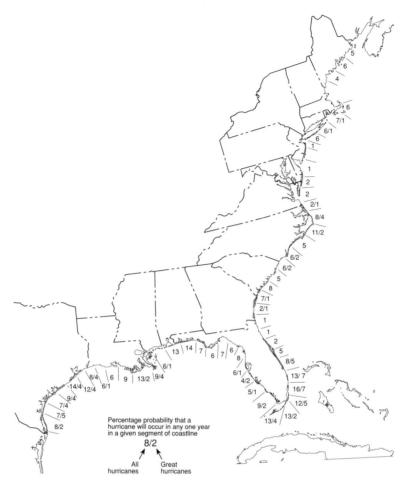

2.4 Hurricane probability map. Numbers are the percent probability that a hurricane (top number) or great hurricane (winds 125 mph or greater) will occur in any one year along 50-mile segments of the coast. Note that the percentages for southeast Florida are the highest for the entire U.S. Atlantic and Gulf coasts!

65). Furthermore, the annual probabilities of hurricanes are calculated from a limited number of records. Such storms are probably cyclic and occur clustered in time. Balsillie notes a deficit of Florida-incident hurricanes since about 1970 and predicts an increased incidence of hurricanes in the near future. Consider this in combination with the fact that the densest coastal population is in southeastern Florida, the area that has the highest hurricane probabilities in the nation!

According to National Oceanic and Atmospheric Administration (NOAA) data, from 1900 to 2002, 167 hurricanes made landfall on the U.S. mainland from Maine to Texas. Of those, 59 affected Florida and 35 affected the

Florida east coast (several affected both the Atlantic and Gulf coasts). When only major hurricanes (category 3, 4, or 5) are considered, the U.S. east and Gulf coasts have been affected by 65 hurricanes, Florida by 24, and the Florida east coast by 11—all in the southeastern Florida area (fig. 2.1). Furthermore, the occurrence of a great hurricane one year does not reduce the likelihood that a similar storm will strike the next year. And several storms can strike the same area in a single year (e.g., the multiple hurricanes Earl, Georges, and Mitch in the Caribbean in 1998).

Death tolls from modern hurricanes have been greatly reduced, thanks to National Weather Service warnings, radio and television communications, and evacuation and sheltering plans. Nevertheless, we must not grow complacent; the storm response can be improved. The hurricane watchers of NOAA track hurricanes and provide advance warning for the evacuation of threatened coastal areas. Yet, as little as 9 to 12 hours of advance warning may be all that is possible given the unpredictable turns a hurricane can take. This is alarming in view of the fact that the estimated evacuation clearance times for many communities exceed the warning lead time (table 2.4). The National Hurricane Center began issuing 5-day forecasts for hurricanes. However, one should regard 5-day forecasts as imperfect.

Clearly, portions of the East Florida coast have population densities that will stretch the system's capacity for storm evacuation. A 1992 study indicated that three of the five worst evacuation problem areas in the United States are in Florida. The more people on the coast, the longer the time

Table 2.4 Evacuation Clearance Times for East Florida Counties

County	Category 1	Category 2	Category 3	Category 4	Category 5
Nassau	10+	12+	13	13+	13+
Duval	9	12	17	20	20
St. Johns	11	14	16	17	17
Flagler	8	8	12	12	12
Volusia	8	8	10	11	11
Brevard	12	12	18	18	18
Indian River	7	7	11	11	11
St. Lucie	8	8	9	9	9
Martin	9	9	14+	18	18
Palm Beach	7	15	14	16	16
Broward	12	12	15	19	19
Dade	10	10	12	15	15
Monroe	12	12	36	36	36

Note: Counties are listed from north to south. Times are in hours. Variability in times reflects the differences in the number of people to be evacuated and the limited number of routes of egress off of barrier islands and flood-prone areas.
Source: Modified from the Florida Department of Community Affairs website, http://www.dca.state.fl.us/bpr/Response/Plans/nathaz/hurricanes/clearance_times.htm.

needed to evacuate them; and evacuation may become dangerous. For example, a hurricane approaching the southeastern Florida coast will trigger the evacuation of tens of thousands of residents and visitors from the Florida Keys into the Miami metropolitan area. These people, plus the metropolitan area population, will then need to be evacuated or sheltered. Add to this the large number of retired, elderly, and special-needs people living in the area, and the emergency preparedness and response teams will be taxed to their limit. Just such a scenario became reality with Hurricane Floyd in 1999. Fortunately, Floyd stayed offshore and never made landfall in Florida, but the chaos of that evacuation is an omen of what will happen in the future.

Sometimes the only possible choice is vertical evacuation—taking shelter on the upper floors of high-rise buildings in the area of the storm. Although a high-rise has never fallen in a storm, do you want to be the guinea pig in the next "test" hurricane?

Has your community exceeded the critical population limits for safe and timely evacuation? You need to be prepared, know your community's storm-response plan, and take appropriate action when the warning comes. Further unsafe development must be prevented, and population growth cannot be allowed to exceed the capacity for safe evacuation. After the traffic gridlock caused by Opal, people demanded more and expanded roads; but more access encourages more development in areas already beyond their evacuation carrying capacity. After Hurricane Floyd, which caused gridlock across the entire Southeast, states were required to review their evacuation plans.

One thing is certain from a review of storm history: storms do not occur in a regular pattern or with regular spacing. One big storm can follow on the heels of another, or several years can go by without a big event. Over the lifetime of a house, however, it is certain that several storms will affect the property (table 2.3). In order to prepare for such storms and attempt to reduce their impact in terms of property losses and potential loss of life, we must understand two things: how our particular part of the coast interacts with storms, and the potential for conflict between nature and development.

Ranking Hurricane Intensities

The National Weather Service has adopted the Saffir/Simpson scale (table 2.5) for communicating the strength and damage potential of a hurricane to public safety officials of communities in the storm's potential path. The scale ranks a storm on three variables—wind velocity, storm surge, and barometric pressure—and communicates quickly the nature of the storm and what to expect in terms of wind, waves, and flooding. The risk for property damage and the property damage mitigation recommendations

Table 2.5 The Saffir-Simpson Hurricane Scale

Scale Number (Category)	1	2	3	4	5
Central pressure					
Millibars	≥980	979–965	964–945	944–920	≤919
Inches of mercury	≥28.94	28.91–28.50	28.47–27.91	27.88–27.17	≤27.16
Winds					
Miles per hour	74–95	96–110	111–130	131–155	>155
Kilometers per hour	119–153	154–177	179–209	211–249	>249
Meters per second	32–42	42–49	50–57	58–68	>69
Surge					
Feet	4–5	6–8	9–12	13–18	>18
Meters	1.2–1.5	1.8–2.4	2.7–3.7	4.0–5.5	>5.5
Damage	Minimal	Moderate	Extensive	Extreme	Catastrophic
East Florida examples	Erin 1995	Cleo 1969 Dora 1962	Betsy 1965 King 1950	Andrew 1992 1928 Lake Okeechobee	1935 Florida Keys

discussed throughout this book are based on moderate category 3 hurricane conditions. Category 4 and 5 storms will cause massive property damage or destruction in spite of mitigation efforts. Do not be misled by such classifications, however. A hurricane is a hurricane. The scale simply defines how bad is "bad." When the word comes to evacuate, do it. The wind velocity may change, or the configuration of the coast may amplify the storm-surge level, so the category rank can change. Don't gamble with your life or the lives of others.

Hurricane History: A Stormy Past

Today, anyone on the coast, particularly on a barrier island, during a hurricane is almost certainly there by choice. In the past, people could not be warned of a hurricane's approach and were not always able to flee to safety before a hurricane struck. The absence of warning made hurricanes even more feared then than they are today and accentuated the need for safe development. Figure 2.1 shows the tracks of several hurricanes that have impacted the Florida coast.

According to the National Hurricane Center, 6 of the 30 costliest storms to strike the Atlantic and Gulf coasts of the United States hit the Florida east coast: Andrew (1992), Betsy (1965), Dora (1964), Donna (1960), the south-

2.5 Coastal erosion and property damage to the Seacrest Hotel, Delray Beach area, from the September 1947 hurricane. Photo from the Photographic Collection of the Florida State Archives.

east Florida storm of 1947 (fig. 2.5), and the 1926 Miami storm (see fig. 1.17). Of the 30 deadliest storms to strike the United States, 7 hit the Florida east coast: Betsy (1965), the southeast Florida storm of 1947, the 1935 Florida Keys storm, the 1928 Lake Okeechobee storm, the 1926 Miami storm, the 1919 Florida Keys storm, and the 1906 southeast Florida storm.

Early Hurricanes
The effects of early storms were generally not well documented because so few people lived on the barrier islands, although personal accounts and reports reflect the storms' intensities and impacts. The following information, taken largely from *Florida Hurricanes and Tropical Storms*, by John M. Williams and Iver W. Duedall (appendix C, ref. 7); *Florida's Hurricane History*, by Jay Barnes (appendix C, ref. 6); and the National Climate Data Center's Internet website (www.ncdc.noaa.gov), summarizes some historical tropical storm and hurricane data for the area.

Among the most significant storms to strike East Florida were the major hurricane of August 1880, which impacted Cocoa Beach and the surrounding area; an October 1906 hurricane that resulted in the deaths of 164 railroad workers in Miami; the September 1926 "Great Miami Hurricane," which hit as a category 4 storm with a storm surge above 13 feet, causing 243 deaths and more than $112 million in damages; a September 1928 category 4 hurricane in the Palm Beach area, which generated winds in excess of 100 mph, a storm surge of 10 to 15 feet, and caused 1,836 deaths and $26 million in damages; and the September 1947 Pompano Beach category 4 hurricane, which had winds recorded at 155 mph and a storm surge above 21 feet, and caused 51 deaths and $704 million in damages.

Before 1941, storms were not named and were referred to by the dates they hit or the areas they affected. From 1941 to 1950, storms were named using the World War II phonetic alphabet (i.e., Able, Baker, Charlie, Dog, Easy, and so on). Beginning in 1953, hurricanes were given female names. Donna (1960), which caused $300 million damage ($1.9 billion in 1990 dollars) and had wind gusts to 150 mph, affected the Florida Keys and both the east and west coasts. In September 1964, Hurricane Dora struck nearly head-on near St. Augustine, crossed the peninsula, and impacted the Florida Panhandle. Dora left five people dead and caused more than $250 million in damage ($1 billion in 1990 dollars). Hurricane Isbell (October 1964) crossed Cuba and the Florida Straits, affected the Ten Thousand Islands area of Florida, and then turned to the northeast, crossed the peninsula, and passed offshore near Fort Lauderdale. The period between 1971 and 1980 saw the lowest number of storms for a 10-year period in Florida, with only three hurricanes and one tropical storm. In 1979, male names were integrated into the lists of female names for hurricanes by the National Hurricane Center.

Recent Hurricanes
The twentieth century closed with an upswing in hurricanes. For the United States in general, it began in the 1980s with several smaller storms. The decade culminated in 1989 with Hugo, which made landfall at Charleston, South Carolina, and continued inland to Charlotte, North Carolina, and beyond.

The 1990s began with Andrew (1992), the costliest natural disaster in U.S. history (fig. 2.6). Andrew was a compact but very powerful storm. Although it affected only a short section of the coast, the winds were so fierce that entire neighborhoods were destroyed. Particularly noteworthy was the devastation of Homestead, Florida, a town that has yet to recover. Winds of more than 175 mph caused 48 deaths and nearly $30 billion in damages.

Subsequently, 1995 was one of the most active hurricane seasons on record; in fact, it was the most active storm season since 1933, the second busiest hurricane season since 1871! Nineteen named storms formed, 11 of which reached hurricane stage. Florida, however, was hit only by Hurricane Erin, which came ashore north of Vero Beach as a category 1 storm (table 2.5). Although Erin generated $700 million in damage, its impact on the Florida Atlantic coast was relatively light.

Then came the 1998 and 1999 seasons, and Nature truly made up for the

2.6 Property damage from Hurricane Andrew (1992) in the Lakes by the Bay development. Photo from NOAA. Andrew's impact was mainly from strong winds rather than storm surge and associated coastal flooding and waves. A good overview of Hurricane Andrew's impact is provided by *In the Eye of Hurricane Andrew*, a book by Eugene and Asterie Provenzo (University Press of Florida, 2002).

lull. Hurricane Georges (1998) was only a category 2 storm, but it did serious damage when it passed over the Keys (see chapter 7). Irene hit the same area a year later, following Floyd (fig. 2.2) in a season that illustrated how the damage from one storm creates greater vulnerability to the next storm. Floyd is an example of a storm that never made landfall but affected long reaches of shoreline in terms of serious erosion. The 1999 storms also revealed the growing problems of evacuating an ever-increasing population and maintaining a strong public commitment to evacuation after a "false alarm" when the storm did not make landfall.

The twenty-first century holds hurricanes, great and small, in store for Florida. An article in the *Palm Beach Post* (May 27, 2001) retelling the story of the 1926 hurricane notes: "If such a hurricane were to take the same path now, head-on into Miami, it would cause more than twice the damage that Andrew would cause if it hit today. It also might kill more people—perhaps a lot more." Individuals may not be able to prevent this potential tragedy, but we can take prudent actions to reduce our own exposure to risk. Selecting lower-risk building sites, using the best construction techniques and materials available, and always taking storm warnings and evacuation orders seriously is a good start.

Winter Storms

Although only a few winter storms affect the east coast of Florida each year, these storms are often larger and more persistent than hurricanes. Hurricanes are typically 300 to 400 miles in diameter (zone of gale force winds), with the greatest winds concentrated in the wall of the eye (the eye may be up to 50 to 60 miles in diameter). A hurricane's exposure to any given area of the coast is usually measured in hours. Winter storms are neither so concentrated nor so brief. A winter storm may cover more than 1,000 miles and may linger for days. Winter storms, also called nor'easters and northeasters, are extratropical cyclones, meaning the storm is a rotating mass of air (counterclockwise rotation in the Northern Hemisphere) born outside the tropics.

Northeasters typically form as low-pressure cells over the Gulf of Mexico or the Pacific Ocean. As they track to the east and north, their counterclockwise rotating winds pull moisture from the Atlantic onto the heavily populated eastern seaboard, and the winds arrive at those locations from the northeast, hence the name "northeaster." These are the same storms that are called "southwesters" when they affect the U.S. Gulf coast. Most often these cells track to the northeast, gaining strength from the warmer waters of the Atlantic Ocean.

The development of destructive winter storms requires the presence of a strong, stable high-pressure system over eastern Canada. This prevents the storm from moving quickly to the north or northeast and ensures that it will remain over ocean water for a longer period, often several days. The longer the storm remains offshore, the more powerful it can become. The result is that storm surge and waves are the most destructive processes along the coast during a northeaster.

The northeaster/southwester of March 12–15, 1993, was named the "Storm of the Century." Although it was not a record-breaking coastal storm, it caused widespread damage that included storm surge and wave erosion along the Florida Panhandle, record-breaking snow cover inland along the U.S. east coast, and cosmetic but costly wind damage to coastal buildings from Florida to Maine. Total damage estimates exceeded $6 billion. The storm was blamed for 44 deaths in Florida, although several deaths were indirect results of the storm (e.g., traffic accidents). Every major airport on the east coast was closed at one time or another by this massive storm. Florida was struck by 15 tornadoes during this storm.

The "Storm of the Century" had associated hurricane-strength winds. The Dry Tortugas, west of Key West, recorded gusts of 109 mph. In fact, on the Saffir-Simpson scale (table 2.5), the storm equated to a category 3 hurricane, based on storm surge and minimum pressure attained.

2.7 Associated storm hazards such as lightning and waterspouts are illustrated by this 1980 photo taken in the Florida Keys. Photo from the Photographic Collection of the Florida State Archives.

Other Storm-Related Hazards

Although the focus here is on site safety and property damage mitigation from coastal processes, any storm can be deadly. Lightning, strong winds, the rare tornado, and waterspouts are potential killers that cause property damage (fig. 2.7). In fact, if you are concerned only with probabilities of being affected by natural hazards, your primary concern probably should be lightning. Lightning kills an average of 10 people a year in Florida, and the state leads the nation in lightning casualties (deaths and injuries). Windstorms also create such hazards as falling trees and flying debris that act as missiles. Waterspouts, although rare, can be a threat to boaters, and tornadoes, which also are rare in Florida, are sometimes generated by hurricanes. Local flash flooding causes property loss and the occasional drowning.

Coastal Storm Processes

Storm processes are natural forces that include wind, waves, coastal and inlet currents, storm-surge flooding, and storm-surge flood and ebb currents. Wind, waves, and rising water account for most storm damage. Currents are responsible for moving vast amounts of sediment during storms. Storm surge, the onshore movement of water, causes flooding and may create scouring currents around and behind structures. The rising water level allows the zone of wave attack to move inland, and sediment to wash over onto the land. Storm-surge ebb, or the seaward return of storm surge, is a less familiar storm process that may erode new inlets and contribute to the overall damage.

Natural Processes: Energy in Motion

Storm processes rarely act separately. That is, wind, waves, and currents all are active at the same time and combine to form secondary processes. For example, storm surge is formed by several processes acting together: wind pushes water toward shore, waves push water toward shore, low pressure allows doming of the sea surface, and the rotating winds of a hurricane actually cause the shallow water near shore to spiral higher. Any one of these processes may be dominant during any given storm or for a given period during a certain storm. Consider the following individual storm processes, but keep in mind their combined actions during storms.

Wind

The most common, and often the most costly, storm hazard that causes damage to buildings is direct wind impact on structures, including damage from flying debris (known as "missiling"). In addition, strong winds can destroy vegetation by uprooting and knocking over trees, by defoliating trees and other vegetation, by blowing down shrubs and grasses, and by damaging leaves directly, either by blasting leaves with airborne sand or by carrying damaging salt spray inland. The same salt-spray pruning effect that produces the nearshore sloping profile of maritime vegetation will kill or damage inland vegetation that is not salt-tolerant. Strong winds can also be responsible for transporting sediment onto and off the shore.

Storm Waves

Structures and property can be damaged by direct wave attack or when they are pummeled by floating debris, a process called "ramrodding." Concrete pillboxes are probably the only type of buildings capable of surviving direct wave assault unscathed. Even lighthouses have toppled under wave attack. Waves are also responsible for shoreline erosion (on bay and lagoon shores as well as ocean shores), dune erosion, overwash, and destruction of vegetation.

Currents

Storm-generated currents transport water, sediment, and storm debris both parallel and perpendicular to the coast. Waves usually approach the coast at an angle, then break to create a current called the longshore current, which moves parallel to the shore. This current can move sediment (and storm debris such as trees, sand fences, and dune crossovers or walkways) for great distances. The sediment loss may be temporary or permanent, depending on many other factors. Rip currents may be intensified during part of the storm, making conditions even more dangerous for those foolhardy enough to try to surf or swim during a storm. Changes in channel positions during storms may cause erosion of, or deposition on, adjacent islands.

Storm Surge

Storm surge is technically defined as "the super-elevation of the still-water surface that results from the transport and circulation of water induced by wind stresses and pressure gradients in an atmospheric storm" (fig. 2.8; appendix C, ref. 10). "Pressure gradient" refers to the lowered atmospheric pressure in storms that by itself can cause a rise in sea level. Such a rise in local sea level extends the zone of wave impact inland, causing flooding and damage to structures. The initial flow over and around obstructions (e.g., pilings) may cause scouring and sediment transport. Storm surges that flood barrier islands may form overwash deposits when they transport beach sand onto the island and across it into the adjacent sound. Storm surge can also float structures off their foundations; float debris inland,

2.8   Florida storm-surge map. Adapted from NOAA data.

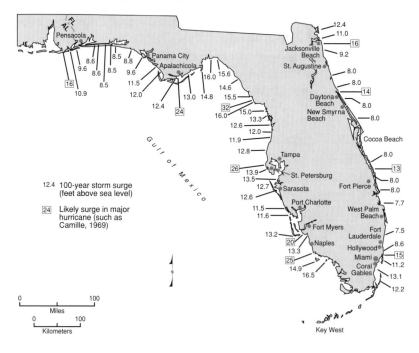

sometimes with ramrod force; and damage inland plants that are not salt-water-tolerant.

While a hurricane is in deep water offshore, storm surge is minimized by currents at greater depths moving water away. As the hurricane moves onto the continental shelf and makes landfall, these currents are eliminated by the slope of the shelf and the shoreline, and the converging water rises or piles up. Maximum storm-surge heights (measured relative to mean sea level) have been recorded at the head of bays or even inland away from the shoreline. Generally, storm surge gradually rises to a peak, then returns to normal, all within 6 to 12 hours. Storm surge, which has been known to reach heights of 20 to 30 feet, has been responsible for some of the largest losses of life associated with hurricanes.

Storm-Surge Ebb

As the storm passes, the "piled-up" storm-surge water flows back to sea, either by the force of gravity alone or when driven by offshore-blowing winds, generating an erosive ebb current. This type of current occurs while the storm is moving out of the area or diminishing. Storm-surge ebb can cause an existing inlet to change shape, create a new inlet, scour shallow cross-island channels (breaches), transport storm debris (including houses) offshore, and cause permanent removal of sand from the beach/dune system to the deeper offshore area.

Human Coastal Modifications:
Altering the Response to Natural Processes

Construction in the coastal zone may enhance or alter the natural processes described above and increase their resulting impacts. Roads and beach access paths that are perpendicular to the shore and that penetrate the dune line will become overwash passes or focal points for storm-surge flood or ebb currents. Seawalls may redistribute wave energy or obstruct sediment movement. Jetties may block great volumes of sand from being transported along the coast, resulting in deposition of sand and beach widening on the updrift side and a long-term sand deficit and erosion on the downdrift side. Groin fields and breakwaters have the same effect of interrupting along-shore sediment transport. Ground-level houses and closed-in ground floors of houses on stilts will obstruct the passage of overwash sand, which is then lost to shorefront erosion. Where vegetation cover has been removed, erosion by wind or water may occur.

Loss of beach sand increases a community's vulnerability to future storms. The protective role of a heavily nourished beach such as Miami Beach is unclear. Claims of communities with replenished beaches to have sustained less damage during recent hurricanes than neighboring beaches may be unfounded. Variability in the storm processes or geologic setting may have had more to do with it than the mitigative effects of a long and costly history of beach replenishment.

Studies conducted after Hurricane Opal (1995, Panhandle) showed that Florida's Coastal Construction Control Line (cccl; see chapter 9) had a positive effect in reducing damage by the storm along the Panhandle shores. About one-quarter of the major habitable structures seaward of the cccl were permitted buildings. Almost half of the nonpermitted structures were seriously damaged or destroyed, while only two permitted structures were seriously damaged. Hurricanes Opal, Fran, and Hugo also demonstrated the important protective role of dunes. In contrast, seawalls did not prevent property damage.

Understanding your shore type, whether barrier island or mainland beach, is important to mitigating storm impact and avoiding property loss.

3   The Variable Coast: Beaches, Barrier Islands, and Coastal Processes

Living with the coast requires an overview that goes beyond the focal point of the beach and an awareness of storms. Knowledge of the suitability of a particular coastal type for development, and how it might change during the lifetime of a cottage or condominium, is essential. Understanding the beach requires some knowledge of the coast that the beach is fringing. East Florida's sandy barrier coast extends approximately 365 miles from the Georgia border to Key Biscayne in Dade County and is more complex than a simple barrier-island coast. Although the East Florida coast does not appear to be particularly complex, differences in the underlying geology, wave and tide dynamics, and sediment supply create regional variations. Like all natural systems, the coast is in balance or equilibrium with the various factors that shape the shore. Coastal types will change in response to even subtle changes in these controlling factors. So, different parts of the coast will respond differently to the same storm.

The East Florida coast is subdivided into four physiographic regions (see figs. 1.7, 1.8, 1.9; appendix C, refs. 39, 43, and 56):

— The Northeastern Florida Coast includes Nassau, Duval, St. Johns, Flagler, and Volusia Counties. This region has several barrier islands fronting low tidal marsh or lagoon, and six tidal inlets separate the islands. The southern end of the barrier system extends into Brevard County and merges with Cape Canaveral. The mean tidal range for this region is 3 to 6 feet, decreasing to the south. Average wave height increases to the south toward Cape Canaveral. The net longshore transport of sediment is to the south, except for local reversals.

— The Central-East Florida Coast extends south from Cape Canaveral through the long stretch of narrow barrier islands fronting the open water of the Indian River and Hobe Sound, south of St. Lucie Inlet. This stretch fronts Brevard, Indian River, St. Lucie, and Martin Counties, and includes four artificial inlets. The mean tidal range is less than 3 feet. The net long-shore transport is to the south.

— The Southeastern Florida Coast stretches across Palm Beach, Broward, and Dade Counties, with mainland beach in the north, narrow barrier islands fronting Lake Worth, and the Intracoastal Waterway giving some of the shoreline a barrier appearance north of the Miami Beach area where islands front Biscayne Bay. Southern Dade County has mainland shores, including some mangrove coast. This southeastern barrier segment is cut by 10 inlets. Average wave height decreases to the south, as does the amount of sediment being transported by longshore drift. In part, this is because the Fort Lauderdale-to-Miami coast is partially protected from Atlantic swell by the Bahamas. The tidal range is low.

— The Florida Keys extend from Dade County into the waters of Monroe County as a chain of limestone islands. There are few beaches and no sandy barrier islands. This fossil reef tract divides the Atlantic Ocean from the Gulf of Mexico.

As noted, the wave energy, tidal range, and net longshore sediment transport vary along the length of the coast. The direction of longshore transport changes seasonally. Florida coastal geologist Charles Finkl provides a nice summary of the complexities of Florida's geological setting in a paper titled "Pre-emptive Strategies for Enhanced Sand Bypassing and Beach Replenishment Activities in Southeast Florida: A Geological Perspective" (appendix C, ref. 56). Dr. Finkl notes that around 1900, 11 natural tidal inlets divided the east coast of Florida. Several of the inlets in the stretch from Ponce de Leon Inlet at Daytona Beach to Jupiter Inlet near Palm Beach were intermittently breached by storm waters. Starting around 1920, some inlets were artificially opened, including Lake Worth Inlet (1920), Bakers Haulover Inlet (1927), Port Everglades (1928), Fort Pierce (1930), and Sebastian Inlet (1948). Where once 11 natural—and often ephemeral—inlets existed, 19 permanent (stabilized) inlets now exist. One of the consequences of introducing the artificial inlets into the system was to alter greatly the sediment transport regimes. Some sediment actually migrates landward and welds onto the mainland.

Dr. Finkl also explains how underlying rock can have a great control on barrier island location and behavior. Ancient coral reefs that once existed in southeastern Florida are now manifested as the rock cores of many of the modern barrier islands, including Hutchinson Island, Singer Island, Hillsboro Beach, Fort Lauderdale Beach, Dania Beach, and Miami Beach. Much of the southeastern Florida shoreline consists of only 3 to 6 feet of beach sand overlying rocks, and rock outcrops are common along this portion of the coast.

Naturally, few tidal inlets behave identically; some are more or less permanent, others open and close with time, and some follow a pattern of lateral migration—bad news for downstream developments. Artificial inlets cut in bedrock are not likely to migrate, but they must be maintained or they will close. Storms have cut new inlets through barrier islands in historical times, and they will cut through islands in the future. Like all barrier islands, the East Florida chains are highly susceptible to rapid change due to shoreline retreat, overwash, dune development or reduction, and inlet formation and movement. The islands vary in elevation, dune and beach ridge development, and, correspondingly, in how frequently they are flooded and overwashed during storms. Few areas are really suitable for sustainable, long-term development, but this coast has some of the densest development found along U.S. shores. Likewise, the associated development on bay shores and the low-lying mainland is often at risk. For the most part, a great hurricane, or even an Opal equivalent, has not tested this development, although the region has a record of hurricanes.

The Significance of Barrier Islands in Hazard Evaluation

All East Florida development fronted by sandy beaches is at risk from coastal hazards, but barrier islands are of greatest concern because of the concentration of people and buildings on these fragile, vulnerable strips of sand. Barrier islands are perhaps the world's most dynamic real estate; they are capable of actually migrating landward when sea level rises. These islands are also some of the world's most sought-after real estate!

By definition, barrier islands are elongate bodies of sand bounded on either end by inlets that allow salt and fresh water to flow to and from the sound or embayment behind the island. Although some of East Florida's inlets are artificial, the result is the same: all create landforms that act as barrier islands. In front of, or seaward, of the island is the shoreface, a surface that dips steeply beneath the water, usually extending to a depth of 30 or 40 feet before leveling out as the slope of the continental shelf becomes more gentle.

Barrier islands form in response to four common factors:
1. Rising sea level
2. Large sand supply
3. A gently sloping mainland coast (a coastal plain)
4. Sufficient wave energy to move sand

All four requirements must be met before islands will form. Changes in one or more of these factors will upset the balance of an existing island. Perhaps the greatest concerns to development are the effects of diminished sand supplies and rising sea level, whatever its cause.

In general, barrier islands form in one of three ways. (1) A rise in sea level floods the mouths of streams and coastal processes, reworking the interstream divide headlands (fig. 3.1). (2) Beach-dune ridges may form along

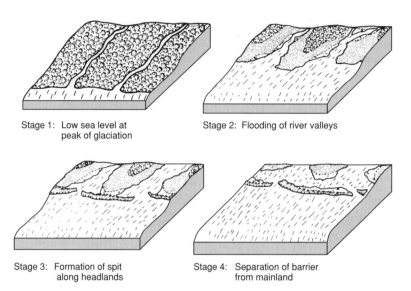

| Stage 1: Low sea level at peak of glaciation | Stage 2: Flooding of river valleys |
| Stage 3: Formation of spit along headlands | Stage 4: Separation of barrier from mainland |

3.1 Barrier island formation during a rising sea level. Stage 1: Straight coast forms during lower sea level. Stage 2: Sea level rises and floods valleys on land, transforming a straight coast into a sinuous coast. Stage 3: Sand eroded from preexisting ridges forms spits. Stage 4: The spits are breached by storms, making them into islands.

straight shorelines and then become barrier islands when the sea-level rise breaches and floods the area in back of the ridges. Such islands tend to be transgressive and migrate shoreward as the sea level continues to rise (see fig. 1.13). Parts of Hutchinson Island and the barriers fronting Indian River may behave in this fashion. (3) Spits may grow parallel to and in front of the mainland shore, sometimes for long distances. Breaching of a spit can result in one or more islands. Some of the East Florida barrier chain may be of breached-spit origin.

Barrier islands often have complex histories. The Sea Islands of Georgia, for example, are Pleistocene-age barrier islands that formed during earlier high stands of sea level and were modified in recent geologic time by the postglacial sea-level rise. Former high stands of sea level have produced barrier islands and shorelines that now make up higher coastal landforms in East Florida. For example, the Atlantic Coastal Ridge, which forms the mainland shore of the Central-East Florida Coast, is the result of a sea level that was around 25 to 28 feet higher than the present sea level 140,000 to 120,000 years before the present (the Pamlico shore). Melbourne is located on this ridge, and you can see other old coastal landforms and ancient shorelines on satellite images of Florida. Amelia Island is an old sea island modified in postglacial time, while Little Talbot Island may be a less complex barrier island in terms of age and origin. Merritt Island is another example of an older landform—in this case, an earlier cape in the Cape Canaveral reach.

Once an island does form, its dynamic nature is expressed almost immediately through changes in island shape, vegetation, and landforms, and in some cases even through migration. Different islands evolve in different ways and at different rates. No two islands are the same, but understanding general island evolution mechanisms is particularly important if you are concerned about living with these short-lived, dynamic features. Know your island. The same is true of mainland shores in Florida. The siting, design, and construction of buildings must be based on the knowledge of coastal processes in order to prevent loss or damage to the structures.

Barrier Island Evolution

Barrier islands form in response to the rising sea level (see figs. 1.6 and 3.1). Although the exact timing is not known, barrier islands had probably formed along the Atlantic seaboard, including Florida, by 3,000 years ago or earlier, although some may have been offshore from their present positions. Once a chain of barrier islands forms, a whole new set of processes takes over. In some cases the islands begin to move landward and/or build upward in response to sea-level rise. This process of island migration is a remarkable mechanism by which the islands can escape drowning by an encroaching sea. We can only speculate that ancestral barrier islands formed early in the postglacial sea-level rise, and that their first few thousand years of existence were marked by rapid landward retreat as the sea level rose at a fairly high rate.

As the rate of sea-level rise slowed around 3,000 to 4,000 years ago, the migration of earlier-formed islands may have slowed; or perhaps this was a time of new island formation as spits elongated along the East Florida coast. No evidence of former barrier islands that would infer migration has been found on the adjacent continental shelf. The fact that much of the East Florida chain is grounded on rock suggests that the islands formed near the positions they occupy at present. As noted above, Amelia Island is a compound island—a modern barrier welded to an earlier Pleistocene barrier. Regardless of their origin and early history, the slower rate of sea-level rise (perhaps less than 2 inches per century) allowed the sandy barriers to stabilize and grow into the island chains that make up the present coast.

As the sea level rises, the mainland shoreline retreats, allowing the barriers to remain islands. Whether migrating or not, these narrow sand islands and sandy shores on which we build our beach cottages and condos are indeed transitory and ephemeral features! The same is true for the South Florida mainland shore. The low elevation of the land, including some in-

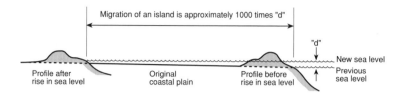

3.2 Ratio of horizontal barrier island migration to the vertical sea-level rise. A very small vertical increase in sea level will lead to a much larger horizontal island migration because the slope of the land surface is very gentle.

land Miami suburbs, means that even a small rise in sea level will cause mainland land loss.

By 2,000 years ago, the islands were close to their present position and were growing in area and elevation. The rate of shoreline retreat and possible island migration is a function of the slope of the inundated land and the rate of sea-level rise (fig. 3.2). Again, the same is true for mainland shores. For example, if the lower coastal plain and shelf has a slope of 1:1,200 (expressed as vertical change over horizontal distance) a 1-foot rise in sea level would cause shoreline retreat of 1,000 feet or more (fig. 3.2)!

The kind of seashells and debris you find on the ocean-side beach may be evidence of island migration. On some beaches, you will find oyster, clam, or snail shells—the remains of animals that once lived in the bay, sound, or marsh behind the barrier island. How did shells from the estuary get to the ocean side? One possibility is that the island migrated over the back marsh and estuary; open-ocean waves eroded the old estuary sands and muds, now exposed on the shoreface, and threw the shells onto the present-day beach. On the other hand, black shells or shells of lagoon species may have arrived on the beach via artificial beach nourishment if nonmarine sands are being used as the nourishment material. In addition, salt marsh peat and mud that formed in back of the islands at some earlier time are occasionally exposed on ocean-side beaches after storms (fig. 3.3). Tree stumps exposed on beaches are the remains of forests that once grew well back from the beach.

Each island and shoreline responds in a differing fashion and at differing rates to its surrounding marine environment. As noted, the reasons for this variability include differences in the amount and type of sand; island orientation; the type, direction, and size of the waves that strike the beach; and the nature of the rocks underlying the coast. All of these factors should be important considerations for people who choose to live on these dynamic strips of sand. Unfortunately, those who set the price of coastal real estate do not always recognize—or care—that islands are different. Regardless of how an island's shoreline formed, change is always the rule on the coast, and the shorelines we see today are the products of the most recent set of

3.3 Evidence of island migration on Big Talbot Island. Severe erosion has downed trees and scarped the back of the beach (extreme right), exposing mud layers just beyond the tree in the foreground (center and left). The muds and old tree roots contained in such deposits are from marshes and forests, indicating that this location was once the back side of the island. The shoreline (beach) retreated landward as it is doing now, and island sand first buried the marsh mud and then the forest that grew in the soil as the island rolled over itself.

events (the last hurricane, changes in sand supply, impacts of engineering modifications, etc.). Some evidence suggests that the rate of sea-level rise has increased in the last several decades; if such is the case, it is bad news for East Florida communities.

Stationary or Grounded Barrier Islands

Islands that have formed by emergence or upward in-place growth and those that have migrated onto a topographic high or obstruction on the seafloor, such as a bedrock ridge, may be held in place. Such islands either cannot or are less likely to migrate. In order to persist as islands in the face of a rising sea level they must build vertically at a rate equal to or greater than the sea-level rise. The two mechanisms for maintaining elevation above sea level by vertical accretion are dune growth and overwash buildup (discussed below under how migrating islands maintain their elevation). Under natural conditions, such islands widen and narrow, are breached by inlets, and reorient in position as the equilibrium controls fluctuate. When densely developed, such an island loses its flexibility, and sometimes even its capability for upward growth. The beach and island then must be maintained artificially to counteract the effects of storms and day-to-day beach erosion.

Rolling Sandbars: How Islands Migrate

Most of the East Florida barrier islands are grounded on rock outcrops, but some are free to migrate. In order for an island to migrate, four things must happen:

1. The front (ocean) side must move landward through shoreline retreat.

2. The back (sound) side must do likewise by landward growth (island widening).

3. The island must continually build up in order to maintain its elevation above a rising sea level.

4. The mainland shoreline must retreat to keep pace with island migration.

Coastal terminology can sometimes be confusing. Such terms as *shoreline retreat* and *island retreat* may be used more or less interchangeably, but in fact they describe different processes. Shoreline retreat, sometimes inappropriately called shoreline erosion, is the landward migration of the shoreline, whether on an island or a mainland shore. Island retreat implies that the entire island is migrating landward.

Landward retreat of the beach occurs for a number of reasons but is due partly to the current sea-level rise of about 1 foot per century. This sea-level rise is a principal worldwide cause of beach erosion, although other local factors, such as the lack of sand supply, can add to the problem. Along specific shoreline segments, humans are responsible for a great deal of the shoreline retreat in recent decades. In some parts of the world, shorelines are retreating because river dams have blocked the flow of sediment to the sea. Examples include dams on the Rio Grande and the Brazos River that are preventing sediment from reaching the Texas coast and are thus contributing to the rapid erosion of the barrier islands there. Loss of Columbia River sands due to dams is causing the barrier spits of Oregon and Washington to retreat. The shoreline may move seaward by accretion at sites where river sediments reach the shore, but no major rivers exist on Florida's east coast. Seawalls, groins, offshore breakwaters, and inlet dredging are likewise significant worldwide contributors to shoreline erosion. The effects of shoreline engineering on beaches are discussed in more detail in chapter 4.

Island retreat requires widening or accretion on the sound sides of barrier islands. Two mechanisms—tidal delta incorporation and overwash—account for such growth. Tidal deltas are the bodies of sand that form outside (seaward) and inside (landward) of an inlet. The open-ocean tidal delta is called the ebb delta. The tidal delta inside the sound is the flood delta (fig. 3.4). These tidal bodies of sand form when a new inlet forms (the sand is moved primarily by tidal currents). If the inlet closes or migrates away, the flood-tidal delta eventually becomes part of the island. Such old tidal inlet

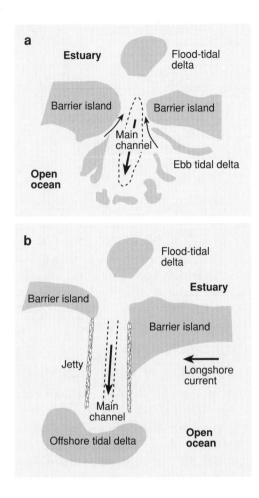

3.4 Flood-tidal and ebb-tidal deltas, bodies of sand moved into and out of the inlet by tidal currents, are found at all barrier island inlets. Flood-tidal deltas, formed in the estuary side of the inlet, are often incorporated into the island once the inlet closes. (a) Ebb-tidal deltas form seaward of the inlet and are part of the lateral sand transport system between islands as well as offshore transport of sand. (b) The ebb-tidal delta moves offshore when inlets are jettied to improve navigation, and its sand is lost from the island system.

deposits are common in parts of Mosquito Lagoon, the Banana River, and the Indian River (e.g., the back side of Hutchinson Island).

Tidal delta incorporation widens only a portion of an island. Other parts of islands migrate via storm overwash. This mechanism is at work today on low islands such as parts of Hutchinson Island. Overwash sand widens islands when it is carried completely across the island and deposited in the sound, as happens on narrow island segments where there are no dunes to block the overwash. Old overwash deposits can be recognized by looking at sediment types and ages.

As the sea level rises, islands maintain their elevation and bulk by two processes: dune formation and overwash fan deposition. Both processes obtain their sand from the beach. In fact, every grain of sand on an island came from the beach at some point in its history.

Dunes are formed by the wind, and if a sufficiently large supply of sand

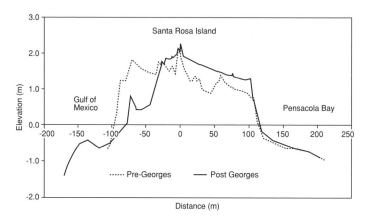

3.5 Cross-section comparison of Santa Rosa Island on Florida's Gulf coast before and after Hurricane Georges (1998). Sand removed from the front of the island was deposited as an overwash terrace on the back side to build the island's elevation. Note that the vertical scale is exaggerated 50 times the horizontal for illustration purposes. After "Studying the Importance of Hurricanes to the Northern Gulf of Mexico Coast," by G. W. Stone et al., 1999, *EOS*, vol. 80, no. 27, p. 305.

comes to the beach by longshore drift or is pushed up by the waves from the continental shelf, a high-elevation island can form. A good example of this type of island is part of Amelia Island with its beach ridge topography. If sand is not supplied from the adjacent shoreface or the prevailing wind direction does not promote sand movement inland, significant dunes will not form. The resulting low-elevation island is then more likely to be affected by overwash. The change in landscape south of Indialantic where the barrier narrows is a good example of the latter. Overwash fans coalesce laterally into an elevated terrace, as well as extending the island's back side into the sound. One of the most recent examples of this process comes from West Florida, where Hurricane Georges's (1998) overwash modified Santa Rosa Island (fig. 3.5).

An island's elevation may be reduced when development removes or scalps dunes, trucks carry away overwash sand after storms, or vegetation that is stabilizing the sediment is removed. Development discourages natural growth in island elevation by blocking sand flow across the island and by paving over the sand supply.

Mainland shore retreat is necessary if open water is to persist in back of the island for continued migration. Again, such retreat over time will occur as the sea level rises, and in proportion to the slope of the land. Shoreline erosion of the mainland shore also contributes to retreat, and the processes of inundation and erosion show no consideration for houses in their path.

If the mainland shore does not retreat or retreats more slowly than the offshore barrier moves landward, the sound will narrow and the island may attach to the mainland (e.g., the south end of Hobe Sound). If the sea level then falls, the barrier island will be left as a ridge on the emergent coastal plain. Such features from the former high stands of Pleistocene and much older sea levels are common on the southeastern U.S. coastal plain (e.g., Atlantic Coastal Ridge, Trail Ridge).

The Role of the Shoreface in Barrier Island Evolution

The shoreface plays a major role in determining how a barrier island behaves. The shoreface along part of East Florida is a relatively gently-sloping surface extending from the shoreline to the innermost continental shelf at a depth of around 30 feet. In effect, the shoreface is the active beach, and the portion we walk on is really only the edge of the zone of active sand movement. The rate of shoreline retreat, the way an island responds and recovers from a storm, the size of the dunes, and even the size of the island are all greatly affected by the nature of the shoreface.

The character of the shoreface is also a central element in the models used by engineers to predict beach behavior. Coastal engineers tend to assume that all shorefaces are composed of a loose pile of sand that forms a predictable "profile of equilibrium." In this view, the shoreface has a profile produced entirely by ocean waves, and the shape of the shoreface is determined by the grain size of the sand. This simplistic concept is the basis of design for most coastal engineering projects (such as beach fill)—and is the reason that coastal engineers generally have a poor record in predicting beach behavior. The life spans of nourished beaches generally are overestimated because the engineers who plan the nourishment do not understand the characteristics of particular shorefaces. In fact, because storms are usually responsible for the demise of nourished beaches, no one can predict accurately how long such beaches will last. As will become clear in the following discussion, the shoreface is much more complex than a loose pile of sand.

Geologic Framework of the Coast: Know Your Shoreface

In Florida, the underlying geologic framework consists of sediment and rock units that range in age from 90 million years to the present (see fig. 1.3). The complex variability in this underlying geologic framework, in consort with the physical dynamics of each specific barrier island, ultimately determines: (1) the three-dimensional shoreface shape, (2) the composition of beach sediments, and (3) shoreline erosion rates.

Old drainage systems that formed on the continental shelf when it was standing as the coastal plain during the lowered Ice Age sea level filled with sediment as the sea level rose. Coastal segments underlain by this less-resistant sediment fill may now erode faster than areas underlain by bedrock. Old barrier-island deposits also are likely to be less resistant to erosion, while former interstream divides, composed of older and harder geologic units, may form headland segments of the coast. These rocks may crop out on the beach (e.g., the reef rock that forms the bathtub at Bathtub Reef Park on Stuart Beach, and Anastasia coquina outcrops along the coast). More commonly, the rocks occur underwater and crop out on the shoreface below sea level. Such resistant shoals modify incoming waves and affect the rates of shoreline erosion on the adjacent beaches.

Where a barrier island is underlain by the fill of either historical or prehistoric inlets, the shoreface is composed of the unconsolidated sands that backfilled the inlets as they migrated or closed. And in areas where low, narrow barrier islands are actively migrating up and over the back-barrier estuary, the shoreface is composed of peat, mud, and clay (e.g., South Hutchinson Island; fig. 3.6). The young sediment units may extend from the estuaries, under the barrier, and crop out within the surf zone and shoreface. In other words, the shoreface is not a simple pile of sand, and often it does not perform in ways simplistic models predict!

The rule is: when locating on the coast, know the type of shoreface, because it is one predictor of future island changes. Also, when a shoreline

3.6 Cross section under South Hutchinson Island. The shoreface includes marsh sediments that formed behind an earlier island more than 1,400 years before the present (B.P.). The island is migrating to the west, over the marsh. Eventually these sediments are exposed on the front of the island, either on the emergent or the submergent part of the beach. Modified from "Late Holocene Erosional Shoreface Retreat within Siliciclastic-to-Carbonate Transition Zone, East Central Florida, USA," by R. W. Parkinson and J. R. White (appendix C, ref. 32).

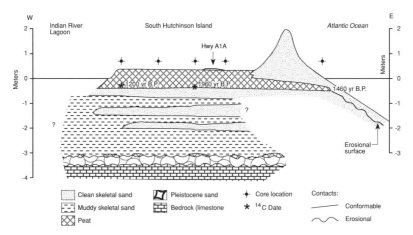

or barrier island changes, as in a hurricane, the appropriate "solution" to mitigate the impact of the changes also should be based on the type of shoreface.

Beaches: Nature's Shock Absorbers

The beach is one of Earth's most dynamic environments. On barrier islands the beach is the source of sand for the entire island. Every grain of sand on the island got there by crossing the beach. The beach, defined as the zone of active sand movement, is always changing. Most beaches are retreating in a landward direction, and as this gradual migration goes on, the beach changes its shape on an almost daily basis.

The natural laws of the beach produce a beautiful, logical structure that builds up when the weather is good and strategically (but only temporarily) retreats when confronted by big storm waves. Beach behavior depends on four factors: (1) wave energy (proportional to wave height), (2) the quality and quantity of beach sand, (3) the shape and location of the beach, and (4) the rate of sea-level change. The beach behaves through a natural balance or dynamic equilibrium of these four factors (see fig. 1.12). When one of the four factors changes, the others all adjust accordingly to maintain a balance. When humans enter the system in opposition to the status quo of natural processes, the dynamic equilibrium continues to function predictably, but in a way that damages or destroys buildings and infrastructure.

Keep in mind that the beach extends from the toe of the dune to an offshore depth of approximately 30 feet; the part on which we walk is only the upper beach. And just like barrier islands, every beach is different. Answers to the following often-asked questions may clarify the nature of the dynamic equilibrium.

How Does the Beach Respond to a Storm?

Old-timers and storm survivors frequently comment on how beautiful, flat, and broad the beach is after a storm. The flat beach can be explained in terms of the dynamic equilibrium: as wave energy increases and sea level rises (as part of the storm surge), materials move about to change the shape of the beach. Beaches usually flatten in response to storm waves, causing the rough waves to expend their energy over a broader and more level surface. On a steeper surface, storm-wave energy would be expended on a smaller area, causing greater change. Beaches do such logical and predictable things that they almost seem to be alive! Figure 3.7 illustrates the way in which the beach flattens. Waves take sand from the upper beach or from the first dune and transport it to the lower beach. If a hotdog stand or beach cottage happens to be located on the first dune, it may be taken along with the dune

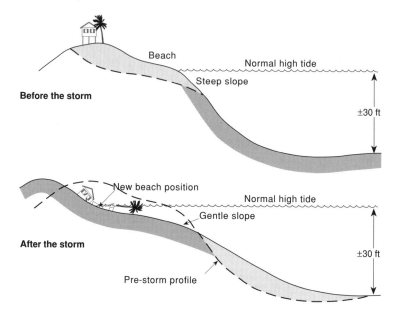

3.7 Beach flattening in response to a storm. The prestorm beach (above dashed line at top) will be eroded and deposited offshore during the storm. This flattened profile will dissipate the storm waves, reducing additional retreat. Natural beaches do not disappear due to storms. In fact, wide beaches are common after storms, even though they have shifted landward.

sands. In major storms this surf-zone sand may be transported beyond the base of the shoreface, and is then lost to the beach forever. An island can lose a great deal of sand during a storm. The sand that remains on the shoreface, however, may return, gradually pushed shoreward by fair-weather waves. This is known as "beach recovery." Beaches with coastal engineering structures (such as seawalls), as well as nourished beaches, generally recover much less sand after a storm than natural beaches do.

How Does the Beach Widen?

Beaches grow seaward principally by the addition of new sand carried laterally by the so-called longshore (surf-zone) currents (fig. 3.8) or by the addition of new sand from the shoreface brought in by the shoreward movement of sandbars. Actually, these two methods of beach widening often occur simultaneously.

Longshore currents are familiar to anyone who has swum in the ocean; they are the reason you sometimes end up far down the beach from your beach towel. Such currents result from waves approaching the shore at an angle, causing a portion of the breaking waves' energy to be directed along

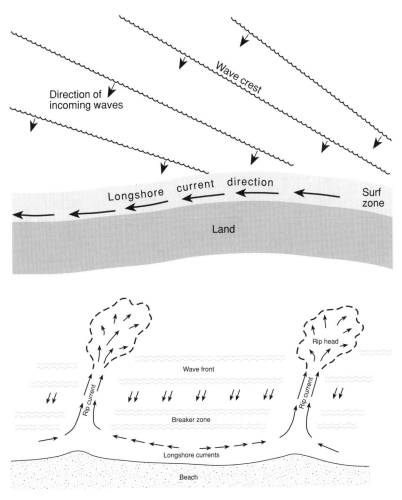

3.8 Longshore currents, sometimes referred to as longshore drift, are formed by waves approaching the shoreline at an angle. The longshore current transports sand parallel to the shore. Obstructions perpendicular to the shore such as jetties and groins will block this shore-parallel sand transport.

3.9 Strong, seaward-flowing rip currents form where the longshore current overcomes wave energy.

the beach. When combined with breaking waves that put sand into suspension, the current is capable of carrying large amounts of sediment for miles along a beach. The direction the sand moves depends on the direction of the winds that produce the waves. Most beaches have a dominant or net direction of sand transport. This is called "downdrift" or "updrift" depending on the direction, and is analogous to downstream and upstream in rivers.

The longshore current does not flow continuously along the shore. The

3.10 Wide beaches often show ridge and runnel systems. The runnels are the troughs that may retain water on the falling tide. This scene from Jacksonville Beach in the 1930s is not unlike what you will find today. Photo from the Photographic Collection of the Florida State Archives.

waves keep pushing water onshore until the longshore current becomes strong enough to move water seaward, against the waves. The resulting seaward-flowing current is a rip current (fig. 3.9), a hazard to swimmers. Rip currents can sometimes be identified as seaward-extending plumes of murky water due to the suspended sediment they carry. They may also be visible as areas in the surf zone where there is less wave activity. Swimmers caught in a rip current should swim parallel to the shore to get out of the current rather than swimming toward the shore against the current.

During the summer, sandbars may be visible within a few tens of yards offshore on many (but not all) beaches. This offshore bar or ridge is usually where the better swimmers and surfers congregate to catch the big wave. The trough between the beach and the ridge, or sandbar, is called the runnel. Multiple ridges and runnels are typically formed during small summer storms. In the quiet weather between storms, the ridges virtually march onto the shore and are "welded" to the beach. The next time you are at the beach, observe the offshore ridge for a few days and verify this for yourself. You will find that each day you have to swim out a slightly shorter distance to stand on the sandbar. During the summer, the beach between low and high tide frequently has a runnel filled or partly filled with water (fig. 3.10). This trough is formed by a ridge that is in the final stages of filling the runnel and welding onto the beach.

Where Does Beach Sand Come From?

As noted in chapter 1, most of the sand in the system was derived long ago from sources that are no longer adding new sand to the overall system. The exceptions are the breakdown of shells that contribute new sand grains and the erosion of older sedimentary deposits that provide small quantities to the sediment budget.

The reservoir of sand in the shoreface, barrier islands, tidal deltas, and mainland beaches is constantly being recycled. Sand is supplied to the beaches from the adjacent shoreface and laterally from inlets, capes, and updrift beaches. The shoreface is an important source of sand for most islands. As noted above, fair-weather waves gradually push the sand shoreward, and storm waves tend to carry it rapidly seaward; additional sand is carried parallel to the beach by longshore currents. Sand moves laterally into and across inlets, which is why the dredging of navigation channels often leads to sand starvation and increased erosion on downdrift islands.

Why Are Our Shorelines Retreating?

There are many causes of shoreline erosion, as discussed above. Anything that influences sand supply to the beaches will cause a change in the rate of erosion. Humans are often the major cause of changes in sand supply. Human activities such as shoreline armoring, construction too close to the shore, and inlet dredging and/or stabilization have significantly contributed to shoreline changes over the past 100 years. Certainly for Miami Beach–type developments, where 100 percent of the shoreline is fronted by seawalls and/or groins and/or is downdrift from jetties, most of the erosion "problem" is the result of human activities. Humans have become one of the principal geologic agents at the shore! Natural coastlines without buildings, infrastructure, and protective fortification do not have perceived erosion problems.

Add the rising sea level to the erosion potential of shorefaces, and you have it all. Shoreline erosion is here to stay. In fact, it is likely to increase in the future as more navigation channels are dredged and as the sea-level rise accelerates. It is important, however, to distinguish shoreline erosion from a shoreline erosion "problem." There is no erosion problem until buildings, roads, and services are built close to the beach.

If Most Shorelines Are Eroding, What Is the Long-Range Future of Beach Development?

Much of Florida's coast is eroding, although sand does accumulate locally and temporary beach growth may occur. As the frequency of storms and the direction of storm tracks vary through time, the local patterns of erosion will vary as well, often depending on the type of shoreface as described above. Erosion rates should definitely be expected to increase because: (1) humans' impacts on barrier sand supplies are increasing, leading to increasing shoreline retreat rates; (2) the rate of sea-level rise will likely increase due to global warming, leading to increasing shoreline retreat rates; (3) and storm frequency is expected to increase due to global warming. For many beachfront and barrier-island property owners, the long-term future, and even the intermediate future, will be an interesting time.

Current state regulations requiring buildings to be set back a specified distance from the shore simply postpone the long-term erosion problem. But setbacks do not postpone the threats to life, limb, and property from hurricanes and storms! And the same three factors of human impacts, sea-level rise, and increased storminess also affect the back shore of the islands and the mainland shores of the associated estuaries. As shoreline erosion threatens more and more property, the pressure will increase to adopt shoreline engineering as a means to hold the line. The question is: Is shoreline engineering—either armoring the coast to repel wave energy or major dredge-and-fill beach projects—a prudent choice?

4 The Fortified Coast: Living with Coastal Engineering

More than 80 percent of the American sandy shoreline, including significant portions of the Florida shore, is eroding because of a variety of processes (appendix C, refs. 57 and 64). On open-ocean shorelines this coastal erosion is persistent because of the sea-level rise and associated shoreline retreat. It is a continuous threat to the coastal development that lies in its path. The effects of storms, inlet formation and migration, loss of sediment supply, and changing coastal conditions magnify the erosion losses. A 1990 state report estimated the amount of coastline and property threatened by a 25-year storm to be 132.9 miles and 4,073 structures; by 2000 the latter number had increased significantly (appendix C, ref. 57). Because more and more static buildings and infrastructure are being placed in the path of this moving and constantly changing line in the sand, our society faces a major problem: How are we to keep the buildings from falling into the sea when we build them on its edge?

Coastal engineering is the usual choice of those attempting to protect property and hold the shoreline in place, but more than a century of experience with seawalls and other engineering structures shows us that trying to anchor the shoreline eventually leads to the loss of the beach. The real issue is how to save both buildings and beaches—a most difficult task. Several approaches address this problem:

1. Areas can be zoned to keep people out of harm's way. There are few areas safe for development on most barrier islands and low-lying coasts, and the coasts will continue to change over the coming decades. Areas that were once relatively suitable for development will become unsuitable.

2. The shoreline can be engineered through armoring in an attempt to stabilize it or hold it in place (hard stabilization).

3. Other beach and dune maintenance methods can be applied to widen the beach or hold the dune line in place (the so-called soft approach). Large coastal dredge-and-fill projects are the most typical approach.

4. Sand transfer plants (STPS) are sometimes used at inlets to artificially maintain the alongshore transport of sand to downdrift beaches.

5. Buildings can be moved back, demolished, or allowed to fall into the sea (relocation/retreat).

6. Combinations of the above can be employed (e.g., prohibiting building near inlets and moving sand past the inlet via STPS).

Most of these approaches involve some aspect of engineering, either through attempting to stabilize the shoreline, moving large volumes of sand, or moving buildings and infrastructure. Even the zoning option usually includes requirements that call for input from construction engineers. Shoreline stabilization through engineering includes armoring, the construction of hard, immovable engineering structures such as seawalls; and so-called beach nourishment, the placement of dredged or hauled-in sediments on the beach. Relocation or retreat involves moving buildings out of the zone of immediate risk or demolishing them when they are claimed by the sea.

Shoreline Armoring: Engineering Structures

Shoreline armoring, commonly referred to as "hard stabilization," generally involves engineering structures designed either to block and dissipate wave energy or to trap sand to widen a beach. Various types and designs of structures exist, but there are three major categories: (1) shore-parallel structures on land such as seawalls, (2) shore-parallel structures offshore such as breakwaters, and (3) shore-perpendicular structures such as groins and jetties. We are only now, after a century of their use, understanding many of the disadvantages associated with such structures. Nevertheless, we continue to build them, and they continue to damage Florida's beaches (fig. 4.1). In 1990 the Florida Department of Natural Resources (FDNR) estimated that 147 miles, or 18 percent, of Florida's 710-mile coastline had shoreline armoring. This percentage is misleading, however, because it includes undeveloped shoreline. The density of armoring is considerably higher when only developed shorelines, with development driving the perceived need to build shore-hardening structures, are considered. Forty-five percent of the developed shoreline on the East Florida coast is armored—nearly the same as the New Jersey coast! For comparison, the figure for West Florida's developed shoreline is 50 percent; for South Carolina, 27 percent; and for the developed North Carolina open-ocean shoreline, only 6 percent. These figures generally do not include parks and national seashores.

The conclusion is clear: parklands that do not allow shore-hardening structures and states that have adopted regulations discouraging engineering structures are maintaining their beaches for future generations. But Florida continues on the road of armoring. A 1990 state study projected

4.1 Old seawalls are often unsafe and unsightly, and many have lost their fronting beaches. The structures become obstacles to beach use, although the upland property temporarily is held in place.

significant future armoring, much of it in areas where sea turtles nest. And the report is proving to be correct; between 1990 and 2001 the Florida Department of Environmental Protection (FDEP) approved 63 new seawalls.

Property owners should be aware of the continued shoreline retreat and beach loss associated with seawalls, groins, and offshore breakwaters. People living within inlet zones should be aware of the effects of jetties as well as natural inlet dynamics.

Shore-Parallel Structures on Land: The Seawall Family

Seawalls and their cousins are shoreline engineering structures built parallel to the shore on the exposed (subaerial) beach. They are the most common type of hard stabilization. Strictly defined, seawalls are free-standing structures near the surf-zone edge. Built of wood, steel, rock, or concrete, they are designed to protect the upland from the impact of waves (fig. 4.2). Seawalls are usually low walls that are not intended to block storm waves, especially those accompanied by storm surge. Such walls instead function mainly to prevent the shoreline from retreating into the line of buildings they protect. Overtopping of seawalls is common in hurricanes, and the walls fail for a variety of reasons, including building up of water pressure (from storm surge) on the landward side, storm-surge ebb flow tearing the wall apart, scouring and undermining by waves and storm-surge ebb, and direct wave attack. Seawalls should extend deep below the ground (beach) surface to prevent undermining.

Bulkheads are generally indistinguishable from seawalls to the general public (fig. 4.3). In theory, the primary purpose of bulkheads is to prevent the land from slumping or eroding into the sea, and not to absorb wave energy. In reality, bulkheads serve both purposes, and the term usually refers to small, low seawalls.

Revetments consist of an armor of rock facing on a dune, beach slope, or in front of a seawall (fig. 4.2). Also known as riprap, their role is to buffer the waves just as a seawall does. As a wave breaks on a revetment, much of the water contained in the wave is absorbed in the interstices between the rocks, reducing erosion-causing backwash. In most storms, however, the difference between a revetment and a seawall is negligible. Revetments are often unsightly structures, especially those made of construction debris. Proper design requires carefully placed, heavy, wave-resistant material for the structure, properly angled and backed by filter cloth, a decay-resistant mesh fabric that allows water to escape but prevents soil loss.

Sandbags are sometimes used for temporary erosion control, but sandbag walls rarely have a foundation and are swept away or moved about by storms (fig. 4.4). Whether they are filled with sand or concrete, sandbags are best viewed as temporary protection, buying time before moving a building back. Sandbags have the advantage of being easier to remove when they fail.

Gabions are rock-filled rectangular steel-wire-mesh cages piled one on top of another to form a wall. Although the wire is plastic coated, the mesh inevitably corrodes, the gabion ruptures, the rocks spill out, and the wall fails, strewing jagged wire and rocks over the beach, creating a hazard for beach strollers.

When properly designed, hard shoreline structures slow shoreline retreat and offer some protection to coastal property. Hard structures do not protect property in major storms, however, as demonstrated by Hurricanes Fran, Hugo, and Opal in other areas; and their disadvantages are many. Walls lead to degradation of the recreational beach, are costly in both the short term and the long term, destroy beach aesthetics, make beach access difficult, and can be dangerous.

All seawalls are subject to numerous hydraulic forces that must be accounted for in wall design and construction materials. Walls intended to prevent wave attack on buildings must be constructed high enough to prevent storm-wave overtopping, but they also must be implanted deep enough in the beach to prevent undermining. In general, the maximum depth of expected scour is roughly equal to the highest-breaking wave at the site. Thus, maximum storm waves of 3 feet require a footing depth of at least 3 feet. Nevertheless, some scour will still occur. Placing large rocks at the foot of the

4.2 Combined stone revetment and concrete seawall south of St. John's City Pier, St. Augustine. Typically, as beaches in front of seawalls narrow or disappear, the seawall needs protecting. The wall halts shoreline retreat but does not preserve the beach.

4.3 Bulkheads such as this wooden structure in the Vero Beach area are designed to hold the land in place. The structures are generally not wave resistant and often fail due to scouring by storm-surge flooding and associated currents.

4.4 This sandbag seawall in the Sailfish Point area failed under wave attack. The advantage of sandbags is that they are easier to remove than hard walls. The beach scarp, downed tree, and sandbags strewn over the beach are evidence of the most recent erosion event.

structure will help reduce this effect but will also further reduce the recreational value of the beach.

Waves often refract around the ends of seawalls, increasing erosion at those points, so the ends should be joined to neighboring structures if possible. Where none exist, wing walls or tie-ins to the adjacent land must be built to prevent wave flanking and erosion at the ends of the wall. Wing walls are only a temporary measure because erosion will continue and extend beyond each successive flank built to "solve" the problem.

Additional wall strength is gained through the use of tiebacks, which should be part of the design of any seawall. Tiebacks are steel cables or rods that anchor the upper part of the wall to anchoring devices (called deadmen) deeply embedded into the beach or bluff. Accumulating water and soil pressure will build behind bulkheads and seawalls. Drainage must be provided to allow water to escape from the landward side of the wall without carrying the backfill material with it. Backfilling with gravel and having numerous openings (weep holes) along the lower part of the wall allow water to escape. Walls should be backed by filter cloth.

This brief discussion of seawalls is not intended to give design advice, but rather to illustrate some construction considerations and indicate why these walls fail. A professional engineer should be consulted prior to any construction. Seawalls and other types of shoreline engineering structures require maintenance. Remember to ask the engineers how much the maintenance will cost, how long they "guarantee" the design, how the wall will perform under expected storm conditions during its design life, and what are the likely impacts to the beach and adjacent properties.

Impacts of Seawalls
Seawalls lead to narrowing of recreational beaches by means referred to as active, passive, and placement beach loss (fig. 4.5).

Passive beach loss occurs in a landward-retreating shoreline situation where a seawall (or highway, or building) acts as a fixed line (fig. 4.6). As the shoreline continues to erode or retreat landward, the beach narrows and eventually disappears in front of that line. This process often takes several decades to complete.

Active beach loss occurs when the seawall reflects wave energy or in other ways intensifies surf-zone processes, leading to beach sand loss in front of the wall (fig. 4.7). A seawall does not absorb all of a wave's energy; some of that energy reflects off the wall, scouring and eroding sediment in front of the wall. Some of the energy is also deflected along the wall to the adjacent unprotected property, where the energy is spent eroding the shore. The mechanisms of active beach loss are poorly understood because of the difficulty in observing and measuring wave/current processes when the "action" is taking place during storms.

Placement beach loss occurs when a seawall is built seaward of the dunes or toe of the upland so that part of the recreational beach is behind the seawall. The placement of the wall causes an immediate loss of recreational beach. Such placement of seawalls has led to beach loss in many locations, perhaps the most famous being Miami Beach prior to its 1981 replenishment.

Seawalls, Sediment Loss, and Narrowing Beaches
The immovable object has another significant effect. Beaches often get part of their sediment from erosion of the land at the back of the beach. Walls cover up that source, starving the beach of its sediment supply either in the area of the wall or downdrift of the wall. Where wall-protected areas form mini-headlands, the waves may be refracted by the wall into the adjacent unwalled shore, again concentrating erosive wave energy. Stroll along the armored shore of a hotel or condominium row almost anywhere and observe where the beach is narrow or missing—the offending walls, bulkheads, or revetments will be obvious. The name of the community is of no consequence; the effects of seawalls are the same. In most cases, the prob-

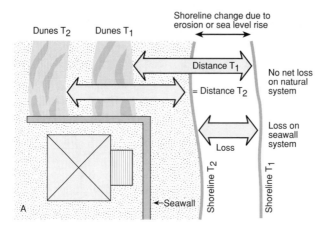

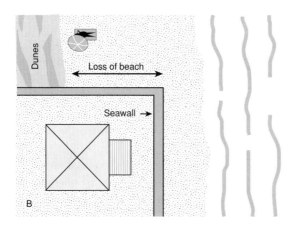

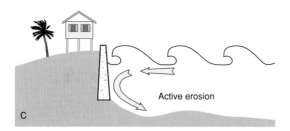

4.5 Seawalls cause recreational beach loss in three ways. (A) Passive loss occurs when the beach and dune line migrate landward (Time 1 [T_1] to Time 2 [T_2]) but the seawall blocks beach migration. (B) Placement loss occurs immediately because the seawall is built seaward of the dune line, narrowing the beach. (C) Active loss occurs when waves reflect off a seawall to scour and erode sediment in front of the wall.

4.6 Probable passive beach loss due to a seawall in the Hollywood Beach area. The wall was once at the back of the beach, but the beach migrated past the wall, as can be seen in the foreground. The beach in front of the wall could not migrate, so it narrowed and disappeared as the profile shifted. If the beach in the foreground was already in this position when the wall was built, then placement loss has occurred. Once the beach is gone in front of the wall, active loss occurs if the waves are removing sand laterally or offshore.

4.7 Wave reflection from seawalls, such as here at Palm Beach, creates turbulence capable of suspending sediments. Erosional scour may result in front of the wall, and refracted waves often increase erosion at the ends of seawalls.

lem began with the imprudent decision to locate a building too close to the shore and was followed by the need to protect the building from processes that should have been obvious prior to its construction. If beaches are the attraction, and walls are built to protect property at the expense of the beaches' sand supply, then the resource that supports the economy is being lost. Regional comparisons of dry beach (recreational beach) widths in front of seawalls with dry beach widths on beaches not altered by engineering structures prove that beaches are consistently narrower in front of seawalls (appendix C, ref. 40).

Shore-Parallel Structures Offshore: Breakwaters

Breakwaters are offshore wall-like structures, usually shore-parallel and typically a few tens of yards seaward of the normal surf zone, designed specifically to reduce wave energy, shelter a portion of the shoreline, and encourage sand accumulation on the beach. Like all shore-hardening structures, breakwaters change the dynamics of the shoreline, and they create no new sand. The structures dampen wave energy to the protected shoreline behind the breakwater, interrupting the longshore current and causing sand to be deposited behind the structure. As the local beach widens, downdrift beaches are starved of sand. Sometimes the beach deposits will accumulate out to the back of the breakwater, creating a feature like a natural tombolo where a sandbar connects an island to the mainland. This tombolo effect is especially likely if the top of the breakwater is emergent. Some breakwaters are designed with the top of the structure below the water level (submergent) to allow some wave energy to reach the shore and maintain partial alongshore sand transport.

In the 1980s and 1990s breakwaters again became "fashionable" with proponents of shore hardening, and new breakwater systems consisting of portable concrete segments were installed along some Florida beaches (see "Alternative" Devices, below). Although it is necessary to observe shoreline structures on a decadal time frame to understand their impact, early reports indicated that these "portable" breakwaters were not as successful as their "inventors" promised. At the same time that concerns were being raised about the ill effects of these new structures, Palm Beach was reversing the trend by removing a breakwater built in the early 1990s. The device may have created more erosion problems than it solved, including in the area behind the breakwater. At Redington Shores in West Florida, five swimmers died near a breakwater in the months after its construction. Apparently, waves or currents generated around the structure knocked the victims into the breakwater. No swimming is allowed near the breakwater now.

Whereas shore-parallel structures are built basically to block wave energy, shore-perpendicular structures are designed to block the alongshore flow of sand. The trapped sand, in theory, is held as a beach deposit.

Groins, walls built perpendicular to the shoreline, are designed to trap and hold sediment flowing in the longshore current, thus slowing beach erosion (fig. 4.8). Made of rock, wood, concrete, steel, or fabric bags filled with sand, groins also are installed to retain sediment already on the beach or to hold sand fill in nourishment projects. Groins are often, but not always, used in conjunction with seawalls and are sometimes used with beach replenishment. Groins can be low or high, long or short, depending on the desired extent of sand trapping. Some designs are referred to as T-groins because the end of the structure terminates in a short, shore-parallel segment (see fig. 1.1). If a groin is working correctly, more sand should be piled up on one side of the groin than on the other. Because groins interrupt the longshore drift, a functioning groin requires downdrift measures for self-defense. The result is often a series of groins, called a "groin field" (fig. 4.8), that may extend for miles. Spacing of groins in a groin field depends on local sand supply and wave characteristics, and is highly variable from one beach to another, as can be seen along many East Florida beaches.

Impacts of Groins
The problem with groins is that they trap sediment on one side and intensify erosion on the other. If abundant sand is moving alongshore, updrift beaches are widened while downdrift beaches are starved of sediment. Property owners claiming increased erosion damage as a result of nearby groin construction have initiated lawsuits.

Often groins are used along shorelines that are already experiencing a shortage of sand. Miami Beach, prior to the 1981 beach nourishment project, illustrated the endpoint of groin usage. Jetties had decreased the sand supply, so the addition of groins was useless for building or maintaining the beach. The shoreline looked like an army obstacle course; groin after groin obstructed both pedestrian and vehicular traffic (see fig. 1.16). Clearly, groins should not be used where there is a low supply of sand flowing laterally along the beach. If no sand builds up, the groins are not doing their job. Over the long term, or very quickly during a storm, the shoreline can retreat past the landward end of groins, causing them to become detached from the shoreline. When this happens, water and sediment pass between the groins and the beach, and the groins become useless obstructions in the water. Per Bruun, the retired director of the Coastal Engineering Program at the University of Florida, has observed that, on a worldwide basis, groins may be a losing proposition; that is, more beach may be lost than is gained by the use

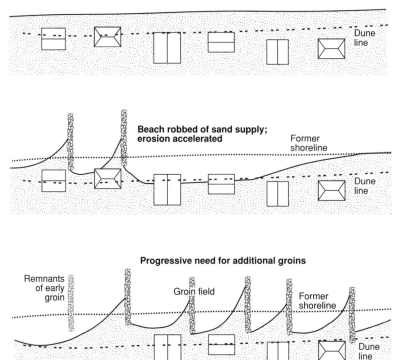

Direction of natural beach sand transport

Dune line

Beach robbed of sand supply; erosion accelerated

Former shoreline

Dune line

Progressive need for additional groins

Remnants of early groin

Groin field

Former shoreline

Dune line

4.8 Map view of the downdrift erosional effect of groins and the typical proliferation of the structures into a groin field. Beach retreat typically continues, and the groins become detached and fail if they are not lengthened.

of groins. The bottom line is that temporary sand buildup in one place simply transfers the erosion problem to another place and worsens the overall erosion problem.

Jetties are analogous to groins but are constructed specifically to stabilize navigational inlets and entrances, not to protect beaches or upland. These structures, which may be thousands of feet long, are intended to make navigation safer and channel maintenance cheaper. A jetty is designed to keep sand from flowing into a ship channel within an inlet. Jetties cause more extreme downdrift erosion than groins because they more completely interrupt the longshore sediment transport system. The great number of jetties along America's shores, particularly on the Atlantic and Gulf coasts, suggests a widespread and significant frequency of associated erosion problems. Most of East Florida's inlets are jettied, and these structures are considered to be the principal human contributor to beach erosion (fig. 4.9). Jetties that extend far out to sea may also channel sand offshore during storms, causing a permanent loss of the sand supply in the longshore drift. Jetties are the antithesis of sand conservation in an island system.

Because jetties are major obstructions to longshore sand transport, sand-bypassing systems (sand transfer plants) are sometimes included in the design of jettied inlets (e.g., Hillsboro Inlet and Lake Worth Inlet; figs. 4.10 and 4.11). In order to get sand to the downdrift beaches, the sand trapped by the updrift jetty and in the inlet must be either pumped or periodically dredged (maintenance dredging) and placed on the opposite side of the inlet. Permanent sand-pumping plants, or sand transfer plants (STPs; fig. 4.11), are discussed below under "Redistributing Sediments." Bypassing systems are useful, but the STPs cannot operate during storms, the time when much of Nature's transport work is being accomplished. Sand transfer plants may represent a preferable design solution for maintaining downdrift beaches in those cases where jetties are a necessity.

4.9 Government Cut was indeed cut to create an inlet, and in the process formed the northern end of the Miami Beach barrier island. Constructed in 1905, the cut began to fill with sand carried by longshore drift and tidal currents; it was jettied in 1912 to keep the channel open. Like most coastal engineering, one modification led to the need for another, and the inlet has been redredged and deepened, and the jetties extended over the years. This 1922 view shows the jetties trapping sand on the updrift (right) side while erosional retreat was taking place on the downdrift side (left). Today, the land adjacent to the inlet is developed, placing more property at risk in a hazard zone. Photo from the Photographic Collection of the Florida State Archives.

4.10 Sand transfer plant (STP) on north side of Lake Worth Inlet (see fig. 4.11).

Engineering Structures: A Final Word

Although once thought to be the ultimate "solution" to shoreline erosion problems, hard stabilization has fallen increasingly out of favor. The story of Cape May, New Jersey, remains the premier lesson for all communities opting for armoring. In 1801 Cape May was the first popular full-fledged beach resort in America, and it sparked the beginning of a rush to the shore. During the next 75 years, U.S. presidents vacationed at Cape May. At the time of the Civil War it was the country's most prestigious beach resort, and its popularity continued into the twentieth century. In 1908 Henry Ford raced his newest-model cars on Cape May beaches. Cape May is no longer found on anyone's list of great beach resorts. The problem is not that the resort is too old-fashioned, but that the beach was lost to seawalls and groin fields, structures built to "save" it. The armoring did not stop the relentless work of the sea. The long-term result was an unsightly, walled, beachless shoreline. No beach remained until a dredge-and-fill project replaced it, temporarily.

Shoreline stabilization is a difficult political issue. Seawalls may take as long as five or six decades to destroy beaches, although it usually takes only one to three decades for the beach to erode to the point where it is entirely gone at mid-to-high tide. Thus it takes a politician with some foresight to endorse prohibition of armoring. Another issue is that there is no room for compromise. Once in place, seawalls are rarely removed. The economic reasoning is that the wall must be maintained, even protected, leading to higher and longer walls (fig. 4.12). Few politicians like issues with no room for compromise.

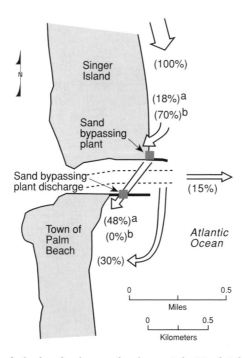

Singer
Island

(100%)

(18%)[a]
(70%)[b]

Sand
bypassing
plant

Sand bypassing
plant discharge

(15%)

Town of
Palm
Beach

(48%)[a]
(0%)[b]

(30%)

Atlantic
Ocean

0   0.5

Miles

0   0.5

Kilometers

4.11 Sand transfer budget for the transfer plant at Lake Worth Inlet. Superscript *a* values represent the plant's effectiveness when in operation from 1960 to 1990. The plant bypassed 48 percent of the sand in the longshore drift, while 18 percent continued to accrete on the northern side of the jetty. Superscript *b* represents postshutdown conditions in which the jetty blocks 70 percent of the longshore transport. The other arrows represent percentages of sediment moved by the U.S. Army Corps of Engineers channel maintenance activities (15 percent offshore, 30 percent placed on southern beach). Modified from figure 3 in M. R. Dombrowski and A. J. Mehta, "Inlets and Management Practices: Southeast Coast of Florida," *Journal of Coastal Research*, special issue 18 (1993): 34 (appendix C, ref. 56).

The emplacement of seawalls and revetments along the Florida coast must be considered an irreversible act. As any long-term observer of Florida beaches knows, the beaches are gone or going in front of walls, except where dredge-and-fill projects have temporarily replaced them. In the meantime, the original walls are often replaced by bigger and "better" walls. The final question is: What is more important, beaches or buildings?

Coastal Armoring Policy

Unlike some other Atlantic coast states, Florida permits shoreline armoring with hard structures (see Florida State Code: 62B-33.0051 *Coastal Armoring and Related Structures*, 161.053 *Coastal Construction and Excavation; Regulation on County Basis*, and 161.085 *Rigid Coastal Armoring Structures*). For

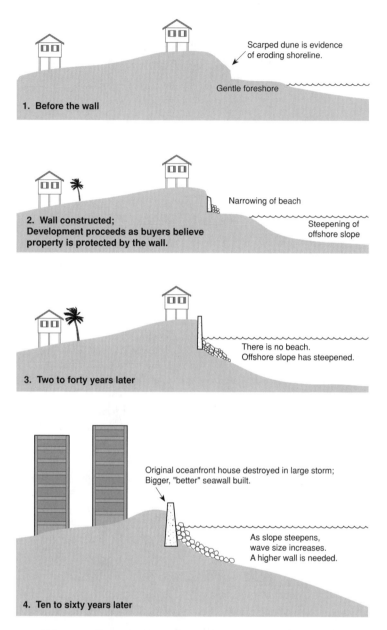

1. Before the wall

Scarped dune is evidence of eroding shoreline.

Gentle foreshore

**2. Wall constructed;
Development proceeds as buyers believe
property is protected by the wall.**

Narrowing of beach

Steepening of
offshore slope

3. Two to forty years later

There is no beach.
Offshore slope has steepened.

4. Ten to sixty years later

Original oceanfront house destroyed in large storm;
Bigger, "better" seawall built.

As slope steepens,
wave size increases.
A higher wall is needed.

4.12 The seawall saga is the evolution from a migrating beach, perceived to be eroding because houses or other structures are threatened; to the construction of the first seawall; to that seawall's contribution to the erosion problem; to its failure and the need for a bigger, better wall. The process may take decades, but it is the ultimate fate of walled shorelines in the face of a rising sea level.

construction of any armoring seaward of the Coastal Construction Control Line (on land that is subject to 100-year storm surge, storm waves, or other unpredictable weather conditions), the property owner must obtain a permit from the Florida Department of Environmental Protection (FDEP) and meet the following conditions:

— The structure is vulnerable to erosion as determined by the FDEP's model described in *Erosion Due to High Frequency Storm Events* (University of Florida, 1995).

— The armoring will not result in complete loss of beach access without providing alternative access.

— The construction will not result in significant adverse impacts.

— The armoring structure should be as far landward as possible and designed to minimize adverse impacts to the beach-dune system, adjacent properties, and marine turtles.

— Construction during marine turtle nesting season should be avoided.

In 1999 Florida's armoring policy was amended (section 161.085(2) *Rigid Coastal Armoring Structures*) to allow armoring on undeveloped private coastal property. Armoring is allowed on undeveloped private property when the property is flanked by existing seawalls and the gap to be armored is less than 250 feet.

"Alternative" Devices

Desperate situations require desperate measures. The ultimate crises of threatened property, faced by communities and individuals in the path of shoreline retreat, create a repeated scenario. Faced with the knowledge that walls, groins, and breakwaters have not held back the sea, and that building such protective structures is very costly, coastal property owners often are attracted to "alternative" or "nontraditional" engineering structures. Like their larger cousins, these devices are intended to prevent shoreline retreat. The structures come in a fascinating variety of names: Beach Builder, Wave Buster, Wave Shield, Sand Grabber, Surge Breaker, Stabeach, PEP Reef, Seascape, Biodune, and "speed bumps." The claim that a particular novel device will protect or save any beach, anywhere (one size fits all), should raise the first red flag. Although such structures may not have the appearance of seawalls, groins, or breakwaters, and thus can sometimes slip under the "no armoring" regulations, they are actually variations on these fundamental shoreline-hardening schemes; that is, they really are not "alternatives."

A review of more than 40 such devices found no hard evidence of successes but did reveal some failures, and also revealed that a disturbingly high percentage of the companies promoting such structures had gone out of business (see www.env.duke.edu/psds/stabilization.htm). A few of these structures may temporarily protect property, but they are no different from traditional armoring in that they cause downdrift erosion and do not stop the eventual loss of the beach.

Often, the inventors of these devices claim that their "invention" (and yes, many have a patent) has worked somewhere else, usually far enough away that the customer isn't likely to visit the "successful" site. In Norfolk, Virginia, the inventors of a shoreline stabilization device claimed success in Australia and New Guinea. A device promoted in Florida was said to have worked in Denmark. Any prudent community will go to the expense to check out "somewhere else" very carefully. Another problem is that most claims of success are short term, and the claimed changes are nothing more than normal cyclical changes in the beach over a few seasons or years. Unfortunately, success must be viewed over the intermediate to long term— that is, beach accretion and sustained property protection for at least five years, and preferably for a decade or more. The majority of victory claims are very premature, some after only a few weeks.

In 1997 the state of South Carolina allowed the emplacement of a device called Stabler Disks on Myrtle Beach. State bureaucrats said that the disks, touted to cause beach sand accumulation, were not shoreline armoring, which was completely incorrect. Representatives from the city manager's office said they had researched the manufacturer's claims and were certain the device would solve the local erosion problem. But apparently they researched it solely by reading the company's literature! Coastal managers in New Jersey, where the device had previously been used, were less than impressed with its effectiveness, but the word had not reached South Carolina. The device was removed for the given reason that a beach user was injured on the structure, but in truth it was not working.

The one major advantage of most of these structures is that they can be removed at a lower cost than a more massive structure if the community is unhappy with them. The use of an alternative type of breakwater at Palm Beach provides a good example. Breakwater units consisting of heavy triangular concrete prisms (Prefabricated Erosion Prevention, or PEP, reef) approximately 6 feet in height were placed in a line just off the beach. Although the "reef" structure was designed to dissipate wave energy and reduce shoreline erosion, it introduced a new set of problems. The structures halted the beachward flow of new sand during fair weather and partially deprived the beach of one source of its sediment. In addition, the "reef" caused erosion rates to increase because water velocity between the beach and the breakwater increased. The Palm Beach reef was removed several years after its emplacement.

Florida coastal policy allows alternative technologies for coastal protection to be employed on an experimental basis, but the permit usually requires that the structure must be removed if it becomes deformed, dislodged, a nuisance, or a public hazard. A "new technology" is any method about which there is insufficient information to predict its performance under a range of operational conditions and its potential environmental impacts. The fact that some of these structures can be removed cheaply is important, and the state has required removals, such as the PEP Reef at Palm Beach and underwater stabilizers at Captiva Island. The manufacturer of the latter sand or concrete-filled geotextile bags claimed that these structures were successful even though they were shown to be ineffective. Large, long, sand- or concrete-filled textile tubes (Geotubes) have been used at the back of some beaches, but these tubes tend to settle, buckle, rotate, dislocate, and rupture, losing their fill, and have little positive effect on the beach, according to a state report. In sum, alternative "beach-saving" devices are generally a waste of money: they rarely live up to expectations and they clutter up the beach when they fail.

The story of how North Carolina's Cape Hatteras lighthouse was saved illustrates the point. The lighthouse had been threatened by shoreline retreat for many years. Groins, emergency revetments, and beach nourishment had failed to hold the shoreline in place. A group of concerned citizens proposed installing Seascape, a form of artificial seaweed consisting of plastic fronds anchored to the bottom and intended to slow wave and current activity enough to cause sand accumulation. Studies indicating that Seascape did not work were ignored, and the "seaweed" was emplaced. Within weeks a small storm swept the coast and the beach widened! The group immediately claimed success; the widened beach was evidence that all could see. But the same storm also widened the beach along much of the 50-mile reach to the north of the lighthouse! The wind direction had caused onshore sand movement and temporarily widened the beaches. In the following weeks and months, the beach again narrowed and storm waves ripped out the seaweed, washing much of it ashore to clutter the beach. Seascape and other coastal engineering devices could not reduce the lighthouse's vulnerability to future storm damage or destruction. In 1999, as the lighthouse was on the verge of falling to the next big storm, it was finally relocated 2,900 feet to the southwest of its original location. The new position placed the light 1,600 feet from the Atlantic Ocean's edge, just about the same distance as when it was built in 1870.

In summary, consider the following points before purchasing nontraditional engineering devices:

No device creates new sand. The sand came from and is going somewhere.

Any structure that traps sand will cause a downdrift shortage.

One size does *not* fit all; no device works on every shoreline.

Treat claims of success elsewhere with great skepticism.

Success implies 5 to 10 years of property protection with no beach loss on adjacent properties.

To measure success, a project must be monitored for 5 to 10 years. Very few such projects are monitored even for 1 to 2 years.

There is no proven low-cost shore protection. If it sounds too good to be true, it isn't true. In fact, the terms *low cost* and *shore protection* are probably mutually exclusive. Effective shore protection is likely to be massive and expensive.

Redistributing Sediment: Dredging/Filling, Trucking, Scraping, and Bypassing

As we noted in chapter 1, vocabulary reflects attitude, and the tone of the terminology adapted to promote beach maintenance has been somewhat misleading. The general alternatives to shore "hardening" are referred to as "soft" solutions, and when sand is added to a beach, it is for "nourishment" and the artificially widened beach is said to be "healthy." In fact, such terminology masks the reality that dredging large amounts of sand and placing it on the shore is not "soft" in terms of its impact on organisms or the changes it introduces into the physical environment. Consider the following. Beach width is not necessarily a measure of the "health" of a beach. Sediment may be incompatible for use as beach fill because of its size or composition, the sorting and angularity of grains, or the way the sediment packs once it is placed on the beach. Even the color of the sediment can contribute to the heating and cooling of the sand or the aesthetics of the appearance of the beach. Fill sediment may be detrimental to the beach as habitat or as a recreational resource.

The terminology used here is meant to reflect the true character of redistributing sediment as a means of maintaining beaches and dunes.

Beach Dredge-and-Fill Projects

Beach restorations usually consist of dredging massive amounts of sand from offshore, pumping or barging it to the shore, and then distributing the sand using bulldozers (see chapter 5). The goals of most communities are to improve their recreational beach, to slow shoreline erosion, and to afford storm protection for beachfront buildings. In order to obtain federal funding for beach nourishment, storm protection is usually a required justification. Beach dredge-and-fill has become the current solution of choice in combating shoreline retreat; many famous beaches in developed areas are now artificial and are consistently refilled through offshore dredging, often near reefs or in other valuable fishery habitats. The national cost of this philosophy is growing in both dollars and impact (appendix C, ref. 38).

Remember that the beach, or zone of active sand movement, actually ex-

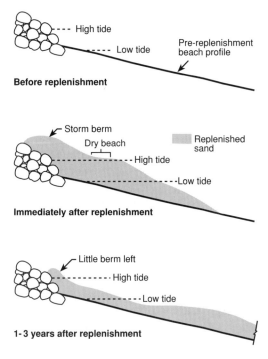

4.13 Replenished beach before sand emplacement (top), immediately after emplacement (middle), and some years after emplacement (bottom). Often the sand from the storm berm disperses offshore, where it plays no role in storm protection and has no recreational value.

tends out to a water depth of 30 or 40 feet. With beach fill, only the upper beach is covered with new sand, so a steeper beach is created (fig. 4.13). This new steepened profile often increases the rate of erosion; in fact, nationwide, replenished beaches almost always disappear at a faster rate than their natural predecessors. Florida may be an exception to this trend because of lower wave energy or the nature of the replenished beach sand (i.e., its size and composition), but a period of quiescence in terms of hurricane history also may account for Florida's better record of fill durability.

Sand for beach fill is available from several possible sources, including lagoons and embayments, nearby inlets and associated tidal deltas, the adjacent continental shelf, and mainland deposits. Availability of sand nearby does not imply that the sediment is compatible for beach fill. Often the sand is too coarse or too fine, and sometimes the fill sediments have a higher than expected component of mud, shells, coral fragments, or rocks (fig. 4.14). On barrier islands, sand from the adjacent lagoon is rarely used now because of the potential for ecological damage in that delicately balanced ecosystem. Taking sand from the tidal delta can increase the rates of shoreline retreat on adjacent beaches. Geologic and oceanographic impacts are lessened if marine sand is taken from locations as far from the beach as possible. In a number of locations (e.g., Grand Isle, Louisiana) the hole dug on the continental shelf to obtain the nourishment sand actually led to the early demise of the beach because it modified the incoming wave pattern. Because creating craters on the shelf can cause wave refraction resulting in unintended erosion of the beach, the Dutch government requires that sand be obtained from more than 15 miles offshore! Dredging offshore sand and filling shallow habitats has serious biological impacts as well (see chapter 5).

Studies conducted by the Duke University Program for the Study of Developed Shorelines found it difficult to obtain exact total costs for beach fill projects, or even the exact number of cumulative projects; however, documented expenditures through 2002 for East Florida were well over $500 million. At the time of this writing, the most replenished beaches along Florida's Atlantic coast are Fort Pierce, Jupiter Island, and Jacksonville Beach. The Program for the Study of Developed Shorelines maintains a summary of beach fill projects on its website (www.env.duke.edu/psds/nourishment). Table 4.1 summarizes the general number of fill episodes, locations, sediment volumes, and costs for Florida's beach fill experience through mid-2002.

The number of beaches being nourished is increasing, so communities opting for beach dredge-and-fill projects face the problem that federal, state, and local governments (the taxpayers) are less inclined to pick up even a share of the costs. In 2002 the majority of U.S. Army Corps of Engineers (USACE) projects were put on hold, and the country may be at a crossroads in its beach fill policies.

Beach fill projects along the U.S. east coast generally use more than 1 million cubic yards of sand per mile. The 10.5-mile long Miami Beach project was given 11.6 million cubic yards of sand between 1978 and 1982. Figure 4.13 illustrates what happens when a beach is "nourished." Immediately after the

Table 4.1   A Summary of Major Beach Dredge-and-Fill Projects for East Florida

Beach Location	Number of Fills	Years	Volume (cubic yards)	2002 Cost
Amelia Island	4	1983–1994	3,985,096	$14,918,107
Anastasia State Park/St. Augustine	3	1963–2000	542,000	$5,789,522
Bal Harbour	5+	1960–1990	2,346,000	$22,049,174
Boca Raton	1	1998	600,000	$3,001,774
Boca Raton North	1	1988	1,102,000	$5,072,077
Boca Raton South	2	1985–1996	549,000	$3,181,732
Boynton Inlet	1+	1961–1973	1,366,229	$1,399,825
Cape Canaveral/Cocoa Beach	5	1966–1995	3,877,000	$9,511,133
Cocoa Beach	1	1996	40,000	$392,089

Beach Location	Number of Fills	Years	Volume (cubic yards)	2002 Cost
Delray Beach	5	1973–1996	5,373,830	$32,469,845
Fernandina Beach	5	1979–1996	2,281,139	$14,494,424
Fisher Island	1	1991	30,263	$175,855
Fort Pierce (South Beach)	10	1971–1995	1,882,940	$11,073,308
Fort Pierce Beach	1	1999	908,000	$6,611,287
Hallandale	1	1971	370,000	$3,187,989
Haulover Park	4	1960–1987	795,000	$4,757,866
Hillsboro Beach	1	1972	500,000	$3,051,535
Hollywood/Hallandale	2	1979–1991	3,030,000	$28,940,294
Hutchinson Island	1	1996	1,340,000	$12,841,821
Indialantic/Melbourne Beach	2	1981–1985	720,000	$7,598,192
Jacksonville Beach	8	1963–1996	5,575,000	$33,247,047
John U. Lloyd State Park	2	1977–1989	1,693,000	$11,512,314
Juno Beach	1	1996	135,000	$1,672,991
Jupiter Inlet (South Beach)	1	no data	60,000	$300,000
Jupiter Island	13+	1957–1996	11,603,552	$45,662,662
Jupiter/Carlin Beach	1	1995	603,000	$2,686,378
Key Biscayne	1	1987	360,000	$2,095,194
Key West, Smathers Beach	2	1960–2000	30,000	$185,837
Lake Worth Inlet (South Beach)	17	1944–1994	4,887,978	$31,614,438
Martin County	1	1996	1,269,000	$9,917,215
Mayport/Kathryn Abby Hanna Park	7	1966–1994	5,229,000	$26,589,327
Miami Beach	2+	1978–1987	12,350,000	$62,333,182
Midtown Beach	1	1996	800,000	$3,679,431
Ocean Ridge	1	1998	939,886	$3,459,135
Palm Beach	8	1944–1987	280,000	$2,545,045
Pompano Beach/ Lauderdale-by-the-Sea	3	1964–1983	2,985,000	$20,028,381
Ponce Inlet (North Beach)	6	1974–1996	2,374,900	$13,952,263
S. Amelia Island	1	1997	325,000	$1,676,515
Sebastian Inlet (South Beach)	6	1972–1993	1,172,842	$4,637,915
South of Matanzas	1	2000	765,000	$4,442,015
St. Lucie Inlet	3	1980–1989	no data	
St. Augustine Beach	1	2000	200,000	$986,803
St. Augustine Beach/Anastasia	2	1996–1998	540,000	$4,110,074
Sunny Isles	2	1988–1990	1,530,000	$22,481,006
Sunny Isles/Miami Beach	1	1997	716,052	$14,074,402
Surfside/South Miami Beach	1	1999	839,175	$14,272,916
Virginia Key–Key Biscayne	1	1969	373,000	$2,293,949
Vero Beach	2	1979–1984	no data	
Virginia Key	1	1974	500,000	$3,040,883
East Florida Totals	155		93,573,812	$550,176,055

Note: A number given with a plus is the minimum number of fill projects. Table does not include inlet maintenance dredging.

Source: Information derived from the Duke University Program for the Study of Developed Shorelines website, updated June 19, 2002; http://www.env.duke.edu/psds/nourishment.htm.

placement of the fill, an artificial berm exists in the form of a wider dry beach (the recreational beach at high tide). The profile also is steepened somewhat, and wave energy begins to redistribute the sand out onto the submerged portion of the beach. The sand is moved out beyond the surf zone and no longer offers much resistance to storm waves, especially if storm surge occurs, which it often does. Eventually the protective storm berm is diminished and the high-tide dry beach is very narrow or absent. Although the claim is sometimes made that the sand is still offshore, offering storm protection, the wide, dry beach is gone; both the recreational value and the original storm protection are lost.

Most beach communities faced with shoreline retreat consider dredge-and-fill projects at some point. Any community considering this option should keep the following generalizations in mind:

1. Beach dredge-and-fill projects are costly (see table 4.1).

2. A dredge-and-fill project is not a one-time solution; beach replenishment requires a long-term financial commitment by the community. The beach must be nourished again and again (e.g., Jupiter Island received 15 nourishments between 1957 and 1997).

3. The environmental impacts of dredge-and-fill projects are poorly understood (see chapter 5). Turtle nesting grounds are altered, dredging and pumping expose hard rock ground, turbidity may kill invertebrates and fish or smother sea grasses. Such impacts must be evaluated before new replenishments are undertaken and must be avoided, minimized, and mitigated.

4. Projects funded by the USACE take 8 to 15 years to come to fruition. A clash between the state and federal agencies often results.

5. A favorable cost-to-benefit ratio is required for federal participation. Recreational benefits usually do not count. The principal justification in most cases must be storm protection.

6. The Corps of Engineers is required to predict long-term (usually 50 years) costs and required sand volumes. These predictions will be highly optimistic; that is, the Corps's estimates of costs and sand volumes are likely to be too low.

7. Each beach fill project is different, but in most cases the community or state will pay the lion's share of the beach design costs, which can be millions of dollars. Offshore geology and oceanography are often more complicated than assumed in the models used to predict the cost and durability of a nourished beach. No one knows when the next big storm will occur.

8. The best estimates of the durability, cost, and sand volumes for a beach project can often be obtained by reviewing previous dredge-and-fill projects on the same beach or the experience of neighboring beaches. This approach is not precise, but it often proves to be as good as a coastal engineering estimate based on oversimplified or unrealistic models.

9. There is little or no difference between a designed beach fill and a

dredge-spoil-disposal beach fill, and dredge spoil is free! Fill sand from navigation dredging projects often works very well, even though it is not "designer" sand. If such material is derived from the mouth of an inlet, it is likely to be compatible beach sand. However, the quality of dredge spoil may not be appropriate for beach maintenance in all cases (e.g., muddy sands, coarse shells, rocks). The Corps of Engineers considers such filled beaches to be dredge-spoil disposal, and thus no design effort is required. In theory, such navigation projects can be done only if beach disposal is the cheapest way to get rid of dredge spoil. In practice, this is a highly politicized process.

10. Beaches constructed from dredge and fill often erode at higher rates than the original natural beaches eroded. As noted, nourishment may increase the state of disequilibrium by steepening the profile or introducing materials that differ from the natural beach in terms of grain size and composition.

11. Beach fill does not recover as well from storms as natural beaches do. The national experience is, at best, that perhaps 10 to 20 percent of nourished beaches might come back, but the more general case is little or no poststorm recovery.

12. A lesson based on the experience of Virginia Beach, Virginia, suggests that frequent small dredge-and-fill repairs may be more effective than less frequent large dredge-and-fill projects in maintaining the beach's width and longevity.

13. The sources and costs of dredge-and-fill sand are highly variable.

14. Sand can be a rare commodity on the continental shelf off East Florida, which is not covered with a blanket of beach-quality sand. Sand deposits are localized, and a search for sand must be carried out using seismic surveys and coring. This aspect of the design process is essential and cannot be avoided. Even when deposits are located, the quality of the deposit may not be uniform.

15. Consider using trucked sand if it is of high quality and compatibility, especially to respond to erosion "hot spots," both before and after replenishment. Every beach fill has "hot spots," or areas that erode more rapidly. Sometimes relatively small amounts of sand—for example, a few hundred truckloads—can repair the "hot spot" until the next fill project.

16. Having its own source of sand is to a community's advantage. Hire a geologist to find a long-term sand supply.

17. Once a dredge-and-fill beach is in place, it is essential to monitor its progress. Monitoring can be done very easily by taking successive photos from the same spot, making sure a sunbather or surfer is in the photo for scale. Alternatively, cross-beach profiles can be taken using elementary leveling techniques to provide a more quantitative view of the loss or gain rate (a good community project for high school classes). The fill being added to

the beach should be checked to see whether it is compatible with the existing beach (e.g., fill is free of rock and coral fragments; see fig. 4.14).

18. Sand located offshore, below the low-tide line, is useless for either recreation or community storm protection. When a replenished beach disappears more quickly than expected (the usual case), the sand is not just offshore providing protection. When the sea level rises with a storm surge, the portion of the beach that is most effective for storm protection is the artificial dune (sometimes called a berm in engineering parlance) at the back or landward side of the beach, as well as exposed beach width.

19. Changing the character of the natural beach through artificial fill (e.g., putting rocks in place of sand) will change the recreational use of the beach (fig. 4.14).

20. Where dunes are part of the natural system, dune building and maintenance should be part of dredge-and-fill beach projects. Dunes are sand reservoirs, and sand entrapment can be encouraged by the addition of vegetation and sand fences.

21. In the community/state/nationwide debate about beach maintenance and rebuilding beaches, keep in mind that the usual impetus behind proposed beach dredge-and-fill projects is that the first row of buildings fronting the water is threatened with destruction. No beachfront buildings, no erosion problem! That being the case, who should pay for the beach?

Trucking Sand

As noted above, an inland source of high-quality, compatible sand for beach fill and maintenance of fill projects is preferable to offshore sources. Trucking sand may be more costly per cubic yard of sand, but the true cost of offshore dredging (e.g., lost habitat and modifications to offshore bottoms that may increase coastal hazards) is likely to be higher. Virginia Beach, Virginia, is an example of a community that maintains its beaches through fill trucking. As offshore sand supplies diminish in Florida, attention will inevitably turn to inland sand sources.

Beach Scraping

Beach scraping (bulldozing) should not be confused with beach fill. Beach sand is moved from the low-tide beach to the upper back beach (independent of building artificial dunes) as an erosion mitigation technique and to offer temporary storm protection. No new sand is added to the system. A thin layer of sand (1 foot or less) is removed from over the entire lower beach using heavy machinery (dragline, grader, bulldozer, front-end loader) and spread over the upper beach. The objectives are to build a wider, higher,

4.14 Waves from Hurricane David (1979) concentrated coral rubble from the Miami Beach fill on the surface of the beach. When broken coral and rock are pumped onto the beach, the recreational quality is degraded. For some communities this problem has added to the cost of beach fill projects because rock removal or crushing was necessary to maintain beach quality. On the other hand, shell collectors may be delighted to peruse the coarse debris.

high-tide dry beach; to fill in troughlike lows that drain across the beach; and to encourage additional sand to accrete to the lower beach. Often the procedure is carried out simply to pile sand at the back of the beach as a berm or dike ("dune" is a misnomer) that offers little or no protection from storm waves (fig. 4.15).

The newly accreted sand can in turn be scraped, leading to a net gain of sand on the manicured beach. An enhanced recreational beach may be achieved for the short term, but the drawback is that no new sand is added to the system. Ideally, scraping is intended to encourage onshore transport of sand, but most of the sand "trapped" on the lower beach is brought in by longshore transport. Removal of this lower-beach sand deprives downdrift beaches of their natural nourishment, steepens the beach profile, and destroys beach organisms. So beach scraping may accelerate beach erosion.

Beach sweeping or raking is not a protective technique; it is mentioned here because of its potentially negative impact on the beach. Beach users prefer clean beaches, and refuse removal certainly is required for safe beaches. The removal or burial of seaweed and other wrack-line flotsam routinely carried out on recreational beaches for aesthetic reasons (fig. 4.16) results in sand loss and may contribute to gradual lowering of the beach profile.

4.15 Bulldozed sand such as that shown here in Brevard County offers little storm protection to the property at the back of the beach. The erosion scarp on the right suggests that the equilibrium position of the back beach should be about on a line with the front of the buildings. Attempting to hold the shoreline in place increases the disequilibrium, and more beach loss is likely.

4.16 Beach cleaning at Miami Beach. When sweeping removes seaweed and other natural wrack components, sand is also lost. Burying natural materials in the beach reduces sand loss and conserves organic content. Some beach aficionados prefer to keep the natural beach, wrack and all.

Sand Transfer Plants

STPS are specific to jettied inlets, as noted in the "Jetties" section above. STPS offer a viable solution for moving the natural sediment past the jetty structure and reducing downdrift erosion. Maintenance dredging of inlets achieves the same goal; however, it may come after the fact in terms of the losses suffered due to downdrift erosion and is more likely to have detrimental habitat impact when a larger amount of sediment is finally moved. Although Florida has experienced operational problems with its two sand-bypassing systems, STPS should be considered for many of the state's inlets.

Dune Building

Dune building is often an important part of beach maintenance design, although it may be carried out independent of beach fill. Coastal dunes are a common back-beach landform and are part of the dynamic equilibrium of barrier beach systems. Although there is extensive literature about dunes, their protective role is often misunderstood. Frontal dunes are the last line of defense against ocean storm wave attack and flooding from overwash; interior dunes may provide high ground and protection against penetration of overwash and against the damaging effects of storm-surge ebb scour.

Wide dune fields (both natural and bulldozed) can be the main line of defense during hurricanes. In actual hurricane experience, wide, high dunes were more effective protection for property than any shore-hardening structure. Nature's price, however, is to take the dunes in a storm. Posthurricane recovery and routine hazard mitigation include artificial dune building and encouraging new dune growth through the use of sand fencing and/or dune grass plantings.

Plugging Dune Gaps

Storms have a way of exploiting weak points. Artificial gaps in dunes are avenues for flooding, overwash, and storm-surge ebb currents. Plugging dune gaps should be a part of beach fill, dune construction, and sand conservation projects. Because dunes are critical coastal geomorphic features with respect to property damage mitigation, they are now protected, right down to the vegetation critical to their growth. Prior to strict coastal-zone management regulations, frontal dunes were often excavated for ocean views or building sites, or notched at road termini for beach access. Wherever dune removal for development has occurred, the probability of complete overwash and possible inlet formation is increased. The combined threats of storm flooding, inlet formation, and the burial of roads by overwash sand make dune-removal areas prime danger zones for evacuation in case of a hurricane warning. The good news is that dune gaps can be refilled (plugged), many with just a few truckloads of new sand. Maintaining dunes in the interior of islands is an equally important way to reduce property damage (also known as property damage mitigation).

Principles of Sand Fencing and Artificial Plantings

Dune gaps and dune lines can be repaired and augmented by encouraging or enhancing natural processes. Typically, such augmentation includes the placement of sand fences and the planting of dune grasses to trap wind-blown sand. Sand fencing also serves as a barrier to foot traffic over dunes, allowing vegetation to gain a foothold and flourish. Effective use of fencing to build dunes should follow these guidelines:

> Do not place fencing on the beach because landward transport of sand may be reduced, the small dunes that build up are out of equilibrium, fencing is likely to wash out in the first storm, and fencing on the face of the dune may encourage seaward dune toe growth.
>
> Do not use double rows of dune fencing, which act as impenetrable rather than permeable barriers (blocks inland sand flow).
>
> Do not attach new fence to old fence as the dune grows upward.
>
> Remove fencing periodically.
>
> Vegetate the newly formed dunes with native species.
>
> Vegetation is just as effective as sand fences in building dunes over the long term.
>
> Trapping sand on the landward side of the dune is as important as trapping sand on the front and top of the dune.

The last guideline is very important because dune width as well as dune height affords protection. The principle is often violated when property owners notch the back side of the dune (e.g., for house construction, driveways, patios, play areas) and during poststorm reconstruction. Instead of placing overwash sand from roads, driveways, and parking lots back onto the dune, the sediment sometimes is removed from the area. Remember: both dune width and height are important; keep all the sand in the system and add new sand if possible; allow the dune to migrate (maintain equilibrium); and vegetate with native species.

Sand fencing and artificial plantings of dune grass to build (or rebuild) dunes are most effective when structures are set back far enough to provide an adequate space for dunes to build and stabilize in a natural equilibrium profile and location. A healthy sand supply also is needed. Shorelines with low sand supplies defy efforts to build dunes artificially.

Dune management must be guided by the principles of dynamic equilibrium. A fundamental rule is that the dune zone may have to migrate if it is to retain its protective characteristics. Unfortunately, some people view dunes as if these natural sand accumulations can be designed, engineered, and constructed in the same fashion as groins and seawalls. If dunes are to function in their natural protective role, a "preserve, augment, and restore" approach must mimic the equilibrium setting. A dune bulldozed or built into a nonequilibrium location will not be stable. In fact, artificially "cemented" dunes (e.g., Biodune) are like seawalls, blocking sediment derivation and migration, and thus creating new problems in other parts of the beach-dune system or island interior on barrier islands. Dunes are not static, rigid, permanent structures, and the dune line must migrate inland as the shoreline retracts.

Similarly, the natural vegetation that stabilizes dunes is in equilibrium with the sediment and biota. The roots of sea oats are home to colonies of vesicular-arbuscular mycorrhizal (VAM) fungi that improve the plants' uptake of nutrients and water. Artificial plantings of these grasses do not fare well in pumped-in nourishment sands or where these sands have been used to construct artificial dunes because the VAM fungus is missing. Plant root systems can be inoculated with the VAM fungus in the nursery to improve chances that the artificial plantings will take hold, but the point is that nature is far more complex than a simple engineering design. Even differences in grain size and sorting between bulldozed sediment and natural windblown sand may influence dune stability and plant growth.

Relocation: Managed Retreat

Moving buildings back or letting them fall into the sea has a long tradition along American shores. Retreating from the shoreline is the best way to ensure preservation of beaches for future generations. Although politically difficult, this is the course of action chosen by states that prohibit seawalls. On a shoreline lined with high-rise buildings, such as Miami Beach, retreat would be very difficult but not impossible to implement. In contrast, retreat would be less difficult on parts of Hutchinson Island where there are fewer and smaller buildings.

In the long run (decades), in a time of rising sea level, decreasing sand supplies, and decreasing funding, communities will have to make a choice. They can have beaches or they can have shorefront buildings on beachless armored shores or they can have short-lived artificial beaches. It will be expensive and perhaps impossible to have both buildings and beaches. If the community opts in favor of buildings, the beaches will be lost, and so, ultimately, will the buildings.

Relocation can be encouraged or implemented in many ways. Federal and state governments can end expenditures in support of beachfront development. Undeveloped beach areas can be acquired, an approach Florida currently is using. In addition, poststorm reconstruction of destroyed buildings could be prohibited, as could reconstruction of buildings that have exceeded their design lives. Developers could be required to purchase and set aside retreat areas in new developments. Strong incentives could be provided to encourage development in low-risk areas and to move development already in existence into low-risk areas. FEMA encourages relocation through partial support for buyouts of residences that have suffered repeated flooding. For example, the FEMA-funded Missouri Buyout Program relocated 4,800 properties off of a hazardous river floodplain. Relocation is the ultimate mitigation; however, support for it is very limited. Continued public education, especially for property purchasers, regarding risks from coastal hazards and the long-term costs of coastal development is essential to change public policy.

Are Variances Eroding Beach Protection Efforts?

The problem of shoreline engineering leading to beach narrowing and degradation is not exclusive to Florida or New Jersey, or to any one part of the coast. On Oahu, Hawaii, 30 percent of the island's sandy beaches have disappeared because of seawalls. The beaches of California are disappearing as well, partly because of dam construction and harbor protection, factors that are also contributing to the erosion of the Puerto Rico coastline. All in all, the Atlantic, Pacific, and Gulf stories are identical. Shore-hardening structures either directly or indirectly cause loss of the beaches.

The stated general policy of the FDEP's Bureau of Beaches and Coastal Systems is to use armoring only as a last resort where no alternative is available to protect habitable and major public structures. Variances abound, of course, because all developed areas have habitable and major public structures, and relocation is not taken seriously as an alternative of less impact. So agencies charged with protecting natural resources yield to political and economic pressure, and opt to protect buildings.

Beaches and dunes are Florida's most valuable natural resources, arguably far more valuable than private condos or cottages. Our shores need help—the help of the public and of far-sighted planners and developers—if they are to be available for today and tomorrow.

Truths of the Shoreline

Studies of long-developed shorelines indicate a set of principles or "universal truths" that are fundamental to low-risk, aesthetically pleasing development. These truths are evident to scientists who have studied the shoreline and to old-timers who have lived there all of their lives.

1. Beach erosion is not a natural disaster. Shoreline retreat is an integral and expected part of beach response to rising sea level, increased wave en-

ergy, or diminished sediment supply. Landward migration of beaches is particularly important to barrier island evolution.

2. Erosion is not a problem until someone builds a stationary structure along the dynamic shoreline. No buildings, no problem. Visit one of the state parks to verify this principle. The once great beaches of the urbanized barriers no longer match the beauty of the near-natural park beaches.

3. Shoreline erosion creates no problem for the beach. The beach simply retreats and changes its position in space. The beach does not disappoint its users. Surfers, swimmers, fishers, and strolling lovers cannot tell the difference.

4. Human activities increase the rate of shoreline retreat. Most shoreline modifications made by humans, including shoreline engineering, dune destruction, building construction, channel dredging, and jetty construction, reduce the sand supply to beaches.

5. Shoreline engineering protects the interests of a very few, often at a very high cost in federal and state dollars. The shorefront property responsible for the erosion problem (truth 2) is owned by relatively few people compared with the number of beach users. Engineering structures protect the interests of those property owners rather than the interests of the thousands or hundreds of thousands of people who use the beaches.

6. Shoreline stabilization, especially beach dredge-and-fill projects, can lead to intensified development. The presence of a new, wide beach replacing a narrow, eroded beach with waves rolling under buildings is a temptation developers will not pass up. The new beach is regarded as a permanent resource rather than an ephemeral feature.

7. Once you begin shoreline engineering, you cannot stop it! Shoreline hardening is rarely removed; instead it usually grows larger and longer. And once a beach is constructed by dredge and fill, then more dredge-and-fill projects will be required to maintain the beach.

8. You can have buildings or you can have beaches, but in the long run you cannot have both. The ultimate truth is that we should avoid the hazards that accompany life at the coast, but if we choose to locate on the coast, then prudence dictates that we evaluate the level of risk. Structures and nourished beaches will not prevent hurricanes or stop the sea-level rise.

The final truth is that it is better to work with Nature than to attempt to out-engineer it. Learning to live by the rules of the sea will save time, money, and lives. If coastal development covers the onshore environment and destroys the offshore environment, what remains to enjoy? *You can't do just one thing.* When we choose coastal engineering over relocation, a chain of events takes place that may have repercussions well beyond the shoreline.

5 Environmental Effects of Beach Management

Declines in coastal area quality are often expressed in terms of erosion, and efforts focus on the protection of shorefront property and maintaining the recreational beach. Too often the animals and plants that make up the coastal ecosystem and the large economic values they provide (e.g., fisheries, diving, etc.) are undervalued. Beach erosion is visible, but the great diversity of life and the effects of human intervention at the margin of the land and ocean often go unseen. Good beach management, particularly when it is based on the offshore dredging and inshore dumping of massive amounts of sediment, must include a sound knowledge of the impacts of construction activities on nearshore ecosystems.

The Shelf Setting

East Florida's long continental shelf includes diverse tropical and temperate habitats that are home to thousands of coastal animal and plant species. These organisms are affected by many human activities including overfishing, various types of water pollution, creating artificial inlets, shoreline armoring, beach scraping, and wetland degradation. The cumulative impacts of some of these activities extend back for more than a century, and many scientists are suggesting a more proactive management approach given the already degraded conditions of many coastal areas in the region (appendix C, ref. 50). Since the late 1970s, engineering efforts to hold the shoreline in place have focused on large dredge-and-fill projects (termed "renourishments" or "restorations"). Such projects often require the dredging of millions of cubic yards of sediments from mid-shelf habitats and subsequent dumping and bulldozing of the fill in shallow waters. Inevitably, these dredge projects are repeated at 4- to 12-year intervals at a cost to taxpayers of tens of millions of dollars.

From St. Augustine to Fort Lauderdale, nearshore hard-bottom reefs are

5.1 Nearshore hard-bottom reef habitats of East Florida support the juvenile life stages of a wide variety of fishes, invertebrates, and plants. Photo copyright David B. Snyder.

often interspersed among sandy intertidal and subtidal nearshore habitats. These reefs, which consist primarily of exposed limestone bedrock, often support diverse communities dominated by fishes (fig. 5.1), invertebrate animals, and algae. More than 500 species of animals and plants have been recorded on the nearshore reefs that are buried or indirectly affected by beach dredging projects (appendix C, refs. 45 and 46).

These shallow environments are important to the coastal system for many reasons. They serve as nursery habitats for many valuable species, as there are typically no other natural habitats in this depth zone to use for shelter and feeding. Some nearshore reefs actually reduce erosional shoreline losses by damping wave energy (appendix C, refs. 44 and 51). Turtle- and manatee-grass beds, abundant only on the eastern sides of several beaches south of Miami Beach (Fisher Island, Virginia Key, and Key Biscayne), are home to numerous species. Beaches are used as nesting habitat by several species of threatened or endangered sea turtles, and juvenile green sea turtles use shallow reefs as nursery and feeding habitats.

Deeper reefs often exist offshore in bands that roughly parallel the shore. These systems differ in geology and biology from nearshore hard-bottom reefs and have a higher percentage of hard corals, sponges, and soft corals that require water relatively free of suspended sediments. The northernmost coral reefs of continental North America are off southeastern Florida.

And some of the finest remaining staghorn coral reefs are located between the offshore dredge and inshore fill areas of a pending 2.5-million-cubic-yard beach dredge-and-fill project in Fort Lauderdale.

How Marine Animals Can Be Affected by Engineering Projects

The environmental consequences of large dredge-and-fill projects are not well known. Dredging of sand plains on the shelf, often near reef habitats, creates large craters ("borrow" pits) and increases turbidity in the water column, blocking light for long periods. When these sediments eventually settle to the bottom, they may cover corals and other organisms that need both light and sediment-free surfaces for survival. At both the dredge and the fill sites, acres of shallow and deeper reefs and associated habitats are routinely buried or subjected to high turbidity, suffocating animals or disturbing their growth patterns. In the year 2000, four proposed projects between Vero Beach and Fort Lauderdale would have buried more than 100 acres of nearshore reef. There is a surprising lack of scientific knowledge about the impacts of such projects, an absence that is ironic given the number that have occurred in southeast Florida over the past several decades. The millions of dollars that have gone into studying their environmental effects have not produced independent journal publications.

Although this chapter cannot characterize all of the ecological aspects of nearshore and mid-shelf habitats and the potential effects on them from beach projects, the following overview summarizes some of the complex issues involved. It will be useful to think of changes in the environment that present challenges to organisms as "stressors," and the response of organisms to these changes as "effects." Individual stressors can produce complex effects in fish and invertebrate animal populations, and they can interact with other stressors to create further effects in cascades of events that are often very difficult to predict. For example, many stressors resulting from the dredge burial of a habitat can affect various aspects of respiration and feeding. Effects can be direct or indirect and may operate over the short term, the long term, or both (table 5.1). Yet, even an "indirect" effect, such as lowered growth rate, may ultimately lead to increased vulnerability to predation or production of fewer eggs. Many effects will vary among different species and life stages; the earliest development stages are frequently the most sensitive to environmental changes. These early stages are common in many of the nearshore habitats most affected by beach dredge-and-fill projects.

Even if impacts from one dredging project are low, the cumulative effects of multiple projects can be amplified over time. A classic example where negative effects cascaded through an entire ecosystem with catastrophic results exists in the Everglades just west of southeast Florida's beaches. Over decades, many modifications were made to the regional environment, par-

Table 5.1 Stressors Associated with Beach Dredge-and-Fill Projects That Affect Marine Organisms: Some Relationships Between Intensity (Lethal/Sublethal) and Duration (Shore Term/Long Term)

| | Duration of Effects | |
	Short-term	Long-term
Intensity of Effects:		
Lethal	—Direct burial of cryptic species or those that flee to crevices (1) —Respiratory trauma (2) (erosion of gill filaments) —Increased predation*	Loss of settlement habitat (1, 3) resulting in: —Increased predation —Increased starvation
Sublethal	—Respiratory stress and reduction in growth (2) —Separation from conspecific schools (2)	—Reduction in growth and thus reduced reproduction* —Residence in new, suboptimal habitat*

Note: Type of stressor inducing the effect: (1) sedimentation, (2) turbidity, (3) mechanical impacts.
*Potentially a combination of all stressors.

ticularly to the natural drainage system feeding the Everglades, for agricultural and development purposes. Most projects were conducted independently of the others, with little or no consideration of the indirect or cumulative impacts of all. Fifty years later, many unanticipated negative effects had surfaced across a vast landscape from Central Florida to the reefs of the Florida Keys. As the twenty-first century began, $8 billion had been budgeted for the USACE to begin a restoration program in an attempt to repair the cumulative, unanticipated ecosystem damage caused by the cascades of many unrelated projects.

Thorough and unbiased consideration of the direct, indirect, and cumulative biological effects of multiple beach engineering projects should be a critical part of environmental planning in large dredge-and-fill projects on Florida's already degraded eastern coast. An examination of the *cumulative effects* of even the most basic stressors, however, is often lacking in the various environmental assessments for dredge-and-fill projects. Discriminating among lethal and sublethal stressors and identifying interactions between the durations and intensities of effects (table 5.1) are particularly important. Each combination of organism, stressor type, intensity, and duration can produce different effects.

The responses of fishes and invertebrates to beach dredge-and-fill projects will be dictated in part by their relative degree of mobility and ability to deal with change (e.g., the animal's ability to move out of harm's way). Can the animal survive long enough to find new habitat? Does it have the sensory abilities to locate new habitat and avoid predators while it searches? How will it respond to decreased food and increased turbidity in its habitat? These factors and others determine whether individuals can survive and repopulate dredge-and-fill sites (table 5.1). Variations in mobility during different growth stages are very important. Animals in earlier life stages are less able to avoid stressors than larger, older animals. Perhaps most important, increased mortality of younger life stages in their nearshore nursery areas can reduce the ultimate size of adult populations, or at least lower reproductive outputs.

Beach Engineering Methods and Some Environmental Effects

A number of technologies have been utilized for beach maintenance in South Florida. Six types involving the deposition of sediment on or near beaches are listed below.

1. Large dredge-and-fill projects: restoration and renourishment
2. Large dredge-and-fill projects: inlet channel maintenance
3. Large dredge-and-fill projects: nearshore berms
4. Placement of quarry sediments using trucks
5. Placement of aragonite sediments using barges
6. Inlet sand transfer plants

Dredging for inlet channel maintenance, which is much less invasive than large offshore dredge-and-fill projects, typically involves the dredging of much smaller amounts of higher-quality sand from within inlets and placement on the adjacent beach. It is considered separately below. Large beach dredge-and-fill projects are considered in more detail because such projects are increasingly common and have a greater likelihood of environmental impacts. Because the higher-quality offshore sand sources available for large-scale dredging are almost gone or limited in some counties (Dade and Broward), the need to evaluate alternative methods is increasing.

Most of these beach maintenance alternatives generate a variety of stressors, which can be subdivided into categories such as (1) sedimentation (direct burial), (2) turbidity (reduced water clarity), and (3) mechanical impacts (direct impacts of machinery on habitats). These stressors are distributed in several areas across the shelf during the dredging process, each area home to hundreds of species of organisms that respond to disturbance in differing ways. From shallow to deep, these areas include the nearshore area (approximately 0–12 feet deep), the intermediate area (12–35 feet), and the mid-shelf area (35–60 feet). These areas correspond to common biological patterns of cross-shelf distribution (e.g., younger life stages are typically in nearshore areas).

Engineering Methods

Large beach dredge-and-fill projects are often based on the dredging of sediments from mid-shelf areas, pumping of the sediments through pipes on the bottom to the shore, and dumping the fill on shorelines and shallow habitats where it is bulldozed into a broader beach. When first done on a highly eroded shore, such projects are termed "restorations." Most involve the excavation and dumping of 1–3 million cubic yards of sediments and are completed in one to three months with 24-hour-a-day dredging, pumping, and bulldozing operations.

Because "restored" beaches such as these are often lost steadily to erosion (see chapter 4), follow-up dredging projects ("renourishments") are usually incorporated into the original design at 3- to 10-year intervals. Whether the project is a restoration or renourishment, it involves large-scale excavations at one or more mid-shelf dredge pits that have been identified as possessing adequate sediments.

Two fundamental types of dredges are employed: cutterhead dredges and hopper dredges. Cutterhead dredges use 5 to 8-foot-diameter terminal heads (baskets) equipped with rotating cutting blades, customized for size and serration, for actually digging into the bottom. Large hydraulic pumps convey the excavated material from the back of the basket into a long series of pipes leading to shore (fig. 5.2). The bow of the dredge, holding the cutterhead

5.2 Dredging operation and associated turbidity plumes. The pipeline carrying fill pumped toward the shore is submerged and not visible. Photo copyright David B. Snyder.

5.3 Burial of approximately 12 acres of nearshore reef in northern Palm Beach County. Muddy sand blown out of discharge pipes is pushed seaward by bulldozers over shallow reef habitats. Photo copyright David B. Snyder.

basket, associated hardware, and discharge pipe, is swung in an arc using a vertical support mounted on the stern (a "spud") as a fulcrum. Large craters on the bottom of the area are the result. Typically, the transport pipes leading away from the dredge platform are tethered on the surface for a short distance and then descend to the bottom for the remainder of the distance to the shore. At the fill site, the dredged material is blown out of a discharge pipe in a slurry, then redistributed by a "dump crew" using bulldozers, sometimes burying nearshore reefs in the process (fig. 5.3).

Unlike the relatively stationary, deep-digging cutterhead dredge, the hopper dredge maneuvers over a predetermined dredge path trailing a suction head that does not dig as deeply into the sediments as the cutterhead described above. Deep, large craters typically do not result from this method, but the surface of the bottom is thoroughly disturbed. Sediments are stored in the open hull (hopper) of the vessel and can be taken near the dump site for offloading by various methods, including hydraulic pumping or dumping from the ship in the nearshore zone. Fill overflowing from the hopper can release enormous amounts of sediments into the water column during the dredging process. Many variations in these basic approaches have been developed, but all have biological impacts.

Historical Perspectives on Beach Dredge-and-Fill
The large-scale offshore dredging and inshore filling of East Florida beaches began in the 1970s with projects at Pompano Beach, Delray Beach, and

particularly Miami Beach. By the early 1980s the state began to view this method as the alternative of choice to maintain beaches. Florida's policy emphasis on frequent large-scale dredging has not changed. The USACE's planning guide for southeast Florida, *Coast of Florida Erosion and Storm Effects Study: Region III* (appendix C, ref. 43), published in 1996, provides comprehensive coastal engineering plans for the next 50 years. The study identifies approximately 20 sites for continued large-scale dredging and filling on the open shelf in Dade, Broward, and Palm Beach Counties, but does not include locally funded projects. More than 50 such projects were already constructed between 1960 and 2000. By 2000 more than 50 million cubic yards of sediments had been dredged from offshore, pumped to shore, and bulldozed into the shallow waters of southeast Florida.

As follow-up dredging is budgeted for almost all sites at 3- to 10-year intervals based on federal authorizations, the *Coast of Florida* study gives information on the number of large-scale dredge "renourishments" that will occur in southeast Florida between 1997 and 2047. A conservative estimate of the total number of projects in this small subregion can be obtained by summing the number of "renourishments" per project site for 50 years (ranging from 4 to 16 based on 3- to 12-year "renourishment" intervals) and dividing by 2 (reducing the project numbers by half to allow for the usual delays in permitting and financing of these projects). Based on this conservative evaluation, approximately 95 additional offshore dredging and inshore fill projects will be constructed within the same 125-mile stretch of southeast Florida by mid-century. If the dredge projects are constructed at the estimated engineering intervals for renourishment presented in the *Coast of Florida* study, that number will double, and well over 100 million cubic yards of fill will be dredged and dumped. Estimating the cost is difficult, but given that past project costs were often underestimated and that the supply of high-quality sediments is diminishing, the costs will certainly be extreme. Unfortunately, estimates of added costs accruing from damage to habitats, fisheries, and other ecosystem factors are not performed.

Environmental Effects
Different areas across the continental shelf support different types of activities associated with large dredge-and-fill operations. Each area can experience its own set of environmental effects.

Mid-shelf Areas (35–60 Feet). Cutterhead dredges mechanically disrupt the seafloor, removing sediment and the many animals that live within, while digging craters as deep as 30 feet into the bottom. Trailing suction heads of hopper dredges remove sediments and organisms within the sediment as well, but with reduced volume and depth compared with cutterheads. Despite some buffer zones between dredges and reefs, cutterhead dredges and associated equipment (e.g., discharge pipelines, mooring chains) can directly damage hard-bottom areas, as has occurred in projects at Miami and Boca Raton.

Because of the excavation and hydraulic pumping of hundreds of thousands of cubic yards of sediment during offshore dredging, turbidity clouds are created that extend both downstream and across large areas of the shelf for miles. Turbidity may be most concentrated at the dredge excavation site or, for hopper dredge barges, at the site of slurry overflow. Heavier sediments settle out, stressing corals and other bottom-dwelling animals and algae that provide food and shelter for fishes.

Assumptions of rapid recovery of sediment-dwelling organisms at offshore dredge sites have been questioned by detailed studies (appendix C, ref. 49), suggesting instead that recovery times from single projects can be at least four to five years at some sites. Among other key issues, few studies consider age-based population responses, which are often disregarded in typical environmental assessments. Long-term cumulative effects remain unstudied.

Dredge-suspended sediments are distributed across the shelf between the dredging and dumping sites by the dredging and filling operations and by currents as well. Wind and waves resuspend these sediments in significant amounts long after the dredging is completed. Chronic wind- and wave-induced sediment that turns the water "to milk" is commented on by fishermen and divers along Jupiter Island immediately north of Palm Beach in Martin County, the site of at least nine major offshore dredge projects over the past 25 years. Again, no long-term studies of such effects have ever been conducted.

Marine populations may respond to reductions in water quality over time scales of decades, masking effects that may be cumulatively large (as was seen immediately inland in the Everglades). This scenario is easily as plausible as the common claims that effects of large-scale dredging are short term or negligible.

Intermediate Shelf Areas (12–35 Feet). Pipelines 24 to 36 inches in diameter typically are used to transport hydraulically pumped fill from excavation sites, across the shelf, to the dump sites. These pipelines are sometimes laid directly across reefs. Although it is well known that the pipelines can shift during storms and further damage the reefs, large dredge projects continue to include the laying of discharge pipes across reef habitats (e.g., the 1997 "renourishment" at Surfside in Miami Beach involving approximately 0.4–0.6 acre of hard-bottom damage).

Leaks from the seams between pipes transporting dredge fill along the bottom can also affect nearby fish and invertebrate habitats. In one pipe leakage event in Miami Beach, 9 acres of reef were buried before the contractor temporarily terminated the fill pumping. Potential effects in the short term, and chronic resuspension in the long term, also apply here.

Nearshore and Onshore Areas (0–12 Feet). More than 325 species of invertebrates have been identified on nearshore reefs buried by "renourishment" dredging. In addition, living colonies of star corals (*Siderastrea* spp.), fire corals (*Millepora* spp.), and large numbers of other attached or cryptic species are commonly buried by dumped fill. Other activities that directly kill or damage corals require specific permits under the Florida Administrative Code, but that is apparently not the case for beach dredging.

Stress related to both sedimentation (eventual settling of sediments on the bottom) and turbidity (sediments suspended in the water column) can have direct and indirect effects (appendix C, ref. 46). A 1999 study examined some direct effects of the burial of 12 to 14 acres of nearshore reef at a beach dredge-and-fill site south of Jupiter Inlet (appendix C, ref. 45). After the burial, the number of fishes at the impact site decreased by 95 percent. Sixty-five species were recorded in the year of preburial sampling; only 8 species were recorded in one year of postburial monitoring, and the decline was still apparent 18 months later. Eighty percent of the individuals originally present at the study site and a nearby nearshore reef that was not buried were early life stages, indicating that the nearshore reefs buried by dredge fill are nursery habitats. This study and other nearshore fish surveys have identified more than 200 species of fishes associated with the nearshore reefs of southeast Florida.

Administrative environmental reviews of dredge-and-fill projects typically assume that fishes will simply swim away to other areas when their habitats are buried and the water is filled with sediments. But juvenile stages of fish and invertebrates (typically less than 2 inches in length) cannot simply swim far away when their habitat is eliminated. Among the species affected by burial of nearshore reefs are juvenile stages of grunts, snappers, porgies, drums, and all life stages of other species such as damselfishes, labrisomids (clinids), and gobies, as well as many crabs, shrimp, worms, and mollusks. Many fish and invertebrates incubate their eggs in nests on the hard-bottom habitats that are buried by the fill. The egg nests of damselfishes, blennies, and other fishes cannot survive burial, and thousands of unhatched fish die in this manner. Plants, important as both shelter and food, are also impacted by dredge projects. The 1987 dredge-and-fill project at Key Biscayne directly buried more than 20 acres of seagrass beds.

Independent publications on fill impacts on invertebrates that live within the emergent beach still do not exist for Florida. However, initial scholarly research from North Carolina focusing on the same key crustacean species that occur within Florida's beaches has identified a number of direct and indirect negative impacts that are rarely considered in dredge-and-fill environmental assessments (appendix C, ref. 52). In addition, respected sea turtle researchers suggest caution in accepting the assumption that large dredge-and-fill projects are a preferred long-term solution for sea turtle nesting (appendix C, ref. 53).

Inlet Channel Maintenance

Almost all of the inlets on Florida's east coast are dredged at several-year intervals to keep them deep and safe for marine traffic. Before 1970, the dredged material (called dredge spoil) was commonly considered waste and was dumped offshore. Now, the fill is usually placed on the southern side of an inlet's south jetty in order to help maintain the downdrift beaches (see chapter 3). These projects, which involve much smaller dredges and lower fill volumes (typically between 25,000 and 100,000 cubic yards) than beach "renourishments," occur at 1- to 4-year intervals at most inlets. Frequencies and fill volumes vary according to inlet widths, depths, sedimentation rates, and boating needs. Turbidity clouds from these projects typically do not reach mid-shelf areas, and if they do, are dispersed relatively quickly. Impacts on fishes are probably limited.

Large-scale inlet expansions of ports, which occur much less frequently than small inlet maintenance projects, can generate very large volumes of sediments which both historically and recently have been dumped on mid-shelf sites (e.g., the dumping of approximately 350,000 cubic yards of fill on mid-shelf reef habitats off Fort Pierce in 1996). Substantial turbidity clouds may also reach these intermediate cross-shelf areas from particularly large inlet channel maintenance projects (e.g., a 400,000-cubic-yard inlet channel dredging at St. Lucie Inlet).

Nearshore Berms

A new alternative for South Florida, nearshore berm construction, was proposed in the USACE's *Coast of Florida* study (appendix C, ref. 43). In this approach, a close relative of large dredge-and-fill projects, fill from offshore is dumped in nearshore waters at depths of 8 to 20 feet, instead of intertidal areas. Inlet maintenance projects can also be a source of fill for berms or bars. Although currently uncommon, berms are theoretically under consideration at approximately 17 sites in southeast Florida alone, according to the *Coast of Florida* study. Proposed dimensions of the berms include lengths ranging from 1,000 to 24,000 feet, widths from 400 to 600 feet, and fill volumes from 40,000 to 480,000 cubic yards. These proposed projects could typically involve the dredging and nearshore dumping of approximately 500,000 cubic yards of fill.

In theory, shallow-water berms, at 10- to 15-foot depths, can have two different effects: as "stable berms" they would attenuate incoming wave energy; as "active berms" they would feed beach sand into the system to migrate inshore and downstream. All of the nearshore berms proposed in southeast Florida would be designed to be active berms. The assumption is that sediments placed nearshore will move mainly onshore because of placement within a "depth of closure," a theoretical nearshore limit beyond which offshore sediment transport is limited. The assumption that sediments will not be transported seaward because of the "depth of closure" is considered unrealistic by many. Storms will continuously resuspend sediments into the water column, and the particles will be transported alongshore, inshore, or offshore depending on a wide array of physical conditions.

Environmental studies on such projects for this region are absent, but it is possible to make logical predictions. Nearshore berms will directly impact bottom fauna in and adjacent to the fill areas. Negative turbidity and sedimentation effects will probably be similar to those associated with typical renourishment projects. The cumulative effects of chronically reduced water quality on tropical nearshore and mid-shelf fauna remain unknown. If berms are placed at least 500–1,000 feet away from reefs, sedimentation may be less of an issue than turbidity.

Sand Trucking

Beach-compatible sand trucked from inland sand pits and dumped on the beach has been used in some smaller projects. Large-scale trucking of inland sands to South Florida beaches has not been common because the costs and logistics have been considered prohibitive, owing in part to relatively long distances to suitable sand sources. But the complete consumption of remaining offshore sand deposits for dredging in Dade County (predicted to occur within several years) may require more inland sand mining.

One of the benefits of trucking sand is that the offshore and intermediate areas are less disturbed because sediments are not being dredged and transported across the shelf. Nevertheless, short-term turbidity clouds will affect bottom-dwelling animals and fishes. Direct burial of the beachface and submerged nearshore habitats will still occur. The increased demand for sand and greater attention to cross-shelf marine impacts may eventually make this alternative more acceptable in some cases in spite of the higher costs.

Importing Aragonite Sand

Another sand source alternative that has received attention in southeast Florida is aragonite sand from the Bahamas. Aragonite is a form of calcium carbonate that is common in Bahamian sand. The aragonite would be purchased from existing mining operations, primarily on the Grand Bahamas shelf, and then barged to South Florida for deposition in shoreline areas. The percentage of silts/clays is reported to be low; however, aragonite sand grains break down into very fine mud-sized particles that can coalesce and harden over time.

Aragonite use raises its own set of environmental issues. The breakdown of aragonite may cause the beach to harden in contrast to East Florida's native beach sediments. Because aragonite reflects light more than native South Florida beach sediments, cooler beachfaces would result. This has created concerns regarding sea turtles because incubation temperatures influence sex ratios of embryos within sea turtle nests. Intermediate shelf areas may be affected by offshore dispersal of turbidity plumes. As of 2000, only one very small project (using 25,000 cubic yards of aragonite sand), at Fisher Island in Miami, had been constructed. Monitoring of this project revealed the loss of less than 1 acre of seagrasses and moderate declines in numbers of both animal species and individuals.

The limited information on the effects of aragonite dredging and filling on sea turtles, in fauna, and other organisms seems to indicate that few negative consequences are likely in South Florida. However, a variety of significant differences in faunal distributions and ecological characteristics exist between Florida and the Bahamian aragonite source areas (e.g., species occurrences, relative abundance). Concerns have been raised that importing aragonite from other regions might introduce harmful nonnative species. The Bahamian government does not at this time support the export of aragonite sands to South Florida. If this policy changes, the number of proposals to dump barges of aragonite sand along East Florida's coasts will likely increase.

Sand Transfer Plants

Sand transfer plants (STPs) are fixed sand-pumping stations situated in shallow water on the north sides of inlet jetties where sand tends to accumulate (see figs. 4.10 and 4.11). Such plants use submerged pipes placed under the inlet to pump naturally accreted sediments from the north side of the jettied inlet to the south side. These plants keep sand in the natural longshore transport system and can be effective long-term tools. For example, the Lake Worth STP bypassed an estimated 2.1 million cubic yards of sediment from 1958 to 1990. Current technology could permit a fully operational STP in South Florida to bypass 100,000 to 150,000 cubic yards of sediment annually. Environmental effects at all scales from this technology are minimal. If STPs using new technology were located at several strategically located inlets, cost-effective beach maintenance in East Florida could be enhanced and fewer large dredge-and-fill projects would be deemed necessary.

Unfortunately, only two STPs, at Lake Worth Inlet and South Lake Worth Inlet, are currently in use in southeast Florida. Both are old (constructed in approximately 1958 and 1937, respectively) and have functioned with quite variable efficiency. The state and local governments have made considerable effort to rehabilitate these existing facilities. The *Coast of Florida* study recommends cost-shared funding to refurbish and operate both plants at full bypassing capacity. In particular, the Lake Worth plant would use newer technology as a demonstration project. Unfortunately, no other STPs are currently under development in this region.

Comparative Environmental Effects of Beach Engineering Methods

All of the beach maintenance alternatives discussed above affect the nearshore zone. "Renourishment" projects and nearshore berms completely bury shallow-water habitats. Dredging for renourishment or berm construction substantially affects both nearshore and mid-shelf sites. Extensive mechanical impacts and turbidity can be present along the path of the cutterhead or trailing suction head (on a hopper dredge). In theory, small buffer zones are maintained between working dredges and nearby reefs. In practice, these buffer zones are not always enforced during operations and reefs have been damaged at many sites. In addition, the pipelines transporting dredged fill shoreward usually lie on the bottom over long distances. Therefore, mechanical impacts and turbidity effects are also possible over long corridors between the excavation and dump sites.

Sand transfer plants have the lowest environmental impact of the beach maintenance technologies currently available. Once operational, such systems can be economically competitive. They create no new environmental problems across the shelf, help keep nearshore sediments out of inlets, reduce the need for both inlet channel and offshore "renourishment" dredging, and therefore reduce the concentration of silts and clays in shallow waters. Because of long-term environmental issues, high dredging project costs, and a shortage of beach-compatible sand from offshore dredge areas, planning to establish several additional, well-maintained sand transfer plants on the east coast of Florida is warranted.

Several unresolved engineering and geology debates have significance for environmental assessments of differing shoreline management options. One issue of importance is the "depth of closure" model, which is the basis for some engineering assumptions that sediments do not show substantial offshore movement beyond a certain water depth. This engineering model has biological relevance because it is the basis for planning and designing the many nearshore berm dredging projects now proposed for southeast Florida. The USACE predicts that sediments from these dump sites will move primarily inshore; however, many coastal geologists well-versed in long-term sediment behavior have raised questions about the validity of these predictions (e.g., appendix C, refs. 38 and 42). Like the cliché "surgeons recommend surgery," engineers likewise recommend engineering, but beach maintenance decisions should come after balanced scientific analyses involving independent biologists, geologists, and oceanographers, in addition to engineering agencies and firms. Surprisingly, very few geologists are employed within the primary beach management agencies and consulting companies in Florida.

The Chronic Absence of Cumulative Impact Assessments

Official environmental assessments of beach dredging projects often conclude that projects will have no long-term effects in spite of literature reviews that identify huge information voids. Among the major problems associated with environmental assessments for Florida beach dredge-and-fill projects are the following:

1. For dozens of biological variables among hundreds of species across the shelf, we have no idea if cumulative impacts are harming populations, particularly in the case of large-scale dredging.

2. Over decades, administrative momentum has built from one environmental assessment to the next, reinforcing optimistic views based on incomplete data that became acceptable "conclusions," and eventually, "facts."

3. Few or no new data are generated, much less published in scholarly outlets, between successive projects—despite substantial monitoring expenditures.

Collectively, such problems undermine the scientific value of environmental impact assessments and cumulatively allow numerous environmental impacts within already degraded systems that have the potential to multiply though time (appendix C, ref. 47). Several approaches for incorporating cumulative effects into environmental assessments have been developed, and such documents should detail, not avoid, logical scenarios of multiple impacts. Such discussions are commonplace now in the *independent* scholarly literature on reefs.

Despite the absence of long-term scientific research on the biological effects of dredging, three assertions may surface to downplay biological questions about large-scale dredging and reef burial. These are considered below.

Natural Stressors

The complete burial of acres of nearshore reef and the induction of months of artificially elevated turbidity are commonly justified by referring to natural storm effects. Evaluations of artificial impacts *should* consider natural stressors in the assessment of potential effects; however, natural storms are not a biological justification for artificially increasing the amount and duration of turbidity beyond what already characterizes Florida's nearshore waters. Long-term estimates of average turbidity values under natural conditions are still absent, so the percentages of animals and plants affected by artificial increases in sedimentation and turbidity are not known. East Florida storms do not last for two months at a time, do not create dredge craters, and do not rapidly push concentrated sediment loads of a million cubic yards through pipes across the shelf to cover shallow reefs under 8 feet of fill, as many dredge projects do. Offshore, the introduction of unusually high concentrations of silts and clays may exceed the tolerance thresholds of organisms both directly (death) and indirectly (lowered growth, lowered egg output).

Although the effects of elevated turbidity on the health of organisms in tropical marine environments are poorly known, some information is available. One study showed that a relatively short period of dredge-induced turbidity caused an abrupt decrease in growth in two species of hard corals and may have a long-term impact on coral reproduction (appendix C, ref. 48). Long-term resuspension of bottom sediments also has been shown to adversely affect an important hard coral, *Montastrea annularis*. A related study demonstrated negative effects of sediment loads on hard corals at turbidity levels well below the maximum allowed by the state during dredging. By the time the threshold turbidity level for temporary shutdowns of dredge operations is reached, corals are already damaged.

Similar studies are badly needed for other animals and plants in order to provide a basis for recognizing the maximum turbidities that should be allowed during dredging. Even well-adapted invertebrates, such as the sabellariid worms that encrust shallow rocks to form "worm reefs," can be adversely affected by burial exceeding 1 to 3 days and by the elimination of the hard structure on which they depend.

In addition to hurricanes, natural high-turbidity conditions also result from winter storms. But winter storms occur during the period of least reef usage by the early life stages of most hard-bottom fishes. Such storms are much more uncommon during the spring and summer, the periods of peak nursery habitat use. Artificial dredge burials of hard-bottom reefs in spring, summer, and fall eliminate the habitat that the larvae and juveniles of many marine organisms require right before or during their peak periods of use. Dredge projects that receive clearance to proceed in the early spring through late summer are most likely to bury nursery habitats at their time of peak value, with effects far exceeding winter storms.

Historical Reef Burials

Direct burials of nearshore reefs south of inlets are sometimes justified by the argument that such reefs are exposed only because the digging and maintenance of inlets during the past century resulted in sediment starvation to the south. These reefs are thus artificially "improved" sites and as such are undeserving of protection. This point has been used to reduce mitigation for the burial of natural reefs (e.g., Ocean Ridge, south Boca Raton). Therefore, it is argued that since there may have been accidental environmental "improvements" from the past construction of these inlets, the elimination of these positive results will not matter today, despite the overall current degraded status of coastal east Florida.

Most recent studies of the fishes, invertebrates, and water quality on the east coast of Florida conclude that many populations and the habitats that sustain them are in decline from a number of factors. The state of Florida and the National Ocean and Atmospheric Administration (NOAA) have recently invested considerable effort in the development and application of ecosystem-wide management strategies that emphasize risk-averse and precautionary management measures.

Nearshore reef habitats are a central component of a wide marine ecosystem that extends from low-salinity tidal creeks out to deep reef habitats. Over time, this broad, yet interconnected, coastal ecosystem has been historically degraded in many more ways than it has been enhanced (e.g., large net declines in wetlands, water quality, and fishery yields). Given the problems at the larger cross-shelf scale, the relatively small areas of these nearshore reefs (among barren areas of sand) may actually increase their value as nursery habitats for fishes and invertebrates migrating in both directions across the shelf. Therefore, invoking a few accidental positive effects from 50 years past to justify continuous burial and turbidity impacts across the shelf for 50 years to come does not appear consistent with state and federal emphasis on ecosystem-scale management policies.

Assertions that large-scale dredge operations are actually restoring Florida's coastal areas to their natural condition ignore many impacts, including the long-term reductions in water clarity resulting from semicontinuous dredging (e.g., Jupiter Island, Miami Beach). The more than 50 large dredge craters dug into the submerged lands off southeast Florida (and the dozens more that are planned) also are not natural. It is only logical to predict that large-scale dredging will increase both the frequency and the duration of negative biological impacts. Well-designed evaluations of cumulative dredging effects should be sought before denying that such effects exist or suggesting that massive dredging is simply returning South Florida to its past.

Mitigation and Artificial Reefs

The construction of artificial reefs to mitigate or offset expected reef loss is often proposed up front in the permit application process for large beach dredge-and-fill projects. As in development applications for wetland filling, such mitigation is often regarded as "the price you pay to obtain a permit." If executed pre-project and if substantial amounts of high-quality materials are used, artificial reefs constructed of limestone or other suitable materials may compensate in part for the burial of nearshore habitats, and less commonly, the mechanical impacts on habitats. However, artificial reefs do little or nothing to reduce the impacts on water quality (e.g., reduce chronic turbidity) or to mitigate any number of negative food web impacts that may cascade in totally unstudied ways. The artificial reefs are often positioned in deeper water than the reefs that are to be buried, despite the evidence that there may be age-specific faunal variations between reefs at 5 and 20 feet. In addition, mitigation reefs provide no compensation for mechanical impacts on fishes and invertebrates at offshore dredging sites. Well-constructed artificial reefs may compensate for some environmental impacts, but they can not compensate for all.

The state does not require a one-for-one loss-to-replacement ratio. For example, a one-half-to-one ratio has been used for many reef mitigation plans. A ratio that is satisfactory in one place may not serve in another because hard-bottom characteristics vary substantially from one site to the next. Although we hesitate to recommend that one standard ratio be adopted, the minimum ratio should be at least one to one. The environmental impact statement (EIS) in the *Coast of Florida* study concludes that it is necessary to build mitigation reefs post-project to allow the beach to reach equilibrium and to determine the time-averaged area of affected hard bottom. These engineering concerns are legitimate. However, the emphasis on post-impact mitigation contradicts the conclusion that "no significant adverse impacts to hardgrounds are anticipated with the implementation of mitigation plans." The more time that passes before the mitigation reef is built, the less likely it is that populations of bottom organisms will survive to repopulate it. Pre-project mitigation (e.g., reef construction) is biologically preferred; but even in this case, replacement of the lost nearshore habitat value may be incomplete, and critically, mitigation for dredge-induced water quality impacts and offshore mechanical impacts is probably nonexistent.

Just the Facts

The public hears about beach fill projects one at a time, and the emphasis is always on the "benefits." Massive dredging is called "renourishment." Large craters that the sediments don't return to are called "borrow" areas. No mention is made of the potential cumulative effects of past projects or the total impacts of future projects combined. The past and future numbers—costs, amounts, and sizes—are rarely provided for southeast Florida. However, if you are going to live with the coast, you should know the context in which the dredging will occur for that next "renourishment."

While the foregoing discussion has focused on southeast Florida, much of this basic summation of the impacts of dredge-and-fill projects is applicable to all of East Florida and some other regions as well. Here are some facts that rarely surface in environmental assessments or impact statements, although these costly documents are required to address cumulative impacts.

The Scale of Past and Future Dredge-and-Fill Projects

— Since 1960, at least 50 large-scale offshore dredge and inshore fill projects have been constructed between Miami and Stuart alone. Conservatively, about 95 additional large-scale dredge projects are planned for this area between 2000 and 2046.

— From 1960 to 2000, at least 50 million cubic yards of offshore sediments, approximating 5 million dump-truck loads, have been dredged and dumped within the intertidal/subtidal corridor of southeast Florida's narrow shelf. Based on USACE projections, at least another 80 million cubic yards of offshore sediments will be dumped within the same corridor of subtropical southeast Florida over the next 50 years.

— Dozens of large dredge craters have been dug among mid-shelf habitats of southeast Florida since 1960, and many more will follow.

— Dozens of acres of nearshore reefs and more than 30 acres of seagrass beds have been directly buried since 1970. Retrospective data on reef impacts are very limited (i.e., acreages of reef buried are unavailable). In 2000, more than 100 acres of shallow reefs were proposed for burial by several projects in the planning stages.

— The dumping of fill directly into shallow waters to build nearshore berms, a relatively new activity in southeast Florida, was examined for 17 southeast Florida sites by the USACE (1996) with no detailed evaluation in the accompanying EIS.

Current Understanding of Faunas and Impacts of Beach Engineering

— More than 515 species of invertebrates, algae, and fishes have been recorded in association with East Florida's nearshore hard-bottom reefs. These habitats often serve as particularly important nursery areas because there are few or no other types of natural bottom structure in nearshore areas of East Florida.

— All of these hard-bottom habitats are classified as Habitat Areas of Particular Concern—the highest level of Essential Fish Habitat protection available under the federal Sustainable Fishery Act.

— Endangered sea turtles use nearshore reefs as nursery areas for feeding and shelter.

— Very few detailed studies of short-term dredge-and-fill effects have been published in independent scholarly journals, despite millions of dollars spent in monitoring. Planning documents invariably conclude that impacts are minimal and that the affected areas have low habitat value.

— No studies of long-term dredge-and-fill effects have been published.

— No long-term water-quality data have been utilized to assess the potential of increased turbidity from wind- or wave-induced resuspension of sediments (chronic turbidity) at either inshore fill sites or offshore dredge pits.

— The biological monitoring requirements for massive beach dredging projects continue to allow studies that lack the statistical power to make rigorous conclusions.

— Population-scale changes in diversity and abundance via dredging-generated habitat shifts, food-web disruption, and associated processes are also unexamined for almost all animals and plants affected by large-scale dredging.

— Interactive effects of repetitive dredging and filling could cumulatively reduce local biological productivity, but this possibility typically is ignored in environmental assessments.

— Reef burial is often justified by reference to natural turbidity, sediment coverage of reefs by storms (usually occurring during winter when recruitment success is not critical for most populations), and mitigation using artificial reefs. Detailed, independent biological analyses of these approaches suggest that none fully justifies or mitigates the long-term potential environmental effects of large dredge-and-fill projects.

— Plans to upgrade existing sand transfer plants in southeast Florida are encouraging. Because of the potential long-term impacts from semicontinuous dredge-and-fill projects, as well as shortages of beach-compatible sand from offshore, additional sand transfer plants should be developed for several other East Florida inlets.

— The common assumption that repeated large dredge-and-fill projects across the shelf of southeast Florida have no long-term environmental impacts is at best premature, and potentially false.

In learning to live with the shore, society cannot ignore the consequences of our collective actions on the larger coastal ecosystems within which the beaches are situated, or the economic and ecological services provided by sustainable fisheries and reefs. If you choose to locate on the coast, you should understand natural processes, storm response, and the collective ecosystem impacts of coastal engineering. Then, you are ready for the next step: to evaluate the property's vulnerability to natural and artificial hazards.

6 The Rules of the Coast: Assessing Hazards

Low-lying coasts and barrier islands are not safe for development! Hurricanes, northeasters, floods, winds, wave erosion, and inlet formation and migration can and will attack any coastal reach. Barrier islands are particularly susceptible to coastal flooding from storm surge. Human activities such as dune or mangrove removal, and particularly construction, reduce the relative stability of the natural environment and increase vulnerability to damage from natural hazards. Built structures are static (immobile); when placed in a dynamic (mobile) system, they disrupt the balance of that system (fig. 6.1). Interference with the sand supply, disruption of vegetative cover, topographic alteration, and similar effects of structures actually create conditions favorable to the damage or loss of those structures. At the same time, site safety clues exist that allow buyers to evaluate the possible risk before making a purchase; likewise, natural features (e.g., dune integrity, vegetation cover, elevation) can be utilized to reduce the risk of property damage. The approach to assessing site safety presented here is modified from *Living by the Rules of the Sea* (appendix C, ref. 55).

Your house should be in the least dynamic zone, the place where it can survive a storm. For example, a condominium built in the forest on the back side of Amelia Island should prove to be in a less hazardous site than the same condominium built on the low and narrow stretch of Orchid Island south of Sebastian Inlet. The idea is to identify the rates and intensities of storm activity for a given segment of shoreline and to use this knowledge as a basis for safe site selection.

Most individuals who move to the shore know very little about the environment they have come there to enjoy. Often their only advice with regard to site safety comes from realtors and developers, who are not known for their objectivity! Home or condominium purchasers often take the attitude that "since thousands of people live on this island, it can't be all that un-

6.1 House located too close to the beach north of Bathtub Reef Park, Martin County. The raised berm and structure will interfere with overwash and dune formation. The sand berm will offer little resistance to storm surge, so the owner's next request will be for a seawall or bulkhead.

safe." To make that assumption when choosing a coastal homesite is a serious and fundamental error.

The Flexible Coast

Among the lessons learned from recent hurricanes is that coastal lands, especially spits and barrier islands, respond to storms and other coastal processes in systematic and somewhat predictable ways. To design to live with the flexibility of the coast, first evaluate the entire system in terms of its physical processes and responses to human activities; second, focus on the characteristics of the neighborhood; and third, evaluate the individual building site. Keep in mind that neither a barrier island nor a low-elevation mainland coast is safe from hurricane winds, storm-surge flooding, wave erosion, overwash, or—for barriers—inlet changes. However, a lower-elevation, potentially migrating island such as Hutchinson Island is more likely to suffer from these hazards than Amelia Island Plantation, which is nestled in relatively high elevation maritime forest. Over the short term, the latter will be subjected to coastal hazards, but with less frequency and probably less intensity than the former.

The elevation and forest cover offer immediate clues to the area's stability. Also, consider how the coastal area has responded to previous storms, and check the area's response to past human activity, particularly construction. For example, an island is not necessarily low risk merely because it has been developed or because there are stabilization structures in place; more likely, the opposite is true. Often, seawalls and groins mask natural shoreline variations, and buildings and roads initially built too close to the shore suffer the consequences: frequent storm damage, continuous structural repairs, and no recreational beach.

As shown in chapter 4, engineering structures create conditions favorable to beach loss and their own destruction. The presence of groins, seawalls, or revetments on the beach indicates an erosion problem, now compounded by the engineering structures (figs. 4.2, 6.2, and 6.3). Such a shoreline certainly is to be avoided, even on a mainland coast.

Removal of vegetation for purposes of construction or to get a better view of the sea increases the potential for storm damage and creates a blow-

6.2 A 1957 view of an area of Miami Beach with dense development. Seawalls built in front of many of these buildings block sand movement, leaving the beach narrow or absent. Low-elevation driveways and parking lots between buildings are potential storm-surge overwash passes or areas where storm-surge ebb may be concentrated. The latter's potential is enhanced by the finger canals cut into the landward side of the barrier. Photo from the Photographic Collection of the Florida State Archives.

6.3 Old "protective" structures, seawalls, pilings, and other structures clutter New Smyrna Beach in the Flagler Avenue area. The structures indicate an ongoing erosion problem.

ing sand nuisance. The removal of mangroves, in particular, leads to rapid shoreline erosion. Roads to the beach built through the dune line act as overwash passes. Removal of dunes invites storm disasters because the elevation is lowered and the protective buffering action of the dune is lost. Hurricanes Hugo (1989, South Carolina), Opal (1995, Florida Panhandle), and Fran (1996, North Carolina) proved the effectiveness of high, wide dunes in preventing or reducing property damage. In contrast, coastal armoring failed to provide equivalent protection in all three cases; the walls were overtopped or breached and became part of the damage statistics.

The political infrastructure of your prospective island or coastal community has a strong bearing on overall safety. Unchecked growth or unenforced building and dune protection codes are examples of social conditions that may create threats to health or safety. Overloaded or inadequate sewage treatment systems, inadequate or unsafe escape routes, loss of natural storm protection, buildings lacking structural integrity, and vulnerable utilities are but a few examples of politically derived development problems. Developers and real estate interests often take a "head in the sand" attitude and are reluctant to face the fact that the beaches are retreating, that development disrupts the natural dynamics, or that the density of development has exceeded the carrying capacity with respect to natural resources and processes.

Potential buyers are not encouraged by words like *hazard, risk, mitiga-*

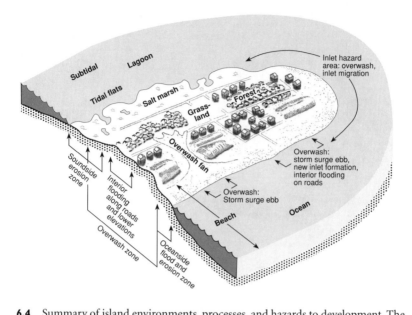

Labels within figure:
Subtidal
Lagoon
Tidal flats
Salt marsh
Grass-land
Forest
Inlet hazard area: overwash, inlet migration
Overwash: storm surge ebb, new inlet formation, interior flooding on roads
Overwash fan
Soundside erosion zone
Interior flooding along roads and lower elevations
Overwash: Storm surge ebb
Overwash zone
Oceanside flood and erosion zone
Beach
Ocean

6.4 Summary of island environments, processes, and hazards to development. The development grid increases hazard potential by removing protective vegetation cover, flattening dunes, providing avenues for overwash, and placing buildings and roadways at low elevations too close to the shoreline.

tion, and *cost.* These terms apply communitywide, not just to individual properties. Eroding beaches, removed dunes, disappearing forest cover, beach nourishment projects, and failing seawalls are examples of community problems for which all individual property owners pay, whether or not their property is directly involved.

Once you are satisfied with an area's natural stability, its response to past storms and property development activities, and the political setting, selecting the general location and specific site are the next important steps. The following site selection guide applies to your specific property; however, property lines are an artificial grid put down over dynamic environments (fig. 6.4). Be sure to look at your site in the context of the developed or developable neighboring properties as well.

Selecting Your Coastal Site

The rewards of coastal living are the amenities of the seashore and other coastal environments, but sunny-day decisions often overlook the realities of risk for property loss. Be aware of the likelihood of coastal hazards and act accordingly. Visiting the coast during a storm would illustrate the point, but there are safer ways to evaluate a site.

Structures placed in the least dynamic zones (stable areas subject to less sediment movement or change) are less likely to be damaged. Identifying areas, rates, and intensities of natural processes gives you a basis for choosing a specific homesite. Consider, for example, an inland river and the adjacent flat land (floodplain). Even casual observation reveals that rivers flood occasionally. If we observed the area for a long period, we would note that the time and size of the floods follow a pattern of sorts. Perhaps the lower area is flooded every spring, but the middle floodplain is flooded only every 5 to 10 years on average. Once or twice in a person's lifetime the flood is devastating, covering an area greater than the adjacent floodplain, although that once or twice may be closely spaced in time. We can predict the frequency and size of floods expected in a given area on the basis of its flood history.

Individual floods are ranked on the basis of the frequency of a given flood level. For instance, if water has reached a certain level only twice during a 100-year period of record, a flood rising to that level is called a one-in-50-year flood. Unfortunately, this terminology leaves the impression that you do not have to worry about such a flood level for another 50 years after its occurrence. Such flood levels are spaced in time randomly; they may occur in successive years or even the same year!

A better way of thinking about such floods is in terms of probability. A 100-year flood is a level of flooding having a 1 percent probability of occurring in any given year. You could have two such floods in successive years and it would not preclude the 1 percent probability of having another the third year. Like flipping pennies, you don't expect to see three heads in a row when you start with the first flip, but after two in a row, the chance that the third flip will be a head is the same as on the first flip—50/50. And while not worrying about the next 100-year flood, you may experience the 70-year flood or the 1,000-year flood, of which we know nothing because we have no weather records of sufficient length to even make a prediction!

Such big floods have occurred and will again. Tens of thousands of people in Minnesota and the Dakotas did not expect the great flood of 1997, and its occurrence does not preclude a repeat event very soon. The same is true for the coastal zone and barrier islands. Flooding of the mainland coast may come from rivers, but more likely the flood is storm surge—the rising of the sea level during a storm—plus winds, waves, and sediments, mixed in the caldron of a hurricane or northeaster.

Of course it would be foolish to build a house in a place that is flooded once every year, or even every 10 years. Given the choice, you might prefer to locate where the likelihood of flooding is 1 percent in any given year. A house is not built to last only a year. We expect its lifetime to be decades, so even a flood level with a 1 percent annual probability is likely to occur at least once during the lifetime of the house. Choosing a site above the 100-year flood level, or at least elevating the house above that level, reduces but does not eliminate the vulnerability to loss. Whether to locate in a flood-prone area at all should be determined by how important it is to choose that site, the level of economic loss you are willing to sustain, and the level of risk to which you are willing to expose family and friends occupying the site.

The frequency and elevation of storm-surge flooding in coastal areas is somewhat predictable (see fig. 2.8). Potential storm surges for hurricanes of all strengths are calculated using a mathematical model called SLOSH (*Sea, Lake, and Overland Surges from Hurricanes*). Flood levels are displayed in a series of maps showing what areas would be flooded in each category of hurricane. The main use of SLOSH maps is for selecting evacuation routes and shelters. SLOSH models are usually run under a cooperative program between the U.S. Army Corps of Engineers (USACE), the Federal Emergency Management Agency (FEMA), the National Hurricane Center, and the local office of the Florida Division of Emergency Management. You should be able to access the SLOSH data from your local community government office or from the agencies just mentioned.

SLOSH maps for the East Florida coastal counties show that potential storm surges for category 1 storms range around 5 feet in Monroe and Dade Counties and 4 feet in Broward and Palm Beach Counties. A category 4 hurricane could bring 13 feet of storm surge to Monroe and Dade Counties (Hurricane Andrew in fact exceeded 15 feet in the area), 9 feet to Broward County, and 8 feet to Palm Beach County. The storm-surge potential is greater where the offshore profile is gentler, and also increases where the shoreline is concave to funnel the surge water.

If the one-in-100-year storm-surge flood level is the basis for planning and is 15 feet for a particular stretch of coast, the elevation of the house should be greater than 15 feet. But in the case of coastal flooding, the surge level is not the only determining factor. Waves will be whipping the surface of the water, so the height requirement for elevating a structure must also allow for storm waves (chapter 8). And if the expectation is that a house will exist for a very long time, a little extra elevation ought to be added to accommodate the sea-level rise.

The 100-year flood level is a standard used for both inland and coastal regions as the basis for building codes and zoning ordinances adopted by communities that participate in the National Flood Insurance Program (chapter 9). Flood-level data and calculated wave heights are available from FEMA or can be obtained from community planning and insurance offices (Flood Insurance Rate Maps, or FIRMS, show these elevations; see appendix B). If you think that using the 100-year flood level is a bit overcautious, by comparison, the Dutch use one-in-500-year and even one-in-1,000-year event probabilities for planning and regulating purposes!

Stability Indicators: Reading Nature's Record at the Coast

Coastal processes often leave a record of past events or reflect the natural dynamic history of an area. The natural attributes of a site can guide prospective buyers and builders when evaluating the site's vulnerability to potentially hazardous processes and events. The primary natural indicators include terrain (landform type), elevation, and vegetation type and cover, but numerous parameters should be considered (table 6.1).

Terrain and Elevation

Terrain and elevation are good measures of an area's safety from various adverse natural processes. Low, flat areas are subject to destructive wave attack, overwash, storm-surge flooding, and blowing sand (fig. 6.4). Be aware that low areas often flood from the landward side. Figure 2.8 shows expected storm-surge levels for Florida.

Vegetation

Vegetation often indicates relative environmental stability, age, and elevation. For example, the maritime forests of Amelia Island Plantation are inundated rarely relative to the mangrove shorelines of many of the Florida Keys, which are subject to frequent flooding. Pine forests do not survive frequent saltwater intrusions, so their presence suggests stability. Salt marsh vegetation, on the other hand, requires frequent saltwater intrusion.

In general, the taller and thicker the vegetative growth, the more stable the site and the lower the risk for development (fig. 6.5). Maritime forests grow only at elevations high enough to preclude frequent overwash. In addition, because a mature maritime forest takes at least 100 years to develop, the homeowner can be assured that such areas are generally the most stable and offer the lowest-risk homesites. Another advantage of construction in a maritime forest is the shelter the trees provide from hurricane-force winds. The problem is that building in these low-to-moderate-risk sites may require disturbing the vegetation, destroying the very aspect that helps reduce risk! Major clearance of such vegetation for large structures or extensive development not only increases vulnerability for the new buildings but also increases the risk to adjacent properties. The exception to the low-risk forest site rule is where rapidly eroding shorelines have advanced into the maritime forest.

Along the southern Florida coast, mangroves fill an ecological niche similar to that filled by marsh grasses farther north. Mangroves are likewise sensitive to the same negative impacts of development and pollution. If your shoreline property is lined with mangroves, do not remove them. The

Table 6.1 Parameters for Evaluating Site-Specific Risks from Coastal Hazards

Parameter	Risk Level		
	High	**Moderate**	**Low**
Site elevation	< 10 feet	10–20 feet	>20 feet
Beach width, slope, and thickness	Narrow and flat, thin with mud, peat, or stumps exposed	Wide and flat, or narrow and steep; not eroding	Wide with well-developed berm; accreting
Overwash	Overwash apron or terrace (frequent overwash)	Overwash fans (occasional overwash)	No overwash
Site position relative to inlet or river mouth	Very near	Within sight	Distant
Dune configuration	No dunes (see Overwash)	Low, narrow, or discontinuous dunes	High (30 feet), continuous, wide, unbreached ridge, dune field
Coastal shape	Concave or embayed	Straight	Convex
Vegetation on Site	Little, toppled, or immature vegetation	Well-established shrubs and grasses, none toppled	Mature vegetation, forested, no evidence of erosion
Drainage	Poor	Moderate	Good
Area landward of site	Lagoon, marsh, or river	Floodplain or low-elevation terrace	Upland
Natural offshore protection	None, open water	Frequent bars offshore	Submerged reef, limited fetch
Offshore shelf	Wide and shallow	Moderate	Steep and narrow
Engineering structures	Shore-hardening structures and/or beach fill	Few structures and infrequent need for beach fill	Natural beach free of engineering structures

Note: This list is designed specifically for shorelines developed in unconsolidated, potentially erodible materials, such as bluffed shorelines or sandy systems (e.g., barrier islands, barrier beaches).

Source: Modified from table 6.2 in *The North Carolina Shore and Its Barrier Islands*, by Orrin H. Pilkey et al.

6.5   An elevated boardwalk in Volusia County protects both vegetation and old dune topography.

intertwining roots buffer erosion, trap and stabilize sediment, and provide critical habitat for juvenile stages of many marine animals.

Salt marshes, ecosystems that also flourish in quiet waters, often line the bay sides of islands as well as the mainland margins of bays. The true salt marsh is a unique botanical environment because it consists primarily of a single plant, *Spartina*. Marshes are important breeding grounds for many marine species and offer considerable protection from wave attack as well. Marshes are very susceptible to flooding from even minor storms. New marsh grasses can be planted on bay shorelines, and such plantings should be considered as an alternative buffer against erosion rather than using bulkheads and walls.

At one time, many Florida salt marshes were filled in for development, a practice that is now regulated. Areas around finger canals often were built up with material dredged from the marsh to form the canal. Such sites have their own resulting problems. Buried marsh provides poor support for building foundations and does not provide a good-quality groundwater reservoir. Thus, such building sites typically have settling problems, an inadequate supply of fresh water, and septic systems that do not function properly. In addition, effluent waste from such sites often has closed adjacent marshes to shellfishing.

If you build in a vegetated area, preserve as much vegetation as possible, including undergrowth. Trees provide excellent protection from flying debris during hurricanes. Remove large, dead trees from the construction site but conserve the surrounding forest, including the undercover, to protect your home. Stabilize bare construction areas as soon as possible with new plantings. Destabilized dunes or the presence of an active, migrating dune field on the margin of a forest may threaten the stability of forest sites. The rule is: protect existing vegetation and use native species when attempting to stabilize a site through artificial plantings.

The introduced *Casuarina* tree, known locally as Australian pine, flourishes along the back beaches of Florida, but is considered an unwelcome intruder. These "pines" have shallow root systems and are easily blown over by storm winds, causing damage or creating obstructions to evacuation and recovery. These trees do not stabilize dunes or help them to grow, and they furnish large amounts of debris to be cleaned up after beach storms. Their toxic needles inhibit undergrowth and discourage a diverse biota. Although they may be considered attractive, it is preferable to remove them and plant native vegetation. Some communities are removing *Casuarinas* because of their tendency to blow over easily in storms.

Seashells

Even seashells can provide clues about stability because both humans and natural processes move them about. A mixture of brown-stained and natural-colored shells often washes onshore on the ocean side during storms. Shells of these colors are like those already on the beach and indicate overwash zones when found inland of the beach. Do not build where overwash occurs; if it is necessary to do so, elevate the building above the overwash channel, enough so as not to interfere with the overwash process.

Mixed black and white shells without brown or natural-colored shells are almost certainly a sign that material has been dredged and pumped from nearby waterways. Such material is used to fill low areas on islands, to fill inlets that break through islands during storms, and to nourish eroding beaches. Thus, such a shell mixture may indicate an unstable area where development should be avoided. Black shells also may be derived from the erosion of older marsh sediments outcropping on the shoreface.

Soil Profiles

A soil profile takes a long time to develop, so a mature soil suggests building-site stability. White-bleached sand overlying yellow sand to a depth of 2 to 3 feet (often found in forest areas) suggests such stability. Note the soil profile by looking in a road cut, finger canal, or a pit that you have dug. Keep in mind that even formerly stable areas can be eroded by a migrating shoreline, so a "stable" soil profile can occur in an unstable position, such as in the wave-cut scarp at the back of a beach. Avoid areas where profiles show layers of peat or other organic materials, which have a high water content and lack the strength to support an overlying structure. The weight of a house can compress the layers, causing the house to sink. Furthermore, such soil conditions are conducive to septic tank problems.

Coastal Environments: Your Site in the Bigger Coastal Picture

Inland developments typically occupy a single environment such as a pine forest or former farm pasture. In contrast, the coastal zone is characterized by small areas of very different environments (see figs. 1.13 and 1.14), and typical developments overlap environmental boundaries without regard to the consequences. By knowing which environment(s) a building site and adjacent properties occupy, prevailing conditions that may or may not be conducive to development can be identified. Typical barrier island and sandy coast environments include primary dunes, dune fields, overwash fans, grasslands, inlets, maritime forests and thickets, marshes (north Florida), and mangroves (south Florida).

Primary Dunes

The next best thing to being at a high elevation is to have some rows of dunes between your property and the forces of the sea (fig. 6.6). Dunes are formed by wind blowing sand in from the beach. Primary dunes are the most important and should be protected at all costs. Primary dunes usually are defined as the row of dunes closest to the ocean, although a distinct line or row may be absent. Such dunes serve as a sand reservoir that feeds the beach, island interior, and back island, and they provide elevation and width as a temporary line of defense against wind and waves.

Although primary dunes offer protection against erosion and storm damage to man-made structures, they rarely present a continuous front because of the overwash passes between the dunes. Storm surge finds its way through, across, and around these passes, transporting dune sand inland; that transport is an important barrier island process. Unfortunately, humans also removed primary dunes for construction sites or simply for a better view of the sea, and cut beach access roads and paths through the dunes, particularly in areas of heavy development. Many existing houses were constructed by notching the landward side of the frontal dune, resulting in built-in destabilization. Vehicles, foot traffic, drought, and fire also destroy vegetation and lead to dune instability. The construction of wooden dune walkovers is encouraged to eliminate interference with dune processes

6.6 House in the Ponte Vedra Beach area well sited to minimize flood and erosion risks. Note the elevation, dune ridges, and walkovers protecting the dune and its vegetative cover.

(figs. 6.5 and 6.6). By prohibiting vehicles on the dunes and by building boardwalks and footbridges over rather than through them, dunes and associated storm protection may be preserved.

Remedial steps can be taken to restore or stabilize dunes artificially in cases where dunes (oceanfront or interior dunes) have been destroyed or are being threatened. Planting dune grasses in bare areas helps to stabilize existing dunes and encourages additional dune growth. Sand fencing also is commonly used to trap sand and increase dune growth.

The high elevation of a dune does not in itself render a site safe. An area adjacent to the shore with a high erosion rate is likely to lose its dune protection during the average lifetime of a house. Even setback ordinances, which require that structures be placed a minimum distance behind the dune, do not ensure long-term protection. Setbacks sometimes are based on historical erosion rates, but nothing guarantees that future erosion rates will be constant (remember the sea-level rise and likelihood of increased storminess). If your home is located on a primary dune, you should expect significant damage during the next major storm.

Dune Fields

Dune fields are open, bare-to-grassy dune areas found between the primary dunes and the maritime forest (if present) or on the back side of the island.

Stable dune fields offer sites that are at relatively low risk from the hazards of wave erosion, overwash, and storm-surge flooding, if the elevation is sufficiently high. Do not build where dunes show bare, unvegetated surfaces; such dunes are active. When blowing sand does accumulate on roads, driveways, and such, the sand should be returned to the area from which it came rather than hauling it away as is sometimes done.

Overwash Fans

Overwash fans develop when water thrown up by waves and storm surge flows between and around dunes or between and under buildings in developed areas. Such washover waters carry sand that is deposited in flat, fan-shaped masses. Stained, bleached, and natural-colored shells also are transported to the inner island. These fans provide sand to form and maintain dunes and to build up the island's elevation. Where primary dunes are high and continuous, overwash is relatively unimportant and restricted to back-beach and nearshore areas. Where dunes are absent, low, or discontinuous, overwash fans may extend across the entire island. During severe hurricanes, only the highest elevations (generally above 15 to 20 feet) are safe from overwash.

Level roads that are cut straight to the beach often become overwash passes during storms, especially in spots where they notch dunes. Roads built to increase development may contribute to the destruction. Such roads should end landward of the dune and curve or cross an island obliquely rather than perpendicular to the shore. Only emergency vehicles should be allowed to go over the dunes.

Try to avoid building on overwash fans, especially if fresh and unvegetated. Such areas may be difficult to recognize, particularly if the last hurricane or storm was years ago and the overwash has revegetated. Similarly, in urban areas you will not see overwash because it is removed after the storm. Fans also are destroyed by bulldozing or sand removal. If no alternative site is available, elevate the building and keep the area underneath open to allow overwash to continue and to build up sand. Use overwash deposits removed from roads and driveways to rebuild adjacent dunes, or return the sediment to the beach. Do not remove the sand from the area. Planting dune grass and other natural vegetation on overwash deposits may help stabilize the deposit and trap additional sand.

Grasslands

Grasslands are located either behind dune fields or on the back side of an island just inside the salt marsh. The area may be relatively flat, built up as a terrace of overwash fans, and generally is subject to future flooding and overwash. Natural grasslands may be difficult to distinguish from areas flattened for development by bulldozers, but the former are characterized by a diversity of plants (e.g., salt meadow cordgrass, yucca, cactus, and thistle).

Inlets

Consider a site's proximity to inlets, the channels that separate barrier islands. Although East Florida's inlets are stabilized with jetties to prevent natural migration, one may have a false sense of security regarding problems associated with nearby inlets. Keep in mind the effects of the jetties and remember that inlets—even stabilized ones—are a dynamic part of the coastal system. For example, as a hurricane approaches a barrier island, strong onshore winds drive storm-surge waters and waves against the island and into the waterways in back of the island. As the storm passes, the wind either stops blowing or shifts to blow seaward, causing surge waters to return seaward. Inlet channels may enlarge or shift, eroding into the end of the adjacent island. If the existing inlets do not allow the water to escape fast enough, water may flow across low, narrow segments of the barrier and a new inlet may form.

Avoid low, narrow island areas that lack extensive salt marsh and are backed by open water or drainage lines (e.g., lagoons, rivers, creeks). Numerous such narrows occur along the Florida coast, including portions of the barriers fronting the Matanzas River, Smith Creek, the Halifax River, Mosquito Lagoon, Indian River, Banana River, Lake Worth, and even parts of the Intracoastal Waterway. A new inlet is unlikely to form where the associated barriers are cored by shallow bedrock; however, this does not preclude severe flooding and erosion. Shallow breaching by small channels, either by the storm-surge flood or more often by strong storm-surge ebb currents, may occur during storms. Spits, common on the ends of barrier islands, are particularly vulnerable to breaching.

The Army Corps of Engineers or Florida Department of Transportation repairs washouts soon after storms. The future property owner may not realize that the site is in the location of such a washout, or that the access route (escape) to and from the property will be cut in future storms!

The Infrastructure Coast: Water Resources, Services, and Utilities

In addition to assessing risks from natural hazards in your site analysis, you should also consider water resources, pollution potential, infrastructure, density of present and future development, and similar human-development aspects of the site (fig. 6.7). Most developed communities have water and septic service, but some more rustic sites may be without

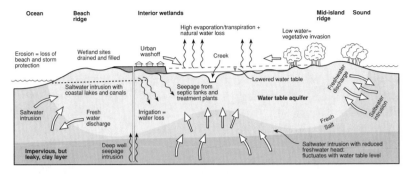

6.7 Barrier islands and spits are vulnerable to several types of environmental hazards. Modified from *Coastal Zone Management Handbook,* by John R. Clark (appendix C, ref. 69).

such services. If you are relying on groundwater, will the supply be adequate and unpolluted? Is the soil suitable for a septic system, and is the septic system compatible with maintaining groundwater quality? If you are relying on service lines (e.g., water, waste disposal, electric, telephone), will they survive a storm? Or are the utility poles lining your escape route potential obstructions when blown down? The more construction in the area, the greater the amount of debris that will be moved about in a storm.

Finger Canals

A common island alteration of the 1960s and 1970s that still causes coastal problems is the finger canal (fig. 6.8), the term applied to channels dug into an island or mainland shore for the purpose of providing additional waterfront lots. Finger canals can be found in many developed coastal communities in Florida. When finger canals are dug, they cut into the natural underground water system and can cause a host of problems (fig. 6.9). Major problems associated with finger canals are: (1) lowering of the groundwater table, (2) pollution of groundwater by seepage of salt or brackish canal water into the groundwater table, (3) pollution of canal water by septic seepage into the canal, (4) pollution of canal water by stagnation resulting from lack of tidal flushing or poor circulation with sound waters, (5) fish kills generated by higher canal water temperatures, and (6) fish kills generated by nutrient overloading and deoxygenation of the water. When finger canals begin to fill with sediment these problems are compounded. This leads to requests for dredging, which is expensive and may not be permitted for all of the above reasons.

Bad odors, flotsam of dead fish and algal scum, and contamination of adjacent shellfishing grounds are symptomatic of polluted canal water. Thus, finger canals often become health hazards or simply places too unpleasant

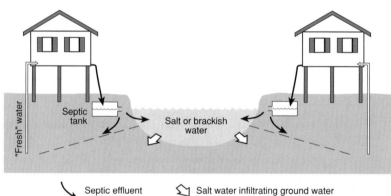

Septic effluent   Salt water infiltrating ground water

6.8 Finger canal, Cocoa Beach. Such canals alter groundwater conditions as well as increasing the flood hazard.

6.9 Cross section of a finger canal. The dredged channel allows saltwater intrusion into the fresh groundwater. Septic effluent and surface runoff pollute the canal water.

to live near. Residents along some older finger canals have built walls to separate their homes from the canal.

If you consider buying a lot on a canal, remember that canals are usually not harmful until houses are built along them. Short canals, a few tens of yards long, generally are less likely to be a nuisance than long ones. Also, while most canals are initially deep enough for small-craft traffic, sand movement from the main channel into the canal can lead to navigation problems. Finally, on narrow islands, finger canals dug almost to the ocean side offer a path of least resistance to storm waters and are therefore potential locations for ebb-surge flooding and even new inlets (fig. 6.2).

Site Evaluation Checklist: Vulnerability and Risk Potential

To determine a site's vulnerability or risk potential, evaluate all of the prevalent dynamic processes. Information on storm surge, overwash, erosion rates, inlet migration, longshore drift, and other processes can be obtained from maps, aerial photographs, scientific literature, or personal observations. Appendix B provides a list of agencies and Internet websites that deal with specific topics. Appendix C provides a list of relevant references. Although developers and planners usually have the resources and expertise to use such information in making decisions, they sometimes ignore it. In the past, the individual buyer was not likely to seek crucial information when deciding on the suitability of a given site. Today's buyer should be better informed.

Buyers, builders, or planners can assess the level of risk they are willing to take with respect to coastal hazards. The discussion of specific dangers and cautions in this chapter provides a basis for taking appropriate precautions in site selection, construction, or evacuation plans. Our recommendation is to avoid extreme- and high-risk zones. Keep in mind, however, that small maps of large areas must be generalized and that every site must be evaluated individually. Low-risk sites may exist in high-risk zones, whereas very dangerous sites may exist in moderate- or low-risk zones.

The following checklist summarizes the characteristics that should be examined for the initial site risk evaluation:

1. The site elevation is above the anticipated storm-surge level.

2. The site is behind a natural protective barrier such as a line of sand dunes, preferably 30 or more feet in height and 100 feet in basal width.

3. The site is well away from any inlet, even if the inlet is stabilized.

4. The site is in an area of shoreline growth (accretion) or low shoreline erosion. Contact the Florida Department of Environmental Protection, Bureau of Beaches and Coastal Systems (see appendix B), for more information on erosion rates. Evidence of an eroding shoreline includes:

    a. sand bluff or dune scarp at back of beach;

    b. stumps or peat exposed on beach;

    c. slumped features such as trees, dunes, or man-made structures;

    d. protective devices such as seawalls, groins, or replenished sand.

5. The site is located on a portion of the island backed by healthy salt marsh or mangrove.

6. The site is away from low-elevation, narrow portions of the island.

7. The site is in an area of no or infrequent historic overwash.

8. The site is away from finger canals that may be subject to flooding or breaching.

9. The site is in a vegetated area that suggests stability.

10. The site drains water readily.

11. The fresh groundwater supply is adequate and uncontaminated. There is proper spacing between water wells and septic systems.

12. Soil and elevation are suitable for efficient septic tank operation.

13. No compactable layers such as peat are present in the soil (i.e., the site is not on a buried salt marsh).

14. Adjacent structures are adequately spaced and of sound construction.

15. The structure's design preserves natural protection.

Escape Routes: Have an Emergency Plan

Florida's experience with hurricanes in the 1990s demonstrated the existence of serious evacuation problems. Some areas simply cannot handle massive evacuation efficiently. Raising road grades to higher elevations and replacing old drawbridges with higher fixed-span bridges will eliminate some bottlenecks, but often the problem is sheer numbers. All of East Florida must pay continued attention to improving evacuation, but it is especially critical in South Florida. Southeast Florida was ranked fourth and the Florida Keys fifth in the 1992 "Worst Case Top Ten Problem Areas" for evacuation clearance times (appendix C, ref. 65). A decade later the problem had not improved. Table 2.4 gives evacuation clearance times for East Florida counties. These times may exceed the maximum warning time for a hurricane. The point is, be informed and have an emergency plan.

The threat of hurricanes makes it essential that there be an egress route that will allow you to go from your site to a refuge location inland within a reasonable length of time. The significance of such a route escalates in areas of high-rise and high-density housing where the number of people to be evacuated, transported, and housed elsewhere is large.

The allure of a vacation may be "getting away from it all" and being out of touch, but coastal vacationers should make one exception. Stay informed: know the evacuation route and what to do in a storm (see appendix A).

Know the Escape Route Ahead of Time

Check the potential escape route for low elevations, which are subject to blockage by overwash or flooding; be aware of alternate routes. Exit routes from islands may be flood-prone. Do not assume that a mainland site is easy to evacuate (e.g., extensive areas of south and west Miami and around Homestead are at low elevations). Note whether there are bridges along the route; the Keys are an obvious example. A low-elevation bridge approach that may flood early or a drawbridge may be a major obstacle. Remember that some residents will be evacuating pleasure boats, and that fishing boats will be seeking safer waters; thus, drawbridges may be accommodating both boats and automobiles. If you are a visitor or new to an area, consult the telephone directory for the evacuation route map and be familiar with evacuation route signage. Heed the directions of law officers during evacuation.

Use the Escape Route Early

Significant areas of the coast, both islands and mainland, have limited escape routes; in some cases the route itself is through an extensive flood zone. In the event of a hurricane warning, leave the hazard area immediately. Anyone who has experienced the evacuation of a community knows of the chaos. Know your designated evacuation route and shelter. Keep alternative destinations in mind in case you find the original refuge filled or in danger. Finally, find a place of last refuge where you can go rather than being stuck in your car. Floors above the first floor on the lee side of high-rise condominiums and hotels may be the last resort (no pun intended). See appendix A for hurricane checklists.

7 The Nitty-Gritty Coast: Evaluating Your Coastal Site

So you want to live at the beach! To evaluate your favorite coast, island, community, neighborhood, existing house, or building site, you will need to know the historical and active coastal processes, hazards, vulnerability, and risks of coastal areas. Observations of Atlantic shores and their communities after several hurricanes and winter storms suggest that property damage can be lessened significantly by prudent site selection and proper location and construction of structures (see chapter 8).

This chapter presents coastal hazard summaries and maps that assess the risks of hurricane and winter storm damage based on the geologic setting and natural processes of Florida's coastal reaches. This *coastal risk mapping* uses physical processes, coastal landform characteristics, and other parameters to rate the overall risk of storm damage to coastal property as "extreme," "high," "moderate," or "low." Coastal and island characteristics considered in making the risk maps (RMs) include elevation and forest cover; island width; frontal and island interior sand dune height, width, and distribution; potential for inlet formation; modern inlet dynamics; erosion or accretion rates; historic storm response; engineering structures and projects; and other human modifications of the natural environment (appendix C, ref. 55). The risk maps also are available for viewing at the website of the Duke University Program for the Study of Developed Shorelines: http://www.env.duke.edu/psds/psds_hazmaps.htm.

Risk maps are based on published data, aerial photographs, maps, and personal communications and observations. The maps present risk zones (extreme, high, moderate, or low) relative to the potential property damage from the passage of a low category 3 hurricane. A low category 3 hurricane will have winds of 111 to 120 mph, and the typical storm surge will range from 5 to 12 feet, depending on coastal configuration and offshore bathymetry.

Risk maps can guide community planning or individual site selection and help determine property damage mitigation alternatives for individual sites. Ultimately, mitigation measures will help reduce storm-loss expenditures, result in more affordable insurance for the property owner, and ease the burden on government disaster response and recovery programs. The risk categories used in the assessments and on the maps are defined below.

Extreme risk areas or sites are at low elevation, within the 100-year flood level, and exposed to open ocean, an inlet, or a wide lagoon, so that waves greater than 3 feet are likely (FIRM V zones; chapter 9). These areas are highly susceptible to wave attack, overwash, storm-surge scour, and flooding, and often are affected by erosional shoreline retreat. Vegetation consists only of sparse growth of beach or dune grasses, and protective dunes are nonexistent. Inlet formation or migration and perilous evacuation routes add to the hazards. Extreme risk makes a site or reach unsuitable for development or for purchase of existing development.

High risk indicates that at least *three* real dangers are present from among flood potential; wave impact; erosion; overwash; inlet migration or formation; poor escape routes; and lack of natural protection from dunes, elevation, or vegetation. These areas are at low elevation and within the 100-year flood zone (FIRM A zones), making them very susceptible to wave attack and flooding by storm surge and heavy rains. High-risk zones are unsafe for development.

Moderate risk implies that the property is vulnerable to *two* of the high-risk processes given above. The area or site is above the 100-year flood zone (FIRM X zone) but lacks maritime forest or dense shrub thicket, resulting in high vulnerability to wind attack. Moderate-risk zones may or may not be subject to flooding and are unlikely to suffer direct wave attack, but the probability of damage to or loss of property is high over the lifetime of the property. Short-term or high-rainfall flooding cannot be ruled out.

Low risk areas or sites are above the 100-year flood zone (FIRM X zone), away from wave attack, and well forested. A low-risk zone is an area where no more than *one* of the high-risk hazards is likely. Keep in mind that one of these processes is all it takes for damage or destruction, so low risk is not risk free!

Many Atlantic coastal communities and individuals have attempted for decades to protect their tourist economies and beachfront properties from natural coastal processes by building walls and other engineered structures. These armored shores are likely to be high- to extreme-risk areas that should be avoided for building sites.

Again, the relative risk zones presented here are based on the risk afforded to property by a low category 3 hurricane hitting at or near the site in question. Virtually all coastal areas are at high to extreme risk from a category 4 or 5 hurricane. Differentiation into risk zones is useless for such storms.

Note that this assessment emphasizes the risk of property damage and does not assess risks to inhabitants. In general, areas with high potential for property damage are also areas of high risk for humans, but low-risk sites are not always safe for their inhabitants either. Difficulty of evacuation is an example of a human risk that may be independent on building site safety (e.g., the only escape route from your moderate-risk site is through a high-risk zone). So, regardless of site location, always evacuate when ordered to do so, and know your evacuation route ahead of time.

The coastal descriptions below are organized geographically by county from north to south, beginning at the Georgia-Florida border in Nassau County and continuing to the Florida Keys in Monroe County (see figs. 1.7, 1.8, and 1.9). Important information for these summaries came from state reports, including the county-specific *Coastal Construction Control Line Review and Reestablishment* studies conducted by the Division of Beaches and Shores (now the Bureau of Beaches and Coastal Systems, Florida Department of Environmental Protection), Department of Natural Resources, between 1982 and 1992; *Critical Beach Erosion Areas in Florida,* 1999 (Report BCS-99-02), by the former Bureau of Beaches and Coastal Systems, Division of Water Facilities, Department of Environmental Protection (www.dep.state.fl.us/beaches); and *Hurricanes Floyd and Irene Report* by Ralph Clark, 2000, Bureau of Beaches and Coastal Systems, Florida Department of Environmental Protection. Other useful reports, such as *Shoreline Change Rate Estimates, Critical Erosion Area Maps* and *Reports,* and *100 Year Storm Elevation Requirements,* are online at www.dep.state.fl.us/beaches/publications. Another excellent source of information on erosion rates and shoreline change is *Characteristics of Shoreline Change Along the Sandy Beaches of the State of Florida: An Atlas* by Robert Dean, Jie Cheng, and Subarna Malakar, 1998, published by the Department of Coastal and Oceanographic Engineering of the University of Florida.

Nassau County (RMs 1 and 2)

Amelia Island, the northernmost island on the east coast of Florida, constitutes the entire coastal reach of Nassau County. The St. Marys River, at the north end of the island, marks the Florida-Georgia border. The southern tip of Amelia Island ends at Nassau Sound, where the boundary with Duval County runs down the center of the Nassau River and out through the Sound. Amelia Island is more than 13 miles long and covers 16,500 acres (table 7.1).

Amelia Island is an island of paradoxes. In some regards it may be Florida's lowest-risk island for development, but examples of development at high risk are present. Much of the old town of Fernandina Beach on the back of the island is above 20 feet in elevation. Only the most disastrous of storms could flood the highest areas of town, and prudent site selection

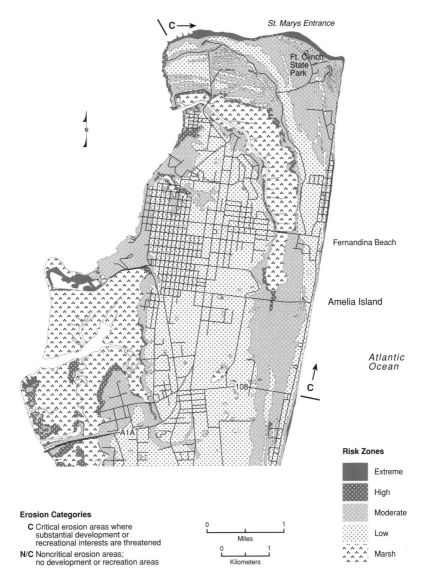

St. Marys Entrance

Ft. Clinch State Park

N

Fernandina Beach

Amelia Island

Atlantic Ocean

C

108

A1A

Risk Zones

Extreme

High

Moderate

Low

Marsh

Erosion Categories

C Critical erosion areas where substantial development or recreational interests are threatened

N/C Noncritical erosion areas; no development or recreation areas

0   1
Miles

0   1
Kilometers

RM 1   Amelia Island north

should be on the high ground. On the other hand, there are sites where houses have encroached onto the protective dunes and into maritime forest, dunes have been lowered, and protective vegetation removed. Streets along Fernandina Beach are built perpendicular to the beach, providing access for storm surge and overwash onto the island.

On northern Fernandina Beach, shorefront houses sit almost astride the surf zone, but south of Florida Highway 108, two rows of dunes usually are present between the houses and the surf, and homesites are at much lower

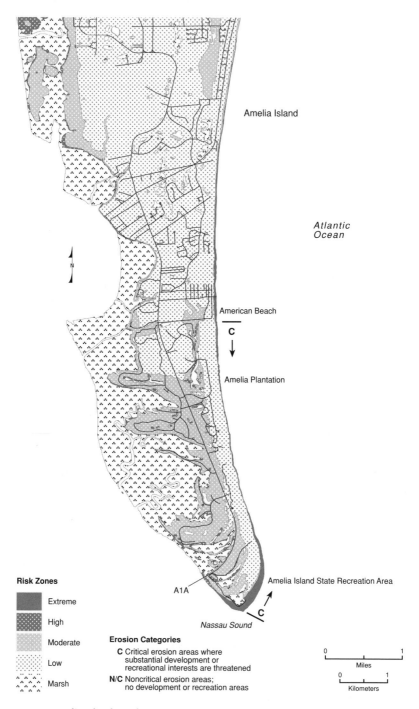

Amelia Island

Atlantic
Ocean

American Beach

_____
C
↓

Amelia Plantation

Amelia Island State Recreation Area

A1A

Nassau Sound

↗
C

Risk Zones

■	Extreme
▨	High
▦	Moderate
⋯	Low
⌃⌃⌃	Marsh

Erosion Categories

C Critical erosion areas where
substantial development or
recreational interests are threatened

N/C Noncritical erosion areas;
no development or recreation areas

0 ⊢————————⊣ 1
Miles

0 ⊢————————⊣ 1
Kilometers

RM 2   Amelia Island south

Table 7.1 Shoreline Summary for Nassau County, Florida

Total ocean shoreline (miles)	15
Critically/noncritically eroding shoreline (miles)	10/0
Erosion rates	
Long term	(1857–1991) 1.78 ft/yr
Short term	(1974–1991) 2.21 ft/yr
Beach maintenance	
Number of fills	9
Volume (cubic yards)	6,266,235
Minimum documented cost	$7,405,230
Density of coastal development	Intermediate
Coastal armoring	Seawalls, groins (Geotubes), revetments, rubble mounds, riprap
Environmental concerns	Sea turtle nesting sites
Comments	Central section of island mostly stable. Critical beach erosion occurs along Fort Clinch State Recreation Area, Fernandina Beach, and Amelia Island State Recreation Area. Beach replenishment along northern parklands ongoing with sand dredged from St. Marys River entrance.

risk as a result. The central section of the island is generally stable and high, but overwash has occurred in the lower areas, as with Hurricane Floyd in 1999. Hurricane Floyd carried large amounts of sand into the street, and storm-surge waters flooded many houses.

Serious beach erosion occurred during the winter of 1983 on the northern and southern thirds of the island, and Floyd caused a considerable amount of erosion. A 2-to-4-foot erosion scarp was evident along this beach in early 2000. Main Beach at the end of Atlantic Avenue in Fernandina Beach has been stabilized by 3.6 miles of rock revetment. The revetment and a sand berm at the back of the beach, along the street, attempt to protect vulnerable houses across the street (fig. 7.1).

American Beach (RM 2) is the last of a vanishing kind of community in the American South. This small town is still owned and frequented almost exclusively by African Americans, mostly from nearby Jacksonville. The shore here is suffering some beach erosion but is mostly stable, and most buildings sit well back from the beach at high elevations.

Amelia Island Plantation (RM 2), a large resort to the south, is often cited as an environmentally sound development because many of its condos are

7.1 Street in Fernandina Beach (February 2000) nearly cleared of sand deposited by Hurricanes Floyd and Irene the previous fall. A duneless backbeach setting such as this is highly vulnerable to coastal hazards.

nestled in maritime forests at relatively high elevations. But if the beach continues to erode at the same high rates of the past few years, some of the most shoreward buildings will be threatened.

Newer construction exists toward southern Nassau County, but both the northern and southern tips of the island are state parks and will not be developed. The southern end of Amelia Island has experienced severe erosion historically and lost more than 400 feet of beach to Hurricane Floyd in 1999.

Between 1837 and 1945, more than 60 storms of hurricane intensity affected Amelia Island's beaches, most notably the storms of September 1896, October 1898, October 1944, October 1950, August 1964 (Cleo), September 1964 (Dora), and September 1999 (Floyd). Northeasters that inflicted major damage include the storms of November 1932, September–October 1947, March 1962 (Ash Wednesday storm), February 1973, winter storms in 1981 and 1983, and Thanksgiving 1984. These hurricanes and northeasters and their associated high tides, storm surge, wave action, and strong winds caused extensive damage to local property by flooding and erosion. In the past, more than 200 feet of beach width and more than 5 to 10 feet of beach/dune elevation have been eroded in a single storm. The 100-year storm-surge levels are 12 to 15 feet above mean sea level. The highest dune on Amelia Island is 45 to 50 feet above mean sea level.

The northern portion of the island at the mouth of the St. Marys River has been changing rapidly since the first jetty was built between 1881 and 1890. The area south of the jetty built seaward along the northern 3,500 feet between 1843 and 1943, but since 1950 this section and the section south of Atlantic Boulevard have eroded. Average erosion rates have been as high as 2 feet per year. The St. Marys entrance is kept navigable by dredging and by a pair of long jetties, south of which erosion threatens Fort Clinch (fig. 1.1) and more than 4 miles of recreational beaches. Dredge material has been used to nourish the dunes and beaches to the south. Shorelines of the state parklands on both sides of Nassau Sound—Amelia Island State Recreation Area to the north and Big and Little Talbot Islands to the south—are fluctuating, as barrier beaches tend to do.

In summary, low-risk building sites exist on the lagoon side of Fernandina Beach where high elevations prevail. The island's least vulnerable sites are atop or behind high dune ridges paralleling the shoreline. Avoid armored sections of the shoreline; in addition to the obvious risk, property owners may have large tax assessments in the future for wall construction and repairs. More than 3 miles of the 9.5 miles of Nassau County developed shoreline are armored. Nevertheless, Amelia Island does offer some relatively low-risk, beautiful sites. Generally, storm evacuation is not a problem for the island; in the event of an evacuation, follow the marked routes or evacuation maps (usually published in the telephone directory).

Duval County (RMs 3 and 4)

Duval County exhibits the northernmost extension of a type of development that characterizes much of South Florida: high-density high-rise condominiums (fig. 7.2). The county also represents the northernmost example of one of the most serious hazards affecting Florida's beachfront development: the problem of storm evacuation. And evacuation will be necessary along much of the Duval shoreline because a major storm will cause widespread flooding. Narrow drawbridges with approach roads at low elevations and the ferry across the St. Johns River at Mayport, the only escape routes, are potential bottlenecks to evacuation traffic.

Duval County's 15 miles of Atlantic beachfront is entirely barrier island shoreline (table 7.2). The shoreline extends south from Nassau Sound, past Fort George Inlet at the mouth of the Fort George River, to the jettied mouth of the St. Johns River. These long jetties (the north jetty is 14,200 feet long and the south jetty is 11,192 feet in length) trap sand, profoundly affecting erosion rates on downdrift beaches. Kathryn Hanna Park, Neptune Beach, Atlantic Beach, and Jacksonville Beach all experience these erosion effects (table 7.2). Fort George Inlet is migrating northward, extending the northern tip of Fort George Island (Huguenot Park) and eroding the southern end of Little Talbot Island. Fortunately, these ever-changing park-

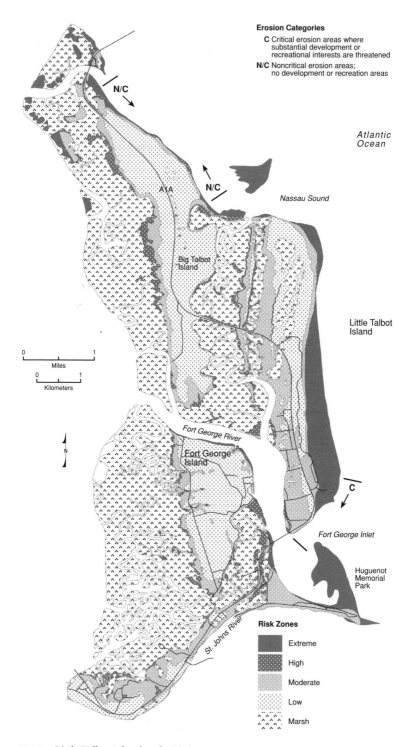

Erosion Categories

C Critical erosion areas where substantial development or recreational interests are threatened

N/C Noncritical erosion areas; no development or recreation areas

Atlantic Ocean

N/C

A1A N/C

Nassau Sound

Big Talbot Island

Little Talbot Island

0 _____ 1
Miles

0 _____ 1
Kilometers

Fort George River

Fort George Island

N

C

Fort George Inlet

Huguenot Memorial Park

St. Johns River

Risk Zones

Extreme

High

Moderate

Low

Marsh

RM 3   Little Talbot Island and vicinity

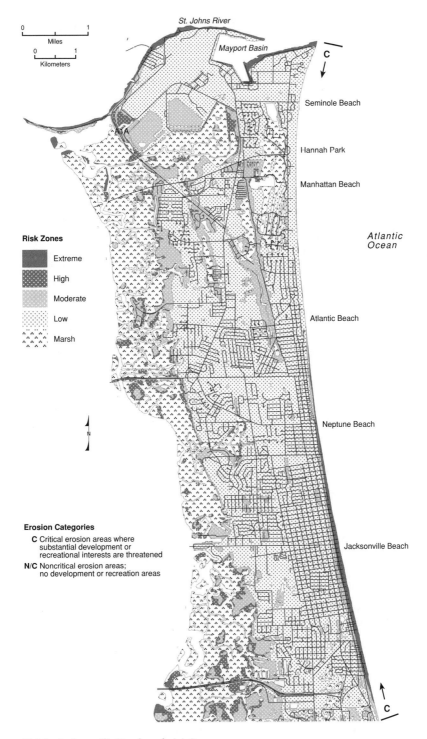

Risk Zones

Extreme

High

Moderate

Low

Marsh

Erosion Categories

C Critical erosion areas where substantial development or recreational interests are threatened

N/C Noncritical erosion areas; no development or recreation areas

RM 4 Jacksonville Beach and vicinity

7.2 Jacksonville Beach shows contrasting development ranging from cottages to high-rises. The riprap boulders to the left are part of an old engineering structure, suggesting past erosion. The fence to the right is an attempt to encourage dune growth on the back of the artificially filled beach.

lands, along with Big Talbot Island on Nassau Sound, will not be developed for private use (see fig. 3.3). South of the St. Johns River jetty and Kathryn Hanna Park, development is intense, with approximately 9 miles of developed shorefront. Beach widths vary with natural erosion and artificial nourishment projects; the barrier island ranges in width from 3,000 to 13,000 feet and in elevation from 10 to 15 feet above the low-water mark. The barrier island (Guana Island) continues uninterrupted for 10 miles in Duval County and for another 23 miles in St. Johns County to St. Augustine Inlet.

Between 1870 and 1972, more than 20 hurricanes passed within a 50-mile radius of Duval County, an average of 1 hurricane every 5 years. However, northeasters generally have been more damaging to Duval County barrier beaches than hurricanes. Particularly severe northeast storms occurred in 1925, 1932, 1947, 1962, 1981, and 1984. Memorable and damaging hurricanes occurred in 1926, 1944, 1964 (Dora), 1968 (Gladys), 1979 (David), and 1999 (Floyd). The 100-year flood tides are estimated to be 11 feet above mean sea level, and storm surge can add another 5 to 7 feet to this flood level. The 1898 hurricane produced water levels 8 to 10 feet above normal in Mayport. The 1944 hurricane produced 11- and 12-foot floods, respectively, in Atlantic Beach and Jacksonville Beach. Twenty years later, Hurricane Dora pushed

Table 7.2 Shoreline Summary for Duval County, Florida

Total ocean shoreline (miles)	15
Critically/noncritically eroding shoreline (miles)	11.1/1
Erosion rates	
Long term	(1853–1990) 3.21 ft/yr
Short term	(1970–1990) 5.00 ft/yr
Beach maintenance	
Number of fills	13
Volume (cubic yards)	10,804,000
Minimum documented cost	$19,821,000
Density of coastal development	Extensive development outside parks
Coastal armoring	Seawalls, revetments, bulkheads, jetties, riprap
Environmental concerns	Sea turtle nesting sites
Comments	Beaches are intensely developed and armored south of St. Johns entrance, excepting parklands. Critically eroded beaches are identified downdrift of jetties at river entrances: along Neptune, Atlantic, and Jacksonville Beaches. The southern 10.1 miles of the county are part of a federal and state beach restoration project and are continually maintained (FDEP).

waters 6 feet deep into those communities. Waves of 20 to 30 feet struck the beaches during the 1944 and 1964 hurricanes! The mean tidal range of the Atlantic here is just over 5 feet, which is sufficiently large that storms striking at high tide will do much more damage than those that hit at low tide.

Beach erosion was noted as early as 1834 in Duval County. When Manhattan Beach and Neptune Beach were first platted, there was another tier of lots seaward of the present concrete bulkheads. Those oceanfront lots were 150 to 175 feet deep, but all became the property of King Neptune by the mid-1930s due to natural recession of the shoreline! The present-day concrete bulkhead and the public right-of-way in these communities are located on the back side of the earlier oceanfront lots. Since the 1920s, seawalls, bulkheads, and riprap revetments have been constructed to protect property and "control" erosion. Timber bulkheads were built in the early 1920s, destroyed in the 1925 storm, and rebuilt, only to be destroyed again in the 1932 storm. After the 1932 storm, Neptune, Atlantic, and Jacksonville Beaches constructed concrete seawalls with federal aid. The seawalls were seriously damaged in 1947, 1956, 1962, 1964, and 1968 storms. After the 1962 storm, granite revetments were emplaced to reinforce the walls, and about 320,000 cubic yards of sand were placed on the beaches. After Hurricane Dora in 1964, more than 25,750 linear feet of granite revetment reinforcement was placed on Jacksonville Beach, Neptune Beach, and Atlantic Beach; and protective beach nourishment was added at Mayport Naval Station. Apparently Hurricane Laura (1979) damaged the structures again, and the USACE placed sand on the beach and over the structures. So the entire 10.1 miles between Jacksonville Beach and Mayport is a nourished reach maintained with federal and state funds. By 1992, about 75 percent of Duval County's developed shoreline was armored, and by 1999 most of it was classified as critically eroding by the FDEP (see chapter 9, "Critical Eroding Areas"). Comparisons of contour maps of the seafloor off these beaches suggest that the nearshore zone is steepening (in places the 18-foot contour receded 1,000 feet between 1874 and 1963), and this may be related to the seawalls.

Largely as a result of the damage caused by the Ash Wednesday storm (1962), planning began in 1964 for a beach nourishment project along 10 or 11 miles of Duval County south of the St. Johns River jetty. The plan was to place 3.75 million cubic yards of sand from offshore borrow sites at an estimated cost of $4.145 million initially, plus $565,000 annually thereafter, to provide a beach 60 feet wide and 11 feet above mean low water. The project was finally initiated in 1977 and completed in 1980. The total cost for 2.25 million cubic yards of beach fill onto 10 or 11 miles of beach exceeded $18 million. That is, when the project was completed, it had cost four times the original dollar estimate to emplace 60 percent of the originally estimated needed sand. Such escalations in cost are almost sure to continue.

The new beach provided improved recreational opportunities and protected structures behind the planted dunes from some storms. However, it also gave developers and potential residents a false sense of security, and many small beachfront cottages and motels were replaced with larger and more expensive residential and commercial buildings. The potential for greater loss of property during a major hurricane increased, and hurricane evacuation problems were created by the increased number of people using the narrow bridges linking the barrier island to the mainland. Erosion is still prevalent; the beach is very narrow to absent at high tide in some areas south of the jetty.

Dune elevations of 20 feet once were present along several reaches before development activities leveled the dunes, making the island more vulnerable to flooding and erosion. A sand ridge more than 10 feet in elevation and about 100 feet back of the mid-tide line ran continuously from south of the St. Johns Inlet jetty to the county line. Automobile access points and open street endings, where the dune elevations have been lowered, provide access for the sea during storms. Such incursions occurred during Hurricane Floyd (1999), causing flooding along Neptune Beach, Atlantic Beach, and Jacksonville Beach. The fishing pier at Jacksonville Beach lost about 140 feet from its seaward end in the same storm. The rule here is: evacuate at first notice from these congested areas.

St. Johns County (RMs 5, 6, 7, 8, and 9)

The St. Johns County shoreline consists of approximately 40 miles of barrier beach fronting tidal marshes and lagoons (table 7.3). The county's communities, from north to south, are Ponte Vedra Beach, South Ponte Vedra Beach, Usinas Beach, Vilano Beach (St. Augustine Inlet), St. Augustine Beach, Coquina Gables, Butler Beach, Crescent Beach (Matanzas Inlet), and Summer Haven, with other developments sprouting up along the back marshes just north of Matanzas Inlet. The salt marshes along the Tolomato River and the Intracoastal Waterway are 3,000 to 9,000 feet wide. For the northern 6 miles, the barrier island is about 3 miles wide and has dunes with heights of 15 to 25 feet. Along much of this reach, public beach access is limited to lateral access from Mickler Landing. Houses stand somewhat protected behind or within the dunes. Forests back a large part of this area. For the next 12 miles, the barrier island has two major dune ridges that are separated by low marshes. The shorefront dune ridge is about 500 to 1,500 feet wide, with elevations of 15 to 44 feet. For the next 7 miles to Vilano Beach (RM 7) and St. Augustine Inlet, the barrier island is about 1,000 to 2,000 feet wide with dunes around 15 feet in height.

Conch Island, south of St. Augustine Inlet, was formed by the coalescing of several small islands after the inlet was stabilized with rocks in 1940. Conch Island is now about 3 miles long and 500 to 4,000 feet wide. The old, natural St. Augustine Inlet was temporarily reopened across Conch Island by the 1962 Ash Wednesday storm. Anastasia Island extends south of Conch Island for about 11 miles to Matanzas Inlet (RM 9). The width of this island varies from about 2 miles at the northern end to less than 1,000 feet at the southern end, and elevations range from 10 to 30 feet above mid-tide. Most of the beach ridge from south of Matanzas Inlet to the Flagler County line, a distance of 3 miles, is very narrow and only 5 to 10 feet in elevation. This area was severely eroded during Hurricane Floyd in September 1999. Sand buried much of Old State Road Florida Highway A1A, and the dune system was completely destroyed south of the Summer Haven revetment (fig. 7.3).

St. Johns County still has miles of beautiful, unspoiled beaches and barrier islands, but the future is arriving fast; development is increasing in intensity almost daily. How well the county controls the development will determine how safe shoreline habitations will be for future homeowners. The St. Johns shoreline has examples of very dangerous homesites south of

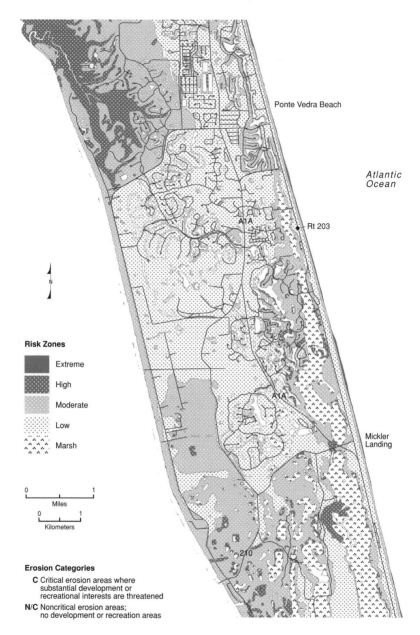

Ponte Vedra Beach

Atlantic
Ocean

A1A

Rt 203

A1A

Mickler
Landing

210

Risk Zones

Extreme

High

Moderate

Low

Marsh

0 _____ 1
Miles
0 _____ 1
Kilometers

Erosion Categories
C Critical erosion areas where
    substantial development or
    recreational interests are threatened
N/C Noncritical erosion areas;
    no development or recreation areas

RM 5   Ponte Vedra Beach and vicinity

Summer Haven, as well as examples of low-risk development in areas such
as Ponte Vedra Beach at the north end of the county and Butler Beach,
about 2 miles south of St. Augustine Beach. In fact, the stretch of Anastasia
Island south of St. Augustine Beach has some of the best-sited shorefront
buildings to be seen in any heavily developed area along the east coast of

Table 7.3 Shoreline Summary for St. Johns County, Florida

Total ocean shoreline (miles)	40
Critically/noncritically eroding shoreline (miles)	7.3 / 0.3
Erosion rates	
Long term	(1858–1992) 2.90 ft/yr
Short term	(1970–1992) 0.61 ft/yr
Beach maintenance	
Number of fills	2
Volume (cubic yards)	342,000
Minimum documented cost	$3,679,360
Density of coastal development	Intermediate to high outside parks
Coastal armoring	Seawalls, revetments, boulder mounds, bulkheads, groins, jetties
Environmental concerns	Sea turtle nesting sites, hard-bottom reefs present
Comments	Shoreline is mostly stable. Severe erosion in Vilano Beach, Anastasia State Recreation Area, St. Augustine Beach, and south of Matanzas Inlet at Summer Haven, where Old A1A is threatened. Dredge disposal is being used to refill these areas.

Florida. Some buildings, including condominiums, along Butler Beach and Crescent Beach stand behind two rows of dunes, but parts of the reach are narrow. A notable exception to this development trend is a cluster of condos just south of St. Augustine Beach built virtually on the beach. An interesting political story probably stands behind these condos, but that story will matter little when the waves begin scouring around the underpinnings.

For long stretches along the St. Johns County coast, the highway sits atop the crest of the most seaward dune, giving developers the choice of siting buildings between the road and the sea, or landward of the road. The narrow areas between sea and road are a poor choice for those seeking sites to mitigate likely property losses (e.g., near South Ponte Vedra). Keep the road between your building site and the sea, but remember, flooding from the back side of the island also can cause damage along low-lying and narrow island reaches. Go for the high ground.

The well-sited development of southern Anastasia Island stands in stark contrast to the very dangerous construction patterns south of Daytona Beach (RMS 13, 14). But all is not well on Anastasia Island, either. At the south boundary of Anastasia State Park, a long stretch of shoreline has been seawalled. Large coquina boulders have been added, and the beach has disappeared in front of several hotels and houses (fig. 7.4). The long-range prognosis is that this stretch of seawall will interrupt beach sand transport to the south, causing increased erosion. The revetment and wall were scheduled to be fronted and covered with sand, or removed and then sand emplaced, as part of a five-year USACE project, using sand from the St. Augustine Inlet to the north.

A beach fill project undertaken in the Anastasia State Recreation Area and along St. Augustine Beach in 1996 used sand dredged from St. Augustine Inlet, but storms carried more than 30 percent of it away (appendix C, ref. 56). In 1999, more sand was pumped onto portions of the beaches of Conch Island for dune restoration, but Hurricane Floyd severely eroded the area, carrying much of the sand away or redistributing it from the dunes to the beach (appendix C, ref. 14).

The barrier islands of St. Johns County are composed of unconsolidated sand and shell material. Underlying this sand and shell in some places is a type of coquina or shelly rock in various stages of consolidation known as the Anastasia Formation. These coquina outcroppings are found sporadically from St. Augustine to Palm Beach, with the most prominent outcrops in this county at Anastasia Island and at Matanzas Inlet as well as farther south (fig. 7.5). The rocks generally occur in thin layers and are easily

7.3   Hurricane Floyd buried this segment of Old A1A north of Marineland in Flagler County. The sand was replaced as an artificial dune, but it provides little protection against the next storm.

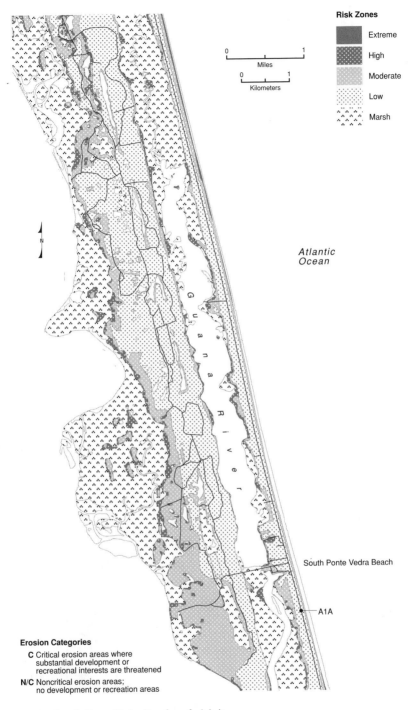

Risk Zones

- Extreme
- High
- Moderate
- Low
- Marsh

0   1
Miles

0   1
Kilometers

N

Atlantic
Ocean

Guana River

South Ponte Vedra Beach

A1A

Erosion Categories

C Critical erosion areas where
substantial development or
recreational interests are threatened

N/C Noncritical erosion areas;
no development or recreation areas

RM 6   South Ponte Vedra Beach and vicinity

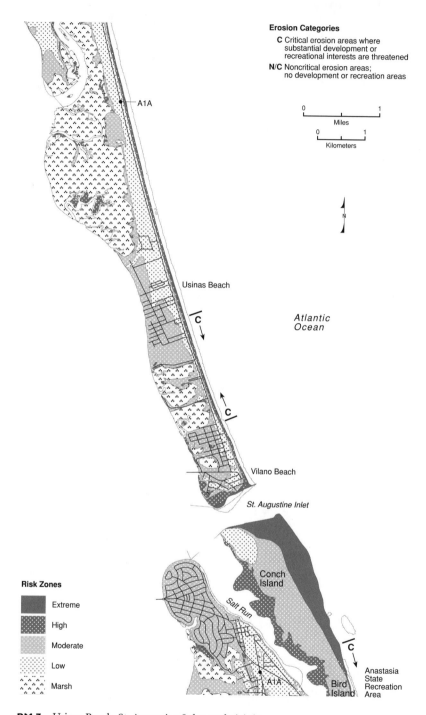

Erosion Categories

C Critical erosion areas where
substantial development or
recreational interests are threatened

N/C Noncritical erosion areas;
no development or recreation areas

0 _____ 1
Miles

0 _____ 1
Kilometers

A1A

Usinas Beach

Atlantic
Ocean

Vilano Beach

St. Augustine Inlet

Conch
Island

Salt Run

Bird
Island

A1A

Anastasia
State
Recreation
Area

Risk Zones

Extreme

High

Moderate

Low

Marsh

RM 7   Usinas Beach, St. Augustine Inlet, and vicinity

7.4 Seawall repair in St. Johns County. Coquina boulders have been added to the top of the wall and sand fill placed behind the wall near the Hampton Inn. In 2000 there was no high-tide beach at this location.

eroded by wave action, thereby contributing large quantities of shell fragments to the beaches.

The St. Johns County coast is subject to frequent northeasters as well as tropical storms and hurricanes. The northeasters, such as the 1962 Ash Wednesday storm, have generally been the more damaging. Hurricane-generated winds and waves are usually of short duration and affect localized areas, whereas a northeaster may cause high winds and waves over a larger area for a longer duration, slowly nibbling away the beaches. But hurricanes can hang around longer than expected, too, as Hurricane Dennis demonstrated along the Atlantic coast in 1999, eroding miles of beaches and dunes. Between 1830 and 1982, 20 hurricanes passed within 50 miles of the St. Johns County shoreline, an average hurricane frequency of 1 every 7.5 years. During the same period, 48 hurricanes passed within 150 miles of the shoreline, an average of 1 hurricane every 3 years.

Damaging storms are common for the county. The October 1944 hurricane caused 50 to 150 feet of beach erosion and 3 to 4 feet of vertical loss in the beach profile at Summer Haven. The October 1956 northeaster caused tides 4 feet above normal, damaged Highway A1A, and dropped the beach profile 3 feet in some places due to erosion. Hurricane Greta (1956) followed on the heels of the previous storm and caused more flooding and erosion. The March 1962 Ash Wednesday storm was followed by another storm in November 1962 that caused extensive damage from high tides and reopened

7.5 The Anastasia Formation outcrops along the shoreline at Ocean Hammock/Hammock Beach, about 6 miles south of Marineland in Flagler County.

an old inlet. A direct hit by Hurricane Dora in September 1964 caused 125-mph winds, tides 12 feet above normal along Anastasia Island, and waves 20 to 30 feet high along the island's beaches! The shoreline at St. Augustine Beach receded more than 100 feet, and 15-foot-high escarpments were eroded at Crescent Beach. Dora destroyed several dwellings along South Ponte Vedra Beach, and damage to structures was estimated at $1.8 million in St. Johns County and $200 to $300 million in all of Florida.

A 1973 northeaster caused 60 to 70 feet of beach recession at St. Augustine Beach and a 3-foot drop in the beach profile at Crescent Beach. Two hurricanes in 1999—Floyd in September and Irene in October—caused extensive erosion and other damage to St. Johns County beaches. In fact, Floyd may have been the worst storm to clobber the area since the Thanksgiving 1984 northeaster. Floyd eroded miles of beaches and dunes at Ponte Vedra, Usinas, Vilano, St. Augustine, Crescent, and Summer Haven.

The 100-year flood-tide levels for St. Johns County are 8.5 feet above mid-tide for the northern half of this stretch and about 8 feet above mid-tide along the southern half. These estimates do not include the wave height on top of the still-water elevations.

The St. Johns County shoreline is characterized by recession of the shoreline and dunes, lowering of beach profiles, and in a few places accretion or building out due to long-term natural processes. The erosion problems were noted as early as 1887, and three reaches were critically eroded as of 1999 (table 7.3; see also appendix C, ref. 30). An interesting historical look at

Risk Zones

■ Extreme
▨ High
▦ Moderate
⬚ Low
△ Marsh

0 ————————— 1
Miles

0 ————————— 1
Kilometers

N

St. Augustine Beach

Anastasia Island

A1A

C

Atlantic
Ocean

Matanzas River
(Intracoastal Waterway)

Butler Beach

Crescent Beach

206

Erosion Categories

C Critical erosion areas where
substantial development or
recreational interests are threatened

N/C Noncritical erosion areas;
no development or recreation areas

RM 8   Anastasia Island, St. Augustine Beach, and vicinity

shoreline changes, the first jetties, and extent of storm erosion in the area can be found in the paper *Shore Erosion from Recurrent Storms Near St. Augustine,* by Peter Kendrick (*Shore and Beach,* July 1933). Beach erosion is a much more critical problem where man-made structures like buildings, parking lots, seawalls, bulkheads, revetments, groins, or jetties have been placed on the shifting and unstable beaches and dunes.

Various structures have been emplaced to stabilize the St. Johns County inlets and beaches, but they have had limited success at great cost. The Corps of Engineers placed three groins on Anastasia Island and Vilano Beach in 1889 (private interests built four additional groins at Vilano Beach) to stabilize the St. Augustine Inlet for navigation. Since 1892, various types of seawalls and bulkheads have been placed along the developed coast of Anastasia Island and St. Augustine Beach. After the 1962 Ash Wednesday storm, the Federal Office of Emergency Planning authorized 50,000 cubic yards of sand fill and 450 linear feet of granite revetment for St. Augustine Beach at a cost of $95,000, as well as 1,800 feet of granite revetment and 1,130 linear feet of road pavement at Summer Haven. After Hurricane Dora (1964), federal emergency funds were provided for more stabilization of both St. Augustine Beach and Summer Haven. At Ponte Vedra Beach, a 2-mile-long, 13.5-foot-tall concrete seawall was built in 1934. In early 2000 the seawall was almost completely buried, and southern Ponte Vedra Beach was wide and flat. Most houses were located in or behind the dune ridge (fig. 6.6).

The most severe erosion problems associated with storms occur in the St. Augustine Beach and Summer Haven areas due to a combination of natural conditions and the impact of man-made structures on the beach. These two areas project seaward and act as headlands where wave energy is concentrated, causing more erosion than that present along a perfectly straight shore. Adding armoring such as seawalls, bulkheads, and revetments to the mix contributes to sediment-supply loss, greater wave scouring, lowering of the beach profiles, higher velocities of the littoral currents, and higher erosion rates.

Automobiles on the county's beaches create several sorts of problems. Automobile access points create openings where overwash and erosion are magnified during storms. The use of automobiles on the beaches, in the opinion of many, interferes with tranquility, peace, and recreational enjoyment; disrupts the nesting of sea turtles and shorebirds; and, most significantly, interferes with dune stabilization by beach grasses that help to trap sand.

Good use of your automobile will be made, however, to get out of the reach of severe storms. Evacuation difficulty is a major hazard for residents along the St. Johns County shoreline. There are five roads leading off county islands to higher ground. The situation is complicated by the fact

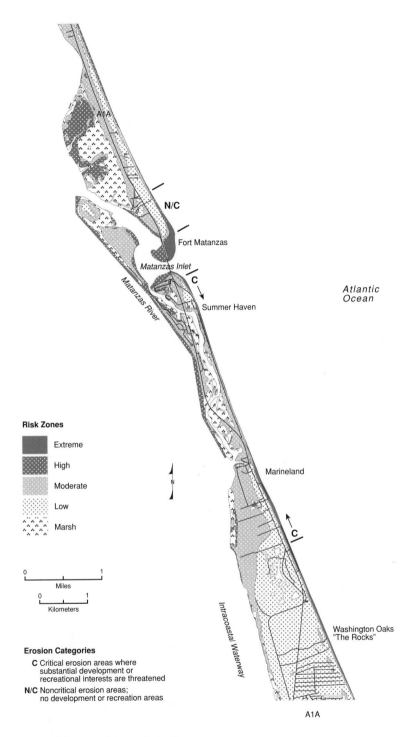

Risk Zones

- Extreme
- High
- Moderate
- Low
- Marsh

0 — Miles — 1

0 — Kilometers — 1

Erosion Categories

C Critical erosion areas where substantial development or recreational interests are threatened

N/C Noncritical erosion areas; no development or recreation areas

N/C

Fort Matanzas

Matanzas Inlet

C

Summer Haven

Matanzas River

Atlantic Ocean

A1A

N

Marineland

C

Intracoastal Waterway

Washington Oaks "The Rocks"

A1A

RM 9 Matanzas Inlet and vicinity

that most of the escape routes are over drawbridges. Florida Highway 312 is a safer fixed-span bridge. People evacuating from Ponte Vedra Beach will have to drive through congested Jacksonville Beach or, alternatively, down long stretches of flood-prone Highway 210. Evacuees from Vilano Beach, St. Augustine Beach, Crescent Beach, and Summer Haven will have to retreat into the congestion and chaos of St. Augustine. Know your designated escape route and destination ahead of time.

Flagler County (RMs 9, 10, and 11)

Flagler County's approximately 19 miles of open-ocean shoreline has no embayments or inlets (table 7.4). From Matanzas Inlet just north of the county line southward to Ponce de Leon Inlet in Volusia County (RM 14), the barrier island extends uninterrupted for a length of 50 miles, making it the longest barrier island in Florida. The portion of the barrier island in Flagler County varies considerably in width. The island is about a mile wide in the northern half of the county and between 800 and 2,000 feet wide in the southern half. A continuous dune ridge with elevations of 10 to 15 feet runs along the entire shoreline of the county. Along the southern half of the county shore, some secondary dune ridges occur. The barrier

Table 7.4 Shoreline Summary for Flagler County, Florida

Total ocean shoreline (miles)	19
Critically/noncritically eroding	2.9/0
Erosion rates	
Long term	(1872–1987) 0.12 ft/yr
Short term	(1972–1987) -0.23 ft/yr (accretion)
Beach maintenance	
Number of fills	0
Volume (cubic yards)	0
Minimum documented cost	0
Density of coastal development	Intermediate to high
Coastal armoring	Revetments, rubble mounds, groins
Environmental concerns	Sea turtle nesting sites, hard-bottom reefs present
Comments	Some stable shoreline. Urban development concentrates along the southern section. Erosion problems at Marineland and Flagler Beach, where A1A is threatened. Flagler County is one of the least armored shores along the Florida Atlantic coast.

island is separated from the mainland by the Matanzas River in the north, by Smith Creek in the south, and by the Intracoastal Waterway along the middle section of the county. Marineland, Painters Hill, Beverly Beach, Silver Lake, and Flagler Beach are the older developed communities. Newer gated residential golf communities, such as Hammock Dunes, are infiltrating the previously undeveloped coast north of Painters Hill (RM 10). These new low-density developments are wisely situated behind dunes, one of the lower risk locales for coastal living. Much of the coastline here is naturally armored by the coquina beach rock (fig. 7.5).

Beaches along the northern 3 miles of Flagler County are quite narrow—30 to 50 feet wide at low tide—as well as steep and soft. Shell material is derived from a large coquina outcrop, part of the extensive Anastasia Formation known at Washington Oaks as "The Rocks." This coquina formation contributes shells for the beaches all the way to Flagler Beach and Ormond Beach in Volusia County and southward to Palm Beach County. The orange color is distinctive. Although in some places the beaches along Flagler County are 100 to 150 feet wide above low tide, at several locations erosion scarps at the toes of dunes are pronounced. Mean tidal range is 4.3 feet with spring tides around 5.1 feet. Overall, shoreline recession rates for Flagler County are rather small, about 1 foot per year (appendix C, ref. 30).

The shoreline fronting Marineland is critically eroded (fig. 7.6) and extensively armored, as are sections of Flagler Beach. The boardwalk and Highway A1A along Flagler Beach are threatened by erosion (fig. 7.7). Fill was added after Hurricane Floyd in September 1999, but much of it was lost during Hurricane Irene one month later! According to Ralph Clark at the FDEP, Hurricane Floyd caused the worst erosion damage in Flagler and other coastal counties since the Thanksgiving 1984 northeaster. Most of the armoring structures were damaged or destroyed, including 3,900 feet of the A1A revetment in Flagler Beach (fig. 7.7). Expect longer and larger revetments to be installed in the future, and the possibility that less or no recreational beach will follow.

Over most of Flagler County, a single ridge line next to the beach is the only land that can be developed with a reasonable level of acceptable risk. Avoid building sites carved out of the narrow strip of land between the beach and the highway. As previously mentioned, the highway itself is threatened in places. The best sites are those with the highway (A1A) between them and the beach. In February 2000, narrow pieces of land were being cleared for new building lots between A1A and the Intracoastal Waterway near Crescent Beach in St. Johns County. Of course, there are no guarantees that a house here will not be flooded by storm surge or damaged by high winds. With the exception of Marineland and Flagler Beach, there is less coastal armoring in Flagler County (about a third of the developed shoreline is armored) than in some other counties.

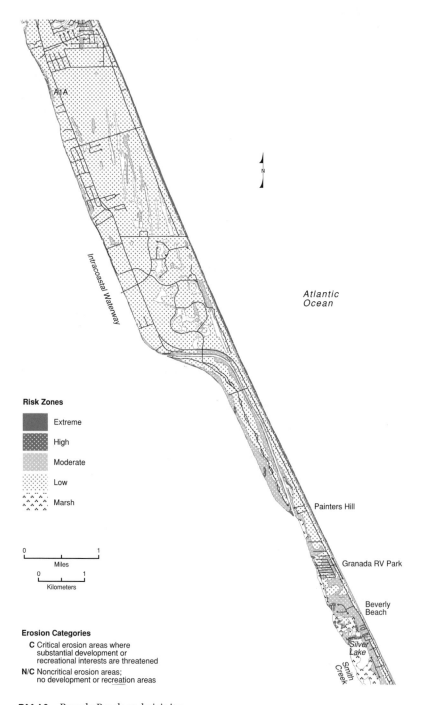

Risk Zones

▮ Extreme

▓ High

▒ Moderate

⋯ Low

∧∧∧ Marsh

```
0                    1
|_____|
       Miles
0                    1
|_____|
    Kilometers
```

A1A

Intracoastal Waterway

*Atlantic
Ocean*

Painters Hill

Granada RV Park

Beverly
Beach

*Silver
Lake*

*Smith
Creek*

Erosion Categories

C Critical erosion areas where
substantial development or
recreational interests are threatened

N/C Noncritical erosion areas;
no development or recreation areas

RM 10   Beverly Beach and vicinity

7.6 The shoreline fronting Marineland is a critical erosion zone that suffered damage from Hurricane Floyd in 1999. The remnants of the damage were still present in 2000. Note that the rubble seawall did not halt erosion.

7.7 Flagler Beach near 24th Street where Highway A1A was threatened by erosion. The fill, as seen in the foreground, was placed by the DOT after Hurricane Floyd (1999), but much of it was lost in Hurricane Irene. The erosion scarp seen here was photographed four months later.

Atlantic
Ocean

Risk Zones

Extreme
High
Moderate
Low
Marsh

| 0 | 1 |
Miles

| 0 | 1 |
Kilometers

Erosion Categories

C Critical erosion areas where
substantial development or
recreational interests are threatened

N/C Noncritical erosion areas;
no development or recreation areas

RM 11   Flagler Beach and vicinity

The county's coastline was approximately 60 percent developed by 1992. Evacuation difficulty is a serious problem that will become worse as development proceeds and the population increases. A toll bridge between Hammock and Palm Coast connects Highway A1A with the road leading to I-95. This route is an important evacuation lifeline from the southern end of the county. Know the escape route and destination well in advance of storm warnings.

Volusia County (RMs 11, 12, 13, 14, 15, 16, and 17)

Volusia County's 50 miles of shoreline (table 7.5) includes the southern portion of the long barrier island extending from St. Johns County to Ponce de Leon Inlet. Communities include Ormond Beach, Daytona Beach, Daytona Beach Shores, Wilbur-by-the-Sea, Ponce Inlet, New Smyrna Beach, and Bethune Beach. This shoreline is the fourth most developed in East Florida (nearly 88 percent).

The prevailing winds are from the northeast during the winter months

Table 7.5 Shoreline Summary for Volusia County, Florida

Total ocean shoreline (miles)	51
Critically/noncritically eroding shoreline (miles)	14.0/1.1
Erosion rates	
Long term	(1873–1989) 1.07 ft/yr
Short term	(1969–1989) -0.08 ft/yr (accretion)
Beach maintenance	
Number of fills	5
Volume (cubic yards)	2,374,900
Minimum documented cost	Costs not sufficiently documented
Density of coastal development	Intermediate to high
Coastal armoring	Seawalls, revetments, groins, jetties
Environmental concerns	Sea turtle nesting sites, hard-bottom reefs present
Comments	Shorelines are mainly stable with one erosion problem area south of Ponce Inlet. Critical erosion affects more than 14 miles of shoreline along New Smyrna Beach, Bethune Beach, Ormond Beach, and Daytona Beach. Intensely developed shorelines are dominant except along the Canaveral National Seashore.

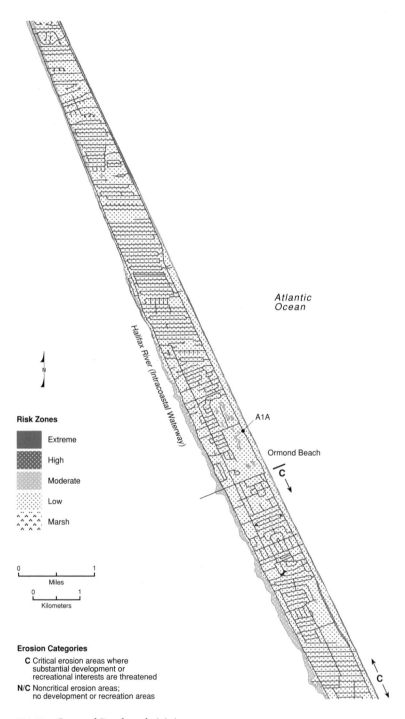

*Atlantic
Ocean*

A1A

Ormond Beach

C

C

Risk Zones

Extreme

High

Moderate

Low

Marsh

0   1
Miles

0   1
Kilometers

Erosion Categories

C Critical erosion areas where
substantial development or
recreational interests are threatened

N/C Noncritical erosion areas;
no development or recreation areas

RM 12   Ormond Beach and vicinity

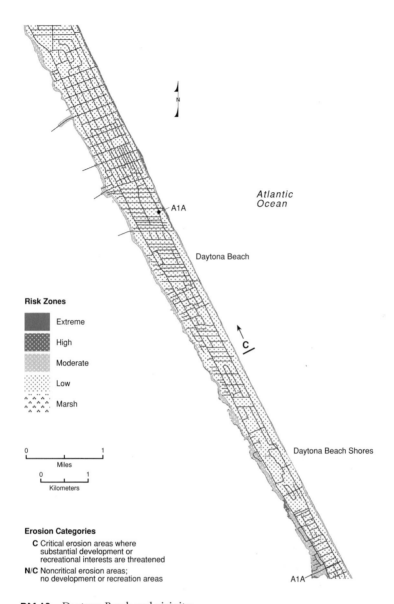

Risk Zones

- Extreme
- High
- Moderate
- Low
- Marsh

0 ——————— 1
Miles

0 ——————— 1
Kilometers

Erosion Categories

C Critical erosion areas where
substantial development or
recreational interests are threatened

N/C Noncritical erosion areas;
no development or recreation areas

*Atlantic
Ocean*

A1A

Daytona Beach

C

Daytona Beach Shores

A1A

RM 13   Daytona Beach and vicinity

and from the east during spring, summer, and fall, as is the case for the
other northeast Florida counties. Wave heights average 4 to 9 feet. The
mean tide range at the Daytona Beach pier is 4.1 feet, with a spring-tide
range of 4.9 feet. The ocean swells approach the coast predominantly from
the northeast and contribute to the net southerly littoral drift of beach
sand—except during June, July, and August, when the prevailing winds and
swells are from the southeast and south, and the littoral drift of sand is

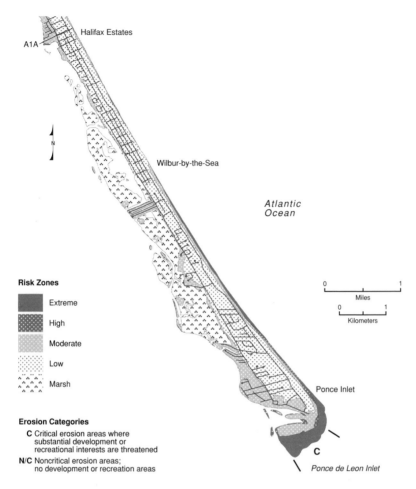

Halifax Estates

A1A

N

Wilbur-by-the-Sea

Atlantic
Ocean

Risk Zones

■ Extreme

▓ High

▒ Moderate

░ Low

⌃⌃⌃ Marsh

Erosion Categories

C Critical erosion areas where
substantial development or
recreational interests are threatened

N/C Noncritical erosion areas;
no development or recreation areas

Ponce Inlet

C

Ponce de Leon Inlet

0 — 1 Miles

0 — 1 Kilometers

RM 14   Ponce de Leon Inlet and north

temporarily to the north (for more information, see appendix C, ref. 30).
The barrier islands off this coast are subject to attack by frequent northeasters during winter and hurricanes and tropical storms during summer.
Records indicate that a hurricane passes within 50 miles of Ponce de Leon
Inlet once every 8 years. Northeasters, which are typically caused by a low-
pressure system located off the coast, may occur several times each winter,
causing chronic beach erosion problems. Some of the more damaging
northeasters and hurricanes occurred in 1848, 1932, 1947, 1956, 1962, 1964,
1973, 1979, 1984, and 1999. The September 1848 hurricane came ashore near
the Flagler County–Volusia County line and caused 11 shipwrecks along the
Florida coast. In July 1926, a hurricane came ashore near Ponce de Leon Inlet and wrecked the Inlet Terrace, a million-dollar hotel then under construction in Ponce Park. In the October 1944 hurricane, the tides were 8.4

Ponce de Leon Inlet

Smyrna Dunes Park

New
Smyrna
Beach

A1A

Atlantic
Ocean

Erosion Categories

C Critical erosion areas where
substantial development or
recreational interests are threatened

N/C Noncritical erosion areas;
no development or recreation areas

0 ──────── 1
Miles

0 ──────── 1
Kilometers

N

Risk Zones

Extreme

High

Moderate

Low

Marsh

RM 15   Ponce de Leon Inlet and south, including New Smyrna Beach

feet above mean sea level at Daytona Beach, and property damage along the
beaches was in the millions of dollars; the total damage to Florida was $60
million. An October 1947 northeaster caused 100 feet of beach retreat and
erosional dune scarps 10 feet in height between Ormond Beach and New
Smyrna Beach, a stretch of shoreline that includes world-famous Daytona
Beach. More than a dozen houses disappeared into the ocean, and roads
and seawalls were destroyed along the developed barrier island. Hurricane
King in October 1950 caused tides 8 feet above normal along the coast from
Daytona Beach north to St. Augustine and in the Halifax River behind the
islands, flooding many homes. The 1962 Ash Wednesday storm caused extensive beach erosion in Volusia, Flagler, and St. Johns Counties, all of
which were declared federal disaster areas. Seawalls were destroyed along
Daytona Beach, and Highway A1A was overwashed and required revetment
reinforcement. Hurricane Dora (September 1964) caused extensive flooding
along the beach and up the Halifax River; beach erosion near the Coast
Guard lighthouse at Ponce Inlet exceeded 100 feet. Tropical Storm Gilda

(October 1973) caused substantial dune erosion north of Ponce Inlet. A northeaster in February 1973 washed away a seawall at the Ponce Inlet Club South condominium, dislodged a rubble mound portion of the north jetty at Ponce de Leon Inlet, and breached a channel on the north side of the inlet. During 1999 and 2000, the north jetty was being extended 800 feet westward by the Army Corps of Engineers, and a 1,540-foot rock revetment was being placed westward into Lighthouse Point Park, at a cost of $5.4 million.

The extensive storm damage caused by the Thanksgiving 1984 storm was equaled or surpassed by Hurricane Floyd's damage in 1999. Floyd caused moderate to major beach and dune erosion throughout most of the northern half of the county. The fishing pier at Daytona Beach lost 300 feet off its seaward end, and pier debris was scattered all the way to the north jetty at Ponce de Leon Inlet, over 12 miles to the south. A 400-foot section of North Atlantic Avenue in Bethune Beach was also destroyed, leaving several homes

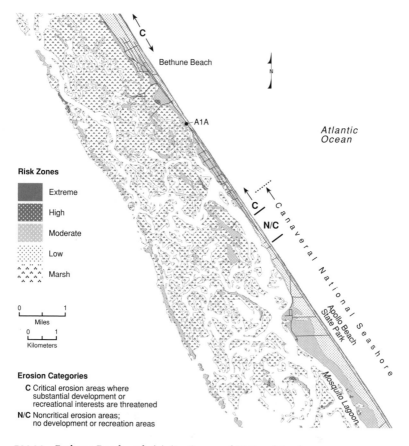

RM 16   Bethune Beach and vicinity, Canaveral National Seashore

in danger. When Hurricane Irene, only a category 2 storm, came along a month after Floyd and again strafed the Volusia County coastline, miles of beaches were left in very critical condition.

FEMA and NOAA estimate 100-year flood levels along this coast at about 8 feet above mean sea level (msl) at the north Flagler County line and 8 feet above msl in Volusia County along the open coast. As previously noted, these estimates do not include wave height, which must be added to the still-water flood level.

Ironically, most of the barrier island area in Volusia County is relatively wide and high, with multiple ridges of sand dunes that make good building sites. However, residents living one or more blocks from the beach should remember that someday they will be asked to help pay to halt the beach erosion caused by imprudent beachfront development.

Ormond by the Sea, which sits on a narrow section of the barrier island that includes dune fields, is made up primarily of gated resorts and residential areas. Ormond Beach and Daytona Beach support oceanfront high-rises with numerous seawalls, particularly along Daytona's famous beach. Wilbur-by-the-Sea and the town of Ponce Inlet, north of the inlet itself, have lower-density development than the crowded Daytona area. South of Ponce de Leon Inlet is New Smyrna Beach, where many condominiums are built behind the dune line. Bethune Beach is armored by a large rock revetment (fig. 7.8). These two southern beaches are on the FDEP's critically eroded list along with portions of Ormond Beach and Daytona Beach. The remainder of Vo-

7.8   Rock revetment and concrete bulkhead wall at Bethune Beach.

lusia County extends southward into the Canaveral National Seashore and will not be developed.

It is fair to say that some of the communities in Volusia County have not done a good job of promoting low-risk shorefront development. Although buildings constructed decades ago were usually set back a prudent distance from the beach, some later development is unsafe, unsound, environmentally damaging, and in violation of at least the spirit of the state's present setback regulations.

An interesting 1938 report of historical beach conditions in the area noted that there were no jetties, groins, or other armoring structures except "isolated bulkheads around private properties to protect them from storm damage" (appendix C, ref. 30). Ironically, the study was done to determine how to save the beach for car racing, which drew tourists to the area!

The use of automobiles on beaches in Volusia County is an old and important tradition. Daytona Beach's wide, flat, compact beach with little or no shell material is unique among U.S. east coast beaches (fig. 1.5). These attributes created conditions suitable for automobile races, the first of which was held in 1906. The name of Daytona Beach became synonymous with speed, and race cars exceeded 200 miles per hour by 1930! However, because of natural storm events and possibly excessive use of the beach, shell pockets began to appear in early 1932. These pockets created hazards for drivers, and later the races were moved to a new racetrack inland. Driving on the beach remains popular today (fig. 7.9).

Laws implemented in the 1990s reduced the amount of beach being used for driving and created "Natural Conservation Zones" along the back of the

7.9   Autos on Daytona Beach illustrate the firmness of this wide, flat beach.

beach to provide turtle nesting sites. Protection of the endangered sea turtles, which nest primarily between May 1 and November 1, is a problem that is being faced in this and other counties.

Storm evacuation problems are another story, and the problems are severe for Volusia County. Evacuation routes on the island north of Ponce de Leon Inlet are less hazardous because most routes are above 11 feet; however, low-elevation (4 feet) bridge approaches on both the island and mainland sides of the Halifax River may flood early. Drawbridges may add to the evacuation problem, but the Fairview Main Street Bridge and the Florida Highway 20 Bridge are fixed spans. It is important to evacuate if requested to do so in the event of a hurricane.

Brevard County (RMs 17, 18, 19, 20, 21, 22, 23, 24, and 25)

The ocean shoreline of Brevard County extends for 72 miles from Volusia County in the north to Sebastian Inlet and Indian River County in the south (table 7.6). The northern 32 miles of county shoreline are in federal ownership and includes Cape Canaveral National Seashore and the Kennedy Space Center, some of the world's most publicized coastal real estate thanks to the space program.

Cape Canaveral is one of the world's largest cuspate forelands, a body of sand very similar in shape and origin to Cape Hatteras, Cape Fear, and Cape Lookout in North Carolina, and Cape San Blas in West Florida. The origin of these features and the large shoal of sand extending seaward from each cape remain somewhat of an enigma to coastal geologists. A widely held idea is that all the Carolina capes are basically river deltas formed when the sea level was lower during the Ice Age. That does not explain Cape Canaveral, however, because there is no river here. Perhaps Cape Canaveral owes its origin to wave bending (refraction) around large sandbars on the continental shelf. Waves striking the beach and pushing sand to a "nodal point" from both the north and the south could have formed the cape.

South of Port Canaveral, the coastline consists of a single barrier island separated from the mainland by Mosquito Lagoon and the Banana and Indian Rivers, all of which are shallow tidal lagoons. The beach communities along the Atlantic include the cities of Cape Canaveral, Cocoa Beach, Satellite Beach, Indian Harbour Beach, Indialantic, Melbourne Beach, and Floridana Beach. Patrick Air Force Base occupies about 4 miles of shoreline south of Cocoa Beach, and the southern 1 mile of the barrier island is in Sebastian Inlet State Recreation Area. Brevard is the most intensively developed coastal county in the state (about 98 percent).

Brevard County's long, narrow barrier island is made up of unconsolidated sand and shell. Elevations are not high, but a more or less continuous 10-foot dune runs along the front of most of the island. Underlying the is-

Table 7.6 Shoreline Summary for Brevard County, Florida

Total ocean shoreline (miles)	72
Critically/noncritically eroding shoreline (miles)	24.6/12.3
Erosion rates	
Long term	(1875–1993) 1.17 ft/yr
Short term	(1969–1993) 15.18 ft/yr
Beach maintenance	
Number of fills	10
Volume (cubic yards)	4,917,000
Minimum documented cost	$6,463,000
Density of coastal development	High
Coastal armoring	Seawalls, revetments/rubble mounds, jetties, bulkheads, Geotube groins
Environmental concerns	Sea turtle nesting sites, hard-bottom reefs present
Comments	Undeveloped shores occur along the Canaveral National Seashore. Coastal armoring is present at Patrick AFB, Cocoa Beach, and elsewhere. Emergency FEMA berms placed at Ballard Pines and Melbourne Beach in 2000. Erosion problem south of the Port Canaveral entrance jetties through Ballard Cove. Beach fill projects at Indialantic, Melbourne Beach, with more proposed.

land and cropping out offshore is the shelly (coquina) rock of the Anastasia Formation. The breakup of this deposit, formed thousands of years ago, furnishes shelly sand to Brevard County's beaches.

The prevailing winds along the coast are from the east, although the strongest winds are from the north. Swells approaching from the north and northeast predominate during winter and spring and produce southerly littoral drift of beach sand. From June through August, the prevailing and predominant swells are from the south and southeast, creating northerly littoral drift of beach sand. An important point to remember is that the net annual drift of sand is to the south. The average tidal range at Cape Canaveral is about 3.5 feet, with a spring-tide range of 4.1 feet. Peak water levels can exceed 9 to 11 feet above mean low water during a major hurricane. The mean tide range at Sebastian Inlet is estimated to be 3.8 feet along the open-ocean beach. According to FEMA, 100-year flood levels range from 7 feet at the north county boundary to 8 feet at the south county line.

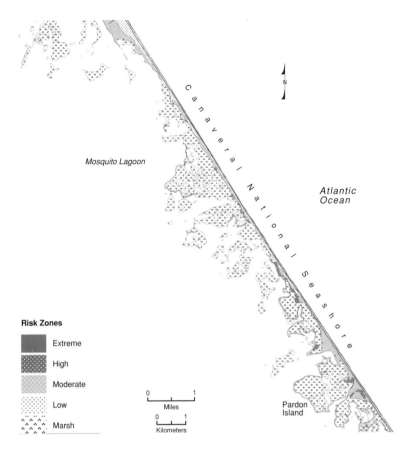

Mosquito Lagoon

Atlantic
Ocean

Canaveral National Seashore

Risk Zones

Extreme

High

Moderate

Low

Marsh

0   1
Miles

0   1
Kilometers

Pardon
Island

RM 17   Canaveral National Seashore

The forces of wind, waves, and tides, as well as hurricanes and storms, cause drastic changes in Brevard County barrier island morphology and can cause severe property damage as well. Although the area seems less hurricane prone than some other counties, major hurricanes have taken their toll. Brevard also seems to get enough northeasters to make up for the lack of hurricanes. The storm history of Brevard County is long and exciting. Most of the early storm-related floods did little damage to buildings or people and caused little loss of life. The earliest storm on record is the July 31, 1715, hurricane that wrecked the Spanish treasure fleet off the east coast of Florida near present-day Sebastian Inlet. McLarty State Museum was constructed in 1970 at the site of an old Spanish ship-salvage camp. The county suffered damage from winds, extensive flooding, and high tides during storms in 1910, 1921, 1924, 1926, 1928, and 1948, particularly in the Titusville area and along the Indian River. An October 1950 storm caused flooding in the Titusville area, breaching the sand dike at Old Sebastian Inlet. Hurricane Donna (1960) caused beach erosion and damaged seawalls at Patrick

Air Force Base. The March and November 1962 storms caused extensive erosion along all Brevard's beaches. The Lincoln's Birthday storm in February 1973 caused dune overtopping and 5 to 25 feet of horizontal beach retreat, accompanied by tides 4 to 6 feet above normal. The October 1974 storm caused severe flooding and beach erosion because of tides 3 to 5 feet above normal and gale-force winds. The winter storms of 1981 and 1983 also caused severe beach and dune retreat. In 1999, Hurricane Floyd caused beach and dune erosion throughout the county, with damage to revetments, walkways, and other structures (figs. 7.10 and 7.11). Hurricane Irene followed Floyd a month later and generated additional erosion and attempts to protect property from future erosion (see fig. 4.15). Severe damage occurred to 17 single-family homes, 15 mobile homes, and 5 commercial buildings countywide, and there was minor damage to 1,074 single-family dwellings, 445 mobile homes, and 555 commercial buildings (appendix C, ref. 14). Irene was southern Brevard County's worst storm since Hurricane

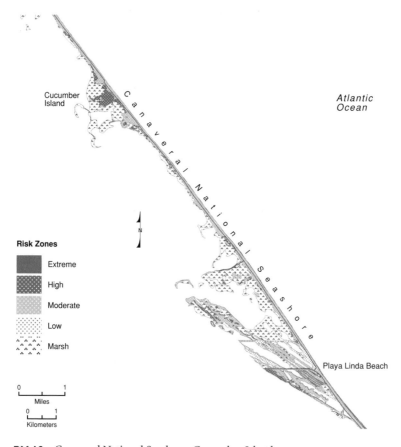

RM 18   Canaveral National Seashore, Cucumber Island area

David in September, 1979. Hurricane David caused severe erosion but was officially only a minimal hurricane at landfall, about 20 miles south of Melbourne, with 90 mph winds.

Generally, northeasters cause more serious beach erosion than do winds and waves from other directions during the rest of the year. If northeasters occur when tides are highest (spring tides), the erosion is spectacular. Large waves from the northeast during high tides for several days appear to cause more sand movement than the average hurricane, probably because the latter have a shorter duration.

The general trend of shoreline changes along the Brevard County barrier beaches is beach and dune recession, as well as lowering and steepening of the offshore beach profiles. In the 1940s, the Army Corps of Engineers believed that northerly littoral drift at the Canaveral Harbor site (to become Port Canaveral) would cause beaches to the south to accrete if a jetty were built at the harbor. Instead, following the construction of jetties there in

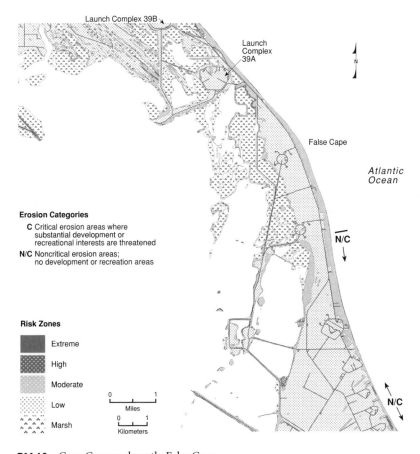

Erosion Categories

C Critical erosion areas where substantial development or recreational interests are threatened

N/C Noncritical erosion areas; no development or recreation areas

Risk Zones

- Extreme
- High
- Moderate
- Low
- Marsh

RM 19 Cape Canaveral north, False Cape

7.10 Cocoa Beach at 12th Street in early 2000 undergoing back-beach armoring and repair following the 1999 hurricanes.

1954, the shoreline of the reach between Canaveral Harbor and Eau Gallie (Canova Beach) retreated an average of 5 feet per year. Net littoral movement is actually to the south, so beach erosion became an ongoing problem south of the jetties. The area south of Port Canaveral has received millions of cubic yards of nourishment sand, both from dredge spoil and from local projects. Some local residents sued the federal government in the early 1990s for damages from beach erosion caused by the Port Canaveral jetties. Final settlement was pending in 2000, but public tax dollars again are being used to protect private beach properties. The estimated cost of the projects to restore about 4.5 million cubic yards of sand to nearly 13 miles of beaches, from Port Canaveral to Patrick Air Force Base and from North Indialantic through Melbourne Beach, is $39 million of federal, state, and local monies.

The construction of the Sebastian Inlet jetties at the southern boundary of the county caused shoreline buildup north of the inlet for a distance of about 4 miles, and retreat of the beaches for approximately 4 miles south of the inlet. The maximum retreat occurred about half a mile south of the inlet. Port Canaveral Inlet and Sebastian Inlet are classic examples of jetties causing the seaward advance of beaches on the updrift (north) side and erosion of the shoreline on the downdrift (south) side of the inlets. This condition can be observed at inlets all along Florida's east coast. Shoreline stabilization is fairly common in Brevard County. Seawalls and revetments abound in South Cocoa Beach, probably the narrowest part of the island, and in Melbourne Beach. Several beach nourishment projects have been carried out, but the replenished sand disappears quickly on most Brevard beaches. The FDEP classifies 24.6 miles of the county's shoreline extending from south of the Canaveral Inlet through the Ballard Cove area as critically eroded (table 7.6).

Evacuation is a major hazard for island dwellers. Immediate evacuation at the first recommendation of local officials is essential. The prudent island dweller will evacuate even before official warnings to do so. The Bennett (A1A) and Merritt (Fla. 520) Causeways that lead to the mainland from Cocoa Beach and Cape Canaveral, both fixed-span bridges, have sections only 5 feet in elevation that are vulnerable to flooding. The Pineda Expressway (Fla. 404) is the evacuation route with the highest elevation in the county. Residents of Floridana Beach and the rest of southern Brevard County will be forced to drive long distances along narrow islands to the nearest bridge. Those who drive south over Sebastian Inlet will have to traverse stretches of low-elevation island and cross the lagoon via Highway 510, which has elevations as low as 4 feet along bridge approaches. The evacuation route north of the Melbourne Causeway (U.S. 192) is along a high sand ridge that is seldom less than 12 feet high. The increased safety of this route, however, is partly negated by the congestion of Melbourne Beach and Indialantic.

The best choice of a homesite near the beach would be one at high eleva-

7.11 Severe back-beach erosion at Shell Street, Satellite Beach, was indicated by this active scarp in February 2000.

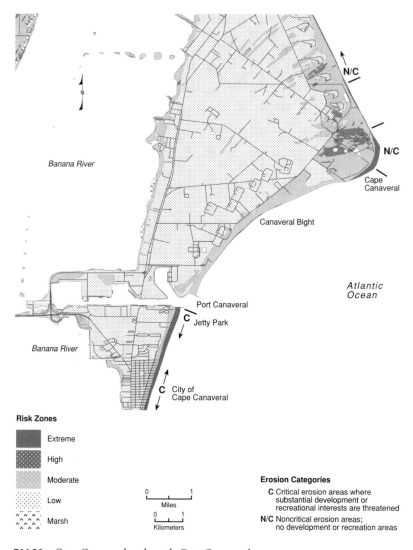

Risk Zones

- Extreme
- High
- Moderate
- Low
- Marsh

Erosion Categories

C Critical erosion areas where
substantial development or
recreational interests are threatened

N/C Noncritical erosion areas;
no development or recreation areas

0 — 1
Miles

0 — 1
Kilometers

RM 20   Cape Canaveral and south, Port Canaveral

tion back from the beach on a wide portion of the island. Finger canals, here as elsewhere, increase the danger of flooding and present an evacuation hazard. Essentially all of Brevard's developed shoreline is in a state of erosion, with long reaches designated as critical. Increasing assessments from the tax collector, both county and local, can be expected to pay for nourishment sand. Simultaneously, the quality of beaches in front of the more heavily developed and armored beach areas can be expected to degrade.

Risk Zones

■	Extreme
▨	High
▨	Moderate
░	Low
∧∧∧	Marsh

```
0                    1
|_____|
        Miles
0                    1
|_____|
     Kilometers
```

Erosion Categories

C Critical erosion areas where
   substantial development or
   recreational interests are threatened

N/C Noncritical erosion areas;
   no development or recreation areas

RM 21   Cocoa Beach and vicinity

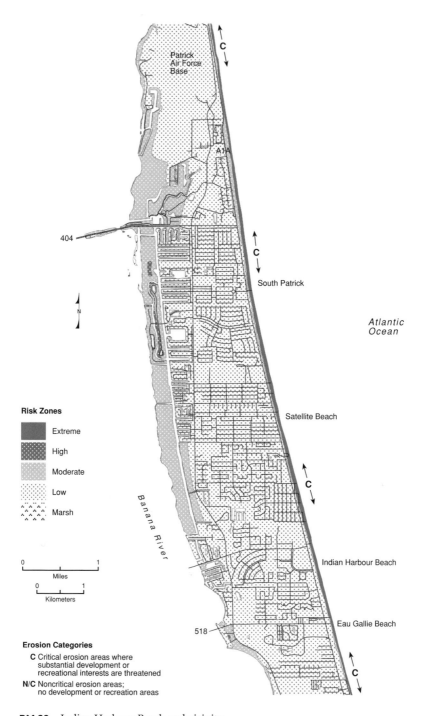

Risk Zones

- Extreme
- High
- Moderate
- Low
- Marsh

```
0                    1
    Miles
0                    1
    Kilometers
```

Erosion Categories

C Critical erosion areas where
substantial development or
recreational interests are threatened

N/C Noncritical erosion areas;
no development or recreation areas

Patrick
Air Force
Base

A1A

404

N

South Patrick

*Atlantic
Ocean*

Satellite Beach

B a n a n a   R i v e r

C

Indian Harbour Beach

Eau Gallie Beach

518

RM 22   Indian Harbour Beach and vicinity

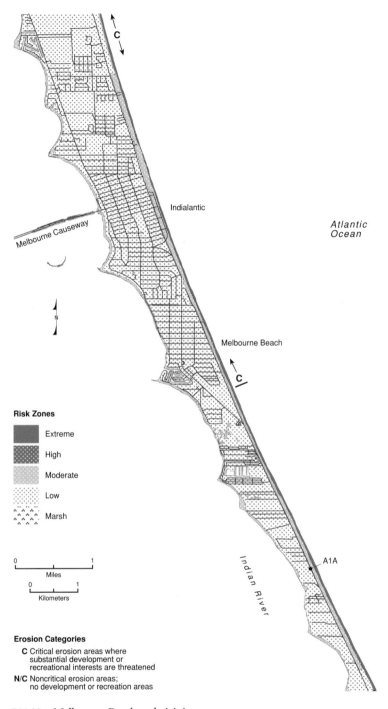

Risk Zones

Extreme

High

Moderate

Low

Marsh

Indialantic

Melbourne Causeway

Atlantic
Ocean

Melbourne Beach

C

C

N

0   1
Miles

0   1
Kilometers

Indian River

A1A

Erosion Categories

C Critical erosion areas where
substantial development or
recreational interests are threatened

N/C Noncritical erosion areas;
no development or recreation areas

RM 23   Melbourne Beach and vicinity

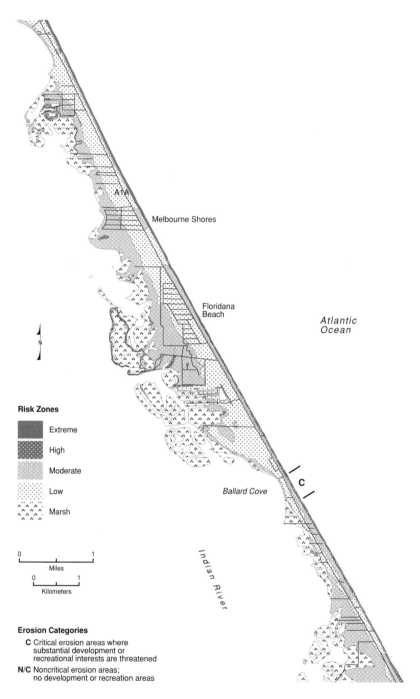

Atlantic
Ocean

A1A

Melbourne Shores

Floridana
Beach

Risk Zones

Extreme

High

Moderate

Low

Marsh

Ballard Cove

Indian River

0   1
Miles

0   1
Kilometers

Erosion Categories

C Critical erosion areas where
substantial development or
recreational interests are threatened

N/C Noncritical erosion areas;
no development or recreation areas

RM 24   Floridana Beach and vicinity

Indian River County (RMs 25, 26, and 27)

Indian River County's ocean coastline consists of low, narrow barrier islands (table 7.7). The northern 3 miles, south of Sebastian Inlet, average 300 to 500 feet in width, with most elevations between 6 to 8 feet. The beach is narrow and steep. Critical erosion predominates in this reach, and in two smaller sections to the south at the Sanderling subdivision and Wabasso Beach on Orchid Island (also known as North Hutchinson Island). In the middle segment, from the Bib Slough area through Wabasso Beach and Indian River Shores, the island width varies from about 1,000 feet to more than 5,000 feet. The elevations in this section range from 8 to 15 feet, with a high point of 24 feet north of Wabasso Beach. Within the Vero Beach city limits, the barrier island is about 1 mile wide, narrowing to the south, and elevations are low, with a 10-foot-high dune running along the beach.

Parklands are an important part of the Indian River County shoreline. The northern 1.8 miles of Orchid Island's shoreline are part of the Sebastian Inlet State Recreation Area. The city of Vero Beach has more than 3,350 feet of

Table 7.7 Shoreline Summary for Indian River County, Florida

Total ocean shoreline (miles)	28
Critically/noncritically eroding shoreline (miles)	7.3/6.3
Erosion rates	
Long term	(1881–1993) 0.59 ft/yr
Short term	(1970–1993) 0.20 ft/yr
Beach maintenance	
Number of fills	6
Volume (cubic yards)	1,172,842
Minimum documented cost	$2,668,720
Density of coastal development	Intermediate
Coastal armoring	Seawalls, revetment, bulkheads/retaining walls, groins, jetties
Environmental concerns	Dense sea turtle nesting sites, many worm reefs (e.g., Riomar Reef at Vero Beach)
Comments	Stable shorelines in some reaches. Coastal armoring along some developed beaches; e.g., steel sheet pile wall in Summerplace subdivision north of Wabasso Beach Park. Critical erosion south of Sebastian Inlet, at Wabasso Beach, Floralton Beach, and Vero Beach. Emergency dune restoration after Hurricane Floyd.

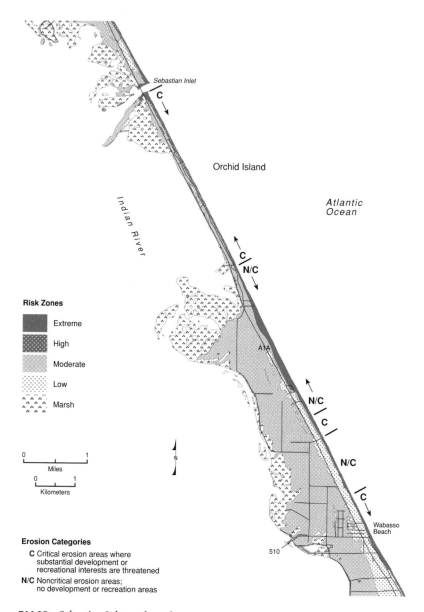

Risk Zones

- Extreme
- High
- Moderate
- Low
- Marsh

0 _____ 1
Miles

0 _____ 1
Kilometers

Erosion Categories

C Critical erosion areas where substantial development or recreational interests are threatened

N/C Noncritical erosion areas; no development or recreation areas

RM 25   Sebastian Inlet and south

oceanfront in public parks, and the county has another 500 feet of ocean frontage in public parks in the northern section. The remaining shoreline is in private ownership, but public beach accesses are widely available. From south of the state park to the northern boundaries of Indian River Shores (across from Barkers Island), the island is designated a barrier island unit under the Federal Barrier Resources Protection Act of 1982. Federal flood insurance and other federal assistance for construction of new structures are not available here. The shores of Indian River County are more than 75 percent developed, with resorts, gated communities, and some single-family homes.

The beaches of Indian River County are characterized by high shell content and coarse grain size when compared with Daytona Beach or Jacksonville Beach to the north. This coarseness results in steep, narrow beaches. In the northern section of the county, the beach width varies from 80 to 100 feet at mean low water; at Vero Beach, the beach width ranges between 20 and 60 feet. The northern 3.1 miles of Vero Beach are categorized as critically eroded. Parts of the area are armored with seawalls. Along the southern section of the county, beach width varies from 50 to 60 feet. Scarp erosion is quite common, and ordinary high tides reach all the way to the vegetation line or toe of the dunes. Longshore currents in the surf zone move sands from north to south most of the time. The predominant wave direction is from the north through the east, and the largest waves approach from the northeast. The average wave height just seaward of the surf is about 2 feet. The mean tide range and spring-tide range are estimated to be 3.3 feet and 3.8 feet, respectively.

Hurricanes and northeasters have altered the county's shoreline over the decades. Between 1830 and 1980, 19 hurricanes passed within 50 miles of the Vero Beach area, or 1 hurricane every 8 years. One of the most remarkable and damaging hurricanes was the September 1928 storm that breached the Lake Okeechobee levees and killed more than 2,000 people; high tides and winds from that storm destroyed most of the wooden beach structures in Indian River County. Tropical Storm Gilda (October 1973) caused 5 to 25 feet of beach erosion. Hurricane David (1979) caused extensive beach and dune erosion along Vero Beach. Hurricane Erin (1995) also dealt a severe blow to the area, damaging homes and beaches. Hurricanes Floyd and Irene (1999) caused beach and dune erosion, caused structural damage to some homes, and left others vulnerable to the threat from future storms. Nourished areas sustained only minor erosion, and more sand fill was brought in after Floyd to restore dunes along several reaches. The beach profile was lowered about 6 feet vertically in the central coast area (appendix C, refs. 14 and 30).

Northeasters are more frequent than hurricanes and tend to last longer, so beach erosion is common in the winter. The Lincoln's Birthday storm of February 1973 caused 5 to 10 feet of beach erosion at Vero Beach. The Thanksgiving storm of 1984 also caused severe damage.

The general trend along the Indian River shoreline is beach and dune retreat and lowering of the offshore depth profile for much of the oceanfront. Average retreat of the shoreline between 1930 and 1972 was 3.2 to 3.7 feet per year for the northern 4 miles of Indian River County, but only 1 to 2 feet per year for the next 6 miles (table 7.7). The 3-mile section of shoreline around Indian River Shores was stable from 1930 to 1972. At Vero Beach, the average

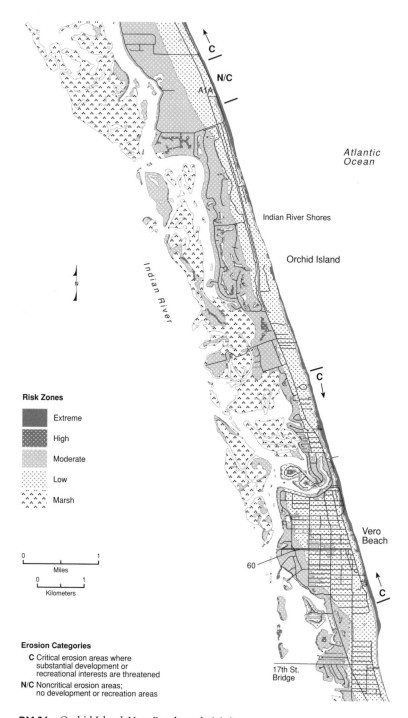

Atlantic
Ocean

Indian River Shores

Orchid Island

Indian River

Risk Zones

Extreme

High

Moderate

Low

Marsh

0   1
Miles

0   1
Kilometers

Vero
Beach

60

17th St.
Bridge

Erosion Categories

C Critical erosion areas where
substantial development or
recreational interests are threatened

N/C Noncritical erosion areas;
no development or recreation areas

RM 26 Orchid Island, Vero Beach, and vicinity

recession rate was estimated at just under 1 foot per year. The southern 5.5 miles of county shoreline experienced 1 to 5 feet of annual seaward advance during that same period.

Vero Beach has stabilized its shoreline over the years with walls, groins, and revetments. One of the shorefront's more notable artificial dunes was built over a backbone of junk cars. Armoring will not improve beach quality, and future beach replenishments are likely. The costs for such projects should be a factor in the decision of anyone planning to buy or build in Vero Beach.

The sites least vulnerable to hazards will be those located at relatively high elevations where one or more dune ridges parallel the shoreline and in areas where forest is left intact. Besides elevation and forest cover, a third factor that should be considered is island width: the wider the better. Wide islands may be less susceptible to flood and overwash, providing their elevation is not low.

By 2000 more than 75 percent of this county's coastline was lined with high-rise resorts, gated communities, and private homes. Increasing population leads to several problems, and storm evacuation is high on the list. Florida Highway 510 near Wabasso Beach has elevations of only 4 feet in the approaches to the fixed-span bridge. However, the bridges to the Vero Beach mainland have higher-elevation abutments. From Vero Beach through southern Indian River County, A1A runs through flood-prone zones. Uprooted trees, particularly where Australian pines line roads, will block potential escape routes.

St. Lucie County (RMs 27, 28, and 29)

St. Lucie County's Atlantic barrier island coast stretches for about 21 miles (table 7.8), broken only by Fort Pierce Inlet. The islands range in width from 700 to 3,000 feet, and a single or sometimes double dune line extends along the back of the beach. This dune line is widest and highest north of Fort Pierce Inlet. The lower-risk building sites are at high elevations and behind dunes.

Hutchinson Island, the barrier island south of Fort Pierce Inlet, has what may be the world's only nuclear power plant located on a barrier island. Hutchinson Island also is the northernmost island on the east coast of Florida with extensive stands of mangroves on its back side (fig. 7.12). This island also has large stands of Australian pines. During Hurricane Irene (1999), many of the pines along undeveloped Blind Creek Beach were toppled by severe erosion. In 2000, the county hired a contractor to remove the rest of the pines, leaving the mangroves in place, with plans to plant native vegetation to replace the pines.

St. Lucie County's barrier islands are subject to frequent winter storms as

Risk Zones

Extreme

High

Moderate

Low

Marsh

0   1
Miles

0   1
Kilometers

Erosion Categories

C Critical erosion areas where
substantial development or
recreational interests are threatened

N/C Noncritical erosion areas;
no development or recreation areas

N/C

Orchid Island

C

Floralton Beach

North Hutchinson Island

A1A

*Atlantic
Ocean*

N

RM 27   North Hutchinson Island and vicinity

Table 7.8 Shoreline Summary for St. Lucie County, Florida

Total ocean shoreline (miles)	21
Critically/noncritically eroding shoreline (miles)	2.3/4.5
Erosion rates	
Long term	(1861–1989) -0.46 ft/yr (accretion)
Short term	(1971–1989) 0.34 ft/yr
Beach maintenance	
Number of fills	12
Volume (cubic yards)	4,130,940
Minimum documented cost	$21,946,800
Density of coastal development	Jetties, seawalls
Coastal armoring	Some intermediate to high outside parks
Environmental concerns	Dense sea turtle nesting sites, hard-bottom reefs
Comments	Stable shorelines dominate. Eroded beaches are identified along Hutchinson Island and south of Fort Pierce Inlet jetties. Beach maintenance ongoing in this area south of the inlet. Armoring occurs along some developed beaches. St. Lucie County has the least urban developed shorelines along the Florida Atlantic coast. Nuclear power plant on Hutchinson Island.

well as tropical storms and hurricanes. Between 1900 and 1962, 17 hurricanes passed within a 50-mile radius of Fort Pierce, a hurricane frequency of 1 every 3.6 years. Two major hurricanes arrived in 1999. Although Floyd passed to the north and had only a minor impact in St. Lucie County, Hurricane Irene exited the Florida east coast right over the county, causing an estimated $6 million in damages (appendix C, refs. 14 and 30). Irene caused the worst erosion since Hurricane David in 1979. In the aftermath of Irene, the county incurred another problem when a 36-inch pipe at the sewage treatment plant inside Fort Pierce Inlet ruptured, releasing 8 million gallons of raw sewage into the Indian River lagoon and the inlet. When the sewage plume reached the ocean and spread, beaches in St. Lucie, Indian River, and Martin Counties had to close (appendix C, refs. 14 and 30). Problems of this nature may seem uncommon, but powerful storms can wreak havoc in a variety of ways. Keep in mind that Hurricane Irene was only a category 2 storm.

Frequent northeasters cause considerable erosion of the beaches. The available storm information indicates that the most memorable and dam-

7.12 A stand of mangrove trees on the back side of Hutchinson Island. The thicket of roots dampens currents, trapping and holding sediment. When such mangrove thickets are cleared, the shoreline sediments quickly erode.

aging storms affected the area in September 1928, September 1933, September 1947, August 1949, October 1964 (Hurricane Isbell), March 1962 (the great Ash Wednesday northeaster), and, to a lesser extent, the winter storm of 1981. The Ash Wednesday storm produced tides of 6.5 feet at Fort Pierce and caused the most severe beach erosion to date.

FEMA estimates 100-year flood tides of 8 feet above mid-tide along the open-ocean shoreline of St. Lucie County. With the addition of waves atop the flooding waters, flood elevations exceed 12 feet above mid-tide along the moderately steep beach slopes. During the 1947 hurricane, the water level in Fort Pierce was 5.8 feet above mean sea level.

Because the dominant direction of sand movement along the shoreline is north to south, the beach has built out on the north side of Fort Pierce Inlet and receded south of the jetty. This beach retreat is as much as 8 feet per year in the immediate vicinity of the jetties, and 3 feet per year 3 miles away. In 1971, 1.3 miles of shoreline south of Fort Pierce Inlet were replenished. Subsequently, the erosion rate of the new fill beach was higher than it ever was for the natural beach. A second beach fill project was carried out by the Corps of Engineers in 1981 at a cost of $5.4 million for 1.3 miles of beach. The sand was obtained during dredging operations to maintain the inlet, which was originally opened in 1921 by developers. More than a third of the sand was lost in a single storm in 1982. The area received another, controversial, nourishment in 1999 when the Corps of Engineers dredged material

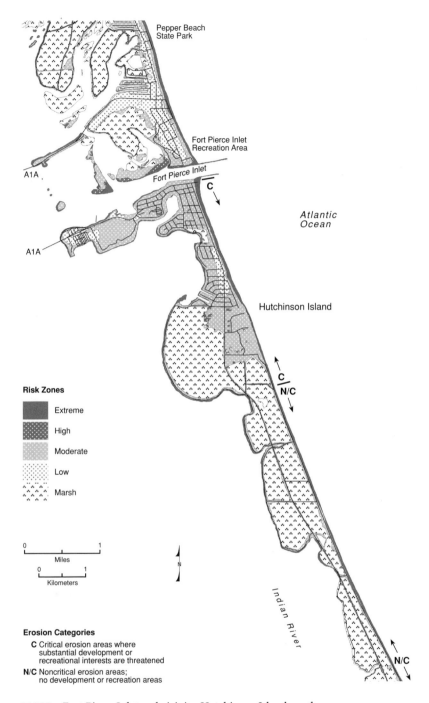

Pepper Beach
State Park

Fort Pierce Inlet
Recreation Area

A1A

Fort Pierce Inlet

C

A1A

Atlantic
Ocean

Hutchinson Island

C
N/C

Risk Zones

Extreme

High

Moderate

Low

Marsh

0   1
Miles

0   1
Kilometers

N

Indian River

Erosion Categories

C Critical erosion areas where
substantial development or
recreational interests are threatened

N/C Noncritical erosion areas;
no development or recreation areas

N/C

RM 28   Fort Pierce Inlet and vicinity, Hutchinson Island north

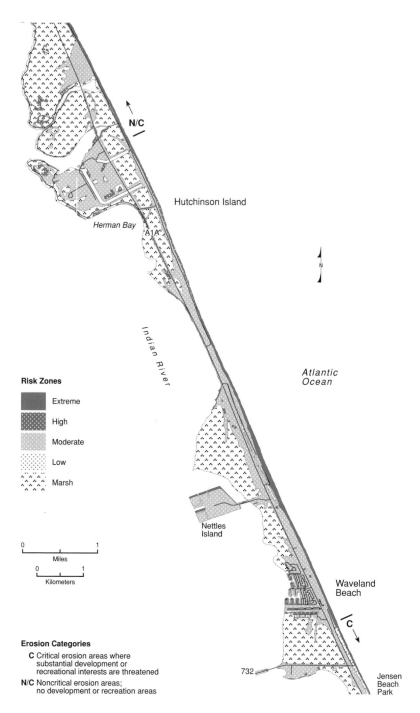

Risk Zones

Extreme

High

Moderate

Low

Marsh

0   1
Miles

0   1
Kilometers

Erosion Categories

C Critical erosion areas where
substantial development or
recreational interests are threatened

N/C Noncritical erosion areas;
no development or recreation areas

N/C

Hutchinson Island

Herman Bay   A1A

Indian River

Atlantic
Ocean

N

Nettles
Island

Waveland
Beach

C

732

Jensen
Beach
Park

RM 29   Hutchinson Island–Waveland Beach area

from nearby Capron Shoal offshore. Scientists and conservation groups obtained a court order to halt the dredging because several new species of microscopic bryozoans were discovered at the dredge site. The cost of the finished project was $5.3 million before delays added $50,000 a day to the total. Hurricane Irene caused significant erosion to the newly nourished beach, leaving a 2-to-3-foot escarpment. By February 2000 the beach to the south of the nourished area had benefited by accreting from about 30 feet to about 100 feet in width, according to local residents.

Evacuation is a major problem for St. Lucie County's islands. Drawbridges, elevations of less than 5 feet along the escape route running the length of the island (A1A), and the route's position near the lagoon shoreline (Indian River) are possible bottlenecks. Flooding will occur from the lagoon side of the island during major storms. The evacuation problem will become more severe as population and development increase. As the present century dawned, development was relatively light, although approximately 50 percent of the coastline was developed. South of the nuclear power plant, numerous large buildings and single-family homes line the beachfront. New building lots on both sides of A1A are being cleared and sold along some reaches, and this will increase the evacuation problems noted above.

During a severe storm there is a strong possibility that new inlets will break through some of the narrow portions of the islands, adding to the problems of evacuation and poststorm recovery. The county's Australian pines are likely to cause the same road blockage problems noted in other areas.

Martin County (RMs 30, 31, and 32)

Martin County's ocean shoreline consists of more than 20 miles of barrier islands: approximately 7 miles of Hutchinson Island from the northern county line to St. Lucie Inlet and 14 miles of Jupiter Island to the southern county line (table 7.9). Hutchinson Island is low and narrow, ranging in elevation from 5 to 10 feet and in width from 200 to 4,000 feet. Jupiter Island varies in width from 200 feet near Peck Lake in the north to 3,600 feet near the Jupiter Island Country Club. The northern 5 miles of Jupiter Island, mostly in St. Lucie Inlet State Park and Hobe Sound National Wildlife Refuge, are below 5 feet in elevation, while south of this section the elevations range between 10 and 15 feet, with the highest point at 24 feet. Thus, on the basis of physical island characteristics alone, the southern third of Martin County's shore is probably the lowest risk, even though the island is quite narrow here and backed by the water of Jupiter Sound.

A single dune ridge runs down the length of Hutchinson Island. Just north of Seminole Shores is one of the narrowest island stretches in all of

Table 7.9 Shoreline Summary for Martin County, Florida

Total ocean shoreline (miles)	24
Critically/noncritically eroding shoreline (miles)	15.8/0
Erosion rates	
Long term	(1883–1989) -4.05 ft/yr (accretion)
Short term	(1970–1986) -2.09 ft/yr (accretion)
Beach maintenance	
Number of fills	14
Volume (cubic yards)	12,872,552
Minimum documented cost	$18,600,960
Density of coastal development	Low to intermediate
Coastal armoring	Seawalls, jetties
Environmental concerns	Dense sea turtle nesting sites, hard-bottom reefs present
Comments	Stable and partially developed shorelines dominate. An 11.5-mile reach south of St. Lucie inlet is eroded, with most critically eroded. This section includes the town of Jupiter Island. Part of Hutchinson Island (4.1 miles) is also experiencing critical erosion and receives beach fill with federal and state monies. Beach fill has also occurred along the developed areas. Inlet formation threat at Pecks Lake. Sand transfer at St. Lucie Inlet. $11 million beach fill project in 1996. Martin County shoreline is the least armored of all the east coast counties.

Florida, a potential site of overwash and new inlet formation, and an evacuation bottleneck for Seminole Shores and Sailfish Point residents. This thin neck (100 to 200 feet wide) has existed for more than 100 years because the well-cemented rocks outcropping on the beach afford protection against erosion (fig. 7.13). Recently, however, the 4-mile-plus length of critically eroded area to the north has extended farther south, ending nearer to this neck of land. Houses are built along both sides of the narrow road just south of Gilbert's Bar House of Refuge in what appears to be a very hazardous location. Gilbert's Bar House of Refuge, now a museum, was once a refuge center for shipwrecked sailors. The building, said to be the oldest structure in the county, has been standing atop the beach rocks since 1875. However, both the nearby Bathtub Reef Park and Sailfish Point areas are showing the detrimental effects of storm activity (see fig. 4.4).

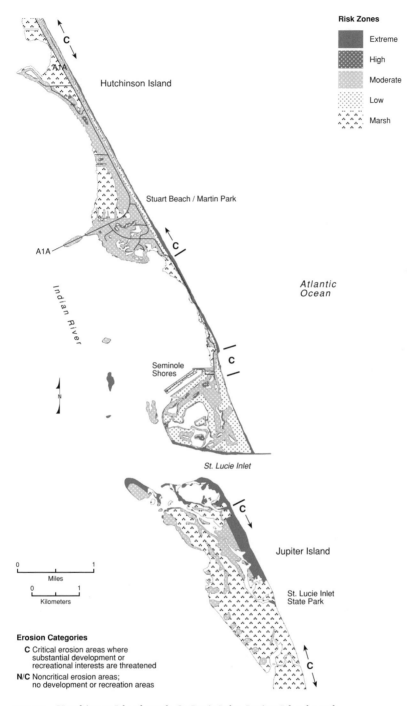

Risk Zones

- Extreme
- High
- Moderate
- Low
- Marsh

Hutchinson Island

Stuart Beach / Martin Park

A1A

Indian River

Atlantic Ocean

Seminole Shores

St. Lucie Inlet

Jupiter Island

St. Lucie Inlet State Park

0   1
Miles

0   1
Kilometers

Erosion Categories

C Critical erosion areas where substantial development or recreational interests are threatened

N/C Noncritical erosion areas; no development or recreation areas

RM 30   Hutchinson Island south, St. Lucie Inlet, Jupiter Island north

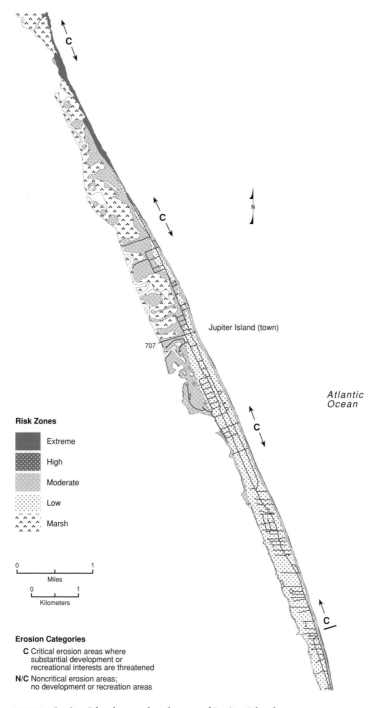

Risk Zones

- Extreme
- High
- Moderate
- Low
- Marsh

Jupiter Island (town)

707

Atlantic
Ocean

0 _____ 1
Miles

0 _____ 1
Kilometers

Erosion Categories

C Critical erosion areas where
substantial development or
recreational interests are threatened

N/C Noncritical erosion areas;
no development or recreation areas

RM 31   Jupiter Island central and town of Jupiter Island

7.13 Rock outcrops on House of Refuge Beach, Martin County.

South of St. Lucie Inlet, the northern 3 or 4 miles of Jupiter Island are being eroded at a very rapid rate as a result of jetty construction on the north
side of St. Lucie Inlet. The jetty has blocked the natural north-to-south flow
of sand and has starved Jupiter Island beaches. Most likely this sand starvation is affecting Jupiter Island over its entire length, even though inlet sand
transfer is ongoing.

The beach over most of the area is 50 to 100 feet wide at low water, with a rather steep slope. At several locations, the mean high water reaches the toe of the dunes, upland trees, or the seawalls. The entire shoreline here has a history of retreat since the 1880s, with the exception of the aforementioned rocky beach on Hutchinson Island. The opening of the artificial St. Lucie Inlet in 1892 and construction of the north jetty (1930), which acted as a littoral barrier for the movement of sediments to the south, contributed significantly to the increased shoreline retreat.

The USACE's beach erosion control study of Martin County indicates that between 1882 and 1964 there was general shoreline retreat for the areas south of both St. Lucie and Jupiter Inlets and shoreline accretion north of the jetties; the 16 miles of shoreline south of St. Lucie Inlet receded 490 feet, or an average of 6 feet per year, with the greatest retreat immediately south of the inlet. The recession for the northern part of Jupiter Island was 1,502 feet for this period, in part due to the jetties.

FEMA estimates that 100-year flood levels along the oceanfront range between 7 and 8 feet above mean sea level. Besides the measured storm surge of 8.5 feet at Stuart, still-water levels of 7 and 6.5 feet were noted during hurricanes at Jupiter Inlet (1945) and St. Lucie Locks (1947), respectively.

Martin County beaches are subject to both hurricanes and winter storms. A hurricane or tropical storm passes within a 60-mile radius of Martin County about once every three years. Damaging storm floods occurred in 1928, 1933, 1947, 1949, and 1964. During September 1933, winds of 125 mph were estimated at Jupiter Inlet just south of the Martin County line. During the August 1949 hurricane, winds of up to 153 mph were recorded in the Stuart-Jupiter area. A high-water mark of 8.5 feet was observed in the St. Lucie River on the railroad bridge near Stuart, and the town suffered the worst damage in its history; 500 people were left homeless. The same storm today would destroy many more hundreds of homes. During Hurricane Isbell (1964), winds reached 80 to 100 mph and the Hobe Sound area was severely flooded. Hurricane Irene (1999) caused about $5.2 million damage in Martin County, of which $3.4 million was the cost for erosion-related beach restoration on Jupiter Island (appendix C, refs. 14 and 30). Northeasters have generally done more beach damage than hurricanes. Severe northeast winter storms occurred here in 1925, 1932, 1947, 1962, 1981, and 1983.

Shoreline retreat and storm damage have prompted property owners and communities to install seawalls, sloping revetments, and groins, and to support beach fill projects. Many of these structures have helped to protect upland property while causing the loss of beaches and steepening of the beach profiles in front of them. Three major beach fill projects in Hobe Sound on Jupiter Island in 1973, 1974, and 1978 placed 2.3 million, 1.0 million, and 1.0 million cubic yards of fill, respectively. There were three earlier nourishment projects in 1956, 1963, and 1967; and later projects in 1983 and 1987 nourished 5- and 3-mile reaches on Jupiter Island. The average life of the beach nourishment projects in the area is about five years. In most cases, local property owners paid for the beach nourishment or other corrective action without any federal funding in order to forgo the required establishment of public beach access points. The total cost of their fill projects is not known, but few communities have the private resources of a Hobe Sound to pay the ongoing cost of repeated fill projects.

Evacuation is a problem in Martin County. Most of the developed areas will be flooded during a major storm, and the roads lined with Australian pines may prove impassable. All Martin County beaches are connected to the mainland by drawbridges. The heavy forests in some developed areas are a plus. As yet, condo development is not heavy on Hutchinson Island and Jupiter Island, in comparison with other South Florida communities, although development is increasing near the southern county line. Overall, the county shoreline is more than 65 percent developed, and as condo development increases, evacuation hazards will increase.

Palm Beach County (RMs 32, 33, 34, 35, 36, and 37)

Palm Beach County's more than 40 miles of open-ocean shoreline (table 7.10) is home to world-renowned Palm Beach (RMs 33 and 34). Only slightly less famous are such names as Delray Beach (RM 36) and Boca Raton (RM 37). It seems as if everybody wants a piece of the Palm Beach shoreline, and the closer the piece is to the beach, the better. As a result, this county has one of the most extensively developed barrier island systems in the world, and beachfront property prices here are astronomical by nearly anybody's standard.

The quality of this much-sought-after environment is highly variable. Only a small amount of beach remains in front of the seawalls at Palm Beach, for example (see fig. 4.7), but that seems to have little impact on the oceanfront's desirability, except when ships wash ashore (fig. 7.14)! In fact, many Palm Beach residents oppose replenishing the beach because a broad new beach might bring an influx of people from the outside world. At the other end of the spectrum are some of the beaches of Boca Raton that are relatively broad and relatively "unspoiled." The aesthetic quality of development varies as well, ranging from the spectacularly beautiful hedge-lined streets of Palm Beach to the endless condo rows fronting South Palm Beach, Highland Beach, and Delray Beach.

In the earlier edition of this book, we asked ourselves where we would want our parents to live along Florida's east coast, and we ranked three areas as low risk for development. The Juno Beach area was one of those locations. Now, however, some shorefront development in Juno Beach is threatened by critically eroding beaches. This increases the flood risk as well. Storm evacuation from this area remains reasonably safe for the prudent.

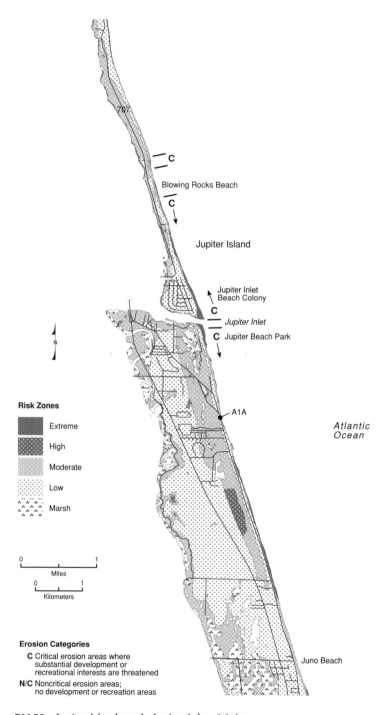

Risk Zones

- Extreme
- High
- Moderate
- Low
- Marsh

0   1
Miles

0   1
Kilometers

Erosion Categories

C Critical erosion areas where
substantial development or
recreational interests are threatened

N/C Noncritical erosion areas;
no development or recreation areas

707

C

Blowing Rocks Beach

C

Jupiter Island

Jupiter Inlet
Beach Colony

C

Jupiter Inlet

C   Jupiter Beach Park

A1A

*Atlantic
Ocean*

Juno Beach

RM 32   Jupiter Island south–Jupiter Inlet vicinity

Table 7.10 Shoreline Summary for Palm Beach County, Florida

Total ocean shoreline (miles)	42
Critically/noncritically eroding shoreline (miles)	27.0/0.9
Erosion rates	
Long term	(1885–1991) 0.19 ft/yr
Short term	(1971–1991) 1.17 ft/yr
Beach maintenance	
Number of fills	38
Volume (cubic yards)	20,215,853
Minimum documented cost	$27,266,143
Density of coastal development	Heavy to extreme
Coastal armoring	Seawalls, groins, jetties, revetments, bulkheads
Environmental concerns	Coral reefs, dense sea turtle nesting sites, hard-bottom reefs present
Comments	Shorelines are extensively developed and armored. Erosional or retreating shorelines occur south of Jupiter Inlet and Lake Worth Inlet, Palm Beach, Juno Beach, Delray Beach, Boca Raton, Highland Beach, and Riviera Beach. Dredging projects continuously in planning or construction stages. Inlet sand transfer is ongoing.

Two other areas, near Delray Beach and Boca Raton, also were classified as low risk, but evacuation now poses somewhat more of a hazard there. Delray Beach has about 3 miles of critical erosion where houses and other interests are threatened, but the beach usually varies between 100 to 200 feet in width. The section of shoreline classified as low risk near Boca Raton has a public park fronting the beach, and the park, along with the highway, acts as a good natural buffer to storm processes. Nevertheless, Boca Raton has areas where private development and Highway A1A are threatened by erosion. The two areas in Palm Beach County classified as high risk in the first edition were Highland Beach and the area south of Lake Worth Inlet. Among other problems, both beachfront areas have particularly severe erosion, which now is classified as critical by the FDEP.

The northern 2 miles of barrier island (the south end of Jupiter Island) in the county range in width from 700 feet to about 2,300 feet near Jupiter Inlet. Jupiter Inlet Beach Colony is located north of the inlet. The beach width in this section varies from 20 to 70 feet at mean low water and has steep

7.14 Another disadvantage of a narrow beach! (Top) During a 1985 storm a small freighter washed ashore at Palm Beach. The fact that the ship was carried clear to the seawall reflects the increased water depth during the storm at this location caused by the storm surge. (Bottom) Close-up of the damage to the seawall.

slopes in the nearshore. The frontal dunes, which have been partially built upon, have elevations ranging from 15 feet to more than 20 feet.

From Jupiter Inlet to Lake Worth Inlet (artificially cut in 1918 and once known as the Port of Palm Beach), the barrier island is about 12 miles long. The towns of Juno Beach, Riviera Beach, and Palm Beach Shores (Singer Is-

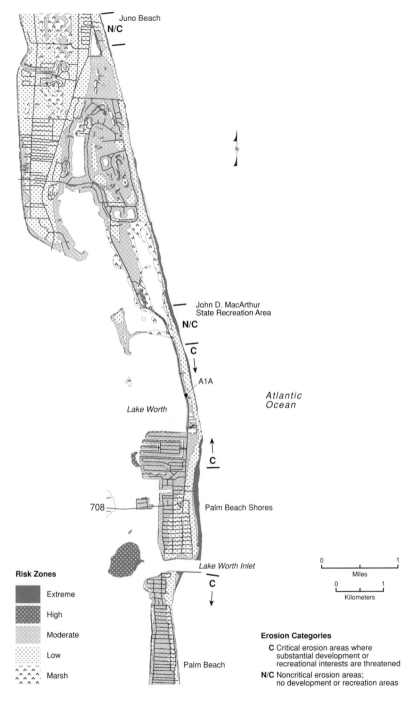

Juno Beach
N/C

John D. MacArthur
State Recreation Area
N/C

C

A1A

Lake Worth

Atlantic
Ocean

C

708

Palm Beach Shores

Lake Worth Inlet

C

Palm Beach

Risk Zones

Extreme
High
Moderate
Low
Marsh

0   1
Miles

0   1
Kilometers

Erosion Categories

C Critical erosion areas where
substantial development or
recreational interests are threatened

N/C Noncritical erosion areas;
no development or recreation areas

RM 33   Juno Beach, Palm Beach Shores, Lake Worth Inlet, to Palm Beach

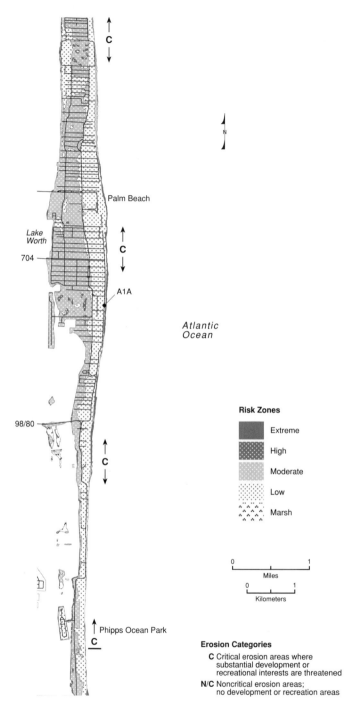

Palm Beach

Lake
Worth

704

A1A

Atlantic
Ocean

98/80

Risk Zones

Extreme

High

Moderate

Low

Marsh

0   1
Miles
0   1
Kilometers

Phipps Ocean Park

Erosion Categories

C Critical erosion areas where
  substantial development or
  recreational interests are threatened

N/C Noncritical erosion areas;
    no development or recreation areas

RM 34   Palm Beach and vicinity

land) are located on this island. The island width varies from 600 feet to about 1 mile. North of the inlet, Riviera Beach varies from no beach to as much as 300 feet wide. Frontal dunes, with elevations of 15 to 20 feet, occur for most of the reach. The natural dunes are particularly well developed on the northern half of this island, and at Juno Beach the largest dune exceeds 50 feet in elevation. The southern 3-mile section of the island has average elevations of only 10 feet above the low-tide mark.

Palm Beach and South Palm Beach are both on the barrier island between Lake Worth Inlet and South Lake Worth Inlet, also known locally as Boynton Inlet, artificially cut in 1927. This island stretches for more than 15 miles and varies in width from about 600 to 4,500 feet. The elevation of the first row of dunes (primary dunes) is less than 13 feet within the Palm Beach city limits and increases to 27 feet on the southern portion of the island. The dunes are steep, and the offshore beach profiles in this section also are steep. Australian pines cover many of these dunes, but, as discussed earlier, do not retain or protect them.

The barrier island between South Lake Worth Inlet and Boca Raton Inlet extends for 14.5 miles and includes the towns of Boynton Beach, Delray Beach, and Highland Beach. The barrier width varies from 750 to about 2,000 feet, and the primary dune elevations range from 15 to 23 feet above mean low water. The beaches are narrow and steep, with seawalls and natural beach rock along some reaches. South of Boca Raton Inlet is about a 1-mile section of island in Palm Beach County that is approximately 700 to 800 feet wide. The elevations are relatively low, about 12 feet above mean low water, and the beach is narrow and steep.

The bay side of the barrier islands was originally lined with mangroves, but these were removed along much of the county's shoreline, and the area was filled. The estuarine and Intracoastal Waterway shorelines are now lined with bulkheads.

Palm Beach County has the second most urbanized barrier island shoreline in East Florida (94 percent developed). On the other hand, almost 9 miles of the county's beachfront are in public ownership, and an additional 4 miles or so have been acquired by state and county agencies to meet public recreation demands and to minimize public hazards and losses from hurricanes and shoreline erosion.

The prevailing winds are from the southeast, but the strongest winds are from the northeast. The highest recorded storm tide in Palm Beach was 11.2 feet above sea level during the 1928 hurricane. The predominant littoral currents are from north to south during winter and spring, and from south to north during the summer and fall, with the net annual movement from north to south. Jetties at the inlets interrupt sand movement along the county shoreline, starving downdrift beaches.

From 1883 to 1983 the county's beaches generally retreated, but at varying rates (table 7.10). As a general rule, stretches of beach 1 to 1.5 miles in length north of the inlets and their associated jetties have either remained stable or have built seaward. The areas immediately south of the inlets have experienced severe retreat due to the blocking of the littoral drift at the jetties and shoaling of the inlet bars. The beaches of Palm Beach Island experienced erosion landward of the 30-foot depth contour amounting to 8 million cubic yards between 1929 and 1955. The beaches south of South Lake Worth Inlet have experienced both retreat and accretion, but retreat exceeds build-out for the entire section, despite the past operation of a sand transfer plant at the inlet (see fig. 4.10). One Army Corps of Engineers estimate of annual sand loss for Palm Beach County was 190,000 cubic yards per year.

Almost one-half of the developed shoreline in this county has been extensively engineered with seawalls, groins, revetments, and jetties. There have been several beach fill projects on Palm Beach Island and at Delray Beach. When operational, the sand bypass systems on Lake Worth Inlet and South Lake Worth Inlet are capable of placing an average of 63,000 cubic yards and 80,000 cubic yards of sand, respectively, on the south side of the inlets annually. Delray Beach was filled in 1973 with 1.6 million cubic yards of sand; the same was done in 1978–79. In 1974, Palm Beach County conducted a study that recommended a beach fill program for 33.9 miles of beaches at a cost of $17.5 million. A Corps of Engineers study recommended improvement for 12.2 miles of beaches at a cost of about $23 million. Between 1975 and 1999 numerous beach fill projects took place at considerable cost (see table 4.1). In spite of frequent and costly beach fill projects throughout this county, Mother Nature still has the upper hand.

Hurricanes and northeasters cause rapid changes in the beaches and dunes as well as property damage and evacuation problems. The frequency of tropical storms and hurricanes passing within a 60-mile radius of Palm Beach County is higher than for the northern counties (see table 2.3). The storm of October 1910 brought severe rain and a 5-foot rise in the Loxahatchee River and Hobe Sound, causing extensive flooding on the bay side. The storm of September 1926 caused considerable damage and loss of beach material. The most severe storm to hit Palm Beach was the September 1928 hurricane, the eye of which passed right over the county. Winds in excess of 100 mph, a barometric pressure of 27.43 inches, and a storm surge or tide of 11.2 feet were recorded. Sections of Highways A1A and 707 were damaged, with millions of dollars worth of property damage in the Palm Beach–Lake Worth area. The 1947 September storm, with winds above 100 mph, caused severe erosion of the beaches and washed out a 1-mile section of A1A in Delray Beach, along with the municipal pavilion. The storm of August 1949 pounded Palm Beach with 130-mph winds and washed out a 3-mile section of A1A from Lantana to Lake Worth. Other highway sections from Boynton Beach to Delray Beach were damaged as well. Hurricane Floyd caused

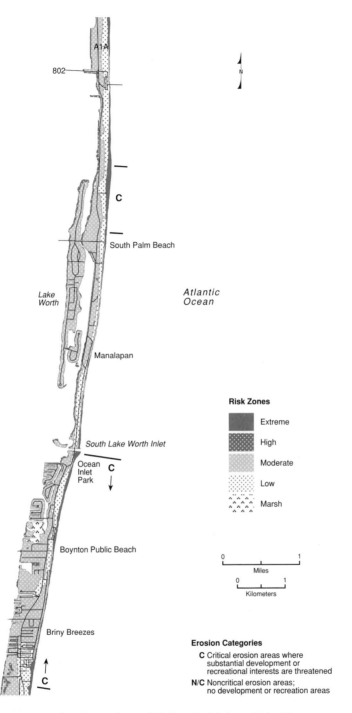

802

A1A

N

C

South Palm Beach

Lake
Worth

*Atlantic
Ocean*

Manalapan

Risk Zones

Extreme

High

Moderate

Low

Marsh

South Lake Worth Inlet

Ocean
Inlet   **C**
Park   ↓

Boynton Public Beach

0   1
Miles

0   1
Kilometers

Briny Breezes

Erosion Categories

C Critical erosion areas where
  substantial development or
  recreational interests are threatened

N/C Noncritical erosion areas;
  no development or recreation areas

↑
C

RM 35 South Palm Beach, South Lake Worth Inlet, to Briny Breezes

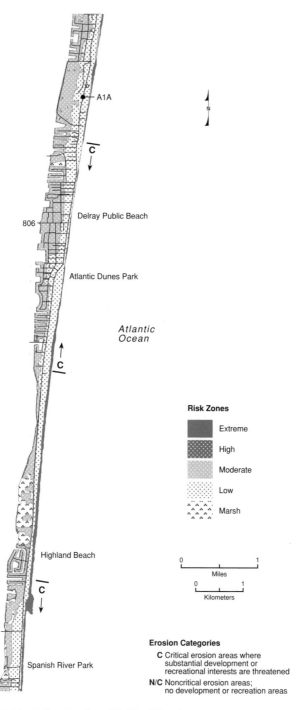

A1A

C

Delray Public Beach

806

Atlantic Dunes Park

Atlantic Ocean

C

Risk Zones

Extreme

High

Moderate

Low

Marsh

Highland Beach

0   1
Miles

0   1
Kilometers

C

Erosion Categories

C Critical erosion areas where
substantial development or
recreational interests are threatened

N/C Noncritical erosion areas;
no development or recreation areas

Spanish River Park

RM 36   Delray Beach to Highland Beach

countywide beach erosion in 1999. In Gulfstream, dunes were eroded, leaving 15 feet of vertical escarpment; and reaches of Boca Raton beaches were left with 2-to-3-foot scarps. When Hurricane Irene struck a month later (1999), the beaches were already damaged, and many areas, such as south of Jupiter Inlet and in Gulfstream south of the Briny Breezes groin, sustained additional erosion from the new storm (appendix C, refs. 14 and 30). If a hurricane struck Palm Beach now, the damage to shorefront property would be greater than ever because there is no natural beach buffer.

Northeasters have caused the most severe and lasting changes along the shoreline. The winter storms of 1957, 1962, and 1981–82 were particularly notable for the considerable damage they did to bulkheads and beach dune profiles.

Evacuation is a serious problem for Palm Beach County. Most areas on the barrier islands are well below the 100-year flood level. Jupiter Inlet Beach Colony residents must escape via Highway 707, which has low-elevation approaches to a drawbridge. Palm Beach has three routes of evacuation to the mainland, all via drawbridges. Locally, Australian pines line streets in northern Palm Beach and should be expected to blow down and block evacuation routes. Much of the evacuation route in South Palm Beach lies below a 5-foot elevation along the back side of the island and is very susceptible to flooding. The two closest routes to the mainland are via drawbridges. On the Delray Beach, Gulf Stream, and Ocean Ridge segments of the shoreline, A1A is on fairly high ground. However, the roads leading back to the mainland lie below 5 feet in elevation and are therefore susceptible to flooding. Florida Highway 804 has a drawbridge over the Intracoastal Waterway; Highway 806 has a fixed-span bridge. The Boca Raton area is best evacuated by the four-span stationary bridges to the north over Lake Rogers.

Broward County (RMs 37, 38, 39, and 40)

Broward County has about 24 miles of open-ocean shoreline (table 7.11). Two inlets break the Broward barrier chain: Hillsboro Inlet north of Pompano Beach and Port Everglades Harbor south of Fort Lauderdale. Broward's open-ocean coast is fronted with barrier islands. Where natural sounds and lagoons do not exist, the Intracoastal Waterway cuts behind the shoreline, isolating the beachfront strip. Widths of the islands in Broward County range from a mere 300 feet or so north of Hillsboro Inlet to 4,500 feet near Fort Lauderdale. Elevations of the Broward County islands are usually less than 15 feet and reach maximums of a little more than 20 feet. There is a more-or-less continuous ridge of sand down the length of the Broward shore, but it is generally lower and less well developed than the ridge of the Palm Beach County shore. Public lands constitute 8 miles of the 24-mile county shorefront.

The county's beachfront communities are, from north to south, Deerfield

Table 7.11 Shoreline Summary for Broward County, Florida

Total ocean shoreline (miles)	24
Critically/noncritically eroding shoreline (miles)	21.3/0
Erosion rates	
Long term	(1883–1987) 0.02 ft/yr
Short term	(1972–1987) 4.47 ft/yr
Beach maintenance	
Number of fills	8
Volume (cubic yards)	8,578,000
Minimum documented cost	$25,473,758
Density of coastal development	High
Coastal armoring	Groins, seawalls, bulkheads, revetments, jetties, boulder mounds
Environmental concerns	Sea turtle nesting sites, coral reefs, hard-bottom reefs
Comments	Shorelines are extensively developed and armored. Two erosion areas are identified, both downdrift of inlets. Nearly all of the county shoreline is classified as critically eroded (21/24 miles) Beaches south of Port Everglades have some of the highest erosion rates of beaches along the southeastern Florida coast.

Beach, Hillsboro Beach, Pompano Beach, Lauderdale-by-the-Sea, Fort Lauderdale, Dania, Hollywood, and Hallandale. This urban corridor makes Broward County's shore one of the most extensively developed in the state—approximately 90 percent in 1992. Thousands of buildings hug the shoreline, and more and bigger structures go up every day (fig. 7.15). Unfortunately, this shoreline has a long history of erosion that has resulted in emplacement of numerous armoring structures along over 60 percent of its length. The already high natural erosion rates have been pushed even higher in some cases by jetties and other structures. For example, prior to 1960, the USACE estimated that the annual shoreline recession rate of the stretch between the county line and Hillsboro Inlet was 4 feet per year. During the 1960s and 1970s the rate accelerated to more than 10 feet per year. Part of the acceleration may have been due to the jetties at Boca Raton Inlet in southern Palm Beach County. Between Hillsboro and Port Everglades Inlet, the recession rates have been much smaller, although Pompano Beach is an exception with its rates of 4 to 8 feet per year. On a shoreline as heavily stabilized as that of Broward County, recession rates may be rather meaningless.

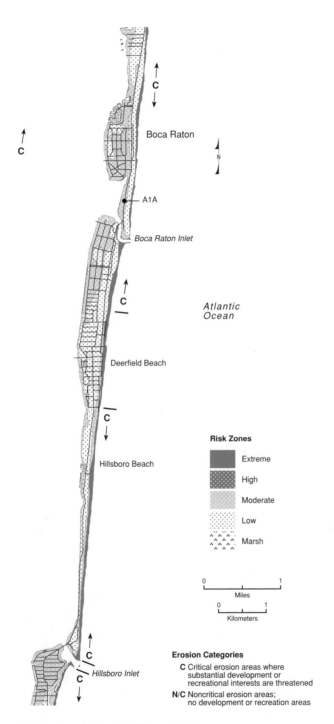

C

Boca Raton

N

A1A

Boca Raton Inlet

C

Atlantic Ocean

Deerfield Beach

C

Hillsboro Beach

Risk Zones

Extreme

High

Moderate

Low

Marsh

0   1
Miles

0   1
Kilometers

Erosion Categories

C Critical erosion areas where
substantial development or
recreational interests are threatened

N/C Noncritical erosion areas;
no development or recreation areas

C

Hillsboro Inlet

C

RM 37   Boca Raton to Hillsboro Inlet

Much of the shoreline retreat now affects replenished or nourished beaches. Almost every community in the county has had, or plans to have, a beach fill project (see table 4.1). Coastal studies indicate that beach fill here disappears very quickly (within three to five years), and thus replenishment will be an ongoing project. In some cases, the reason for the quick loss of sand may be the use of incompatible sand for fill. Potential beachfront property owners will attempt to find out what their future tax bills may be, because of the community's beach stabilization projects. Nearly all of Broward County's beaches are critically eroding (appendix C, ref. 14).

Broward County has an active storm history. Since 1870 the eyes of several hurricanes have passed through the county (see fig. 2.1). At least half of these made landfall along the county shore, but some exited here as well. Exiting storms can cause severe wind damage, but as a rule they do not cause major flooding. The flooding problems are much greater when a storm moves onto land from the sea. Expected 100-year flood levels from such storms are in the range of 7 to 12 feet. Maximum hurricane water levels actually recorded at Fort Lauderdale include a high of 12.6 feet above sea level in the 1926 storm, and 8 feet in the "Yankee" storm (1935), so named because it actually moved ashore from the north. A 1947 storm produced a 9.8-foot storm surge at Hillsboro Inlet. Hurricanes Dennis and Floyd (1999)

7.15 New construction along Broward County's urbanized shore. Even as the New Diplomat Hotel was being constructed, high-tide waves were washing at its doorstep. Note wrack at base of seawall. Such development increases pressure to spend public monies on beach fill to try to protect private property.

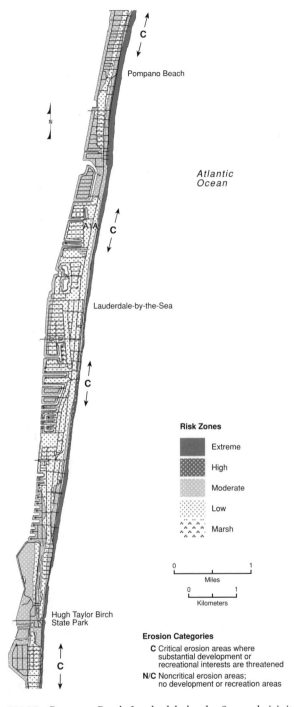

Pompano Beach

N

Atlantic Ocean

A-1-A

Lauderdale-by-the-Sea

Risk Zones

Extreme

High

Moderate

Low

Marsh

0 _____ 1
Miles

0 _____ 1
Kilometers

Hugh Taylor Birch
State Park

Erosion Categories

C Critical erosion areas where
substantial development or
recreational interests are threatened

N/C Noncritical erosion areas;
no development or recreation areas

RM 38   Pompano Beach, Lauderdale-by-the-Sea, and vicinity

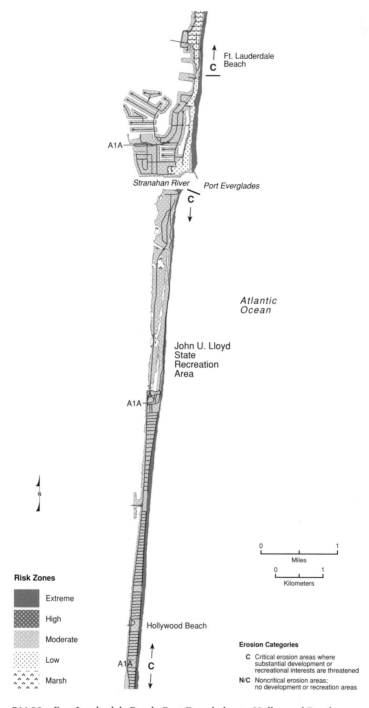

Ft. Lauderdale
Beach

C

A1A

Stranahan River   *Port Everglades*

C

*Atlantic
Ocean*

John U. Lloyd
State
Recreation
Area

A1A

N

Risk Zones

Extreme

High

Moderate

Low

Marsh

Hollywood Beach

A1A   C

0   1
Miles

0   1
Kilometers

Erosion Categories

C   Critical erosion areas where
    substantial development or
    recreational interests are threatened

N/C Noncritical erosion areas;
     no development or recreation areas

RM 39   Fort Lauderdale Beach, Port Everglades, to Hollywood Beach

7.16 As the beach retreats past this walled property on Surf Road in Hollywood, erosion undermines the wall (left).

narrowed Fort Lauderdale's beach, and storm tides carried sand onto Highway A1A. Hurricane Irene (1999) caused more damage when it flooded streets and undermined houses along Surf Road in northern Hollywood and also carried sand back onto A1A (fig. 7.16).

Heavily developed urban shores often have few remaining indicators of site stability, but as a rule the higher ground well away from the beachfront is the lower-risk zone. Wide beaches will provide some storm protection, but artificial beaches from fill projects give a false sense of security. One of the anomalous developments is Dania, a community of single-family dwellings almost surrounded by high-rises. The beach is relatively broad here, but the low elevation of the island dictates a need for attention to storm evacuation. Another striking anomaly in beachfront development in Broward County is the Marriott Hotel in Fort Lauderdale. For some reason, the hotel was given a variance to the coastal setback line, and the building sits far out on the beach relative to adjacent, more prudently sited buildings. The seawall in front of the Marriott Hotel may contribute to downdrift beach loss.

Broward County beach evacuation routes are all via bridges across the Intracoastal Waterway to the mainland. The large number of people living in low-elevation, high-flood-risk zones, including extensive finger canal developments, means that when a big storm threatens, many thousands will be trying to escape simultaneously from the Broward shore. Vertical evacuation into high-rise buildings may become a frightening alternative if roads are impassable.

Dade County (RMs 40, 41, 42, 43, and 44)

Dade County's open-ocean shoreline, about half of which is made up of barrier islands (table 7.12), includes Golden Beach, Sunny Isles, Bal Harbour, Surfside, Miami Beach, South Beach, Key Biscayne, and Biscayne National Park. Dade County, especially Miami Beach, is one of the world's most densely developed barrier island shorelines—about 85 percent in 1992. High-rise buildings interspersed with small parks line Collins Avenue, Miami Beach's main street. At the other end of the development spectrum are Sands Key, Elliott Key, and Rhodes Key. At the southern end of Dade County, all three lie within Biscayne National Park and will not face development pressure.

Table 7.12 Shoreline Summary for Dade County, Florida

Total ocean shoreline (miles)	21
Critically/noncritically eroding shoreline (miles)	17.0/1.7
Erosion rates	
Long term	(1851–1987) 0.98 ft/yr
Short term	(1972–1987) 10.41 ft/yr
Beach maintenance	
Number of fills	19
Volume (cubic yards)	19,839,490
Minimum documented cost	$112,879,149
Density of coastal development	Extensively developed
Coastal armoring	Seawalls, groins, jetties
Environmental concerns	Sea grass beds, sea turtle nesting sites, coral reefs, hard-bottom reefs
Comments	Densely developed, critically eroded shorelines with extensive beach maintenance projects. Nearly half of the developed reaches are armored. Areas formerly regarded as eroded (e.g., Miami Beach) are now classified as stable or accreted due to semi-continuous beach dredging projects. Nearly all of the county shoreline is critically eroded, from the county line to Government Cut, and also the southern half of Key Biscayne.

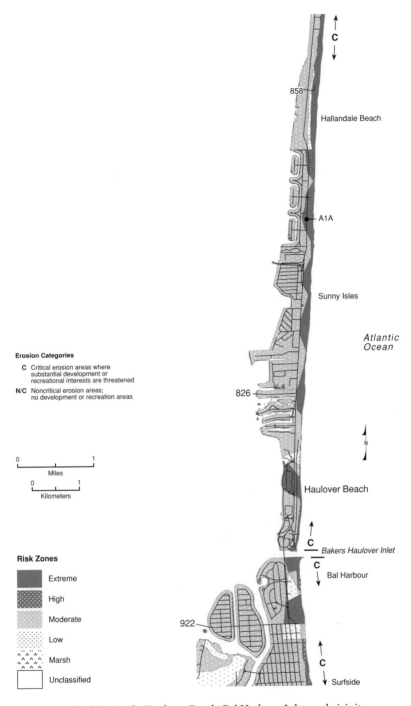

Erosion Categories

C Critical erosion areas where
substantial development or
recreational interests are threatened

N/C Noncritical erosion areas;
no development or recreation areas

0   1
Miles
0   1
Kilometers

Risk Zones

Extreme

High

Moderate

Low

Marsh

Unclassified

Hallandale Beach

A1A

Sunny Isles

*Atlantic
Ocean*

N

Haulover Beach

C
Bakers Haulover Inlet
C

Bal Harbour

C

Surfside

RM 40   Hallandale Beach, Haulover Beach, Bal Harbour Inlet, and vicinity

7.17 A 1960s view of Bakers Haulover Bridge and Inlet in North Miami Beach. Note the different land uses for this high-risk zone on a narrow barrier island: open space versus high-rise buildings and dense residential development. By the 1960s the beaches to the south of the jetties (left background) were narrow to absent in front of the seawalls, and the groins were only partially successful at holding sand. Very little sand was reaching the beaches to the south. Photo from the Photographic Collection of the Florida State Archives.

Miami Beach and Bal Harbour are on the island that is bordered to the north by Bakers Haulover Cut (fig. 7.17) and to the south by Government Cut, the main channel for the Port of Miami. Jetties have been built at both inlets, causing erosion to the beaches south of the jetties because the dominant direction of sand movement along this shore is from north to south. Essentially no sand escapes to reach the shorefront south of the Government Cut jetties (see fig. 4.9), and the islands there show the effects. South of Government Cut lie Fisher Island (Norris Cut), Virginia Key (Bear Cut), and Key Biscayne, plus a few smaller islands farther south. Norris Cut and Bear Cut are natural tidal inlets between the Atlantic and Biscayne Bay.

The barrier islands range from 0.2 to 1.5 miles in width. Elevations are generally quite low. A more or less continuous sand ridge parallels the beach, with elevations ranging from 5 to 12 feet. Behind the narrow frontal sand ridges the islands tend to be flat and low, with much of the area less than 5 feet in elevation. The islands are made up of a shell and quartz mixture. Some beaches have received nourishment sands several times, particularly Bal Harbour and Key Biscayne (see table 4.1).

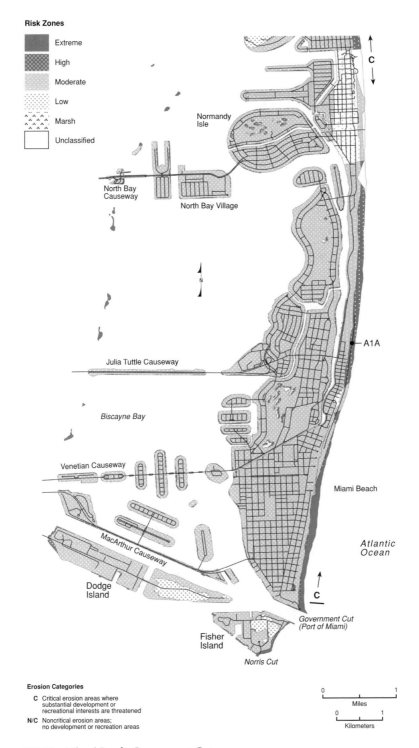

Risk Zones

- Extreme
- High
- Moderate
- Low
- Marsh
- Unclassified

Normandy Isle

C

North Bay Causeway

North Bay Village

N

A1A

Julia Tuttle Causeway

Biscayne Bay

Venetian Causeway

Miami Beach

MacArthur Causeway

Atlantic Ocean

Dodge Island

C

Government Cut (Port of Miami)

Fisher Island

Norris Cut

Erosion Categories

C Critical erosion areas where substantial development or recreational interests are threatened

N/C Noncritical erosion areas; no development or recreation areas

0 _____ 1
Miles

0 _____ 1
Kilometers

RM 41 Miami Beach, Government Cut

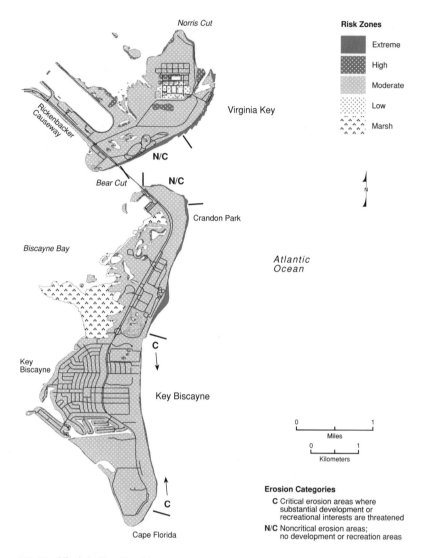

Risk Zones

- Extreme
- High
- Moderate
- Low
- Marsh

Norris Cut

Rickenbacker Causeway

Virginia Key

N/C

Bear Cut   N/C

Crandon Park

Biscayne Bay

Atlantic Ocean

C

Key Biscayne

Key Biscayne

0 ___ 1
Miles

0 ___ 1
Kilometers

C

Cape Florida

Erosion Categories

C Critical erosion areas where substantial development or recreational interests are threatened

N/C Noncritical erosion areas; no development or recreation areas

RM 42   Virginia Key, Key Biscayne

Although the shoreline elsewhere in Dade County has generally re-treated, the Miami Beach shoreline has been held in place since 1920 by a more or less continuous seawall. The beach was first jeopardized as a result of buildings built too close to the shore. When updrift jetties cut off the sand supply, the beach began to narrow. The storm of 1926 left some shore-front hotels partly in the water. Groins were constructed shortly afterward, but there was limited sand to trap and hold for the beach. The seawalls holding the land in place to protect the buildings blocked any local sediment that might have been provided by shore erosion. So Miami Beach disappeared (see fig. 1.16). A $6 million-per-mile beach fill project ($68 million total) constructed between 1979 and 1981 widened the beach to 300 feet. Most of the stretch of barrier island fronted by the filled Miami Beach falls in the moderate-risk category because of the protective effect of the wide, albeit artificial, beach (fig. 7.18). If the wide beach is not maintained, the risk factor will increase.

All of the Dade County shoreline from the northern county line to Government Cut (14.5 miles) is currently classified as critically eroded, as is the southern half (2.5 miles) of Key Biscayne. Central Key Biscayne is heavily developed. Some Key Biscayne condos and hotels are fronted with seawalls —and in some cases lack a beach (fig. 7.19). The southern end of the island is home to the Cape Florida lighthouse and Bill Baggs Cape Florida State Recreational Area. Cape Florida was shaped by a series of southward-arching, sandy beach ridges, each at one time the southern tip of the island. This area is undeveloped and will remain so. The lighthouse built here in 1825 is said to be the oldest building in South Florida (fig. 7.20). Crandon Park at the north end of the island, populated by mangroves, also will not be developed. The beach profile throughout has been lowered as well as narrowed, leaving the entire shore more vulnerable to storm waves.

Prior to the hurricane of 1835, Virginia Key was connected to Miami Beach. The north end of this island contains a sewage treatment facility, and

7.18 Miami Beach, although not as wide as when the original beach fill was completed, still has a wide beach and vegetated zone that provide storm protection to the urbanized barrier.

7.19 Development on Key Biscayne Beach.

7.20 A hurricane survivor, the Cape Florida lighthouse on Key Biscayne was built in 1825 and in service until 1878. The tower was refurbished through the Dade County Heritage Trust and relit in 1996 for the Miami centennial celebration.

an outfall pipe is built out beyond the shelf edge so that effluent ends up in the Straits of Florida. Virginia Key is undeveloped except for a marina and a small restaurant and fish shop. Beaches here have been nourished several times, but the sand does not stay long. This is a concern because of the location of the sewage treatment facility.

Fisher Island, north of Virginia Key, was created by the dredging of Government Cut in 1905. This island can be reached only by boat and is home to relatively few people, who should evacuate early. As noted, the jetties at Government Cut starve the beaches to the south of sand, affecting Fisher Island and perhaps Virginia Key, and northern Key Biscayne to a lesser extent (see appendix C, ref. 33).

During the last 100 years or so, more than a dozen hurricanes have passed through Dade County, the majority making landfall in the county, and some also exited back to the Atlantic here. The most destructive in memory is Andrew (1992), a small category 4 hurricane that struck the coast head-on just north of Homestead Air Force Base with incredible winds. The storm's minimum pressure was 27.23 millibars. The maximum storm surge exceeded 15 feet between Cutler and Kings Bay, south of Miami, but storm surge affected a relatively short distance of shoreline. The billions of dollars of damage was largely due to wind, and Andrew demonstrated once again that hurricanes carry their destruction inland. This is especially true in Florida, and hurricanes that only brush the Dade coast on their way north also can be a threat. Earlier hurricanes that caused significant damage to Dade County occurred in 1903, 1906, 1926 (the big one), 1929, 1935 (two storms), 1941, 1945, 1947 (two storms), 1948, 1949, 1950, 1964, 1965, and 1966. After a lull, Andrew and other recent hurricanes of mass destruction in the Southeast have resensitized Floridians to the dangers posed by such storms, and more people have experienced evacuations even though the storms of the late 1990s were mostly "brushes" for South Florida.

Other than minor beach erosion and the loss of some Australian pines on Virginia Key, the county was spared by Floyd and Irene in 1999. In contrast, the September 1926 hurricane, which killed hundreds, injured more than 4,000, and left 15,000 families homeless, was called the "Most Terrific Storm in the World's History" by a Miami newspaper. Accounts at the time said that the citizens had received a shock that would take years to eliminate from their memory. In fact, the storm was forgotten in less than a generation, a type of selective memory loss that persists in today's coastal communities. It is interesting that a Corps of Engineers evacuation study indicates that numerous South Florida citizens think they have survived an important hurricane, even though no such storms may have occurred since their arrival in the sunny South. The problem is that such people may treat the next real storm with undue apathy.

Hurricanes are not the only storms that cause shoreline damage in Dade

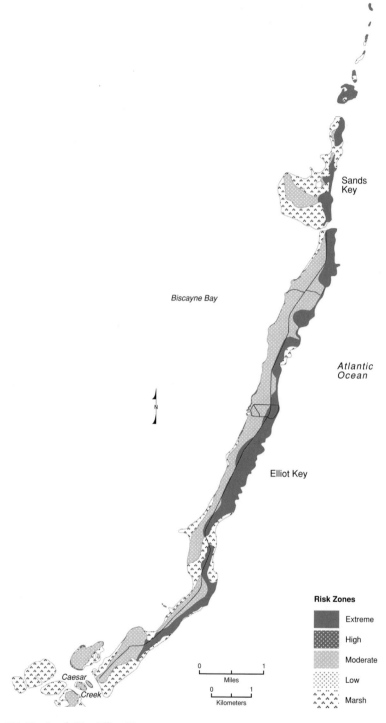

Sands
Key

Biscayne Bay

Atlantic
Ocean

Elliot Key

Caesar
Creek

0   1
Miles
0   1
Kilometers

Risk Zones

Extreme

High

Moderate

Low

Marsh

RM 43   Sands Key, Elliot Key

230   Living with Florida's Atlantic Beaches

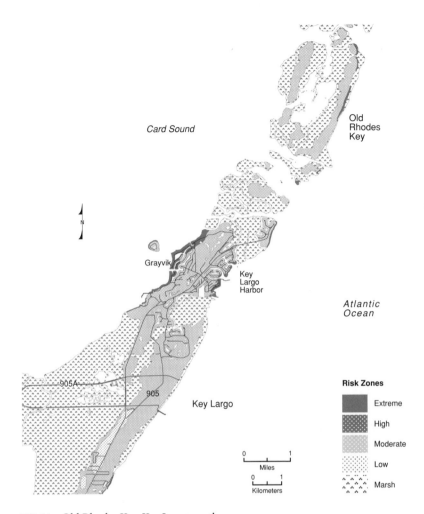

Card Sound

Old Rhodes Key

Grayvik

Key Largo Harbor

Atlantic Ocean

905A

905

Key Largo

0   1
Miles

0   1
Kilometers

Risk Zones

Extreme

High

Moderate

Low

Marsh

RM 44 Old Rhodes Key, Key Largo north

County. Winter storms, most often from the northeast, cause both property damage and erosion.

Evacuation is, as usual in South Florida, a major problem. Dade County's beachfront communities rely on bridges to the mainland for storm egress, but few of these are high, fixed-span bridges with high-elevation approaches.

Once you have escaped to the mainland, your troubles are not over. Much of the Miami area is very low in elevation and will almost certainly be flooded in the next big storm. It is critical for all residents of the Dade shoreline to plan ahead. Go to your local city hall and examine the evacuation routes, then make plans for your family. What shelters can you reach in time? We think the best advice is to leave your island abode more than 24 hours before the storm strikes. At that stage, of course, you cannot even be certain that the storm will strike your community. But it is better to take an early trip to Orlando or Tallahassee than be caught in a last-minute traffic jam fleeing a monster storm.

Miami Beach: The Endpoint

Miami Beach is the end of East Florida's barrier island chain and an example of the endpoint of coastal development—a completely urbanized barrier island. The dense high-rises hold a population that far exceeds the carrying capacity of the island. The water supply must come from the mainland, and waste must be sent to the mainland or be pumped offshore and released in the adjacent marine environment in which we recreate. Only shoreline armoring can hold the island in place, and only artificial beach fill maintains a beach that is unlike the quartz-rich sand that attracted the first tourists to this island. The sand supply is an ever-diminishing resource coming from ever more distant sources at ever-increasing prices. The ecosystems of both land and sea—the area's original attractions—have been stressed and degraded or completely lost. And even if the island continues to be artificially maintained, the sea-level rise is an ongoing phenomenon that will be addressed again and again as the island communities try to cope with beach loss, storm flooding, and evacuation planning. The infrastructure of beach fill, walls, groins, and breakwaters cannot protect the populace or guarantee their safe evacuation. Previous hurricanes contributed to the depression of the Miami economy, and now the stage is set for the greatest property loss in history due to a hurricane.

Monroe County/Florida Keys (RMs 44, 45, 46, 47, 48, 49, 50, 51, 52, 53, 54, 55, and 56)

The Florida Keys are a different kind of island chain, but their development problems are similar to those of barrier islands. "Key" comes from the Spanish word *cayo,* meaning "small, low-lying island." The Florida Keys are variously called a tropical paradise, enchanted, blissful, stunning, a fisherman's paradise, and a place to get away from it all. In terms of origin and evolution, they are quite different from the beach and barrier island systems of East Florida. The Keys are a long chain of low-lying limestone islands extending for over 220 miles (table 7.13) in an arc around the tip of the Florida peninsula, from Soldier Key (Dade County) near Miami to the Dry Tortugas some 65 to 70 miles west of Key West. Key Largo is the northeasternmost key in Monroe County. The Keys are divided into three sections: the Upper Keys include Key Largo, Plantation Key, and Windley Key; the Middle Keys include the Matecumbes (Upper and Lower), Long Key, continuing south to Vaca Key and Pigeon Key (a national historic district); and the Lower Keys

Table 7.13 Shoreline Summary for Monroe County, Florida

Total ocean shoreline (miles)	The Florida Keys stretch for 220 miles from near Miami to the Dry Tortugas, with sandy beaches totaling about 52.5 total miles. Most sandy beaches are composed of material brought in from other locales.
Critically/noncritically eroding shoreline (miles)	7.3/3.5
Erosion rates	
Long term	Not known
Short term	Not known
Beach maintenance	
Number of fills	1 (poorly documented, actual number unknown)
Volume (cubic yards)	30,000
Minimum documented cost	$23,697
Density of coastal development	Ranges from low to high
Coastal armoring	Seawalls, revetments, groins, bulkheads, breakwaters, jetties (terminal groins)
Environmental concerns	Coral reefs, sea grasses, mangroves
Comments	No studies have determined the percentage of developed or armored shoreline in the Keys. Erosion dominates nearly all of the south coast of Key West, particularly the east end, as well as parts of several other keys. The Upper Keys have no natural beaches. Long beaches are found on Long Key and Bahia Honda Key. Most beaches are private pocket beaches nourished as needed with private funding. Extensive development on Vaca Key, Key West, Duck Key, Plantation Key, and Big Pine Key, and other keys.

extend from the Seven-Mile Bridge at Little Duck Key to Key West, the best known of the little islands. The islands west of Key West include the "Sand Keys of Florida," the Marquesas Keys, and the Dry Tortugas, all of which are federal parklands or preserves and will not be developed. Numerous state and federal parks dot the Keys and conserve areas for all people to use. The portions of several keys that are home to military installations, such as Boca Chica Key and Key West, hopefully will not be sold to developers either.

Much has been written about the amazing history and geology of the Keys. The story of the construction of the Overseas Railway (much of which

7.21 The old railroad bridge at Bahia Honda Key was later part of the Overseas Highway.

was destroyed in the Labor Day hurricane of 1935), followed by its conversion to the Overseas Highway, is itself remarkable and has been told elsewhere (fig. 7.21). You may wish to peruse the following books for more information: *Environmental Quality by Design: South Florida*, by A. R. Veri and others, 1975; the *Key Guide to the Florida Keys and Key West*, by George B. Stevenson, 1993; *Yesterday's Florida Keys, A Pictorial Record*, by Stan Windhorn and Wright Langley, 1998; or, for a nontechnical view, *Florida Beaches*, by Parke Puterbaugh and Alan Bisbort, 1999. For a thorough official discussion of the Keys, their beaches, and the beach erosion problem areas, see *The Carbonate Beaches of Florida: An Inventory of Monroe County Beaches*, by Ralph R. Clark, 1990, Florida Department of Natural Resources Beaches and Shores Technical and Design Memorandum 90-1.

The islands and some barely submerged banks in between are composed of two formations of limestone: the Key Largo Limestone and the Miami Oolite, both of which formed during the Pleistocene ice ages. Most of the Upper and Middle Keys are exposures of the Key Largo Formation. The limestone that makes up this old coral reef, which built up to 200 feet, is composed of a variety of fossil coral heads, the shells of many different snails and clams, and the calcareous remains of associated organisms. The southernmost exposure of the Key Largo Limestone is on Bahia Honda Key. The Miami Oolite Formation that forms the Lower Keys is composed of fragments of shells and of particles called oolites—sand-sized spherules of calcium carbonate that precipitated out of seawater in a shallow-water envi-

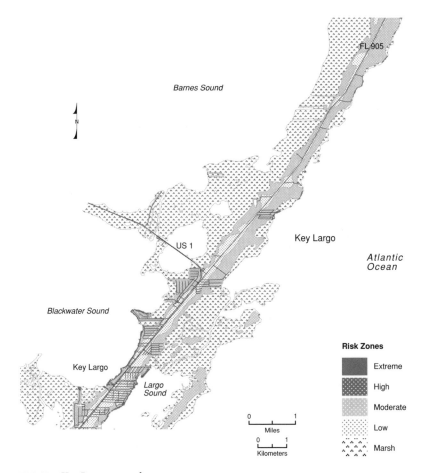

Risk Zones

▨	Extreme
▨	High
▨	Moderate
░	Low
ᴧᴧᴧ	Marsh

RM 45 Key Largo central

ronment subject to wave activity. This formation can be seen at the east end of Big Pine Key near Spanish Harbor.

Along some of the Keys, longshore transport is to the north or east, but the net longshore transport throughout most of the islands is estimated to be to the west or southwest. Along with the pocket beaches, natural rocks, and mangroves that line the shores, many of the islands have been armored with some form of riprap, bulkhead, breakwater, seawall, or groin. Several stretches of the Overseas Highway (U.S. 1) are protected by revetments and walls.

The Environment

The natural environment of the Florida Keys, where it still exists, is breath-takingly beautiful, the product of many unique and fragile interrelated ecosystems. Figure 7.22 is a generalized cross section of a typical key. Barrier reefs grow on the seaward edge of the limestone platform, and behind these reefs are smaller, more or less circular, patch reefs. These two types of reefs make up the only large living reef systems found in the continental United States. Mixed among the patch reefs are shifting shoals of calcareous sand made up mostly of reef fragments broken up during storms. The beautiful reefs can be viewed at John Pennekamp Coral Reef State Park off Key Largo. Besides providing beauty for divers to enjoy, the reefs, especially the barrier reefs, provide the Keys with some protection from waves.

The islands themselves are the high points of ancient coral reef systems exposed during the last major drop in sea level. A few natural beaches dot the Keys, but much of the shoreline is bare limestone. Some Keys beaches are artificial, composed of either dredged material or sand trucked in or even barged in from other locales, and erosion is a problem (fig. 7.23). Before 1926, a small beach was present at Key West, but a seawall constructed behind the beach caused its rapid disappearance. An artificial beach made up of crushed limestone and dredged sand was emplaced in 1960 for $285,000. Most of it disappeared within a decade. Smathers Beach on Key West was filled in 1989. Erosion plagues the east end of Key West, which now is fronted only by a seawall along South Roosevelt Boulevard.

There are no natural beaches in the Upper Keys. The Middle Keys have several narrow natural beaches, like Calusa Cove on Lower Matecumbe Key, and a few beaches created by dredge-and-fill projects, such as Key Colony Beach and Coco Plum Beach south of Fat Deer Key. Beaches fronting the Straits of Florida occur along most of the Lower Keys, with the most notable at Bahia Honda Key, where the third-longest beach in the Keys is experiencing critical erosion. Many of the Keys beaches are privately owned, with little or no public access. The state hopes to acquire and manage more properties in the Keys, which should benefit the public in the future. Beaches here are primarily of the pocket variety, with lengths more often measured in feet than in miles, although the range is from 180 feet on Boot

7.22 Generalized cross section of a key. Individual keys are a complex of numerous environments that provide a variety of habitats for plants and animals.

7.23 A beachless reach on Key West. Development, seawalls, and rock revetments have cut off the natural erosion and longshore transport that might have maintained a beach.

Key to more than 15,000 feet along Long Key. Beach width varies from 15 feet to 100 feet, with the majority averaging 15 feet.

Many of the islands are fringed by mangroves instead of beaches. The mangrove habitat is very important in that it provides a nursery for the larvae of many forms of marine life. Red mangroves lie at the edge of the shore and have roots that tolerate being permanently submerged in seawater. Black mangrove trees grow on slightly higher elevations with roots submerged by every high tide. The third species of the mangrove troika, the white mangrove, is found farther inland and has roots that are flooded only by storms or spring tides. The islands are crowned with a "tropical hammock," a typical West Indies assemblage of exotic trees and bushes not found on mainland America (fig. 7.22). Florida Bay lies behind the Keys. This shallow bay, dotted with numerous mud banks, is an important nursery area for commercial species of shrimp. Mangroves are found on some of these mud banks as well, providing valuable habitat for a variety of marine species.

Look What They've Done to Our Keys!

A large portion of Keys acreage is parkland, but the population on the remainder continues to rise. In addition to the 60,000 or so year-round residents, thousands of tourists flock to the plentiful campgrounds, motels, hotels, and a few large resorts, seeking nirvana. One can only assume that those who decide to stay in the Keys have not considered the implicit dangers they may face, particularly when tropical storms also decide to move in. People have moved to the Florida Keys for many reasons, the foremost being the natural beauty of this delicate ecosystem. Unfortunately, but certainly not surprisingly, development is rapidly destroying the very environment that people are moving to the Keys to enjoy. Development has been especially heavy in the Upper and Middle Keys. The towns of Islamorada (Mile Marker [MM] 83 area) on Upper Matecumbe Key and Marathon (MM 51–52 area) on Vaca Key are examples, but development seems to be increasing all along the Keys. Duck Key is nearly completely developed, and the Torch Keys, Summerland Key, Cudjoe Key, Sugarloaf Key, and Big Coppitt Key are filling up, some with mobile home and RV parks. Big Pine Key (MM 130–31), home of the famous little Key deer, is probably experiencing the most development. Everywhere in the Keys, parcels of land have been stripped of their unique West Indian vegetation, built up, flattened, and re-landscaped, often unsuccessfully. Introduced plants often do poorly in the poor to nonexistent soils; thus fertilizers and topsoil from elsewhere must be introduced. Unfortunately, development also is accompanied by dredg-

RM 46   Key Largo south to Rock Harbor area

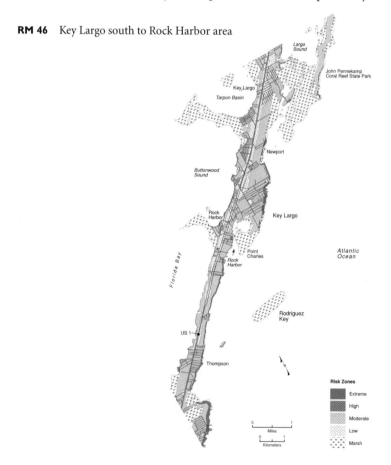

Risk Zones

Extreme
High
Moderate
Low
Marsh

ing and filling (for example, Key Colony Beach) that muddies the adjacent waters. Fortunately, one large area on the north end of Key Largo that was scheduled for development was saved by the state in 1988.

Houses with septic tank systems generate effluent that, along with fertilizers, seeps into the porous and permeable limestone, causing these pollutants to be introduced rapidly into the adjacent marine environment, putting the barrier reefs in jeopardy. The reefs provide natural protection from storm waves as well as critical habitat. The impacts from human development, boating, and fishing are combining with global climate change phenomena—such as warming of sea water and possibly dust from African dust storms carried into these waters—to stress and kill the reef-building organisms. The Florida reef tract has sustained serious losses in terms of reef kill, and there is considerable concern for the future.

The human population on the Keys may be just as threatened. Drinking water arrives via pipeline from the mainland—a long, tenuous lifeline. Both electricity and water were first brought out in the 1940s. How is life on the Keys when power and water supplies are interrupted by storms? How is

RM 47   Key Largo south, Tavernier,
Plantation Key, Windley Key

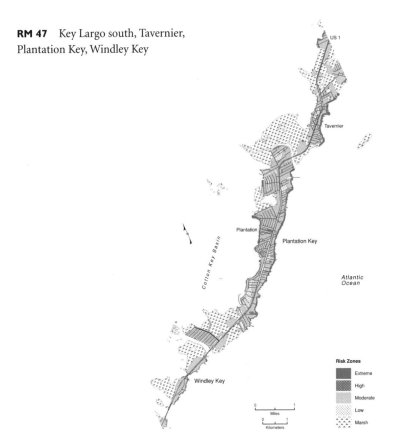

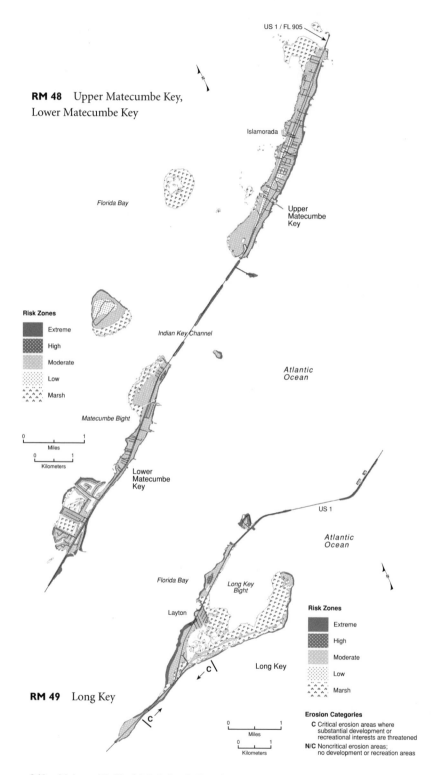

RM 48 Upper Matecumbe Key,
Lower Matecumbe Key

US 1 / FL 905

Islamorada

Florida Bay

Upper
Matecumbe
Key

Risk Zones

Extreme

High

Moderate

Low

Marsh

Indian Key Channel

Atlantic
Ocean

Matecumbe Bight

0   1
Miles

0   1
Kilometers

Lower
Matecumbe
Key

US 1

Atlantic
Ocean

Florida Bay

Long Key
Bight

Layton

Long Key

Risk Zones

Extreme

High

Moderate

Low

Marsh

RM 49   Long Key

c

c

Erosion Categories

C Critical erosion areas where
substantial development or
recreational interests are threatened

N/C Noncritical erosion areas;
no development or recreation areas

0   1
Miles

0   1
Kilometers

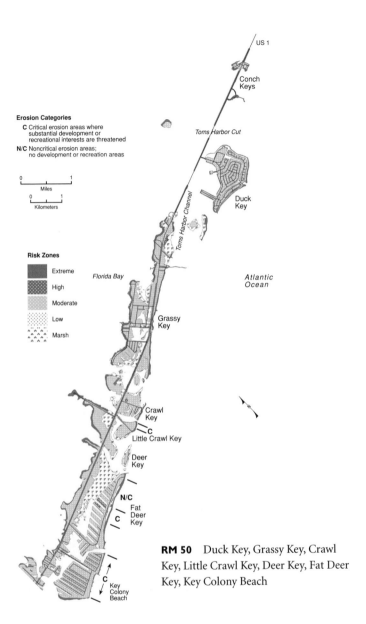

Erosion Categories

C Critical erosion areas where substantial development or recreational interests are threatened

N/C Noncritical erosion areas; no development or recreation areas

0   1
Miles

0   1
Kilometers

Risk Zones

- Extreme
- High
- Moderate
- Low
- Marsh

US 1

Conch Keys

Toms Harbor Cut

Toms Harbor Channel

Duck Key

Florida Bay

Atlantic Ocean

Grassy Key

Crawl Key

C
Little Crawl Key

Deer Key

N/C
C Fat Deer Key

C Key Colony Beach

RM 50   Duck Key, Grassy Key, Crawl Key, Little Crawl Key, Deer Key, Fat Deer Key, Key Colony Beach

waste safely managed under such limited conditions for a growing number of people? And what about hurricanes?

The Storm Threat

Hurricanes pose an enormous threat to people on the Florida Keys. U.S. 1, the four-lane highway that connects the Keys all the way from the mainland (MM 126) to Key West (MM 0), is the only land connection. It is the primary route of egress; boats and planes are the other ways off the islands, but none of these options look attractive in a storm. Complete evacuation before a big storm may be virtually impossible because U.S. 1 in the Keys is low and crosses more than 40 bridges. Flooding may close escape route access early, and you can be sure there will be accidents and stalled vehicles blocking the road as residents and visitors try to evacuate.

Compounding the danger is the fact that many residents of the Keys live in mobile homes that can be destroyed by even a modest hurricane. Finger canal developments such as those at Key Largo, Plantation Key, Big Coppitt Key, and Summerland Key also increase vulnerability to storm flooding and overwash.

Finally, the Keys themselves offer no place of refuge. The average elevation is only 3 feet, and the maximum elevation in the whole chain is only

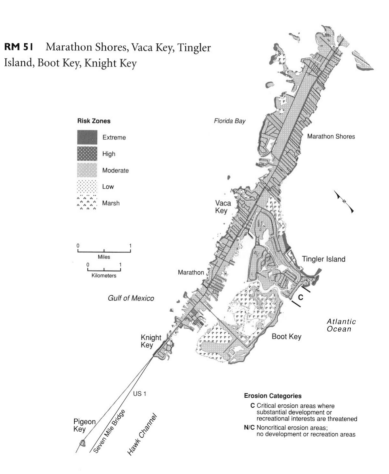

RM 51   Marathon Shores, Vaca Key, Tingler Island, Boot Key, Knight Key

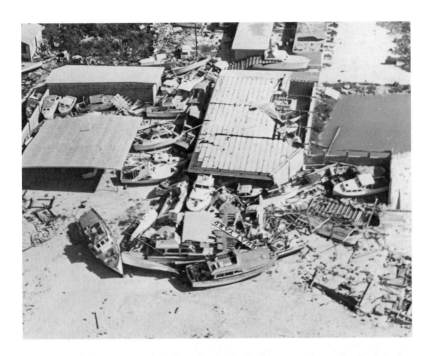

7.24 Damage at Marathon from Hurricane Donna (1960). Photo from the Photographic Collection of the Florida State Archives.

7.25 Foundation damage due to wave erosion during Hurricane Georges (1998).

about 18 feet. More than 99 percent of the land area of the Keys is below the 100-year flood level, and 90 percent is below 5 feet in elevation. Before 1998, residents had been lulled into a false sense of security for many years because the Keys had not suffered a direct hit since Hurricanes Donna and Betsy ravaged the area in 1960 (fig. 7.24) and 1965, respectively. When Hurricane Georges, only a category 2 hurricane, delivered a blow to the Keys in 1998, causing widespread damage from storm surge and wave flooding, the danger once again became evident. At least 1,566 buildings were destroyed or damaged, and private and public beaches were moderately or severely eroded (fig. 7.25). Sand was transported across several islands. Two people were killed as a result of the storm. On Cudjoe Key, the tide was 5 to 6 feet above normal. Sandspur Beach on Bahia Honda Key, designated the "Best

RM 52   Bahia Honda Key, West Summerland Key, No Name Key

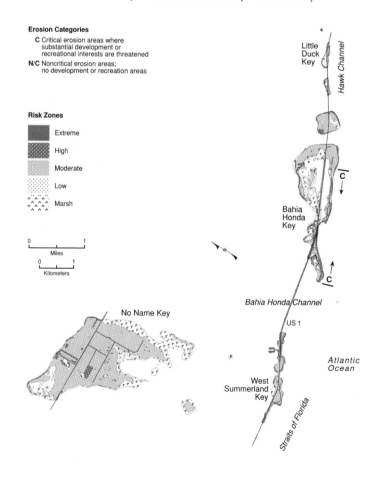

Beach in America" in 1992, sustained major beach and dune erosion. On Key West, South Beach was destroyed and all of the other beaches were damaged.

While the Keys were still repairing the damage from Georges, Hurricane Irene passed over Key West on October 15, 1999, with a peak wind gust of 103 mph measured on Big Pine Key. Peak storm tides were only just over 3 feet at Key West and Vaca Key, but substantial flooding and beach erosion occurred nevertheless.

Imagine the impact on today's overdeveloped Keys when future storms

RM 53   Big Pine Key and vicinity

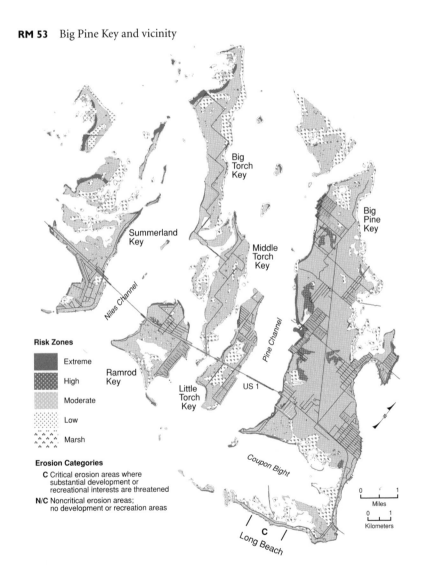

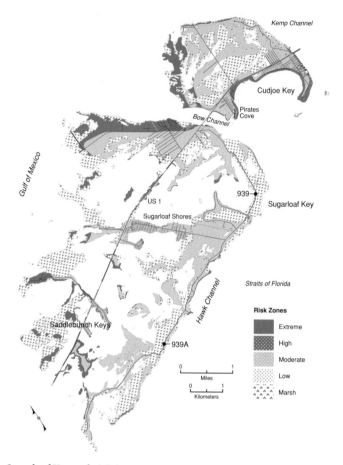

RM 54 Sugarloaf Key and vicinity

repeat the events of 1846 and 1935. In 1846, a hurricane destroyed Key West. Water was 5 feet deep in the main street, and survivors who clustered at the highest point in the area (only about 17 feet) were nearly washed away by waves. The worst storm by far ever to hit the Keys occurred on September 2, 1935, when a hurricane with sustained winds estimated at 200 mph struck, causing massive damage and killing 400 people, even though the strip of maximum devastation was only 40 miles wide. Some victims were decapitated by flying debris, others were impaled, and some were actually sandblasted to death. Incredible winds were followed by an 18-foot tidal wave that smashed houses and drowned occupants, scattering bodies everywhere. The article that describes this hurricane should be required reading for anyone living on the Keys, contemplating moving to the Keys, or even visiting there during the hurricane season (see appendix C, ref. 62). No one knows when such a storm will strike a coastline again—perhaps in this year's season, possibly in the next few years, and almost certainly within this century.

Many of the designated shelters listed for the Keys would be flooded in a category 5 hurricane, and some would be inundated by a Saffir-Simpson category 3 storm. A 1992 FEMA report states that "there will be no official shelters open in the Keys during a Category 3, 4, or 5 event." The implication is clear: in the event of any warning it is time to evacuate—unless that option has already expired.

A previously discussed study of hurricane evacuation risks points out a serious misconception among South Florida and Florida Keys residents. Some current residents believe they already have survived a significant hurricane, but most of those living in the Keys today are recent arrivals or are

RM 55 Boca Chica Key and vicinity

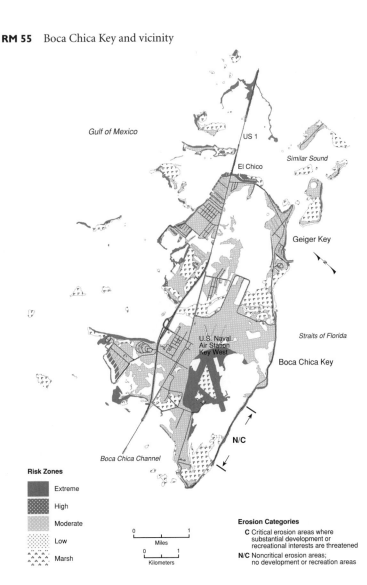

Risk Zones

- Extreme
- High
- Moderate
- Low
- Marsh

0   1
Miles

0   1
Kilometers

Erosion Categories

C Critical erosion areas where substantial development or recreational interests are threatened

N/C Noncritical erosion areas; no development or recreation areas

too young to have experienced the 1935 storm, and are not even aware of its consequences. Civil Defense and other officials involved with evacuation are understandably concerned that many people will not heed warnings until it is too late.

The entire length of the Florida Keys is at high risk for development. The reasons for this classification include storm frequency, low elevation and storm-surge flooding, wind damage potential, and erosion, but the principal risk is the extreme difficulty of evacuation. Perhaps a new, very large Fort Taylor should be designed and constructed to withstand a great hurricane—and designated as the storm refuge!

The Next Step

If, after prudent review of the coast, you are not discouraged and have selected the site for your dream home or prospective condominium, the next step is to consider structural mitigation. What are your choices in construction techniques and materials to build stormworthy housing or improve an existing residential structure?

RM 56   Key West, Fort Taylor

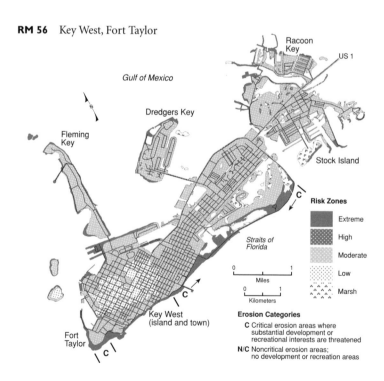

Risk Zones

- Extreme
- High
- Moderate
- Low
- Marsh

Erosion Categories

C Critical erosion areas where substantial development or recreational interests are threatened

N/C Noncritical erosion areas; no development or recreation areas

8   The Built Coast: Construction Guidelines

Low-risk sites are not a guarantee against property loss or damage in the coastal zone. Sound, storm-resistant construction is the last line of defense against wind, wave, and flood. Hurricane Andrew (1992) taught a hard lesson in regard to ignoring wind-resistant construction and contributed to Florida's insurance crisis in the 1990s. Hurricane Opal (1996) provided the complementary lesson of buildings' vulnerability to storm surge, waves, overwash, and flooding. These two great storms and associated impacts of Tropical Storms Alberto and Beryl (1992), the northeaster "Storm of the Century" (1993), and Hurricane Erin (1995) led to the reform of Florida's building codes with the passage of the statewide Florida Building Code in 2001 and its implementation in 2002. And the learning process continues. When you choose your house, the rule is: be aware of the construction, the materials, how the house is built, and the potential for retrofitting to improve stormworthiness.

Can We Learn from Past Experience?

Memories of hurricanes quickly fade, but coastal property owners in Florida would be foolish to ignore the problems that Andrew and Opal brought to light. Similarly, hurricanes in other areas (e.g., Fran, Hugo, Georges, Gilbert, and Iniki) have taught lessons that must be heeded as well. Posthurricane damage inspections have been very revealing and have led to useful recommendations (see appendix C, under "Coastal Construction").

Coastal Realty versus Coastal Reality

Buyer beware. Coastal property is not the same as inland property. The reality of the coast is its dynamic character. Property lines are an artificial grid superimposed on this dynamism. If you choose to place yourself or others in this zone, prudence is in order.

A quick glance at the architecture of the structures on our coast provides convincing evidence that the sea view and aesthetics were the primary considerations in their construction, not the reality of coastal processes. Except for meeting minimal building code requirements, no further thought seems to have been given to the safety of many of these buildings. Failure to follow a few basic architectural guidelines may have disastrous results when structures are required to stand up to major storms.

The Structure: Concept of Balanced Risk

A certain chance of failure exists for any structure built within the constraints of economy and environment. The objective of the building design is to create a structure that is economically feasible and functionally reliable with a reasonable life expectancy. To obtain such a house, a balance must be achieved among financial, structural, environmental, and other special conditions. These conditions are intensified on the coast: property values are higher, the environment is more sensitive, the likelihood of storm hazards is increased, and greater pressure to develop exists as more and more people want to move into the coastal zone.

Anyone who builds or buys a home in an exposed coastal area should fully comprehend the risks involved and the chance of harm to their home and family. The risks should then be weighed against the benefits. Similarly, the developer who is putting up a motel or apartment building should weigh the possibility of destruction and deaths during a hurricane against the advantages to be gained from such a building. Only with an understanding of the risks should construction proceed. For both the homeowner and the developer, proper construction and location reduce the risks.

The concept of balanced risk should take into account six fundamental considerations:

1. A coastal structure exposed to high winds, waves, or flooding should be stronger than a structure built inland.

2. A building with a planned long life, such as a year-round residence, should be stronger than a building with a planned short life, such as a mobile home.

3. A building with high occupancy, such as an apartment building, should be stronger than a building with a low occupancy, such as a single-family dwelling.

4. A building that houses elderly or sick people should be safer than a building housing able-bodied people.

5. Construction costs that incorporate a higher-than-usual margin of safety will be higher than the costs for an average home.

6. The risk of loss may make the project unfeasible.

Using the principles of structural engineering, structures can be designed and built to resist all but the largest storms and still be economical. These principles utilize an estimate of the forces to which the structures will be subjected as well as an understanding of the strength of building materials. The effectiveness of structural engineering design is reflected in the aftermath of each new hurricane: buildings not based on structural engineering principles suffer a much greater percentage of destruction and serious damage than structurally engineered buildings. The importance of building codes requiring standardized structural engineering for buildings in hurricane-prone areas is apparent.

Can We Rely on Building Codes?

That Florida has revised its building codes several times in recent history and that individual communities have implemented the codes' more stringent requirements reflect the fact that building codes represent minimum safety requirements. The 2001 Florida Building Code (appendix C, ref. 97), which went into effect in 2002, reduced some of the shortcomings of the earlier codes, but it is not the final word in building safety. The old Florida Building Codes Act required that each locality adopt one of the State Minimum Building Codes, which included codes such as the Standard Building Code and the South Florida Building Code in addition to the One- and Two-Family Dwelling Code for residential structures. In part to comply with the National Flood Insurance Program regulations, new codes such as the International Building Code 2000, the International Residential Code for One- and Two-Family Dwellings 2000, and the 2001 Florida Building Code were developed. These codes reflect the special needs of areas subject to hurricanes and coastal storms.

Check with local officials to identify construction requirements and the current code in use. Storms will demonstrate areas where the new code is inadequate, and changes will be introduced again in the future. Past failures have proven that pilings must be embedded deeper than called for in earlier codes and that cross-bracing between pilings is required to improve stability against wind. Minimum wind velocities for design also have been raised. In other words, older structures are often below the present code standards, and the code is only a minimum.

Coastal Forces: Design Requirements

Hurricane winds can be categorized in terms of the pressure they exert. The pressure varies with the square of the velocity of the wind. That is, doubling the velocity of the wind corresponds to increasing the pressure by a factor of four. A 50-mph wind exerts a pressure of about 10 psf (pounds per square foot) on a flat surface. A 100-mph wind would exert a pressure of 40 psf, and a 200-mph wind would exert a pressure of 160 psf.

You can estimate the wind force that can be expected to be applied to a flat wall of a house by multiplying the expected force times the exposed area of the side of the house receiving that force. If the wall facing the wind is 40 feet long and 16 feet high, the area of the wall is 640 square feet. A 100-mph wind exerts a force of about 40 psf. Thus the total force on the wall will be 640 feet x 40 pounds per foot = 25,600 pounds, or about 13 tons of force. A 200-mph wind would exert a force of more than 50 tons on the wall! The amount of force the wind exerts on a building can be modified by several factors, which must be considered in the building design (e.g., the pressure on a curved surface is less than the pressure on a flat surface). Also, wind velocities increase with the height above the ground, so a tall structure is subject to greater pressure than a low structure. The pressures presented above were computed for a structure with a height of 33 feet.

A house or building designed for inland areas is built primarily to resist vertical, and mostly downward, loads. Generally, builders assume that the foundation and framing must support the load of the walls, floor, and roof, and relatively insignificant horizontal wind forces. A well-built house in a hurricane-prone area, however, must be constructed to withstand a variety of strong wind and wave forces that may come from any direction. Although many people think wind damage is caused by uniform horizontal pressure, most of the damage is caused by uplift (vertical), suctional (pressure-differential), and torsional (twisting) forces. High horizontal pressure on the windward side is accompanied by suction on the leeward side. The roof is subject to downward pressure and, more important, to uplift (fig. 8.1). Often, roofs are sucked up by the uplift drag of the wind.

Houses usually fail because the devices that tie their parts together fail.

8.1 Wind-exerted pressures on a house.

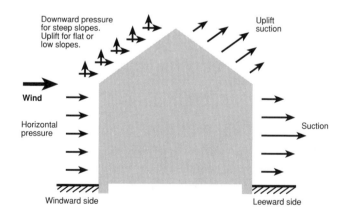

All structural members (beams, rafters, and columns) should be fastened together on the assumption that about 25 percent of the vertical load on each member may be a force coming from any direction (sideways or upward). Structural integrity is also important if it is likely that the building may be moved to avoid destruction by shoreline retreat. In a fanciful way, structural integrity means that you should be able to pick up a house, turn it upside down, and shake it without it falling apart.

Storm surge and the accompanying storm waves cause much of the property damage and loss of life. The offshore storm pushes water into the inlets and backwater areas already swollen from the exceptional rainfall brought by the hurricane. Islands sometimes are flooded from the bay side. This flooding is particularly dangerous when the wind pressure keeps the tide from running out of inlets, so that the next normal high tide pushes the accumulated waters back and higher still.

Proper coastal development takes into account the expected level and frequency of storm surge. Building standards require that the first habitable level of a dwelling be above the 100-year flood level, the level at which a building has a 1 percent probability of being flooded in any given year, plus the added height requirement due to expected waves.

Hurricane waves cause severe damage by forcing floodwaters onshore and by carrying boats, barges, piers, houses, and other floating debris inland and "ramrodding" it against standing structures. In addition, waves can cause coastal structures to collapse by scouring away the underlying sand. Buildings can be designed to survive crashing storm surf. Many lighthouses, for example, have survived hurricane waves. But in the balanced risk equation, it usually isn't economically feasible to build ordinary houses to withstand powerful wave forces. Houses can, however, be constructed to meet most of the challenges of the dynamic coastal environment.

The force of a wave may be understood by considering that a cubic yard of water weighs more than three-fourths of a ton. A breaking wave moving shoreward at a speed of 30 or 40 mph can be one of the most destructive elements of a hurricane. A 10-foot wave can exert more than 1,000 pounds of pressure per square foot, and wave pressures higher than 10,000 psf have been recorded. Figure 8.2 illustrates some of the actions a homeowner can take to deal with the forces just described.

Lessons from Previous Storms

According to the old South Florida Building Code, a structure should be able to withstand wind speeds of at least 120 mph at a height of 30 feet. During hurricane Andrew, a peak two-minute sustained wind speed of 141 mph was reported. The National Hurricane Center experienced peak wind gusts in excess of 160 mph at an elevation of 150 feet. So the first lesson is that

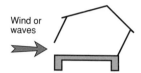

A. Lateral collapse
Remedy: Install bracing, such as diagonals and plywood sheets securely nailed to studs and floor plates. In masonry houses, use reinforcing.

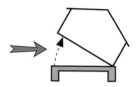

B. Overturning and lateral movement
Remedy: Anchor house to foundation.

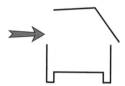

C. Loss of parts of house
Remedy: Install adequate connectors.

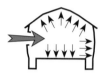

D. Higher pressure inside than out
Remedy: Put vents in attic to equalize pressure. Secure windows and doors before storms.

E. Penetration by flying or floating debris
Remedy: Construct walls and roof solidly. Use high-quality windows for greater strength.

8.2 Modes of failure and how to deal with them.

building codes represent an acceptable minimum standard, not the maximum forces to be dished out by nature!

Storm experience indicates that damage to utilities such as water, sewer, electricity, telephone, and cable TV can often be avoided by proper installation. Appendages to houses such as porches or decks, whose support columns tend not to be deeply embedded, are particularly vulnerable to damage or destruction. Problems with breakaway walls include the following: breakaway wall panels installed seaward of cross-bracing can damage the cross-bracing when they break away; utilities such as air conditioners installed on or next to breakaway panels can inhibit a clean breakaway, resulting in damage to the utilities; and sheathing, when installed so that the breakaway panels are connected to the foundation columns, can retard clean breakaway of the panels.

Many houses have a slab-on-grade floor for the breakaway area below the elevated structure. A solidly constructed slab (with wire mesh or without sufficient contraction joints) may not break into fragments small enough to avoid damaging the foundation system when waterborne.

Mobile homes, manufactured homes, and permanently installed RVs are particularly vulnerable to coastal hazards. The usual installation system of concrete-block foundations and metal tie-down straps with anchors to the ground performs poorly. Scour undermines the blocks, while the corrosion-weakened straps often fail, and the anchors are often pulled out.

The National Flood Insurance Program

The National Flood Insurance Program's (NFIP) Flood Insurance Rate Maps (FIRMS) available for Florida communities in the 1990s led to a false sense of security. The buildings that suffered the greatest damage in Hurricane Andrew conformed to the FIRM specifications. The storm surge was a full 50 percent higher than the base flood elevation (BFE) specified on the FIRM. The first floor of many buildings sustained significant damage. In fact, the FEMA *Coastal Construction Manual* recommends exceeding the NFIP requirements. So it is important to examine the FIRM to determine the vulnerability of your chosen locality.

Construction Type

Building materials and construction methods determine a structure's vulnerability to storm damage. Single-family homes typically are built of wood, masonry, or a combination of wood and masonry. Newer structures are elevated on wooden pilings or cinder-block footings. Generally speaking, the older the structure, the less elevated it is likely to be.

When cinder-block houses in West Florida failed during Opal, they broke into small pieces that were tossed about and caused damage to other structures through missiling and ramrodding. Inadequately elevated houses were knocked off their foundations and carried some distance from their original locations, and in the process collided with other houses.

House Selection

Some types of houses are better suited than others for the shore, and an awareness of the differences will help you make a better selection, whether you are building a new house or buying an existing one.

Poorest of all are unreinforced masonry houses, whether they are brick, concrete block, hollow clay tile, or brick veneer, because they cannot withstand the lateral forces of wind and waves and the settling of a foundation. Extraordinary reinforcing, such as concrete-block stucco reinforced with tie beams and columns, will alleviate some of the inherent weaknesses of unit masonry, if done properly. Reinforced masonry performed well in Hurricane Andrew. Reinforced concrete and steel frames are excellent but are rarely used in the construction of small residential structures. Reinforced concrete construction typically is not considered aesthetically or economically appealing in the United States, although it is used in Florida, Hawaii, and Puerto Rico.

It is hard to beat a wood frame or concrete house that is constructed properly, with bracing and connections for the roof, wall, and floor components, as well as anchors for the foundation. A well-built wood house will hold together as a unit even after it is moved off its foundation, when other types of structures disintegrate.

Strengthening the Exterior Envelope

The term *building envelope* refers to the entire system by which the building resists wind penetration. A breach in the envelope occurs when an exterior enclosure fails, as when the garage door or a window is open. When this happens during a strong wind, pressure may build up inside the structure and roof uplift or wall suction may occur, leading to the failure of the entire system (figs. 8.2 and 8.3). The most susceptible parts of the house are the windows, garage doors, and double entry doors.

8.3 Building envelope breach due to failure of external doors or windows. From *Building Performance: Hurricane Andrew in Florida* (appendix C, ref. 83).

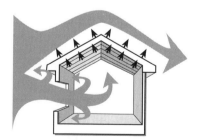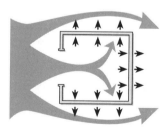

Wind pressure on roof.
Internal pressure adds to roof uplift.

Wind pressure on walls.
Internal pressure adds to wall suction.

Doors

All doors in a home—especially garage doors and double entry doors—should be certified by the seller as to their strength under a given design wind load. The strength must be adequate to prevent damage from projectiles or flying objects such as tree limbs. To upgrade existing doors, a dead bolt added to the locking system can be used for reinforcement. The dead-bolt will act as an additional rigid connection to the house frame. If the house has a double entry door, one door should be fixed at the top and bottom with pins or bolts. In most cases, the original pins are not strong enough to resist heavy wind forces. Homeowners should consider installing heavy-duty bolts.

Garage doors also pose a risk to the building envelope, failing because of inadequate thickness, and tending to bend when subjected to strong winds. Double-wide or two-car garage doors are especially susceptible to high winds. When purchasing a new garage door, check the manufacturer's certification of its strength to verify the adequacy of the system. Retrofit existing garage doors by installing horizontal girts on each panel. A temporary strategy to reinforce a garage door during a windstorm is to back your car up against the inside of the door, providing extra support against bending. To prevent the garage door from falling off its tracks during high winds, strengthen the track supports and glider tracks. The rotation of the door along its edges can be reduced by chaining the door pin to the glider track connections.

Windows

All windows, including skylights, sliding glass doors, and French doors, must be protected from projectiles that could penetrate the building envelope. Protect windows by using storm shutters or precut plywood that is screwed to the outside of the window frame (fig. 8.4). Strong windows are important in protecting the structure against high winds. Pay close attention to manufacturers' specifications of wind resistance for shutters and windows. All windows and doors should be anchored to the wall frame to prevent them from being pulled out of the building. After missile impacts, this is the second most common mode of failure of the building envelope.

Structural Integrity

Building Shape

A hip roof, which slopes in four directions, resists high winds better than a gable roof, which slopes in two directions (fig. 8.5). The reason is twofold:

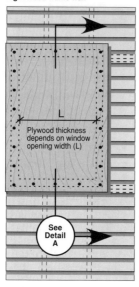

Light wood-frame wall

Plywood thickness depends on window opening width (L)

See Detail A

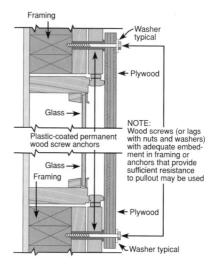

Framing

Washer typical

Plywood

Glass →

Plastic-coated permanent wood screw anchors

NOTE: Wood screws (or lags with nuts and washers) with adequate embedment in framing or anchors that provide sufficient resistance to pullout may be used

Glass →
Framing

Plywood

Washer typical

Detail A : Typical attachment of plywood over openings to add protection to wood-frame building

8.4 Typical installation of plywood over openings of wood-frame building. From *Building Performance: Hurricane Andrew in Florida* (appendix C, ref. 83), which also shows how to install plywood to masonry building.

the hip roof offers a smaller surface for the wind to blow against, and its structure provides better bracing in all directions.

The horizontal cross section of the house (the shape of the house as viewed from above) can affect the wind force exerted on the structure. The wind pressure exerted on a round or elliptical shape is about 60 percent of that exerted on a square or rectangular shape; the pressure exerted on a hexagonal or octagonal cross section is about 80 percent of that exerted on a square or rectangular cross section (fig. 8.5).

The design of a coastal building should minimize structural discontinuities and irregularities. Minimize exterior nooks, crannies, and offsets because damage to a structure tends to concentrate at these points. Award-winning architecture will be a storm loser if the design has not incorporated the technology for maximizing structural integrity with respect to storm forces. A house without irregularities reacts to storm winds as a complete unit (fig. 8.5).

Roofs

When a roof fails, either by losing its shingles or by flying off the house, it spells disaster for the rest of the house and its contents. In high-wind areas, roof failure is often due to inadequate tie-downs of roof framing and poor

Hip roof

Gable roof

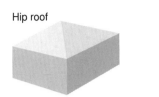
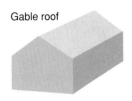

Hip roof is better than gable roof.

Wind has less effect on curved surfaces than on flat surfaces.

Avoid irregular shapes.
Keep it simple so it will act as a unit.

8.5 The influence of building and roof shape on wind resistance.

connections of the roof to the wall components. Poorly attached roof sheathing or poorly placed asphalt-on-roof shingles also cause roof failure.

To protect the contents of your home, judiciously select and adequately attach its roof covering. Shingles can be rated by the manufacturer and recommended as satisfactory for high-wind areas. Metal is the least acceptable of all roof coverings. Asphalt shingles tend to perform poorly because poor fastening techniques are often used. If your roof is covered with metal or asphalt, it might be wise to change to wood shingles, which have a history of performing well in high-wind areas. Look around the neighborhood: what has worked in the past? Consult the building code.

Galvanized nails (two per shingle) should be used to connect wood shingles and shakes to wood sheathing, and they should be long enough to penetrate through the sheathing. Threaded nails should be used for plywood sheathing. For roof slopes that rise 1 foot for every 3 feet or more of horizontal distance, exposure of the shingle should be about one-fourth of its length (4 inches for a 16-inch shingle). If shakes (thicker and longer than shingles) are used, less than one-third of their length should be exposed. If asphalt shingles are used in hurricane-prone areas, they should be exposed somewhat less than usual. Use a mastic or seal-tab type, or an interlocking heavy-grade shingle, along with a roof underlay of asphalt-saturated felt

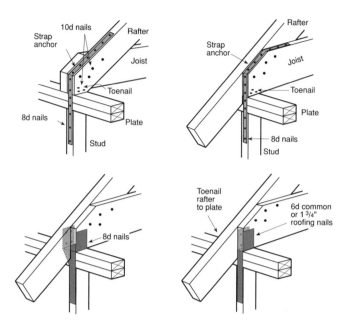

8.6 Roof-to-wall connectors. (Top) Metal strip connectors: (left) rafter to stud; (right) joist to stud. (Bottom left) Double-member metal plate connector, in this case with the joist to the right of the rafter. (Bottom right) A single-member metal plate connector.

and galvanized roofing nails or approved staples (six for each three-tab strip).

As indicated in figure 8.5, the shape of the roof is an important consideration. Aerodynamic building shapes are advantageous (e.g., when feasible, use a low-angled hip roof rather than a steep-angled gable-end or clerestory roof).

Roof trusses must be strong enough to withstand design wind loads. Structural rigidity can be obtained by using bracing and connectors (fig. 8.6 in general, and figs. 8.7 and 8.8 for hip roof framing). Secondary bracing within the truss system can help the roof resist lateral wind forces. Substituting hip roofs for gable roofs is an inherent method of bracing. Retrofitting gable roofs may be necessary to strengthen them. In addition to strengthening the trusses, the overhang must be considered. Overhangs should extend only the distance required for proper drainage; larger overhangs promote roof failure. Finally, roof venting is necessary to relieve internal pressures. The venting must exclude the entry of any uncontrolled air flow, which could result in a buildup of internal air pressure (fig. 8.2).

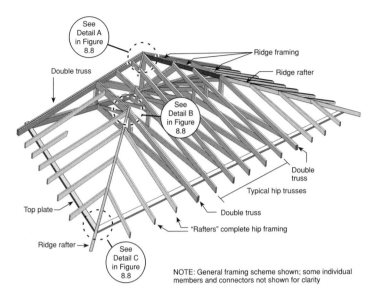

8.7 Recommended hip roof framing. From *Building Performance: Hurricane Andrew in Florida* (appendix C, ref. 83).

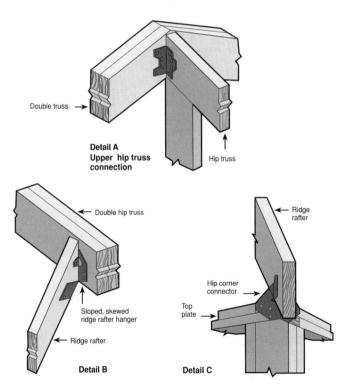

8.8 Hip roof framing connectors. Adapted from *Building Performance: Hurricane Iniki in Hawaii*, FEMA-FIA-23, 1993.

A continuous load-transfer path is needed if a house is to remain structurally intact under extreme loads (fig. 8.9). Everything must be connected to the foundation. Use fasteners and connectors at all the joints. In high-wind areas, these connectors are commonly called hurricane straps if they hold the roof to the walls (fig. 8.10), and tie-downs or anchor bolts if they hold the house to the foundation (figs. 8.11 and 8.12). High winds cause uplift and lateral forces on the girders, trusses, and beams of the structure. Proper connectors can transfer the load away from these vulnerable areas, reducing the potential for structural damage and perhaps even saving the house. During windstorms, wood structures reinforced with metal connectors perform better than unreinforced structures.

A shear wall is an important addition to help a house resist lateral loads. Plywood is an excellent shear wall when nailed to the building frame accurately and completely. The larger the nails and the closer together they are, the better the plywood will perform as a shear wall. The use of nail guns during construction, which do not allow the carpenter to sense whether or

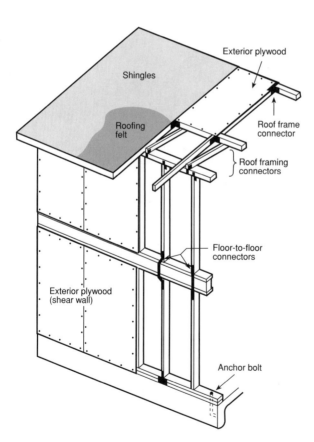

8.9 Recommended wood-frame construction. Continuous load path. Adapted from figures in *Building Performance: Hurricane Andrew in Florida* (appendix C, ref. 83).

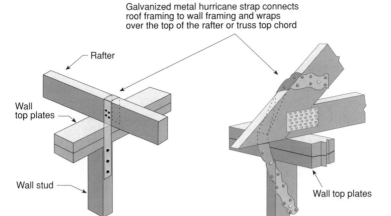

Galvanized metal hurricane strap connects roof framing to wall framing and wraps over the top of the rafter or truss top chord

Rafter

Wall top plates

Wall stud

Wall top plates

8.10 Typical hurricane strap-to-roof framing detail for rafter or prefabricated roof truss. From *Building Performance: Hurricane Andrew in Florida* (appendix C, ref. 83).

not nails are going into the framing, sometimes results in whole rows of nails that miss the framing. When inspecting, make sure the plywood is attached at all levels of the building.

A multistory house must have floor-to-floor connectors to transfer the load path correctly. The first floor should be connected to the second floor with either nailed ties or bolted hold-downs to transfer the uplift forces from the upper stud to the lower stud. In addition, all houses must have connectors in the rafters and trusses. The load-transfer path must include a tie-down to the foundation of the building; generally the house frame is attached to the concrete foundation by metal rods. Have a professional check the foundation of an existing house for termite infestation and dry-rot damage and to make sure it is compatible with the planned tie-down system. Remember, if any component of the house is not connected, the whole house could fail.

Keeping Dry: Pole or "Stilt" Houses

In coastal regions subject to flooding, the best and most common method of minimizing damage is to raise the lowest floor above the expected highest water level. The first habitable floor of a house must be above a prescribed level to comply with regulations. Most modern structures built in flood zones are constructed on pilings that are well anchored in the subsoil. Elevating the structure by placing it on top of a mound is not suitable in coastal zones because mounded soil is easily eroded. Construction on piles or columns is a required design criterion for pole house construction under

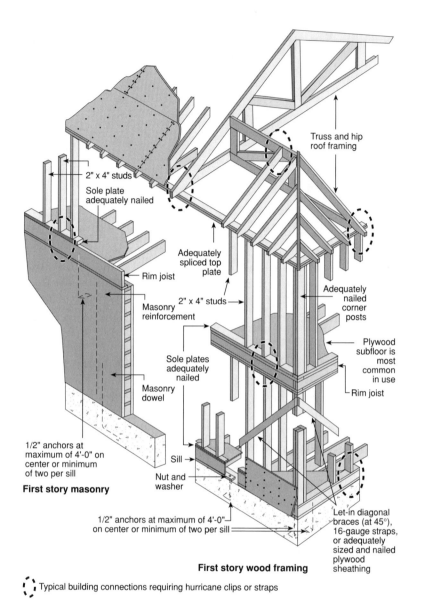

Truss and hip roof framing

2" x 4" studs

Sole plate adequately nailed

Rim joist

Adequately spliced top plate

2" x 4" studs

Masonry reinforcement

Adequately nailed corner posts

Plywood subfloor is most common in use

Sole plates adequately nailed

Masonry dowel

Rim joist

1/2" anchors at maximum of 4'-0" on center or minimum of two per sill

First story masonry

Sill

Nut and washer

1/2" anchors at maximum of 4'-0" on center or minimum of two per sill

Let-in diagonal braces (at 45°), 16-gauge straps, or adequately sized and nailed plywood sheathing

First story wood framing

Typical building connections requiring hurricane clips or straps

8.11 Primary wood framing systems: walls, roof diaphragm, and floor diaphragm. From *Building Performance: Hurricane Andrew in Florida* (appendix C, ref. 83).

the National Flood Insurance Program. Pole-type construction with deeply embedded poles is best in areas where waves and storm surge will erode foundation material. The materials used in pole construction include piles, posts, and piers, but all three are called "poles." Piles and posts are also often referred to as "piling."

Pole construction can be of two types. First, the poles can be cut off at the

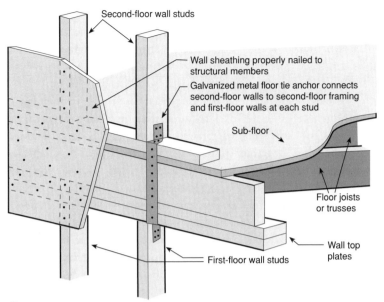

Second-floor wall studs

Wall sheathing properly nailed to
structural members

Galvanized metal floor tie anchor connects
second-floor walls to second-floor framing
and first-floor walls at each stud

Sub-floor

Floor joists
or trusses

Wall top
plates

First-floor wall studs

Note:
1. Horizontal sheathing joints should be minimized along second-floor line.
2. Straps should be sized appropriately for each building, i.e., maximum allowable uplift load resistance may
   vary from 300 lbs. to 950 lbs., for 20-gauge to 16-gauge thickness, respectively.

8.12 Upper-floor tie to lower floor for two-story buildings. From *Building Performance: Hurricane Andrew in Florida* (appendix C, ref. 83).

first floor to support the platform that serves as the dwelling floor. In this case, piles, posts, or piers can be used. Second, the poles can be extended to the roof and rigidly tied into both the floor and the roof, thus becoming major framing members for the structure and providing better anchorage for the house as a whole (fig. 8.13). Sometimes both full-height and floor-height poles are used, with the shorter poles restricted to supporting the floor inside the house (fig. 8.13).

Piling Embedment

Erosion and scour can be devastating to coastal piling foundations. The loss of soil around a slender vertical member can have several deleterious effects. First, the unsupported length of the member is increased, resulting in more deflection or instability of that member. Second, there is less soil to oppose applied lateral piling loads, including the flow of the storm surge, wave forces, debris impact, and even the load of the building itself. Third, there is less friction surface to transfer loads between the piling and the ground, and hence less resistance to uplifting by the wind. The goal in coastal foundation design is to withstand the 100-year flood and long-term erosion.

Coastal buildings must be elevated so that water can pass underneath them. Buildings placed in coastal high-hazard areas—that is, the v zones and coastal A zones on the National Flood Insurance Program FIRMS—must be constructed so that the lowest floor is at or above the base flood elevation (BFE). No obstructions are allowed below the buildings.

Cross-bracing below elevated buildings can be an obstruction that is counterproductive in terms of structural strength. Piling foundations should be designed to avoid cross-bracing by using thicker, longer pilings; placing pilings closer together; or utilizing an unroofed deck that increases the building footprint. If cross-bracing is necessary, design it to be adequate for possible wind and water loads, and use as little as possible, especially where the cross-bracing might be perpendicular to wave and debris forces.

Solid-perimeter masonry foundation walls, which are supported on a continuous footing, are not acceptable in v zones. Away from high-hazard areas such walls should be viewed with caution and, at a minimum, should be professionally designed. Walls are susceptible to scour on both seaward and landward faces.

8.13 Tying floors to poles. Supplied by the Southern Pine Association.

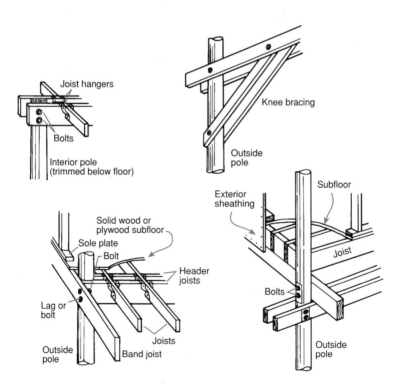

Connection of Pilings to the Floor and Roof

The floor and roof should be securely connected to the poles with bolts or other fasteners. Connections are especially important if the floor rests on poles that do not extend to the roof. Metal straps are commonly used fasteners. Another method is to attach beams to piles with at least two bolts of adequate size. Unfortunately, builders sometimes simply attach the floor beams to a notched pole with one or two bolts. Hurricanes have proven this method to be unacceptable. During the next Florida hurricane, many houses will be destroyed because of inadequate attachments.

Building codes may specify the size, quantity, and spacing of the piles, ties, and bracing, as well as the methods of fastening the structure to them. Again, these are minimal requirements; however, building inspectors are usually amenable to allowing designs that are equally or more effective.

Breakaway Walls below Elevated Buildings

The space under an elevated house must be kept free of obstructions in order to minimize the impact of waves and floating debris. If walls are constructed below elevated buildings, they should be made of panels that break away when loaded by flood forces. That is, breakaway wall panels should be installed to successfully withstand wind loads but break away under flood loads. The exterior wall sheathing should not extend over the foundation posts, should not be placed immediately seaward of cross-bracing, and should be "weakly" attached to the permanent structure.

Concrete Slabs below Elevated Buildings

Slabs below elevated buildings should be designed so as not to harm the building foundation when subjected to flood forces. These slabs should be no thicker than 4 inches, should be frangible so that they can break into relatively small pieces, and should not have reinforcing wire mesh extending through the joints which prevents the slab from breaking into pieces. The slab should not be connected to the vertical foundation members, especially if the soil is liable to be affected by erosion and scour.

Utility Systems

On-site utilities, such as air-conditioner/heat pump compressors, electrical meters, and septic systems, must be installed carefully. The local or state health department will have regulations that control the installation of septic systems. Like the building they serve, compressors must be elevated on a platform that is at or above the level of the BFE. Make sure utilities do not interfere with breakaway panels and are not placed adjacent to vertical foundation members. Service connections, including sewer and water risers, should be located on the landward side of the most landward foundation posts.

Dry Flood-Proofing

NFIP regulations do not permit construction of walls that are impervious to the passage of floodwaters—referred to as "dry flood-proofing"—in coastal high-hazard areas. However, regulations do allow dry flood-proofing of nonresidential buildings in lower-risk areas.

An Existing House: What to Look for, Where to Improve

When considering an existing house in an area subject to storm surge, waves, flooding, and high winds, consider the following factors: (1) where the house is located (2) how well the house is built, and (3) how the house can be improved.

Location

Evaluate the site of an existing house using the same principles you would use to evaluate a building site. The elevation of the house, frequency of high water, escape route, and lot drainage should be emphasized, but you should go through the complete 14-point site-safety checklist given in chapter 6 (also see table 6.1).

The house can be modified after purchase, but hurricanes and northeasters cannot be prevented. First, stop and consider: Do the pleasures and benefits of this location balance the risks and disadvantages? If they do not, look elsewhere for a home; if yes, then proceed to evaluate the house itself.

How Well Built Is the House?

In general, the principles used to evaluate an existing house are the same as those used in building a new one. Remember that many houses were built prior to the enactment of improved standards that have increased the hurricane-worthiness of newer buildings. Also, building codes are generally updated after devastating storms. Thus, a house built after Andrew or Opal, or after 2001 will meet stricter hurricane standards than one built before. In the case of an older house, it is up to the buyer to have someone check for deficiencies.

Before thoroughly inspecting the house, look closely at the adjacent buildings. If poorly built, they may float against your house and damage it in a flood. Consider the type of people you will have as neighbors: Will they "clear the decks" in preparation for a storm, or will they leave items in the yard to become windborne missiles? During Hurricane Andrew, accessory structures such as sheds, carports, porches, and pool enclosures contributed to the windborne debris. The house itself should be inspected for the following features.

The house should be well anchored to the ground, and the walls well anchored to the foundation. If the house is simply resting on blocks, rising water may cause it to float off its foundation and come to rest against a neighbor's house or out in the middle of the street. If the house is well built and well braced internally, it may be possible to move it back to its proper location, but chances are great that the house will be too damaged to be habitable.

If the house is on piles, posts, or poles, make sure that the floor beams are adequately bolted to them. If the house rests on piers, crawl under it, if space permits, and see if the floor beams are securely connected to the foundation. If the floor system rests unanchored on piers, do not buy the house.

Whether or not a house built on a concrete slab is properly bolted to the slab is difficult to discern because the inside and outside walls hide the bolts. If you can locate the builder, ask if such bolting was done. Better yet, if you can get assurance that construction of the house complied with the provisions of a building code serving the needs of that particular region, you can be reasonably sure that all parts of the house are well anchored: the foundation to the ground, the floor to the foundation, the walls to the floor, and the roof to the walls.

The roof should be well anchored to the walls to prevent uplifting and separation from the walls. Visit the attic to see if such anchoring exists. Simple toe-nailing (nailing at an angle) is not adequate; metal fasteners are needed. Depending on the type of construction and the amount of insulation laid on the floor of the attic, these connections may or may not be easy to see. If roof trusses or braced rafters were used, you should be able to see whether the various members, such as the diagonals, are well fastened together. Again, simple toe-nailing will not suffice. A collar beam or gusset at the peak of the roof (fig. 8.14) provides some assurance of good construction.

Good-quality roofing material should be well anchored to the sheathing. A poor roof covering will be destroyed by hurricane-force winds, allowing rain to enter the house and damage the ceilings, walls, and contents.

With regard to framing, the fundamental rule is that all the structural elements should be fastened together and anchored to the ground in such a manner as to resist all forces, regardless of the direction from which they come. This prevents overturning, floating off, racking, or disintegration.

Masonry-walled houses merit special attention. Some architects and

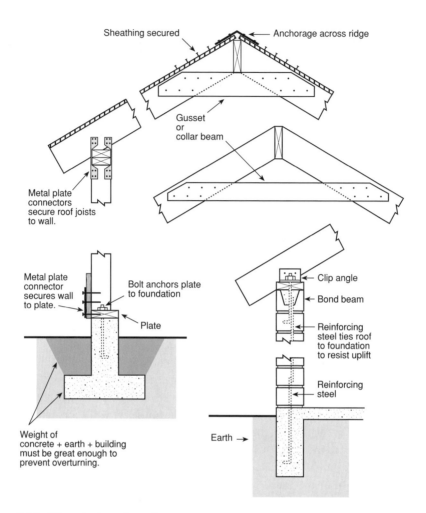

8.14 Where to strengthen a house.

builders use a stacked bond (one block directly above another) rather than overlapped or staggered blocks because they believe it looks better. The stacked bond is definitely weaker than overlapped or staggered blocks. Unless you have proof that the walls are adequately reinforced to overcome this lack of strength, avoid this type of construction. Some masonry-walled buildings have completely collapsed in hurricanes, resembling the flattened buildings associated with earthquakes.

In hurricanes, brick veneer walls tend to separate from the wood frame, even when the house remains standing. Gypsum-board cladding (covered with insulation and stucco) also performs very poorly, typically suffering wind damage and removal. Such cladding should not be used on any building more than 30 feet tall along the coast of Florida.

Windows and large glass areas should be protected, especially those that face the ocean. Many newer coastal houses have large areas of glazing. Windows and doors can fail when subjected to positive pressures and suction, and often are the weak link in the integrity of a structure. Objects thrown through a window during a storm cause dangerous flying glass and weaken the building's structural resistance. Windblown sand can very quickly frost a window and thereby destroy its aesthetic value. Both of these problems can be avoided if the house has storm shutters. Check to see that they are present and functional.

Consult a good architect or structural engineer for advice if you are in doubt about any aspect of the house. A few dollars spent early for wise counsel may save you from later financial grief.

To summarize, a beach house should have the following:

1. Roof tied to wall, walls tied to foundation, and foundation anchored to the earth (the connections are potentially the weakest link in the structural system)

2. A shape that resists storm forces

3. Shutters for all windows, but especially those facing the ocean

4. Floors sufficiently elevated to be above most storm waters (usually the 100-year still-water flood level plus 3 to 8 feet to account for wave height)

5. Piles of sufficient depth or posts embedded in concrete to anchor the structure and withstand erosion

6. Well-braced pilings

What Can Be Done to Improve an Existing House?

The structural integrity of any house can be improved. Suppose the house is resting on blocks but not fastened to them, and thus is not adequately anchored to the ground. Can anything be done? One solution is to treat the house like a mobile home and screw anchors into the ground, then fasten them to the underside of the floor systems. Figures 8.15 and 8.16 illustrate how ground anchors can be used. The number of ground anchors will be different for houses and mobile homes, because each is affected differently by the forces of wind and water. Recent practice is to put these commercial steel-rod anchors in at an angle in order to align them better with the direction of the pull. If a vertical anchor is used, the top 18 inches or so should be encased in a concrete cylinder about 12 inches in diameter. This prevents the top of the anchor rod from bending or slicing through the wet soil from the horizontal component of the pull.

Diagonal struts, either timber or pipe, may also be used to anchor a house that rests on blocks. The upper ends of the struts are fastened to the floor system, and the lower ends to individual concrete footings substantially below the surface of the ground. These struts must be able to take both tension and compression, and should be tied into the concrete footing with anchoring devices such as straps or spikes.

If the house has a porch with exposed columns or posts, install tie-down anchors on their tops and bottoms. Steel straps should suffice in most cases.

When accessible, roof rafters and trusses should be anchored to the wall system. Usually, the roof trusses or braced rafters are sufficiently exposed to make it possible to strengthen joints (where two or more members meet) with collar beams or gussets, particularly at the peak of the roof (fig. 8.14).

A competent carpenter, architect, or structural engineer can review the house with you and help you decide what modifications are most practical and effective. The Standard Building Code says: "lateral support securely

8.15 Tie-downs for mobile homes. From *Protecting Mobile Homes from High Winds* (appendix C, ref. 101).

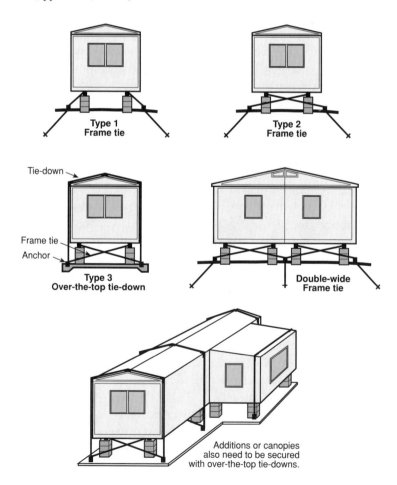

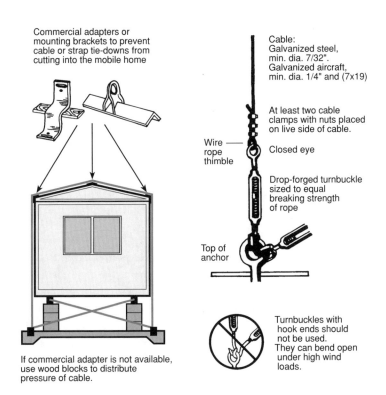

Commercial adapters or mounting brackets to prevent cable or strap tie-downs from cutting into the mobile home

Cable:
Galvanized steel, min. dia. 7/32".
Galvanized aircraft, min. dia. 1/4" and (7x19)

At least two cable clamps with nuts placed on live side of cable.

Wire rope thimble

Closed eye

Drop-forged turnbuckle sized to equal breaking strength of rope

Top of anchor

If commercial adapter is not available, use wood blocks to distribute pressure of cable.

Turnbuckles with hook ends should not be used. They can bend open under high wind loads.

8.16 Hardware for mobile home tie-downs. Modified from *Protecting Mobile Homes from High Winds* (appendix C, ref. 101).

anchored to all walls provides the best and only sound structural stability against horizontal thrusts, such as winds of exceptional velocity." The cost of connecting all of the elements securely adds very little to the cost of the frame of the dwelling, usually less than 10 percent, and a very much smaller percentage to the total cost of the house.

If the house has an overhanging eave and there are no openings on its underside, it may be feasible to cut openings and screen them. These openings keep the attic cooler (a plus in the summer) and may help to equalize the pressure inside and outside the house during a storm with a low-pressure center.

A house also can be improved by modifying a room to be used as an emergency refuge in case you are trapped in a major storm. Note that this precaution is not an alternative to evacuation before a hurricane! The best refuge room is a small, windowless room such as a bathroom, utility room, den, or storage space; such a room is usually stronger than a room with windows. A sturdy inner room with more than one wall between it and the outside is safest. The fewer doors, the better; an adjoining wall or baffle wall shielding the door adds protection.

Consider bracing or strengthening the interior walls. This may require removing the surface covering and installing plywood sheathing or strap bracing. Where wall studs are exposed, bracing straps offer a simple way to achieve needed reinforcement against the winds. These straps are commercially produced and are made of 16-gauge galvanized metal with pre-punched holes for nailing. These should be secured to studs and wall plates as nail holes permit (figs. 8.6 and 8.9).

If you agree that something should be done to your house, do it now. Do not put off the work until the next hurricane or northeaster is about to hit you!

Mobile Homes: Limiting Their Mobility

Their light weight and flat sides make mobile homes exceptionally vulnerable to high winds. High winds overturn unanchored mobile homes or smash them into neighboring homes and property. Nearly 5,000 mobile homes are damaged or destroyed by wind every year. Mobile homes suffered complete destruction during Hugo (1989) in areas where wind gusts exceeded 100 miles per hour. An analysis of mobile homes after Hurricane Andrew (1992) showed that, in general, conventional residences suffered less damage than all types of manufactured homes, including mobile homes. Manufactured homes built using stricter construction standards fared better than those built before the standards were created.

Mobile homes should be properly located. Locating a mobile home in a hilltop park greatly increases its vulnerability to the wind. A lower site screened by trees is safer from the wind, but the elevation should be above storm-surge flood levels. Fewer low-risk locations exist for mobile homes than for stilt houses.

A second lesson taught by past experience is that the mobile home must be tied down or anchored to the ground to avoid overturning in high winds (figs. 8.15 and 8.16). Simple prudence dictates the use of tie-downs, which are required by most community ordinances. A mobile home may be tied down with cable, rope, or built-in straps; or it may be rigidly attached to the ground by connecting it to a simple wood-post foundation system. A mobile home should be properly anchored with both ties to the frame and over-the-top straps; otherwise, it may be damaged by sliding, overturning, or tossing. The most common cause of major damage is the tearing away of most or all of the roof. When this happens, the walls are no longer adequately supported and are likely to collapse. Total destruction is more likely if the roof blows off, especially if the roof blows off first and then the home overturns. The necessity for anchoring cannot be overemphasized: mobile homes need both over-the-top tie-downs to resist overturning and frame ties to resist sliding off the pier foundations. A study of tie-down systems after Hurricane Andrew reached the distressing conclusion that most anchoring systems are inadequate. In particular, anchors tended to pull out at force levels below values recommended by the standards.

Hurricanes Fran and Georges proved that corrosion-weakened straps are vulnerable to relatively small tensile loads. Straps can be weakened in a few (less than 6) years if they are exposed to salt spray and are not frequently cleansed by rainfall. Anchor pullout appeared to be related to the saturation of the sand during flooding; the saturated soil could not resist the pullout of the anchors with small-diameter, shallowly embedded helical augers.

Hurricane experience also suggests that foundations should exceed the anticipated scour depths by at least 1 foot. If significant flow is possible in a region without highly dense sand, anchors should be at least 4 feet long and 0.75 inch in diameter, with helical plates at least 6 inches in diameter.

There remains a question as to the proper angle at which an anchor should be set. To limit possible horizontal displacements, place anchors at an angle so that they are more in line with the direction of pull. Anchors are sometimes set at angles *not* in the direction of the pull, either because the anchor is tucked behind the skirt that is placed around the base of the mobile home or the soil is such that the anchor cannot be properly set.

High-Rise and Medium-Rise Buildings: The Urban Shore

Any multistory building you see on the beach was probably designed by a qualified architect and a structural engineer who were aware of the requirements for buildings on the shoreline. Still, tenants should not assume such a building is invulnerable to storms. Despite the assurances that come with an engineered structure, life in a high-rise has definite drawbacks that stem from high winds, high water, and potentially poor foundations. In addition, fire is particularly hazardous in high-rises.

Pressure from the wind is greater near the shore than it is inland, and it increases with height. If you are living inland in a two-story house and plan to move to the eleventh floor of a high-rise on the shore, you should expect five times more wind pressure than you are accustomed to. High wind pressure can actually cause unpleasant motion of the building. Before you buy, check with current residents of the high-rise to find out if it has undesirable motion characteristics. A more serious problem is that high winds can break windows and cause other damage that results in injury. Tenants of severely damaged buildings must relocate until repairs are made, typically for longer periods than would be required for single-family dwelling repairs.

If you own a condominium, you should encourage your homeowners' association to have the building inspected. The inspector should be a qualified engineer with experience in coastal construction codes and knowledge of water and wind loading. The inspector should be able to propose corrective retrofits to improve the safety of the building.

Modular Unit Construction: Prefabricating the Urban Shore

The method of building a house, duplex, or larger condominium structure by fabricating modular units in a shop and assembling them at the building site is common in shoreline developments. The largest prefabricated structures are commonly two to three stories tall and may contain a large number of living units.

If the manufacturer desires it, shop fabrication can permit a high-quality product. Inspection and control of the whole construction process are much easier in the shop. For instance, there is less hesitation about rejecting a poor piece of lumber when a good supply is nearby than when there is only just the right amount of lumber available on the building site. On the other hand, because so much of the work is done out of the sight of the buyer, the manufacturer has the opportunity to take shortcuts if so inclined. Again, buyer beware; carry out your own inspection.

Approach the acquisition of a modular unit with the same caution you would use for other structures. If you are contemplating purchasing a modular dwelling unit, you are well advised to take the following steps:

1. Check the reputation and integrity of the developer and manufacturer.
2. Check to see if the developer has a state contractor's license.
3. Check the state law to find out who is required to approve and to certify the building.
4. Check that building codes are enforced.
5. Check to make sure the state fire marshal's office has indicated that the dwelling units comply with all applicable codes. Also check to see if this office makes periodic inspections.
6. Check to see that smoke alarms have been installed, that windows are the type that can be opened, that the bathroom has an exhaust fan, and that the kitchen has a vent through the roof.

As with all other types of structures, also consider site safety and escape route(s) for the location.

What Should Be Done to Protect Property along the East Florida Coast?

The public's growing desire for less "big government" and less regulation has left coastal property more and more vulnerable—not just to natural hazards, but also to minimal or poorly enforced building codes; to construction cost reduction through the use of low-quality materials that at best meet minimum code requirements; and to rushed construction and use of unsupervised and inexperienced labor, which leads to poor-quality workmanship or, even worse, to shortcuts that render buildings unsafe. The adage "Buyer beware!" goes double for coastal property. After Hurricane Georges (1998), some of FEMA's suggestions for both coastal and inland houses included the following:

Relocate or elevate water heaters, heating systems, washers, and dryers to a higher floor or at least 12 inches above the expected high-water level.

Anchor fuel tanks to walls with noncorrosive metal straps and lag bolts, preferably elevated as above.

Install a floating floor-drain plug at the lowest point of the lowest finished floor (again to prevent backup of sewage and flood water).

Elevate or relocate electrical boxes to a higher floor or at least 12 inches above the high-water mark.

Coastal property owners and residents should insist that state and local governments follow the recommendations of postdisaster investigation teams. For example, the post-Andrew recommendations (appendix C, ref. 83) apply to all of Florida, particularly the following:

1. The quality of workmanship needs to be improved. Both the construction industry and the building inspection and enforcement people need to be sure their personnel are properly trained.

2. Building codes must be improved and better enforced.

3. Guidance on correct methods of transferring loads must be provided to building contractors.

4. Licensed design professionals should have more participation in the inspection of construction.

5. Inspector supervision and accountability should be improved.

These activities should be ongoing and evaluated after each storm. Many of the same recommendations made after Hurricane Andrew had been made, but ignored, after earlier hurricanes! In 1998 FEMA launched "Project Impact," a short-lived program that was designed to encourage community-based damage-reduction initiatives for all hazards. Jacksonville/Duval County, Volusia County, Brevard County, Deerfield Beach/Broward County, and Miami/Dade County were designated Project Impact Communities. The program was intended for all communities to follow. The legacy of Project Impact lives on in current FEMA mitigation activities.

The toll in both lives and dollars lost to natural disasters is rising. To assess tasks and vulnerability to hazards, to identify actions to reduce future impact, and to take those necessary actions are the responsibilities of individuals, neighbors, and communities. Given that such responsibilities are not always met and that poor choices continue to be made at the shore, legal regulations are necessary for our own protection.

9 The Managed Coast: Living with Coastal Regulations

The 1984 edition of *Living with the East Florida Shore* made two obvious predictions: "Coastal dwellers should expect future changes in the laws and regulations, just as they should expect future changes in the beaches and dunes" (p. 176). Both have come to pass since 1984. And because the coast is a highly dynamic environment, the laws and regulations have proliferated to the point that only a brief overview can be presented here. Thanks to the Internet and World Wide Web, however, one can find summaries, updates, permit procedures, and related information on federal, state, and community regulations via the computer. For information on regulations, visit MyFlorida.com and the National Oceanographic and Atmospheric Administration's (noaa) Coastal Services Center, Ocean Planning Information System (opis), at www.csc.noaa.gov/opis/.

Coastal interests in vital natural resources and in recreational development are often in opposition. Numerous regulatory controls are designed to help the two coexist—to protect the natural environment from development, and development from natural hazards. A sound philosophy is that if development must exist on our coasts, it must be in harmony with the coasts' natural processes and environments. Development should be prohibited in some critical areas. Land-use philosophies range from the extremes of pristine preservationism to completely unplanned urbanization. Like other decisions affecting the public, decisions on land use are controlled in part by the government. Special-interest groups create political pressures that often lead to "legislation of compromise." In this manner, regulations have been and will continue to be established with the intention of ensuring reasonable multiple use of the coastal zone and the protection of inhabitants as well as the natural environment.

Coastal management plans addressing flooding, beach erosion, inlet migration, and wind hazards are an effective way to mitigate against property damage over the short to intermediate term. Unfortunately, there is no single "best" approach for all coastal segments, other than avoidance of hazardous areas through strict land-use planning incorporating no-build zones. Thus, a management program should provide general guidelines on how to handle the consequences of natural hazards. These guidelines would provide local communities with the flexibility and latitude to adopt rules suited to their unique conditions.

Important factors to be addressed in coastal management plans include defining setbacks for new development, establishing restrictions on the type of new construction on the shoreline, determining funding sources for coastal protection, establishing a statewide inventory of erosion and other hazard problem areas, and setting priorities for protection, plus creating a shortcut through the bureaucratic path to obtain permits for the implementation of projects. Current and prospective owners of coastal property should be aware of their responsibilities under the current laws with respect to development and land use, and of the likelihood of future regulation.

A partial list of current land-use regulations in Florida follows. Appendix B lists many of the agencies that will supply more specific information regarding these regulations and permit processes. Always remember to check county and community codes, regulations, and laws before starting any project, as these may have changed or may be stricter than those of the state. The best place to start with questions is your local city or town hall.

National Flood Insurance Program

The National Flood Insurance Program (NFIP) is one of the most significant legal pressures applied to encourage land-use planning and management in the coastal zone. Private insurance companies, realizing how hazardous the coastal environment is and the high risk of doing business in flood-prone areas, either do not provide flood insurance or charge extremely high premiums. In the past, the federal government had to step in and offer disaster relief to those unable to purchase or afford insurance coverage. In an effort to reduce disaster relief costs from floods, Congress passed the National Flood Insurance Act of 1968 (Public Law [P.L.] 90-448), which established the NFIP.

Amended by the Flood Disaster Protection Act of 1973 (P.L. 92-234), the NFIP requires homeowners to meet certain conditions to be eligible to purchase flood insurance. Persons living in flood zones who do not purchase such insurance may not, in the event of a flood, receive postflood federal financial assistance. Most banks will not provide a mortgage loan for a structure that does not have flood insurance. To encourage involvement in the program, flood insurance rates are kept at an affordable level.

Communities must adopt certain land-use and control measures in order to make NFIP flood insurance available at reasonable rates. Federal funds

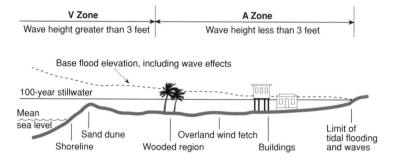

9.1 The v zone and a zone in a coastal flood zone as defined by the Federal Emergency Management Agency. Modified from *Managing Coastal Erosion* (appendix C, ref. 70).

for shoreline engineering, waste disposal, or water-treatment systems are available only when the individual and community involved comply with the requirements of the law. The Community Rating System was implemented so that communities that exceed the minimum standards set by the NFIP can receive reduced rates.

Insurance rates are determined by two main factors: the community's insurance rating and the flood zone within which the building is located. Many Florida coastal communities are subject to both river flooding and coastal flooding due to storm surge and wave run-up. The focus here is on coastal flooding. Flood zones are represented on Flood Insurance Rate Maps (FIRMS) and are designated as v, a, or x zones (v, a, b, or c zones on older maps). These zones represent different flood events with different flood-level heights. The v and a zones are the most hazardous and represent the area inundated by what is commonly referred to as the 100-year flood (fig. 9.1).

As noted in chapter 6, the implication is that the most hazardous zones have a 1 percent chance in any given year that a storm of that magnitude will occur. The 100-year flood level (how high the flood will reach) is a theoretical still-water level. In reality, storm winds cause waves on top of this still-water level so that the true impact of high water plus waves is much greater than just still-water flooding. In order to designate that part of the a zone (the 100-year flood zone) that is susceptible to high waves, FEMA also maps the v zone (velocity zone). v zones are areas where the exposure to wind can theoretically cause waves 3 feet or greater in height on top of the 100-year flood level; a zones have waves smaller than 3 feet. x zones on the FIRMS are divided into two categories: the x zone, the area with elevations between the 100- and 500-year floods (b zone on older maps); and the x500 zone, which is above the 500-year flood level (c zones on older maps; fig. 9.2). x zones have higher elevation and thus generally are less hazardous places to build than v or a zones.

Most flood zones on FIRMS are divided into different subzones with a number in parentheses below, such as A7 (EL14). The EL14 in this example refers to the minimum base elevation of the structure that FEMA requires; in this case, 14 feet above sea level. Note that the standard used in one program (e.g., base flood elevation for the NFIP) may not be the same in another program (e.g., the higher base flood elevation estimate used for Florida's CCCL determination). For more information on how to interpret FIRMS, see appendix C, reference 78. Other FEMA building regulations include requirements for ground-floor breakaway walls, which help reduce overall damage by allowing storm-surge waters to pass unobstructed under the building. For further details, see chapter 8 and appendix C, references 80, 81, and 98.

In 1987, the Upton-Jones Amendment to the National Flood Insurance Program allowed owners of threatened buildings to use up to 40 percent of the NFIP-insured value of their homes for building relocation. The law recognized that relocation is a more economical, more permanent, and more realistic way to deal with long-term erosion problems. The federal government (taxpayers at large) would pay a relatively small amount to assist with re-

9.2 Portion of a Flood Insurance Rate Map (FIRM) for Flagler County, Florida. The FIRMS show flood zones as illustrated in figure 9.1 (V and A zones) as well as X zones, which are above the 100-year flood level. These maps are used to determine NFIP flood insurance rates and for management and zoning decisions and are available for public examination in town and city halls.

locating a threatened house rather than paying a larger amount to help rebuild it, only to see the rebuilt house destroyed in a subsequent storm, and paying to rebuild again . . . and again. Although the Upton-Jones Amendment was terminated, the National Flood Insurance Reform Act of 1994 replaced part of the relocation option through the National Flood Mitigation Fund. Financed from penalty revenues collected for noncompliance with NFIP requirements, the program provides state and local governments with grants for planning, as well as mitigation assistance for activities that will reduce the risk of flood damage to structures covered under the NFIP. Demolition and relocation activities are eligible for grant assistance under the program, although they compete with other mitigation approaches, including elevation and flood-proofing programs, acquisition of flood-zone properties for public use and beach nourishment activities.

The NFIP program undoubtedly has flaws. Some feel that requirements for insurance eligibility should be more stringent and suggest denying flood insurance and federal disaster assistance to current owners of property located in coastal high-hazard areas if their houses and buildings do not meet the standards for new construction. Other problems include establishing actuarial rates, funding the necessary coastal studies to define high-hazard areas, and understanding the effects of long-term federal subsidies. Perhaps the greatest obstacle to the success of the program is the uninformed individual who stands to gain the most from it. A study that examined public response to flood insurance found that many people view insurance as an investment with the expectation of a return rather than a means of sharing the cost of natural disasters. Perhaps the greatest shortcoming is that the policy of "no federal assistance" to the uninsured is circumvented under political pressure in the poststorm relief/reconstruction period, undermining the law and increasing the cost of disaster relief.

Purists may debate the merits of taxpayer-subsidized federal programs, but the NFIP's objectives are worthwhile because the program applies pressure to ensure wiser management of hazardous flood zones. Currently there is a very low percentage of participation in the NFIP. The same applies to inland and upstream residents and property owners. As taxpayers, we hope that in the long run this program will cost less than the growing expense of national disaster relief generated by flooding.

Coastal Barrier Resources Act

The Coastal Barrier Resources Act (COBRA; P.L. 97-348) was passed in 1982 and is administered by the U.S. Department of the Interior. Its goals are to minimize loss of life, stop wasteful expenditure of federal funds, and minimize damage to natural resources. COBRA denies federal subsidies to development-related projects on undeveloped coastal barriers on the U.S. Atlantic and Gulf of Mexico coasts. Coastal areas included become part of the Coastal Barrier Resources System (CBRS). The CBRS originally included 666 miles of the Atlantic and Gulf coasts. COBRA does not prohibit development, but it shifts the financial responsibility for such development to state, local, and private coffers. COBRA represents an effort to stop federal subsidies for development in erosion and flood-prone areas. No federal funds are available within the CBRS for (including, but not limited to) infrastructure, roads, airports, boat docks/landings, bridges, causeways, shore hardening, or flood insurance. COBRA prohibits federal funding for new construction of roads, bridges, or any other related infrastructure development that would promote the urbanization of undeveloped coastal barriers. In addition, federal funds cannot be applied toward erosion or stabilization programs that indirectly encourage development. However, communities existing prior to the enactment of COBRA are protected under exemptions and still receive federal funds; thus, development in high-risk coastal areas continues despite the enactment of COBRA.

Under COBRA, an undeveloped coastal barrier is defined as a depositional geologic feature that consists of unconsolidated sedimentary materials subject to wave, tide, and wind. The law protects landward aquatic habitats as well as back-barrier environments (adjacent wetlands, estuaries, inlets, and nearshore waters). Undeveloped areas contain few man-made structures, none of which "significantly impede geomorphic and ecologic processes." Many COBRA zones in Florida, as elsewhere, are undeveloped marsh lands, state and federal parks, and military base property. However, this should not cause coastal residents to ignore the location of COBRA zones. Future development may occur in COBRA zones, and established residents should be wary of those who build in nearby COBRA zones. How will those unprotected communities respond to disasters? Will they be able to rebuild? Do you want a poststorm ghost town located a few miles from your vacation home?

The Coastal Barrier Improvement Act (CBIA or COBIA) of 1990 (P.L. 101-591) amended the Coastal Barrier Resources Act by expanding the Coastal Barrier Resources System. The CBIA broadened the definition of *coastal barrier* to include barriers composed of consolidated sediments, allowing the inclusion of some of the Florida Keys (CBIA now covers the 66,500 acres of undeveloped land in the Keys). For a list of CBRS units in East Florida, visit the U.S. Fish and Wildlife Service website at http://www.fws.gov/cep/cbrtable.html.

Flood insurance is not available in CBRS units. FEMA and the U.S. Geological Survey published special maps, effective August 3, 1992, to indicate such areas. Make sure you check with local officials to determine precise CBRS unit boundaries.

Rivers and Harbors Act of 1889

The U.S. Army Corps of Engineers is the federal agency responsible for regulating dredging and filling, as administered through the Rivers and Harbors Act of 1889 (33 U.S.C. 403) and the Federal Water Pollution Control Act of 1972 (P.L. 92-500)—as amended, known as the Clean Water Act (see below). Under section 10 of the Rivers and Harbors Act the Corps may authorize activities that could affect navigable waters of the United States. If your project is within the Corps's jurisdiction, you must obtain one of the following authorizations: (1) a nationwide permit—a streamlined permit issued by the Chief of Engineers; (2) a regional general permit—a permit issued by the district office of the Corps authorizing certain minor activities in specific geographic areas within Florida (Jacksonville District jurisdiction); or (3) an individual permit—necessary if your project exceeds the scope of the nationwide and regional general permits. The latter typically requires consultation with the National Marine Fisheries Service and the U.S. Fish and Wildlife Service.

Coastal Zone Management Act

The federal Coastal Zone Management Act of 1972 (czma) established a national initiative for coastal management and encouraged states to develop coastal management programs. Congress promulgated the czma to protect, preserve, develop, and—where possible—restore and enhance our nation's coastal resources. Under this Act, coastal states are given incentives to create comprehensive management plans that balance the need for coastal resource protection with economic growth and development within the coastal zone. Later reauthorization amendments expanded the program. Key requirements of the czma are coastal land-use planning and protection of critical environments. Under the act, individual states established their own coastal zone management programs. Florida's coastal management is governed by several specific programs (table 9.1). The Florida Coastal Management Plan (fcmp) was approved by noaa in 1981 and consists of 23 Florida statutes.

Florida Beach and Shore Preservation Act

Florida regulations applying to the coastal environment are found in legislation ranging from marine animal protection to the state building code. Perhaps the most important part of the Florida Statutes for coastal residents is chapter 161, the Beach and Shore Preservation Act and the Coastal Zone Protection Act of 1985. The complete Florida Statutes should be available in most city halls and/or libraries. A complete and searchable copy of the statutes is available online.

Table 9.1 Primary Programs for Coastal Zone Management in Florida and Associated State Administrative Agency

	CBZ	CCCL	NFIP
Name of program/ zone and agency responsible	Coastal Building Zone (CBZ) (chap. 161, part 3, Fla. statutes) Local enforcement Department of Community Affairs (DCA) is the oversight agency and provides assistance with implementation, training, and enforcement.	Coastal Construction Control Line (CCCL) program (chap. 161, part 1, Fla. statutes) Department of Environmental Protection	National Flood Insurance Program (NFIP) FEMA and local governments
Area defined	SHWL* to 1,500 feet landward of the CCCL or to the most landward of the v zones on non-CCCL program shores fronting the Gulf, Atlantic, and Straits of Florida. For barrier islands, this area is from the SHWL to 5,000 feet landward of the CCCL or the entire island, whichever is less.	Up to the landward limit of a 100-year storm surge (generally east coast) or up to the landward limit of a 3-foot wave associated with 100-year storm surge (generally west coast)	Special Flood Hazard Areas determined to be impacted by 100-year storm event. v zones = likely to experience a wave greater than 3 feet high with 100-year storm event (consistently results in lower elevation requirements than the 100-year storm event used in the CCCL program) A zones = likely to experience a wave less than 3 feet high with 100-year storm event
Objective	Protection of coastal areas; protection of life and property	Protection of beaches and dunes; protection of life and property while assuring reasonable use of private property Originally a setback	Protection of life and property; loss/ coast reduction

(table continues)

Table 9.1 continued

	CBZ	CCCL	NFIP
Wind standards	Standard Building Code 1997 wind design standard of 110 mph and 115 mph for Keys	American Society of Civil Engineering 7-88, sect. 6, wind design standard for 110 mph, 115 mph for Keys including peak pressures. This design standard is 20% stronger than those in the Standard Building Code (for buildings less than 60 feet)	The most restrictive wind requirements in place in that area
Water standards	NFIP requirements of local flood ordinance requirements, whichever is most restrictive. Also, foundations are designed to withstand a 100-year storm event, including effects of waves and scouring.	Foundation design to withstand a 100-year storm, including the effects of surge, waves, and scouring. Pilings/elevation is based on wave crest height associated with a 100-year storm event. Breakaway walls below state's crest elevation; some shear walls	For V zones Pilings; elevation for wind-driven water. Limited permitted uses— unfinished parking, access, and storage below BFE per 100-year storm event model.** For A zones Pilings or elevation on fill, flood proofing of building area below BFE. (If the A zone is seaward of the CCCL, breakaway construction needs to be included below the state's wave crest elevation.) However, NFIP requires hydrostatic openings in walls of all enclosures below BFE.

*Seasonal high water line (SHWL) is the line formed by the intersection of the rising shore and the elevation of 150% of the local mean tidal range above local mean high water.
**"Uses" allowed below base flood elevation (BFE) vary between the CCCL and NFIP programs.

The following brief summary of some important aspects of Florida's coastal regulations is not a substitute for a thorough reading of the state and local regulations, which can change. Always check with the local building inspector before starting any project; the statutes may have changed since the time of this writing, and local ordinances may be stricter. Remember always to use federal, state, and local standards as minimum requirements, and exceed them whenever possible.

Coastal Construction Control Line and Coastal Building Zone

The cornerstone for state coastal regulation in Florida is the Coastal Construction Control Line (CCCL), which is administered by the Florida Department of Environmental Protection (FDEP). Initiated in 1970 with a construction prohibition line for sandy shorelines only, Florida's CCCL established a setback line 50 feet landward of the mean high-water line. The CCCL was established to require state permits for all construction beyond the control lines. The CCCL was modified the following year and adopted as the Coastal Construction Setback Line (CCSL). This control line was established based on the consideration of a number of factors, including erosion, elevation, and construction type. In 1978, the CCCL was adopted not as a line of prohibition, as was the CCSL, but as a line of jurisdiction. The CCCL is based on a computer model of expected flooding from a 100-year storm, and structures and construction seaward of the line are subject to specific rules and regulations.

The CCCL zone also includes a 30-year erosion setback based on the FDEP's determination of the erosion rate from historical measurements (the rate of sea-level rise is not considered). Major structures are not eligible to receive a CCCL permit seaward of this projected 30-year erosion line; however, single-family dwellings may receive a variance if specific siting requirements are met.

The Coastal Zone Protection Act of 1985 (part 3 of the Beach and Shore Preservation Act) created the Coastal Building Zone (table 9.1), which expanded the state's construction jurisdiction to a line 1,500 feet landward of the CCCL. On Florida's barrier islands, the Coastal Building Zone extends 5,000 feet landward of the CCCL or the entire width of the island, whichever is less. Structures located within this zone must comply with the specific rules in the state building code and be in compliance with NFIP regulations. In addition, mobile homes in the Coastal Building Zone are required to meet the specifications of either the Federal Mobile Home Construction and Safety Standards or the Uniform Standard Code. The Coastal Building Zone also extends to the tip of the V zone for nonsandy shorelines along major bodies of water that have no CCCL.

The CCCL is not a true setback because construction is not prohibited seaward of the line. Variances can be obtained through a permit process, and the construction must follow certain standards. Some of the factors considered in permit approval include structure footprints, ability to withstand a 100-year storm event, proximity to the shoreline, erosion rate, and vegetation disturbance.

The establishment of the Coastal Building Zone created the necessary space for a new setback provision. This setback rule prohibits new construction and regulates rebuilding from the seasonal high-water mark landward to the 30-year erosion setback line. Along vegetated coastlines where a CCCL has not been established, a 50-foot prohibitive setback exists. Like other states that are effectively using setbacks for new construction, Florida has not been very specific in determining what to do when buildings within the setback limit are threatened by erosion or what happens when structures built following current setback guidelines are lost. Although all permitted construction is supposed to meet design and site standards, the CCCL program has merely become an institutionalized system for permitting hazardous development along the fragile coast (appendix C, ref. 33).

National Environmental Policy Act

The National Environmental Policy Act of 1969 (NEPA) is considered by some to be the Magna Carta of U.S. environmental law. In theory, NEPA requires all federal agencies to proactively consider direct, indirect, and cumulative environmental effects of federal actions in their decision-making process.

Every recommendation or report on proposals for legislation and other major Federal actions that significantly affect the quality of the human environment is required to include a detailed statement on:

1. The environmental impact of the proposed action,

2. Any adverse effects which cannot be avoided should the proposal be implemented,

3. Alternatives to the proposed action,

4. The relationship between local short-term uses of man's environment and the maintenance and enhancement of long-term productivity, and

5. Any irreversible and irretrievable commitments of resources which would be involved should it be implemented.

The aforementioned "detailed statement" is in the form of an environmental impact statement (EIS) or environmental assessment (EA). EA's and EIS's are frequently prepared to address anticipated environmental impacts stemming from proposed coastal construction. The thoroughness of these documents and the independence and rigor of their construction have been questioned many times, across many national ecosystems, since the inception of NEPA. Legal and technical challenges occur with considerable frequency.

Fish and Wildlife Coordination Act

The Fish and Wildlife Coordination Act of 1958 (FWCA; P.L. 85-624) mandates the preparation of Fish and Wildlife Coordination Act Reports (CARS). The FWCA authorizes the U.S. Fish and Wildlife Service (USFWS) to coordinate with the Army Corps of Engineers in the preparation of CARS addressing the effects that beach renourishment projects will have on reefs and the fish and wildlife resources they support. The FWCA requires CARS to be based on surveys and investigations conducted by the USFWS. A CAR prepared for a beach renourishment project will likely list USFWS recommendations for minimizing any adverse effects on the environment. These recommendations could include reducing the length of shoreline to be nourished in order to avoid direct burial of reefs, constructing artificial mitigation reefs to replace lost habitat, or establishing buffer zones near sensitive resources.

Magnuson-Stevens Fishery Conservation and Management Act

In 1996 Congress amended the Magnuson Fishery Conservation and Management Act of 1976 (16 U.S.C. 1801) to address declining fishery resources due to habitat loss and overfishing. The amended act, renamed the Magnuson-Stevens Fishery Conservation and Management Act (MSFCMA), is important for beach renourishment projects that significantly impact fish habitat. The MSFCMA requires federal fishery management councils to identify habitats needed for sustainable fisheries and include these areas in comprehensive fishery management plans. The South Atlantic and Gulf of Mexico Fishery Management Councils regulate federal fishery resources offshore of Florida. MSFCMA defines *essential fish habitat* (EFH) as "those waters and substrate necessary to fish for spawning, breeding, feeding or growth to maturity." The federal fishery management councils also identify *habitat areas of particular concern* (HAPCS), the highest level of EFH designation. An EFH is designated an HAPC if it meets one of the following criteria:

1. It has an important ecological function.
2. It is sensitive to human degradation.
3. There is a probability of impact from development activities.
4. The habitat is rare.

Almost all of the habitats routinely affected by beach maintenance projects in East Florida are designated EFH-HAPC by the South Atlantic Fishery Management Council. The MSFCMA also requires important interagency coordination requirements. Any federally funded, assisted, or permitted project (e.g., a beach renourishment project) requires coordination with the National Marine Fisheries Service when EFH impacts may occur. Applicants are required to prepare an Essential Fish Habitat Assessment to the satisfaction of the NMFS, who then provide EFH conservation recommendations to avoid and mitigate impacts to the EFH.

Endangered Species Act

The Endangered Species Act of 1977 (ESA; 16 U.S.C. §§ 1531 et seq.) requires federal agencies to assess the effect on endangered species of projects in areas where such species may be present. The enabling legislation for marine turtle protection provides for interagency coordination in that each federal agency shall "insure that any action authorized, funded, or carried out by such agency does not jeopardize the continued existence of any endangered species or threatened species or result in the destruction or adverse modification of habitat of such species." In addition, all persons, including federal agencies, are specifically instructed not to "take" endangered species, meaning that no one is "to harass, harm, pursue, hunt, shoot, wound, kill, trap, capture, or collect" such life forms. The Secretary of the Interior lists the loggerhead turtle (*Caretta caretta*) as threatened and the green (*Chelonia mydas*) and leatherback (*Dermochelys coriacea*) turtles as endangered under the ESA. These three federally protected species utilize the nearshore hard-bottom areas (areas frequently impacted by beach dredge-and-fill projects) as juvenile foraging habitat. The ESA mandates the preparation of biological opinions by the USFWS to address dredge-and-fill project-related effects on threatened or endangered marine turtles. Biological opinions list terms and conditions to avoid and minimize adverse impacts for endangered and threatened species and conclude whether or not the proposed project will likely jeopardize the continued existence of such species.

Clean Water Act

Section 404 of the Clean Water Act (CWA; 33 U.S.C. 1344s) establishes a permit system for the Army Corps of Engineers program regulating the discharge of dredge and fill materials into navigable waters. An important subsection 404(c) of the CWA gives the Environmental Protection Agency (EPA) authority to override an USACE decision to authorize a permit if the EPA determines that the discharge will have an unacceptable effect on Aquatic Resources of National Importance (ARNI), which may include municipal water supplies, shellfish beds, fisheries, wildlife, or recreation areas. Water quality is a serious issue for several reasons, and it has emerged as a major environmental concern in several past beach restoration projects in southeast Florida. Beach dredging results in elevated levels of sedimentation and turbidity. Lowered water quality can significantly damage resources, including reefs. Persistent long-term turbidity caused by beach renourishment may have significant biological consequences.

Critical Eroding Areas

In 1988, the state mandated the designation of "critical eroding areas" for the purpose of implementing long-term erosion management plans. These areas are broadly defined as sites where erosion poses a threat to the recreational beach, structures or buildings, wildlife and/or wildlife habitat, or cultural features. Thus, a coastline with a 15 feet per year erosion rate on an uninhabited island would not necessarily be considered a critical eroding area. This designation by the state triggers erosion mitigation programs such as hard stabilization or artificial beach construction.

The presence of development or engineering structures along the coast should be used to establish the best management practice to deal with coastal erosion instead of being the leading factor in the definition of erosion problem areas. The result of this approach is that critically eroding areas are rapidly expanding as uninhabited beaches become developed. For example, about 218 miles of Florida beaches were classified as critical eroding areas in 1989; this figure had increased to 227 miles by 1991 and to 328 miles by 1999 according to the FDEP, representing an increase of over 66 percent in ten years!

The Bureau of Beaches and Coastal Systems, which is part of the FDEP, determines and periodically updates the critically eroding areas. There is erosion data for most of the barrier coastline of Florida going back some 20 years, and many reaches have some historical shoreline data for the last 100-plus years.

State of Florida and federal coastal laws and regulations are numerous and complex. Again, the short overview presented here is not intended to replace a thorough reading of the statutes. A more extensive examination reveals a system that, although well intended and implemented, can often fall on the side of preserving buildings rather than beaches, via loopholes, variances, and the influence of local developers. Unlike some states where legislative efforts have attempted to preserve beaches *despite* development, Florida's efforts sometimes have the effect of preserving beaches *for* development.

A comprehensive coastal management plan should include:

1. A statewide inventory of erosion problem areas
2. A list of priorities for beach protection based on state needs

3. A long-term erosion mitigation plan for erosional areas

4. A guide specifying funding sources for coastal protection

5. Guidelines for planned occupation along undeveloped shores and measures to be taken when developed areas are in danger

6. A standardized monitoring method for every shoreline stabilization project

Florida's beach erosion control program is administered by the FDEP as a grant-in-aid to local governments, and has not effectively managed beach erosion despite significant shore protection efforts. At present, the state depends on the initiative of local governments to submit shore protection projects for approval. Thus, erosion control projects are implemented not on the basis of statewide needs, but on coastal communities' perception of beach erosion.

Highly developed communities lead the search for shore protection support (e.g., the southeastern coastal segment). Meanwhile, other erosion problem areas have not been protected and may eventually expose larger areas to erosion threats. Additionally, funding for beach protection along Florida's beaches is based on annual general revenue appropriations and on interest earnings, and has been insufficient to promote a comprehensive coastal management plan.

The current system encourages inefficiency because shore management is segmented; that is, adjacent coastal communities may respond to beach erosion differently, based solely on their perceived problems, without concern that their activities may cause or accelerate erosion in neighboring communities. As the health of any shoreline is dictated by updrift processes, the coast must be viewed regionally or over reasonably long lengths that are not restricted by political boundaries. More legislation is necessary to improve the state's role in coastal protection, particularly if a comprehensive coastal management plan is to be implemented. Coastal management in undeveloped areas is not a difficult task, although the best management practice can be established only on the basis of comprehensive knowledge of coastal processes.

Natural processes should be allowed to dominate undeveloped or partially developed shores where retreat may be the most feasible response because any other approach would be too costly. However, erosion should be monitored to determine the potential risk it will pose to adjoining areas, and to evaluate its cost and the future need for mitigation.

Legislative measures are very important in regulating land occupation along eroded shorelines to avoid increasing costs arising from land and structure loss on a long-term basis. Programs of beachfront acquisition by local or state governments are an effective way to prevent development in erosion problem areas, maintain public beach access, and preserve natural habitats (e.g., the FDEP's Conservation and Recreation Lands Program;

CARL). Costs may be high initially, but such areas may become a revenue source based on their recreational use (i.e., entrance and parking fees). Other suggested legislative measures include restrictions on reconstruction of damaged buildings or protective structures within the setback zone (as in Texas and South Carolina); restricting flood insurance availability (Coastal Barrier Resources Act); giving tax incentives to beachfront owners who develop property for uses compatible with beach preservation (e.g., Delaware Beaches 2000 plan); and considering sea-level rise in engineering projects (e.g., San Francisco Bay Conservation and Development Commission).

Prediction: Coastal Regulation Will Increase

Coastal zone management is as old as human occupation and development within the coastal high-hazard zone. The consequences of unfettered development and overutilization of resources demonstrate the need for integrated management with a focus on sustainability. Modern management was and is, for better or for worse, influenced by changing styles of government and politics. However, as our knowledge and experience of coastal dynamics and change increase, so do the levels of regulation. Proper management of the coastal zone is vital not only to natural environments and resources, but also to the economy, the welfare and safety of the population, and the long-term investment in the coast.

Before building or buying a home, an individual should ask these basic questions:

1. What permits are needed?
2. Is the community where I am locating covered by the NFIP program? If not, why?
3. Is my building site above the 100-year flood level plus added wave height?
4. What are the limits of NFIP coverage?
5. What is the town's Community NFIP Rating? What is the town doing to improve its rating?
6. Is my building or community in a COBRA or CBIA zone?
7. What are the structural requirements for my building?

New and existing development in the coastal zone must meet or exceed the minimum requirements of prudent management. Whether you are a developer or an individual planning to build/live in the coastal zone, you must seek the necessary permits. Expect stricter enforcement of existing regulations in the near future, and new, "tighter" regulations in the years to come as more and more people choose to live with the East Florida coast!

Appendix A
Hazard Safety Checklists

Natural disasters such as those described in this book can strike at any time, often with little warning. Even with modern prediction and warning capabilities, it is impossible to make perfect watch, warning, and evacuation calls every time. Always be prepared for the worst.

The following checklists give guidelines to preparing for, riding out, and recovering from natural disasters. Some precautions and preparations are the same for all disasters, and these are included as the "General Disaster Preparation Guide." Specifics for hurricanes, floods, and earthquakes follow the general information. Inland dwellers may be at risk, too. Destructive winds, heavy rains, and inland flooding are always a possibility when a hurricane or northeaster strikes the coast.

General Disaster Preparation Guide

Find out what natural hazards are likely to affect your community (or vacation rental site). Check your telephone book for the local evacuation route, or call the nearest town, township, or county office. Learn the evacuation route. Have a plan.

Do hurricanes occur here? Tornadoes? Are earthquakes possible? Are they likely? Are you located on a floodplain, and have heavy rains been predicted or have they recently occurred? Have you moved your family into your dream vacation home right on the oceanfront just as a tropical disturbance is forming or intensifying out to sea that you want to keep tabs on via television, radio, or NOAA weather radio?

You should have a disaster supply kit already put together that contains the essentials needed for any emergency from power outages to hurricanes, including some ready cash.

Stock adequate supplies:

—battery-powered radio
—weather radio with alarm function for direct National Weather Service broadcasts
—fresh batteries
—flashlights
—portable halogen lamp (you will need more light than just the emergency flashlight when the power goes off)
—hammer
—boards (for securing windows and doors against hurricanes)
—pliers
—hunting knife
—tape
—first-aid kit

—prescribed medicines
—candles
—matches
—nails
—ax (to cut an emergency escape opening if you go to the upper floor or attic of your home)
—rope (for escape to the ground when water subsides)
—plastic drop cloths, waterproof bags, and ties
—containers of water
—canned food, juices, and soft drinks
—enough food for at least three days and enough water for more than three days (select
   food that does not require cooking or refrigeration)
—water purification tablets
—insect repellent
—chewing gum, candy
—life jackets
—charcoal bucket, charcoal, and charcoal lighter
—buckets of sand
—disinfectant
—hard-top headgear
—fire extinguisher
—can openers and utensils (knives, forks, spoons, cups)

Make sure you know how to shut off electricity, gas, and water at main switches and valves. Know where the gas pilots are and how the heating system works. Be ready and able to secure your property before you leave so your belongings won't cause harm to others and you will be able to reenter your home safely.

Make a record of your personal property. Photograph or videotape your belongings and store the record in a safe place.

Keep insurance policies, deeds, property records, and other important papers in a safe place away from your home.

Hurricane Safety Checklist

When (or before) a Hurricane Threatens

—Most important, know the *official evacuation route* for your area. You will not be asked to
   evacuate unless your life is in danger, so *evacuate as directed* by local emergency preparedness officials. Do not react to rumors.
—Many local telephone books contain community information about hurricane preparedness
   and evacuation. Check to see if the information is there and make sure everyone in the
   house is familiar with it.
—Read your newspaper and listen to radio and television for official weather reports and an-
   nouncements.
—Secure reentry permits if necessary. Some communities allow only property owners and
   residents with proper identification or tags to return in the storm's immediate wake.
—Pregnant women, the ill, and the infirm should call a physician for advice.
—Be prepared to turn off gas, water, and electricity where it enters your home.
—Make sure your car's gas tank is full.
—Secure your boat; use long lines to allow for rising water.
—Secure movable objects on your property:
   —doors and gates
   —outdoor furniture

—shutters
—garden tools
—hoses
—garbage cans
—bicycles or large sports equipment
—barbecues or grills
—other
—Board up or tape windows, glassed-in areas, and glazing. Close storm shutters. Draw drapes and window blinds across windows and glass doors, and remove furniture in their vicinity.
—Check mobile home tie-downs.
—Your primary line of defense is *early evacuation*. If you are unable to evacuate, you should also do the following:
   —Know the location of the nearest emergency shelter. Go there if directed by emergency preparedness officials.
   —When a flood or hurricane is imminent, fill bathtubs and containers with water enough for one week (a minimum of one quart per person per day).

Special Precautions for Apartments/Condominiums

—Designate one person as the building captain to supervise storm preparations.
—Know your exits.
—Count stairs on exits: you may be evacuating in darkness.
—Locate safest areas for occupants to congregate.
—Close, lock, and tape windows.
—Remove loose items from your terrace (and from your absent neighbors' terraces).
—Remove (or tie down) loose objects from balconies or porches.
—Assume other trapped people may wish to use the building for shelter.

Special Precautions for Mobile Homes

—Pack breakables in padded cartons and place on the floor.
—Remove bulbs, lamps, and mirrors, and put them in the bathtub (you are leaving, so the bathtub will not be a water reservoir).
—Tape windows.
—Turn off water, propane gas, electricity.
—Disconnect sewer and water lines.
—Remove awnings.
—*Leave*. Do not stay inside for *any* reason unless you can absolutely determine that the hazards from rising floodwaters are greater than those from wind.

Special Precautions for Businesses

—Take photographs of your building and merchandise before the storm.
—Assemble insurance policies.
—Move merchandise away from plate glass.
—Move merchandise to the highest location possible.
—Cover merchandise with tarps or plastic.
—Remove outside display racks and loose signs.
—Take out file drawers, wrap them in trash bags, and store them in a high place.
—Sandbag spaces that may leak.
—Take special precautions with reactive or toxic chemicals.

If You Remain at Home

—*Never* remain in a mobile home; seek official shelter.
—Stay indoors. Remember, the first calm may be the hurricane's eye. Do not attempt to change your location during the eye unless absolutely necessary. Remain indoors until an official all-clear is given.
—Stay on the *downwind* side of the house. Change your position as the wind direction changes.
—If your house has an inside room (away from all outdoor walls), stay there; it may be the most secure part of the structure.
—Monitor official information on radio and television continuously.
—Keep calm. Your ability to meet emergencies will help others.

If Evacuation Is Advised

—Leave as soon as you can. Follow official instructions only. Ignore rumors.
—Follow predesignated evacuation routes unless those in authority direct you to do otherwise.
—Take these supplies:
  —reentry permit
  —change of warm, protective clothes
  —first-aid kit
  —baby formula
  —identification tags: include name, address, next of kin (wear them!)
  —flashlight
  —food, water, gum, candy
  —rope, hunting knife
  —waterproof bags and ties
  —can opener and utensils
  —disposable diapers
  —special medicine
  —blankets and pillows, in waterproof casings
  —battery-powered radio
  —fresh batteries (for radio and flashlight)
  —bottled water
  —purse, wallet, valuables
  —life jackets
  —games and amusements for children
—Disconnect all electric appliances except refrigerator and freezer; their controls should be turned to the coldest setting and the doors kept closed.
—Leave food and water for pets. Seeing-eye dogs are the only animals allowed in the shelters.
—Shut off water at the main valve (where it enters your home).
—Lock windows and doors.
—Keep important papers with you:
  —driver's license and other identification
  —insurance policies
  —property inventory
  —Medic Alert or other device to convey special medical information

During the Hurricane

—Stay indoors and away from windows and glassed areas.
—If you are advised to evacuate, do so at once.

—Listen for weather bulletins and official reports.

—Use your telephone only in an emergency.

—Follow official instructions only. Ignore rumors.

—Beware the eye of the hurricane. A lull in the winds does not necessarily mean the storm has passed. Remain indoors unless emergency repairs are necessary. Be cautious. Winds may resume suddenly, from the opposite direction and with greater force than before.

—Be alert for rising water. Stand on furniture if necessary.

—If electric service is interrupted, note the time. Take the following steps when the electricity goes out:

  —Turn off major appliances, especially air conditioners.

  —Do not disconnect refrigerators or freezers. Their controls should have been turned to the coldest setting and the doors kept closed to preserve food for as long as possible.

  —Keep away from fallen wires. Report the location of such wires to the utility company.

If You Detect Gas

—Do not light matches or cigarette lighters or turn on electrical equipment, not even a flashlight.

—Extinguish all flames.

—Shut off gas supply at the meter. Gas should be turned back on only by a gas service professional or licensed plumber.

Water

—The only *safe* water is the water you stored before it had a chance to come in contact with floodwaters.

—Should you require more, be sure to boil water for 30 minutes before using it.

—If you are unable to boil water, treat it with water purification tablets. These are available at camping stores.

Note. An official announcement will proclaim tap water safe. Boil or treat all water except stored water until you hear the announcement.

After the Hurricane Has Passed

—Listen for official word that the danger has passed. Do not return to your home until officially directed to do so.

—Watch out for loose or hanging power lines as well as gas leaks. People have survived storms only to be electrocuted and burned. Fire protection may be nonexistent because broken power lines and fallen debris in the streets are blocking access.

—Walk or drive carefully through storm-damaged areas. Streets will be dangerous because of debris, undermining by washout, and weakened bridges. Traffic lights may not work; street signs may have been blown down. Approach every intersection as if it had a stop sign.

—Watch out for animals that may act irrationally after being driven out by floodwaters.

—Looting may be a problem in certain areas. Police protection may be nonexistent. Do not participate in such illegal acts and do not try to stop others. Wait for police, National Guard, or other officials to arrive.

—Eat nothing and drink nothing that has been touched by floodwaters.

—Place spoiled food in plastic bags and tie them securely.

—Dispose of all mattresses, pillows, and cushions that have been in floodwaters.

—Contact relatives as soon as possible.

—If you use an electric generator for home power, make sure your house's main circuit breaker switch is off. This will prevent your home-generated electricity from "leaking" out to the main power lines. After Hurricane Hugo in 1989, several power line repairers were electrocuted by electricity from the home generators of thoughtless individuals. Save a life! Make sure your main circuit breaker is off!

Note: If you are stranded, signal for help by waving a flashlight at night or white cloth during the day. If you have no cloth to wave, wave both arms (waving just one arm is an "OK" greeting).

Riverine and Flash Flood Safety Checklist

What to Do Before a Flood

—Know the terminology:

—*Flood watch: flooding is possible.*

—Stay tuned to NOAA weather radio or commercial radio or television.

—*Flash flood watch: flash flooding, which can result in raging waters in just a few minutes, is possible.*

—Move to higher ground; a flash flood could occur without any warning.

—Stay tuned to radio or television.

—*Flood warning: flooding is occurring or will occur soon.*

—If evacuation is advised, do so immediately.

—*Flash flood warning: flash flood is occurring.*

—Seek higher ground on foot immediately.

—Find out from your local emergency management office whether your property is in a flood-prone area. Learn the elevation of your area. Learn about the likely flooding scenario of your lot/neighborhood/community.

—Purchase flood insurance (flood losses are not covered under your homeowner's insurance policy); it is widely available through the NFIP. Your local private insurance agent can help you find the proper coverage. Have your agent also advise you on complete insurance coverage even if you do not live on a river floodplain.

—Prepare a family plan:

—Have a portable radio, flashlight, and emergency supplies.

—Be prepared to evacuate.

—Learn local evacuation routes.

—Choose a safe area in advance.

—Plan a family meeting place in case you are separated and cannot return home.

During a Flood

—Flood watch (2–3 days for flood; 2–12 hours for flash flood)

—*If you have time,* bring outdoor garden equipment and lawn furniture inside or tie it down.

—*If you have time,* move furniture and other items to higher levels (for flood).

—Fill your car's gas tank (for flood).

—Listen to radio or TV for up-to-the-minute information.

—Flood warning (24–48 hours for flood; 0–1 hour for flash flood)

—Evacuate, if necessary, when flood warning indicates, and follow instructions.

—Do not walk or drive through floodwaters.

—Stay off bridges covered by water.

—Heed barricades blocking roads.

—Keep away from waterways during heavy rain; if you are driving in a canyon area and hear a warning, get out of your car and get to high ground immediately.

—Keep out of storm drains and irrigation ditches.

—Listen to radio or TV for up-to-the-minute information.

After a Flood

— Stay away from floodwaters; they could be contaminated.

— Stay away from moving water.

Postdisaster Recovery

Both coastal and inland residents should prepare an emergency handbook or plan for postdisaster recovery: what to do and how to do it. Start with a disaster addendum to your phone book. List contact numbers not just of relatives and disaster agencies, but also the names of insurance representatives and contractors you will need to do repair work (e.g., utilities, water, house repairs, tree clearance, etc.).

Unfortunately, the postdisaster period is a time of social "hazards." People are dazed, confused, and in need of help that is in short supply. Unscrupulous individuals may appear at your door in the guise of construction or clearance contractors. Numerous people, particularly the elderly, are bilked after each hurricane or other natural disaster. Do not accept bids for work unless the contractor provides evidence that the company is bonded and insured (it's best to have established contact with known contractors in advance).

Your telephone service is likely to be out. Know in advance where you might go to find a public phone that is in service (e.g., there is usually a public phone at or near fast-food restaurants or quick-marts). Have enough gasoline to get there (gas stations generally do not have mechanical pumps; when the electricity is off, so are the pumps). When communications are out, rumor takes over. Word-of-mouth rumors spread misinformation, and people feel out of touch. Do not listen to or act on rumors. Get the "official" word. A limited number of radio or TV stations may be in service after the disaster. Make sure you have a portable radio or TV with fresh batteries.

Water may be your greatest need. Store water before the storm (see checklists above), and know in advance where emergency supplies are likely to be available. Power outages and flooding may result in contaminated water supplies for days. In the case of flooding, everything that has come in contact with the floodwater is likely to be contaminated (i.e., household furniture and other belongings may not be salvageable).

Debris clearance and disposal is one of the biggest poststorm problems. Victims often expect government help in the cleanup, but the U.S. Army Corps of Engineers and FEMA cannot go on private property to remove debris. Most likely, there will be no place immediately available for private individuals to put debris. Expect the cleanup to take weeks, more likely months, after the storm or flood.

Finally, people are not the only creatures displaced by these events. You may have to deal with some unwanted invaders. Be particularly cautious in regard to poisonous snakes, fire ants, bees, and other venomous, poisonous, or stinging animals. Dogs and cats also are more likely to bite or scratch when displaced, frightened, and disoriented.

Appendix B
Guide to Local, State, and Federal Agencies
Involved in Coastal Development

Numerous agencies at all levels of government are engaged in planning, regulating, permitting, or studying coastal development and resources. These agencies provide information on development to the homeowner, developer, or planner, and in some instances issue permits for various phases of construction and information on particular topics. Contacts and agencies are listed here by topic, and topics are listed alphabetically.

**Aerial Photography, Coastal Construction Control Line Maps,
Orthophoto Maps, and Remote Sensing Imagery**

Surveying and Mapping Office
Florida Department of Transportation
Aerial Survey Section
Lafayette Building
605 Suwannee Street, MS 5-L
Tallahassee, FL 32399-0450
(850) 488-2250

Bureau of Beaches and Coastal Systems
Florida Department of Environmental Protection (FDEP)
3900 Commonwealth Boulevard
Tallahassee, FL 32399-3000
(850) 488-3181
http://www.dep.state.fl.us/ beaches
Beach and Coastal Ecosystem Management: (850) 487-1262
Coastal Protection and Engineering: (850) 487-4475
Coastal Data and Analysis: (850) 487-4469
Environmental Permitting: (850) 487-4471

Earth Science Information Center
U.S. Geological Survey
12201 Sunrise Valley Drive
Reston, VA 20192
(703) 860-6045; book and map sales: (703) 648-6892
http://info.er.usgs.gov

U.S. Geological Survey, Florida District Office
227 North Bronough Street, Suite 3015
Tallahassee, FL 32301
(850) 942-9500

Nautical charts at several scales contain navigation information on Florida's coastal waters. A nautical chart index map is available from:

Distribution Branch N/CG 33
National Ocean Service
National Oceanic and Atmospheric Administration
Riverdale, MD 20737-1199
(301) 436-6990

Local county or municipal governments also have maps. Address your inquiry to the attention of your county engineer or planning, zoning, or building department. Many local government permit requests to the state of Florida and to the U.S. Army Corps of Engineers are handled by the county engineer, often at the direction of the county commission.

Beach Erosion

Information on barrier beach erosion, inlet migration, and erosion control alternatives is available from the following agencies:

National Oceanic and Atmospheric Administration (NOAA)
Office of Ocean and Coastal Resource Management
1305 E-W Highway
Silver Spring, MD 20910
(301) 713-3115

Bureau of Beaches and Coastal Systems
Florida Department of Environmental Protection
3900 Commonwealth Boulevard
Tallahassee, FL 32399-3000
(850) 488-3181
http://www.dep.state.fl.us/beaches

University of Florida Coastal Engineering Archives
Department of Coastal and Oceanographic Engineering
433 Weil Hall
University of Florida
Gainesville, FL 32611
(352) 392-2710

Florida Institute of Technology
Department of Marine and Environmental Systems, Ocean Engineering Program
150 West University Boulevard, Melbourne, FL 32901-6975
(321) 674-8096; fax: (321) 674-7212; email: dmes@fit.edu

Division of Marine Geology and Geophysics
Rosenstiel School of Marine and Atmospheric Science
University of Miami
4600 Rickenbacker Causeway
Miami, FL 33149
(305) 361-4662; fax: (305) 361-4632; email: mgg@rsmas.miami.edu

Coastal Zone Studies
Department of Government
University of West Florida
11000 University Parkway
Pensacola, FL 32514
(904) 474-2337

U.S. Army Corps of Engineers
Jacksonville District Office
400 West Bay Street
P.O. Box 4970
Jacksonville, FL 32232
(904) 232-2234 or (800) 291-9405

To contact local county or municipal governments regarding beach erosion, direct your inquiry Attn: planning or engineering departments.

Bridges and Causeways

The U.S. Coast Guard has jurisdiction over permits to build bridges or causeways that will affect navigable waters.

Commander, 7th Coast Guard District
909 S.E. First Avenue, Room 954
Miami, FL 33130-3050
(305) 536-4108

Building Codes, Planning, and Zoning

Most communities have adopted comprehensive plans and building codes. Check with your county or city building department for permitted uses and building codes. If you intend to build on a barrier island, you should obtain and follow all local and state codes. The website of the Bureau of Beaches and Coastal Systems (see below) has access to the Florida Building Code.

Coastal Construction Building Code Guidelines

Bureau of Beaches and Coastal Systems
Florida Department of Environmental Protection
3900 Commonwealth Boulevard
Tallahassee, FL 32399-3000
(850) 488-3181
http://www.dep.state.fl.us/beaches

Coastal Regulations

The complete Florida Statutes are available online at http://www.leg.state.fl.us/.

Coastal Zone Planning and Management Program

Florida adopted the Coastal Management Program (CMP) pursuant to the Florida Coastal Zone Management Act of 1978 (chap. 380, Florida Statutes) and the Federal Coastal Zone

Management Act of 1972. Florida's CMP did not create a new agency but provides for coordination and consistency in the implementation of various federal and state programs affecting coastal areas and barrier islands. For information on the CMP and designated barrier islands, contact:

Florida Coastal Management Program
Florida Department of Environmental Protection
3900 Commonwealth Boulevard
Tallahassee, FL 32329-3000
(850) 245-2161 or (850) 245-2163

Construction

American Society of Civil Engineers (ASCE)
1801 Alexander Bell Drive
Reston, VA 20191-4400
(800) 548 2723 (ASCE)
http://www.pubs.asce.org

Federal Emergency Management Agency (FEMA)
Region IV
Mitigation Division
3003 Chamblee Tucker Road
Atlanta, GA 30341
(770) 220-5200
http://www.fema.gov/regions/iv

Dredging, Filling, and Construction in Coastal Waters

Florida laws require all those who wish to dredge, fill, or otherwise alter wetlands, marshes, estuarine bottoms, or tidal lands to apply for a permit from the appropriate state, federal, and local governments. For the standard state permit on dredging and filling, contact:

Florida Department of Environmental Protection
Submerged Lands and Environmental Resources
Environmental Resource Permitting
2600 Blair Stone Road
Tallahassee, FL 32399
(850) 245-8474
http://www.dep.state.fl.us/water/wetlands/erp/index.htm

For short-form dredge-and-fill application permits, contact the appropriate district offices of the Department of Environmental Protection.

For erosion control structures and coastal construction control line permits, write or call:

Bureau of Beaches and Coastal Systems
Florida Department of Environmental Protection
3900 Commonwealth Boulevard
Tallahassee, FL 32399-3000
(850) 488-3181
http://www.dep.state.fl.us/beaches/programs/ccclprog.htm

Easements and submerged land leases for docks, piers, etc., must be obtained from:

Division of State Lands
Florida Department of Environmental Protection
3900 Commonwealth Boulevard
Tallahassee, FL 32399-3000
(850) 245-2555
http://www.dep.state.fl.us/lands

Federal law requires any person who wishes to dredge, fill, or place any structure in navigable water (almost any body of water) to apply for a permit from the U.S. Army Corps of Engineers—Permit Branch.

U.S. Army Corps of Engineers (USACE)
Planning and Regulatory Divisions
400 West Bay Street
P.O. Box 4970
Jacksonville, FL 32232
(904) 232-2234 or (800) 291-9405

The U.S. Army Corps of Engineers has many additional field offices in Florida; 7 of them are located on the east coast. Consult the white pages of your area telephone directory for the U.S. government listing.

The American Shore and Beach Preservation Association publishes a quarterly journal, *Shore and Beach,* which features articles concerned with dredging and construction along the U.S. coasts. For more information, write:

American Shore and Beach Preservation Association
1724 Indian Way
Oakland, CA 94611
http://www.asbpa.org
The Florida chapter can be contacted at:

Florida Shore and Beach Preservation Association
2952 Wellington Circle
Tallahassee, FL 32308
(850) 906-9227; fax: (850) 906-9228
http://www.fsbpa.com

Dune Alteration and Vegetation Removal

Florida laws limit the destruction, damaging, or removal of seagrasses, sea oats, or sand dunes and berms. Individual counties or cities may have ordinances pertaining to dune alteration and vegetation removal as well. Permits for certain work and alterations may be obtained from local county or city planning and building departments. For permits to clear or alter dunes or beaches seaward of the CCCL, write or call:

Bureau of Beaches and Coastal Systems
Florida Department of Environmental Protection
3900 Commonwealth Boulevard
Tallahassee, FL 32399-3000
(850) 488-3181
http://www.dep.state.fl.us/beaches

Geological Information

Earth Science Information Center
U.S. Geological Survey
12201 Sunrise Valley Drive
Reston, VA 20192
(703) 860-6045
http://ask.usgs.gov

Coastal Education and Research Foundation (CERF)
P.O. Box 21087
Royal Palm Beach, FL 33421
(561) 753-7557
http://www.cerf-jcr.com

Health, Sanitation, and Water Quality

All concerns about septic systems should be directed to:

Department of Water Resource Management
Florida Department of Environmental Protection
2600 Blair Stone Road
Tallahassee, FL 32399-2400
(850) 245-8335
http://www.dep.state.fl.us/water

A permit for any discharge into navigable waters must be obtained from the U.S. Environmental Protection Agency. Recent judicial interpretations of the Federal Water Pollution Control Amendments of 1972 (also known as the Clean Water Act) extend federal jurisdiction above the high-water mark for protection of wetlands. Federal permits may now be required to develop land that is occasionally flooded by water draining indirectly into a navigable waterway. Information may be obtained from:

Water Management Division
U.S. Environmental Protection Agency
Region 4
Atlanta Federal Center
61 Forsyth Street s.w.
Atlanta, GA 30303
(404) 562-9345
http://www.epa.gov/region4/water

History and Archaeology

If you suspect that your property may have an archaeological or historical site, write or call:

Bureau of Archaeological Research
Florida Division of Historical Resources
R. A. Gray Building
500 South Bronough Street
Tallahassee, FL 32399-0250
(850) 245-6444
http://dhr.dos.state.fl.us/bar

Hurricane Information and Planning

The National Oceanic and Atmospheric Administration is the best agency from which to request information on hurricanes. NOAA storm flood evacuation maps are prepared for vulnerable coastal areas. For details, call or write:

National Hurricane Center
Tropical Prediction Center
11691 s.w. 17th Street
Miami, FL 33165-2149
(305) 229-4470
http://www.nhc.noaa.gov

National Oceanic and Atmospheric Administration (NOAA)
Office of Ocean and Coastal Resource Management
1305 E-W Highway
Silver Spring, MD 20910
(301) 713-3115
http://www.noaa.gov

Hurricane Evacuation and Disaster Assistance

Contact your local county or city civil defense or disaster preparedness office for hurricane evacuation and hurricane shelter information. Local radio and TV stations provide hurricane warnings and evacuation bulletins when storms threaten an area. For information on hurricane disaster response, recovery, and assistance, contact:

Florida Department of Community Affairs
Division of Emergency Management
Bureau of Preparedness and Response
2225 Shumard Oak Boulevard
Tallahassee, FL 32399-2100
(850) 413-9900
http://www.floridadisaster.org

American National Red Cross
Washington, DC 20006
(202) 728-6400
http://www.redcross.org

Federal Emergency Management Agency (FEMA)
Region IV
3003 Chamblee Tucker Road
Atlanta, GA 30341
(770) 220-5200
http://www.fema.gov/regions/iv

Department of Housing and Urban Development Services
(202) 708-1422

Federal Emergency Management Agency Disaster Services
(800) 262-9029

Federal Emergency Management Agency Information Line
(800) 621-FEMA

Federal Emergency Management Agency Main Office
(202) 646-2500 or (800) 427-4661

Insurance

In coastal areas, special building requirements must often be met to obtain flood or windstorm insurance. To find out the requirements in your area, check with your local building department and your insurance agent. Further information is available from:

Federal Emergency Management Agency (FEMA)
National Flood Insurance Program
(800) 427-4661
http://www.fema.gov/nfip

Florida Department of Insurance
The Capitol
Tallahassee, FL 32399-0301
(850) 922-3100
http://www.doi.state.fl.us/index.htm

Federal Insurance Administration
National Flood Insurance Program
Department of Housing and Urban Development
500 C Street s.w.
Washington, DC 20472
(202) 646-2500

For v zone coverage or structure rating, contact:

National Flood Insurance Program
ATTN: v-Zone Underwriting Specialist
P.O. Box 6468
Rockville, MD 20849-6468
(800) 638-6620

For flood maps, etc., contact:

Federal Emergency Management Agency (FEMA)
Flood Map Distribution Agency
6930 (A-F) San Thomas Road
Baltimore, MD 21227-6627
(800) 358-9616

Other agencies:

Department of Housing and Urban Development Services
(202) 708-1422

Federal Emergency Management Agency Disaster Services
(800) 262-9029

Federal Emergency Management Agency Information Line
800-621-FEMA

Federal Emergency Management Agency Main Office
(202) 646-2500 or (800) 427-4661

Property loss information is available from:

Institute for Business and Home Safety (IBHS)
(formerly the Insurance Institute for Property Loss Reduction)
73 Tremont Street, Suite 510
Boston, MA 02108-3910
(617) 722-0200
http://www.ibhs.org

Land Planning and Land Use

Local county and municipal governments have adopted comprehensive land-use plans and zoning and building codes under the state law. It is advisable to contact the appropriate county or city agency, preferably before you buy land on a barrier island or coastal area. Regional planning councils distributed around the state may also be contacted. For additional information, contact:

Division of Community Planning
Florida Department of Community Affairs
2555 Shumard Oak Boulevard
Tallahassee, FL 32399-2100
(850) 487-4545
http://www.state.fl.us/fdcp/DCP

Land Preservation

Several barrier beaches are being considered by the state for public acquisition under three state programs: the Environmentally Endangered Lands Program, the Save Our Coast Program, and the Conservation and Recreational Lands Program. If you own large parcels of environmentally sensitive land on barrier islands or coastal areas and want to have it preserved for future generations to enjoy, contact one of these agencies. On the other hand, if you plan to buy barrier island property, it would be advisable to contact the local government agency as well as the appropriate state agencies to determine if there could be development and permitting problems.

Land Purchase and Sales

When acquiring a property or condominium, whether in a subdivision or not, consider the following: (1) Owners of property next to dredged canals should make sure that the canals are designed for adequate flushing to keep waters from become stagnant. Requests for federal permits to connect extensive canal systems to navigable waters are frequently denied. (2) Descriptions and surveys of land in coastal areas are very complicated. Old titles granting fee-simple rights to property below the high-tide line may not be upheld in court; titles should be reviewed by a competent attorney before they are transferred. A boundary described as the high-water mark may be impossible to determine. (3) Ask about the provision of sewage disposal and utilities including water, electricity, gas, and telephone. (4) Be sure any promises of future improvements, access, utilities, additions, common property rights, etc., are in writing. (5) Be sure to visit the property and inspect it carefully before buying it.

Land Sales—Subdivisions

Subdivisions containing more than 50 lots and offered in interstate commerce must be registered with the Office of Interstate Land Sales Registration (as specified by the Interstate Land Sales Full Disclosure Act). Prospective buyers must be provided with a property report. This office also produces a booklet entitled *Get the Facts . . . Before Buying Land* for people who wish to invest in property. Information on subdivision property and land investment is available from:

Office of Interstate Land Sales Registration
U.S. Department of Housing and Urban Development
451 Seventh Street s.w.
Room 9146
Washington, DC 20410
(202) 708-0502
http://www.hud.gov

Florida office:

U.S. Department of Housing and Urban Development
Jacksonville (904) 232-2627
Miami (305) 536-4456
http://www.hud.gov/localfl/working/localoffices.cfm

Marine and Coastal Zone Information

Many of the agencies mentioned in related sections, many local universities, and the following organizations can provide various types of information.

Caribbean Conservation Corporation
4424 N.W. 13th Street, Suite A1
Gainesville, FL 32609
(352) 373-6441

Coast Alliance
210 D Street, S.E.
Washington, DC 20003
(202) 546-9554

Environmental Defense
14630 S.W. 144th Terrace
Miami, FL 33186
(305) 256-9508; fax: (305) 256-4488

Florida Sea Grant College Program
University of Florida
Building 803 McCarty Drive
P.O. Box 110400
Gainesville, FL 32611-0400
(352) 392-5870; fax: (352) 392-5113
http://www.flseagrant.org

National Sea Grant Library (NSGL)
Pell Library Building
University of Rhode Island
Narragansett Bay Campus
Narragansett, RI 02882-1197
(401) 792-6114
http://nsgd.gso.uri.edu/

NOAA Coastal Services Center
2234 South Hobson Avenue
Charleston, SC 29405-2413
(843) 740-1200; fax: (843) 740-1224
http://www.csc.noaa.gov

The Ocean Conservancy
One Beach Drive, S.E.
Suite 304
St. Petersburg, FL 33701
(727) 895-2188; fax: (727) 895-3248

Public Employees for Environmental
Responsibility (PEER)
2001 S Street, N.W.
Suite 570
Washington, DC 20009
(202) 265-7337; fax: (202) 265-4192
http://www.peer.org

ReefKeeper International
Suite 5, PMB 162
2829 Bird Avenue
Miami, FL 33133
(305) 358-4600; fax: (301) 371-6188

Surfrider Foundation USA
P.O. Box 6010
San Clemente, CA 92674-6010
(949) 492-8170
http://www.surfrider.org

Water Supply and Pollution Control

If your plan involves draining land or a large water supply system, contact the appropriate Florida Water Management District office for information on the rules and permit process. Construction of any sewage or solid waste disposal facilities requires permits from the Florida Department of Environmental Protection. Contact the appropriate district office of the FDEP. (See "Dredging and Filling" listing, above, for addresses.)

Wildlife and Habitat Protection

For the conservation and protection of fish and wildlife species and their habitat, contact the office of the Florida State Game and Fresh Water Fish Commission in your area. Also contact:

U.S. Fish and Wildlife Service
Department of the Interior
1360 U.S. Highway 1, Suite 5
Vero Beach, FL 32960
http://southeast-fws.gov
(561) 562-3909

National Marine Fisheries Service
Southeast Regional Office
Habitat Conservation Division
9721 Executive Center Drive North
St. Petersburg, FL 33702
(727) 570-5301
http://caldera.sero.nmf.gov

Appendix C
101 Useful Coastal References

The following publications are listed by subject and arranged in the approximate order in which they appear in the text. Sources are included in most citations. Scientific literature (books and journal articles) can be found in the libraries of colleges, universities, and some agencies. Popular books should be available through your local bookstore. Government publications are available from the agency listed or from the U.S. Government Printing Office (www.gpo.gove). Another source of information is the "information superhighway." More and more agencies and organizations are creating their own home pages on the World Wide Web. A good first stop is MyFlorida.com, which has links to just about every state agency.

Floridians who wish to delve into the more detailed literature are referred to the outstanding libraries in the Department of Coastal Engineering at the University of Florida in Gainesville and the Rosentiel School of Marine and Atmospheric Sciences at the University of Miami. Other important sources include the U.S. Army Corps of Engineers' district offices in Jacksonville, offices of the Federal Emergency Management Agency, and various state and county agencies concerned with coastal management.

Abbreviations used in this appendix and elsewhere in the book are given below:

ASBPA	American Shore and Beach Preservation Association
ASCE	American Society of Civil Engineers
CERF	Coastal Education and Research Foundation
CSO	Coastal States Organization
CZMP	Coastal Zone Management Program
DOE	Department of Energy
EPA	Environmental Protection Agency
FDCA	Florida Department of Community Affairs
FDEP	Florida Department of Environmental Protection
FDNR	Florida Department of Natural Resources (no longer in existence)
FEMA	Federal Emergency Management Agency
FIA	Federal Insurance Administration
FSBPA	Florida Shore and Beach Preservation Association
NAS	National Academy of Sciences
NFIP	National Flood Insurance Program
NHC	National Hurricane Center
NHRAIC	Natural Hazards Research and Applications Information Center
NOAA	National Oceanic and Atmospheric Administration
NRC	National Research Council

USACE   U.S. Army Corps of Engineers; may also be abbreviated as USACOE and ACOE
USACOE   see USACE
USGS   U.S. Geological Survey

History and Geology

1   *A History of Florida*, by Charlton W. Tebeau, 1971, covers natural events such as hurricanes, droughts, and floods, and their influence on the state's history. From the earliest Spanish exploration through the twentieth-century land booms and busts, natural hazards have played a significant role in altering the course of the state's history. The 502-page book, published by the University of Miami Press, is available through your library.

2   *A New History of Florida*, edited by Michael Gannon, 1996, was published by the University Press of Florida, Gainesville. This 480-page book is a collection of chapters by various experts on the history of Florida.

3   *Florida's Geological History and Geological Resources*, by the Florida Geological Survey, 1994, provides a short (64-page) introduction to a wide variety of geological topics. Of particular interest is the section on geological hazards, including global warming and the sea-level rise, by Ed Lane and K. M. Campbell. Available from the Florida Geological Survey as Special Publication 35.

4   *The Geomorphology of the Florida Peninsula*, by W. A. White, 1970, is a 164-page report published as Geological Bulletin 51 by the Florida Bureau of Geology, Tallahassee. The author discusses barrier islands, headlands, sand, and Florida geology/geomorphology in general. *Land from the Sea*, by John Edward Hoffmeister, 1984, is also a definitive and readable guide to the geologic history of southeast Florida. Published by the University of Miami Press.

5   *Sinkhole Type, Development, and Distribution in Florida*, by W. C. Sinclair and J. W. Stewart, 1985, is a map that shows the distribution of four categories of bedrock type and cover thickness, and the associated sinkhole types for the state. Although not a risk map, the information conveys a general regional sense of where collapse sinkholes are likely. Available from the Bureau of Geology, Florida Department of Environmental Protection, Map Series 110.

Hurricanes and Storms

6   *Florida's Hurricane History*, 3d ed., by Jay Barnes, 2001, contains well-written, in-depth accounts of just about every hurricane or significant tropical storm to have struck Florida through 1999. This 319-page book was published by University of North Carolina Press and should be available at university libraries or through your local bookseller.

7   *Florida Hurricanes and Tropical Storms*, rev. ed., by John M. Williams and Iver W. Duedall, 2003, covers the period 1871–2001, summarizing the hurricanes and tropical storms that have struck Florida; organized by historical periods. Published by the University Press of Florida, Gainesville.

8   *Hurricane! A Familiarization Booklet*, by NOAA, 1993, gives a descriptive and nontechnical overview of U.S. hurricanes. Also includes sections on hurricane anatomy, storm surge, forecasting, and lists of the most intense and destructive hurricanes through 1992. A hurricane checklist is provided. The 36-page document, NOAA/PA 91001, is available through NOAA.

9   *The Deadliest, Costliest, and Most Intense United States Hurricanes of This Century (and Other Frequently Requested Hurricane Facts)*, by Paul J. Hebert and Glenn Taylor, 1988, updated in 1997, is NOAA Technical Memorandum NWS-TPC-1. This pamphlet contains a discussion of hurricane facts and several tables summarizing deaths, costs, and hurricane

intensities. Available from NOAA, National Weather Service. Lists can be viewed online at the National Hurricane Center's website: http://www.nhc.noaa.gov/.

10 *Hurricane Andrew: South Florida and Louisiana, August 23–26, 1992*, is a Natural Disaster Survey Report published in November 1993 by NOAA. The 131-page report contains several appendixes summarizing immediate poststorm field investigations by teams of experts covering fields such as meteorology of the storm, public response, communications, damage assessments, and recommendations on how to do things better next time.

11 *Hurricane Andrew Storm Summary and Impacts on the Beaches of Florida*, is a special report produced in May 1993 by the U.S. Army Corps of Engineers, Jacksonville District, and the former Florida Department of Natural Resources, Division of Beaches and Shores. The 61-page report provides detailed accounts of the storm and photographs and beach profiles of impacted beaches.

12 *Lessons of Hurricane Andrew* is a 92-page compilation of excerpts from the 15th Annual National Hurricane Conference held on April 13–16, 1993, in Orlando, Florida. The document was compiled by Lawrence S. Tait. Contact FEMA or the National Hurricane Conference executive director, David Tait, at 2952 Wellington Circle, Tallahassee, FL 32308; (850) 906-9224; fax: (850) 906-9228; mail@HurricaneMeeting.com. For a more complete discussion of Hurricane Andrew, see *In the Eye of Hurricane Andrew*, by E. F. Provenzo Jr. and A. B. Provenzo, 2002, published by the University Press of Florida, Gainesville.

13 Additional hurricane-related reports produced by the U.S. Army Corps of Engineers, Mobile District, are available through that office: *After Action Report on Hurricane Camille, 1970*; *Hurricane Camille, 1970*; *Report on Hurricane Survey of Alabama Coast, 1972*; *Post-disaster Report: Hurricane Eloise, 16–23 September 1975, 1976*; and *Feasibility Report for Beach Erosion Control and Hurricane Protection—Mobile County, AL, 1978* (includes Dauphin Island). Although these reports deal with Gulf coast storms, the studies are pertinent to East Florida.

14 Ralph Clark, an engineer with the FDEP Bureau of Beaches and Coastal Systems, has written several documents regarding the effects of Hurricane Opal on the Florida Panhandle and beach conditions in the entire state. His *Hurricanes Floyd and Irene Report*, FDEP Bureau of Beaches and Coastal Systems, is among several FDEP studies that provide details on storm impacts and coastal erosion problem areas in the state (see chapter 7). See also those listed in this appendix under "Coastal Management: General."

15 "Nor'easters," by Robert E. Davis and Robert Dolan, 1993, is one of the best and most thorough treatments of winter storms available. It includes a scale for ranking these storms patterned somewhat after the Saffir-Simpson scale for hurricanes, as well as information on storm formation and tracking, along with good historical accounts of storms. Published in *American Scientist*, vol. 81, pp. 428–39.

16 *The Weather Book*, by Jack Williams, 2d ed., 1997, explains weather phenomena in easily understood language with many diagrams and photographs. Published by Vintage Books, Random House, New York.

Barrier Islands and Beaches

17 *Geology of Holocene Barrier Island Systems*, edited by Richard A. Davis Jr., 1994, is a technical reference on U.S. barrier island systems. Chapter 1: "Barrier Island Systems—A Geologic Overview" (pp. 1–46), by Dr. Davis, gives background information on the geology and dynamics of barrier islands. A chapter by Miles Hayes, "The Georgia Bight Barrier System," discusses part of the East Florida shoreline. Published by Springer-Verlag, New York, 464 pp.

18   *Quaternary Coasts of the United States: Marine and Lacustrine Systems,* edited by C. H. Fletcher III and J. F. Wehmiller, 1992, is a collection of technical papers that contains some of the most detailed work to date on shoreline evolution of the United States. There is only one entry specific to Florida: "Holocene Coastal Development of the Florida Peninsula," by Richard A. Davis, Albert C. Hine, and Eugene A. Shinn (pp. 193–212), but the volume contains general information about shoreline erosion and marine coastal evolution of interest to the serious investigator. Published as Special Publication 48 by the Society for Sedimentary Geology, Tulsa, Okla.

19   *The World's Coastline,* edited by Eric C. F. Bird and Maurice L. Schwartz, 1985, includes a chapter on Florida (pp. 163–67) written by William F. Tanner that contains a general description of the geology of the state's shoreline, including the effects of wave energy and littoral drift, formation and location of beach ridges on islands, and descriptions of reef types and mangroves. Published by Van Nostrand Reinhold, New York.

20   *At the Sea's Edge: An Introduction to Coastal Oceanography for the Amateur Naturalist,* by W. T. Fox, 1983, is an excellent, nontechnical, richly illustrated introduction to coastal processes, meteorology, environments, and ecology. Published by Prentice-Hall, Englewood Cliffs, New Jersey. This 317-page book is available at local and university libraries.

21   *Coastal Environments: An Introduction to the Physical, Ecological and Cultural Systems of Coastlines,* by R. W. G. Carter, 1988, is an excellent text for almost all aspects of the coastal zone although management of coastal environments is emphasized. Published by Academic Press, New York, 617 pages.

22   *Coasts: An Introduction to Coastal Geomorphology,* by Eric C. F. Bird, 3d ed., 1984. This introduction to coastal types and their classifications discusses tides, waves, and currents; changing levels of the sea; cliffed coasts; beaches, spits, and barriers; coastal dunes; estuaries and lagoons; deltas; and coral reefs and atolls. Published by Basil Blackwell, London.

23   *Waves and Beaches,* by Willard Bascom, 1964, provides a good introduction to beaches and coastal processes. Published by Anchor Books/Doubleday, Garden City, New York.

24   *Florida's Sandy Beaches: An Access Guide,* 1985, is a detailed though somewhat dated report on how to reach Florida's sandy beaches and what amenities and resources are available. This 218-page book, full of detailed maps, presents information on facilities and the environment in an easy-to-read format. It is a compilation by the Beach Access Project, Office of Coastal Studies, University of West Florida.

25   *Islands of the South and Southeastern United States,* 1989, by Sarah Bird Wright. This 215-page book, published by Peachtree Publishers of Atlanta, gives information on location, size, access, history and description, points of interest, sightseeing tours, parks, beaches, camping, marinas, restaurants, lodging, rentals, and contacts. It is not comprehensive, but it does cover several Florida beaches.

26   *America's Best Beaches,* 1998, by Stephen P. Leatherman, a.k.a. Dr. Beach, includes a discussion of the Atlantic coast. Several of East Florida's beaches have been listed on Dr. Leatherman's Top 10 Best Beaches list. East Florida beaches included as some of the best in the Southeast are Daytona Beach (best sports beach), Miami Beach (best city beach), Cape Florida Beach on Key Biscayne (best swimming beach), and Sandspur Beach on Bahia Honda Key in the Florida Keys (best overall beach). Available through bookstores, or contact http://www.topbeaches.com.

27   *Against the Tide: The Battle for America's Beaches,* by Cornelia Dean, science editor of the *New York Times,* 1999. This "must" read illustrates how we rescue buildings at the expense of beaches and puts the problem in a national perspective. Published by Columbia University Press, New York, 296 pages.

28   *Using Common Sense to Protect the Coasts,* by Michael Weber, 1990. This brief pamphlet (24 pp.) contains basic information on the geology and ecology of barrier islands, the de-

structive effects of development on these areas, and legislation passed concerning their protection and management. Produced and distributed by the Coast Alliance.

29 *The Coastal Almanac for 1980—the Year of the Coast,* by Paul L. Ringold and John Clark, 1980, is a comprehensive tabulation of the state of the U.S. shoreline as a whole and by state as of 1980. Included is such information as length of the shoreline, water temperatures, environmental and pollution data, energy production, resources, recreation, and hurricanes. This 172-page book was published by W. H. Freeman and is available through university libraries.

30 There are several references specific to East Florida counties. *Shoreline Change Rate Estimates—Flagler County, July 1999,* by E. R. Foster, D. L. Spurgeon, and J. Cheng, is one of several reports available online at the Bureau of Beaches and Coastal Systems website. It is Florida Department of Environmental Protection, Bureau of Beaches and Coastal Systems, Report BCS-99-02, 43 pp. See the report online at http://bcs.dep. state.fl.us/counties/HSSD/reports/flasre.pdf. For several technical and general online publications by the bureau, see http://www.dep.state.fl.us/beaches/publications/publc-sns.htm. See also "Shore Erosion from Recurrent Storms near St. Augustine," by Peter Kendrick, 1933, published in *Shore and Beach,* July, for an interesting historical look at shoreline changes, the first jetties, and the extent of storm erosion in St. Johns County. On Volusia County, see *Evaluation of the Volusia County Coastline: Dominant Processes, Shoreline Change, Stabilization Efforts, and Recommendations for Beach Management,* 1989, by A. C. Hine, Department of Marine Science, University of South Florida, St. Petersburg, FL 33701; and *Study of Beach Conditions at Daytona Beach, Florida, and Vicinity; Being a Synopsis of a Report of the Beach Erosion Board of the Office of the Chief of Engineers of the War Department with Comments and Digest,* by W. W. Fineren, 1938, University of Florida Engineering Experiment Station Bulletin 4, University of Florida, Gainesville.

31 "Holocene Evolution of Indian River Lagoon in Central Brevard County, Florida," by Sharon Bader and Randall Parkinson, 1990, is a technical paper dealing with impacts of sea-level rise on the coast of central Brevard County. Published in the journal *Atmospheric and Oceanographic Sciences,* vol. 53, no. 3, pp. 204–15; available through university libraries.

32 "Late Holocene Erosional Shoreface Retreat within Siliciclastic-to-Carbonate Transition Zone, East Central Florida, USA," by R. W. Parkinson and J. R. White, 1994, *Journal of Sedimentary Research,* vol. B64, pp. 408–15, provides an example of barrier island transgression.

33 "Protecting Undeveloped Barrier Islands—a Florida Case Study," by M. Benedict and T. Bernd-Cohen, provides an example of how to protect what is becoming a rare resource —an undeveloped barrier island. This paper and selected others from the American Society of Civil Engineers' Coastal Zone '89 symposium was published in *Barrier Islands: Process and Management,* edited by D. K. Stauble and O. T. Magoon. See also "Regional Beach Restoration Plan for Three Consecutive Barrier Islands in South Florida," by Paul Lin, Harvey Sasso, and Anthony Spell, 1997, in *New Insights into Beach Preservation,* Proceedings of the 10th National Conference on Beach Preservation Technology, St. Petersburg, January 22–24, 1997.

Recreation and Nature

34 *The Audubon Society Field Guide to North American Seashells,* by Harold A. Rehder, 1995. This well-illustrated reference, published by Alfred A. Knopf, New York, is an excellent handbook for the serious shell collector.

35   *A Field Guide to Southeastern and Caribbean Seashores: Cape Hatteras to the Gulf Coast, Florida, and the Caribbean,* by Eugene H. Kaplan, 1988, is one of the Peterson Field Guide series sponsored by the National Audubon Society and the National Wildlife Federation and published by Houghton Mifflin, Boston. This 425-page guide probably describes most of the wildlife you will encounter in Florida.

36   *The Audubon Society Field Guide to North American Fishes, Whales, and Dolphins,* by H. Boschung, J. Williams, D. Gotshall, D. Caldwell, and M. Caldwell, 1983, provides detailed species descriptions for fishes and marine mammals of North America. Published by Alfred A. Knopf, New York.

37   *The Audubon Society Field Guide to North American Seashore Creatures,* by N. Meinkoth, 1995, gives detailed species descriptions and an overview of the taxonomy of the major shore animals of North America. Illustrated with color photographs. Published by Alfred A. Knopf, New York.

Shoreline Engineering and Environmental Issues

38   *The Corps and the Shore,* by Orrin H. Pilkey and Katherine L. Dixon, 1996, delves into the role of the U.S. Army Corps of Engineers in U.S. beach management, including dredge-and-fill projects, and documents the need for independent peer reviews of Corps activities. Published by Island Press, Washington, D.C., 286 pages.

39   "Evaluation of Shore Protection Measures Applied to Eroding Beaches in Florida," by Luciana Slomp Esteves, 1997, is a graduate thesis presented at Florida Atlantic University, Boca Raton, Florida. The study characterizes almost every Florida beach based on urban development, shoreline changes, environmental factors, and shoreline engineering structures. Contact Florida Atlantic University, Department of Geography and Geology, at (561) 297-3250.

40   *The Effects of Seawalls on the Beach,* edited by Nicholas C. Kraus and O. H. Pilkey Jr., 1988, is a technical volume (146 pages) published as special issue no. 4 of the *Journal of Coastal Research* that explores the nature of the impacts of seawalls on beaches. See the paper by Pilkey and Wright titled "Seawalls versus Beaches," which discusses how seawalls contribute to narrowing of beaches.

41   "An Analysis of Replenished Beach Design Parameters on U.S. East Coast Barrier Islands," by Lynn Leonard, Tonya Clayton, and Orrin Pilkey, 1990. This scientific paper, published in the *Journal of Coastal Research,* vol. 6, no. 1, pp. 15–36, concludes that replenished beaches north of Florida generally have life spans of less than five years. Storm frequency is a major factor in the loss of such beaches. The authors document overestimates of beach life spans by the USACE. See the website of the Duke University Program for the Study of Developed Shorelines (http://www.env.duke.edu/psds/nourishment.htm) for updates of this study.

42   "A 'Thumbnail Method' for Beach Communities: Estimation of Long-Term Beach Replenishment Requirements," by Orrin H. Pilkey, 1988. This short paper demonstrates that current methods of estimating long-term volume requirements for replenished beaches are inadequate. Published in *Shore and Beach,* vol. 56, no. 3, pp. 23–31.

43   *Coast of Florida Erosion and Storm Effects Study: Region III, with Final Environmental Impact Statement,* 3 vols., including appendixes A–I, U.S. Army Corps of Engineers, 1996, Technical Report, Jacksonville District. This remarkably detailed set of documents provides planning options for beach engineering at more than 20 sites between Miami and Palm Beach from 1997 to 2047. Well over 100 dredge-and-fill projects are projected from these plans, yet the cumulative impacts section of the accompanying environmental impact assessment totals a *single* paragraph.

44 "Sabellariid Worms: Builders of a Major Reef Type," by D. W. Kirtley and W. F. Tanner, 1968, is a technical scientific paper published in the *Journal of Sedimentary Petrology*, vol. 38, no. 1, pp. 73–78, that documents the biology of East Florida's worm reefs and their geological significance.

45 "Nearshore Hardbottom Fishes of Southeast Florida and Effects of Habitat Burial by Dredging," by K. C. Lindeman and D. B. Snyder, 1999, *Fishery Bulletin*, vol. 97, no. 3, pp. 508–25, quantifies the effects on fishes of the burial of 12–14 acres of nearshore reef, the importance of nearshore reefs to juvenile fishes, and age-specific variations in impacts.

46 "Beach Nourishment and Hard Bottom Habitats: The Case for Caution," by W. G. Nelson, is a report by a leading academic researcher explaining why the routine burial of reefs needs more careful examination. For some reason it is not referenced in the great majority of environmental assessments. Published in 1989 in the *Proceedings of the 1989 National Conference on Beach Preservation Technology*, pp. 109–16.

47 "Environmental Degradation and the Tyranny of Small Decisions," by W. E. Odum, 1982, is a classic explanation of how the effects of individually "insignificant" construction projects multiply through time to degrade entire ecosystems in unanticipated ways. Published in *BioScience*, vol. 32, no. 9, pp. 728–29.

48 "Effects of Turbidity on the Photosynthesis and Respiration of Two South Florida Reef Coral Species," by G. J. Telesnicki and W. M. Goldberg, 1995, is a technical report discussing controlled experiments which demonstrate that even turbidity levels below Florida's state standards can degrade coral health. In addition, the technological ability to actually measure turbidity "standards" is tenuous at best. Published in the *Bulletin of Marine Science*, vol. 57, no. 2, pp. 527–39.

49 "A Re-examination of Infaunal Studies that Accompany Beach Nourishment Projects," by P. Wilber and M. Stern, 1992, is a rare study that actually considers age-specific and food-web responses to dredging, and recommends more research and precautionary management approaches. This important report is routinely underreferenced in environmental assessments. Published in the *Proceedings of the 1992 Conference on Beach Preservation Technology*, pp. 242–56.

50 "Reefs since Columbus," by J. Jackson, 1997, examines 400 years of information from the Caribbean and concludes that (1) most coastal ecosystems of the greater Caribbean and Florida were already heavily damaged, compared with their original state, by the late 1800s; and (2) scientists and managers are typically working on improper time scales, thinking that reefs from two or three decades ago represent virgin systems, and that it is possible to restore or maintain full ecosystem functioning while underestimating the cascade effects of hundreds of years of effects in some regions. Published as a supplement to *Coral Reefs*, vol. 16, pp. S23–S32.

51 "Roles for Worms in Reef-Building," by J. Pandolfi, D. R. Robertson, and D. Kirtley, 1998, is a technical paper documenting the long- and short-term geological significance of worm reefs. It was published in the journal *Coral Reefs*, vol. 17, p. 120.

52 "Short-Term Consequences of Nourishment and Bulldozing on the Dominant Large Invertebrates of a Sandy Beach," by C. H. Peterson, D. Hickerson, and G. Johnson, 2000, is one of the few statistically strong studies of the impacts of dredging and filling on beach animals. The authors conclude that key populations of beach animals are negatively impacted and that numerous cascade effects are totally unstudied despite the routine assumption of no impacts. Published in the *Journal of Coastal Research*, vol. 16, no. 2, pp. 368–78.

53 "Beach Renourishment and Loggerhead Turtle Reproduction: A Seven Year Study at Jupiter Island, FL," by M. Steinitz, M. Salmon, and J. Wyneken, 1998, offers long-term data from a study by leading turtle researchers. The authors conclude that artificially filled beaches show complex utilization patterns by nesting sea turtles and that renour-

ishment may not be an adequate long-term management option. Published in the *Journal of Coastal Research*, vol. 14, no. 3, pp. 1000–1013.

Hazard Evaluation

54 *Living on the Edge of the Gulf: The West Florida and Alabama Coast*, by David M. Bush and others, 2001, 340 pp., is the Living with the Shore series companion volume to this East Florida book. Published by Duke University Press, Durham, NC. See also other books in the series on other coastal states of interest.

55 *Living by the Rules of the Sea*, by D. M. Bush, O. H. Pilkey, and W. J. Neal, 1996, is the umbrella volume for the Living with the Shore series. This 179-page book discusses coastal hazards, risk assessment, and property damage mitigation, outlining what both individuals and communities can do now to reduce the impact of the next storm.

56 *Beach/Inlet Processes and Management: A Florida Perspective*, edited by Ashish J. Mehta, 1993, is special issue 18 of the *Journal of Coastal Research*. This 308-page technical compilation includes 15 papers and four short technical communications. Among the many entries pertinent for East Florida are "An Overview of Southeast Florida Inlet Morphodynamics," by D. K. Stauble (pp. 1–27); "Inlets and Management Practices: Southeast Coast of Florida," by M. R. Dombrowski and A. J. Mehta (pp. 29–58); and "Pre-emptive Strategies for Enhanced Sand Bypassing and Beach Replenishment Activities in Southeast Florida: A Geological Perspective," by C. W. Finkl (pp. 59–89). Available from the Coastal Education and Research Foundation (http://www.cerf-jcr.com); the *Journal of Coastal Research*, P.O. Box 210187, Royal Palm Beach, FL 33421; or at university libraries. Also see *St. Augustine Beach Nourishment Project: Anastasia State Park, St. Augustine Beach, 1996 Phase I Report*, 1997, by K. A. Donohue and R. G. Dean, Coastal and Oceanographic Engineering Department, University of Florida, Gainesville, FL 32611.

57 *Evaluation of Erosion Hazards*, 2000, is a collaborative project of the H. John Heinz III Center for Science, Economics and the Environment prepared for FEMA. This 204-page report, prepared by an 18-member steering committee chaired by Stephen Leatherman, summarizes the coastal erosion hazard in the United States, reviews how we have dealt with erosion in the past, and offers several recommendations for developing coastal management options for the future. The report can be viewed at http://www.heinzcenter.org; or copies are available from FEMA.

58 "Identification of Unseen Flood Hazard Impacts in Southeast Florida through Integration of Remote Sensing and Geographic Information System Techniques," by Charles W. Finkl, 2000, is a technical paper published in the journal *Environmental Geosciences 7*, no. 3, pp. 119–36. This study used satellite images to classify land uses within flood hazard zones specifically for Broward County, Florida.

59 *Facing the Challenge* is the U.S. National Report on the International Decade of Natural Hazard Reduction, a world conference on natural hazard reduction held in Yokohama, Japan, on May 23–27, 1994. This 78-page report was published by the National Academy Press, Washington, D.C.

60 *Citizen's Guide to Geologic Hazards*, by E. B. Nuhfer and others, 1993. Written for the general public, this book discusses geological hazards in understandable terms. Available from the American Institute of Professional Geologists, 7828 Vance Drive, Suite 103, Arvada, CO 80003-2124, (303) 431-0831.

61 *Coastal Hazards: Perception, Susceptibility, and Mitigation*, edited by Charles W. Finkl Jr., 1994, is special issue 12 of the *Journal of Coastal Research*. This 372-page book features coastal issues such as hazard recognition and evaluation, sea-level rise, storms, tsunamis, effects of humans on coastal environments, effects of coastal hazards on natural features, and hazard mitigation. Published by the Coastal Education and Research Foundation;

available from the foundation (http://www.cerf-jcr.com); by writing to the *Journal of Coastal Research*, P.O. Box 210187, Royal Palm Beach, FL 33421; or at university libraries.

62 "Surviving the Horrific Hurricane of 1935," by Gene Burnett, April 1984, in *Florida Trend*, reprint 90.51.06 B8 s8 at the University of Florida Coastal Engineering Archives, is a "must" read for anyone who wants to live in the Keys. *Disasters by Design: A Reassessment of Natural Hazards in the United States*, by Dennis S. Mileti, 1999, presents the conclusions of the National Assessment of Research and Applications on Natural Hazards and discusses building disaster-resistant or sustainable communities as a basis for mitigation. It is available from the National Academy Press, Washington D.C., (800) 624-6242; it can be ordered online at http://www.nap.edu.

63 *Disasters and Democracy: The Politics of Extreme Natural Events*, by Rutherford H. Platt, 1999, delves into the evolution of natural hazard public policy in the United States. A wealth of information is contained in this 339-page book, published by Island Press of Washington, D.C., about the increase in the number of presidential disaster declarations and the federalization of the cost of disasters. Platt, one of the foremost authorities on natural hazard policy and legislation, asks whether federal involvement has helped or hurt in the long run.

64 *The Hidden Costs of Coastal Hazards: Implications for Risk Assessment and Mitigation* is a report from the H. John Heinz III Center for Science, Economics and the Environment. Published in 2000 by Island Press, Washington, D.C., this 220-page book presents the findings of a panel of experts convened to address the problem of the spiraling and often hidden costs of weather-related coastal hazards.

65 *Coastline at Risk: The Hurricane Threat to the Gulf and Atlantic States, 1992. Excerpts from the 14th Annual National Hurricane Conference.* Published by FEMA but compiled by and available from Lawrence S. Tait, National Hurricane Conference, 864 East Park Avenue, Tallahassee, FL 32301, (904) 561-1163. This 102-page booklet has five sections, including a report by Bob Sheets, former director of the National Hurricane Center, on the hurricane problem in the United States. See also "Expedient Assessments of Coastal Storm and Hurricane Damage Potential," by J. H. Balsillie, 2002, in *Environmental Geosciences*, vol. 9, pp. 102–8.

Coastal Management

General

66 *Beach Conditions in Florida: A Statewide Inventory and Identification of Beach Erosion Problem Areas in Florida*, 5th ed., 1993, Beaches and Shores Technical and Design Memorandum 89-1, pp. 1–17, 50–61; and "Beach Conditions in Florida: A Statewide Inventory and Identification of the Beach Erosion Problem Areas in Florida for Beach Management Planning, 1989," in *Proceedings of Beach Preservation Technology '89*, Tampa, FL, pp. 219–28. These detailed reports and revisions (1990, 1991, 1992), written by Ralph R. Clark of the FDEP Bureau of Beaches and Coastal Systems, systematically identify the beach erosion areas in all open-water coastal counties along the Atlantic and the Gulf of Mexico. Beach erosion problem areas are classified as either "critical" or "noncritical" according to whether or not substantial development or recreational interests on the shore are threatened. Beach lengths affected by erosion are given in miles on a county-by-county and island-by-island basis, and beaches affected by inlets are also noted. These reports are important tools for coastal engineers, public planners and managers, and anyone interested in the state of the coast. Updated in April 2002 and available online at http://www8.myflorida.com/beaches/publications/pdf/errptall.pdf. See also the Bureau of Beaches and Coastal Systems home page at http://www8.myflorida.com/beaches/.

67 *Florida Assessment of Coastal Trends—FACT,* 1997, prepared by the Florida Center for Public Management, G. T. Bergquist Jr., project director, is loaded with summary data on population growth, urban development, infrastructure, disruption of coastal processes, coastal impacts and hazards, changes and trends in ecosystems, water resources, recreational value, and related topics. Data are presented for the entire state without any breakdown by county or coast. The general trends, however, are sobering because more and more people and property are at risk at the expense of the natural environments and resources that are the basis of Florida's economy. This document is available on the Internet at http://www.fsu.edu/_cpm/FACT/index.html.

68 *Introduction to Coastal Zone Management,* by Timothy Beatley, David J. Brower, and Anna K. A. Schwab, 2002, published by Island Press, Washington, D.C., is a new edition of a comprehensive reference book useful for anyone working or interested in coastal management. Available from www.islandpress.org, in university libraries, or through your bookseller.

69 *Coastal Zone Management Handbook,* by John R. Clark, 1996, is a detailed manual and reference source for coastal resources planners and managers. This 694-page book was published by CRC Press, Inc., Boca Raton, FL, (800) 272-7737. In it you will find everything you want to know about the coast from development impacts to beach management to biotoxins to sewage treatment. Not for the casual reader, but recommended for your local coastal community's reference library.

70 *Managing Coastal Erosion,* by the Committee on Coastal Erosion Zone Management for the NRC, 1990, is a 182-page report on coastal erosion and its management written by a blue ribbon panel of experts. Chapters include "Coastal Erosion: Its Causes, Effects, and Distribution"; "Management and Approaches"; "The National Flood Insurance Program"; "State Programs and Experiences"; and "Predicting Future Shoreline Changes." Available from the National Academy Press, Washington, D.C.

71 *Coastal Erosion Mapping and Management,* edited by Mark Crowell and Stephen Leatherman, 1999, is special issue 28 of the *Journal of Coastal Research.* This 196-page compendium of 17 technical papers is a result of studies commissioned by FEMA. Papers pertinent to East Florida include "Evaluation of Coastal Erosion Hazards: An Overview," by Mark Crowell, Howard Leikin, and Michael K. Buckley (pp. 2–9); "Coastal Flood Hazards and the National Flood Insurance Program," by Doug Bellomo, Mary Jean Pajak, and Jerry Sparks (pp. 21–26); and "Projected Flood Hazard Zones in Florida," by Robert Dean and Subarna Malakar (pp. 85–94), which deals with three Florida counties including Brevard County on the east coast.

Storm Damage Mitigation

72 *Florida's History of Beach and Coast Preservation: The Early Years, 1910–1974,* by J. H. Balsillie, Florida Geological Survey, 1996, is an interesting in-depth report of beach and coast preservation activities in Florida that covers much of the twentieth century. Balsillie includes historical accounts of coastal work accomplished in other states (e.g., New Jersey) and by various federal, state, and local agencies and associations (e.g., the Florida Shore and Beach Preservation Association, established in the 1950s). He also describes the steps leading up to the establishment of Coastal Construction Setback Lines and lists the dates they were established for each county. Published in the *Proceedings of the 9th National Conference on Beach Preservation Technology,* pp. 350–68.

73 *Catastrophic Coastal Storms: Hazard Mitigation and Development Management,* by D. R. Godschalk, D. J. Brower, and T. Beatley, 1989, contains extensive information on mitigation and development management in at-risk coastal locations. This 450-page reference book was published by Duke University Press, Durham, NC.

74 "Hurricanes Gilbert and Hugo Send Powerful Messages for Coastal Development," by E. R. Thieler and D. M. Bush, 1991. This article, which appeared in the *Journal of Geological Education,* vol. 39, pp. 291–99, compares the characteristics and impacts of Hugo and Gilbert and discusses how the types and designs of buildings contributed to the damage.

Coastal Law and Public Involvement

75 *Florida Coastal Program Guide and Reference Book, 1997 Revision,* by the Florida Coastal Management Program, Department of Community Affairs, Tallahassee, outlines various programs relative to management and names the pertinent statutes.
76 The 1987 Florida Beach Management Act (chap. 161.161, Florida Statutes) mandated innovative and environmentally responsible approaches to erosion control.

Coastal Flooding

77 *Projected Impact of Relative Sea Level Rise on the National Flood Insurance Program,* by FEMA, 1991, concludes that coastal flood hazard areas will require periodic mapping to stay abreast of the sea-level rise, but that elevation requirements of the present NFIP program provide at least a 20-year cushion [to 2010] for study and adjustment of those construction elevation requirements. The 72-page report includes projections of numbers of households in the coastal floodplains through the year 2100. Produced by FEMA and the Federal Insurance Administration, Washington, D.C.
78 *How to Use a Flood Map to Protect Your Property: A Guide for Interested Private Citizens, Property Owners, Community Officials, Lending Institutions, and Insurance Agents,* 1994, is a 22-page tabloid-sized publication designed to help readers understand Flood Insurance Rate Maps (FIRMs), which establish the extent of flood hazards within a flood-prone community. Available from FEMA as publication FEMA-258. Also check the FEMA website (www.fema.gov) for publications available over the Internet.
79 *Questions and Answers on the National Flood Insurance Program,* by FEMA, 1983, publication FIA-2 (updated March 1992), explains the basics of flood insurance and provides addresses of FEMA offices. Also check the FEMA website (www.fema.gov) for publications available over the Internet.

Coastal Construction

Design

80 *Coastal Construction Manual: Principles and Practices of Planning, Siting, Designing, Constructing, and Maintaining Residential Buildings in Coastal Areas,* by FEMA, 2000. This complete guide to the coastal environment provides recommendations on site selection and structure design. Building codes, coastal environments, hazards, siting, and loads are discussed and examples included for all calculations. The work is the result of what has been learned from building failures in numerous hurricanes. Available on CD-ROM (publication FEMA-55CD) and as hard copy (publication FEMA-55) from FEMA or the U.S. Government Printing Office in Washington, D.C.
81 *Free of Obstruction: Requirements for Buildings Located in Coastal High Hazard Areas,* FEMA Technical Bulletin 5-93, considers the prevention of damage to coastal buildings resulting from obstructions underneath the buildings. Complies with NFIP requirements. Available from FEMA.
82 *Hurricane-Resistant Construction for Homes,* by Todd L. Walton Jr. and Michael R. Barnett, 1991, gives guidelines for wood-frame, masonry, and brick construction; pole

houses; and special considerations such as roofs, doors, glass, shutters, and siding. Available as Bulletin 16 (MAP-16) from Florida Sea Grant College Program, University of Florida, Gainesville.

83 *Building Performance: Hurricane Andrew in Florida; Observations, Recommendations, and Technical Guidance,* by FEMA and Federal Insurance Administration, 1992. This booklet includes background information about the storm, on-site observations of the damaged area, and recommendations for reducing future damage. Available from FEMA as publication FIA-22.

84 *Building Performance Assessment: Hurricane Fran in North Carolina; Observations, Recommendations, and Technical Guidance,* by FEMA, 1997, assesses the problems that occurred during Hurricane Fran in North Carolina. The recommendations on how to avoid similar problems in the future are particularly useful. Available from FEMA as document FEMA-290.

85 *Building Performance Assessment Report: Hurricane Georges in the Gulf Coast; Building on Success—Observations, Recommendations, and Technical Guidance,* 1999, is a report similar to the one listed in reference 84. Of particular note are the separate treatments of each state affected and the detailed illustrations. Publication FEMA-338, 110 pp.; free from FEMA.

Wind Resistance

86 *Connectors for High Wind–Resistant Structures: Retrofit and New Construction,* 1992, Simpson Strong-Tie Company, Inc.

87 *Hurricane Resistant Construction Manual,* 1988, Southern Building Code Congress International, Inc., Birmingham, Alabama.

88 *Wind and the Built Environment: U.S. Needs in Wind Engineering and Hazard Mitigation,* report of the Panel on the Assessment of Wind Engineering Issues in the United States, for the Committee on Natural Disasters, NRC, 1993, 110 pp. State-of-the-art report on wind hazards by a panel of experts. Chapters include "The Nature of Wind"; "Wind Engineering Research Needs"; "Mitigation, Preparedness, Response, and Recovery"; "Education and Technology Transfer"; and "Cooperative Efforts." Available from National Academy Press, Washington, D.C.

89 *Against the Wind,* 1993, is a six-page brochure with summary information about protecting your home from hurricane wind damage. Developed jointly by the American Red Cross, FEMA, Home Depot, the National Association of Home Builders of the United States, and the Georgia Emergency Management Agency, it briefly discusses roof systems, exterior doors and windows, garage doors, and shutters. Available from the American Red Cross (publication ARC-5023) and FEMA (publication FEMA-247).

90 "Wind Conditions in Hurricane Hugo and Their Effect on Buildings in Coastal South Carolina," by P. R. Sparks, *Journal of Coastal Research,* special issue 8, pp. 12–24, gives a good evaluation of how and why buildings failed in Hurricane Hugo and why the Standard Building Code's wind-resistance requirements were inadequate. Available through university libraries.

91 *Wind-Resistant Design Concepts for Residents,* by Delbart B. Ward. Vivid sketches and illustrations explain construction problems and methods of tying structures to the ground. This pamphlet offers recommendations for relatively inexpensive modifications that will increase the safety of residences subject to severe winds. Out of print, but may still be available at major libraries.

92 *Interim Guidelines for Building Occupant Protection from Tornadoes and Extreme Winds,* TR-83A, and *Tornado Protection-Selecting and Designing Safe Areas in Buildings,* TR-83B, are supplements to reference 91 and are available from the same addresses.

93 *Retrofitting and Flood Mitigation in Florida,* 1995. Available from the Florida Department of Community Affairs, State Assistance Office for the National Flood Insurance Program.

94 *Minimum Design Loads for Buildings and Other Structures,* American Society of Civil Engineers, 1995, ASCE standard 7-95. Contains criteria for calculating flood loads and for combining these with other loads. This standard meets, and in some cases exceeds, the National Flood Insurance Program requirements. Builders and design engineers should be familiar with this highly technical set of standards for construction. Available from the American Society of Civil Engineers, 345 E. 47th Street, New York, NY 10017-2398.

95 *Mitigation of Flood and Erosion Damage to Residential Buildings in Coastal Areas,* by FEMA, 1994. This report on flood-proofing investigations includes some case studies and is a good starting point to review flood-proofing techniques; includes additional reading list. Available from FEMA as publication FEMA-257.

96 *Flood Resistant Design and Construction Practices,* 1997, ASCE standard. This standard provides recommendations for design and construction of buildings that will resist flood loadings. These recommendations meet or exceed the minimum requirements of the National Flood Insurance Program. Available from the ASCE; see reference 94 for address.

Building Codes

97 *Florida Building Code,* 2001, is published as chapter 2001-186 in *Laws of Florida.* Several building codes, with varying jurisdictions, have been in effect over the years in Florida. The 2001 code was an attempt to provide a unified building code for Florida with up-to-date hurricane-resistant construction design requirements. See links from the MyFlorida.com website for details and future updates.

Pole-House Construction

98 *Elevated Residential Structures,* prepared by the American Institute of Architects Foundation (1735 New York Avenue N.W., Washington, DC 20006) for FEMA, 1984. This report outlines coastal and riverine flood hazards and the need for proper planning and construction, and discusses the NFIP, site analysis and design, design examples, and construction techniques. It includes illustrations, glossary, references, and worksheets for estimating building costs. Available from FEMA as FEMA-54.

99 *Pole House Construction and Pole Building Design.* Available from the American Wood Preservers Institute, 1651 Old Meadows Road, McLean, VA 22101.

Mobile Homes

100 *A Study of Reaction Forces on Mobile Home Foundations Caused by Wind and Flood Loads,* by Felix Y. Yokel and others, 1981. This technical report from the National Bureau of Standards emphasizes that diagonal ties resist wind forces while vertical ties are more effective for resisting flood forces. NBS Building Science Series 132, available from the U.S. Government Printing Office, Washington, D.C.

101 *Protecting Mobile Homes from High Winds,* document TR-75, prepared by the Civil Defense Preparedness Agency, 1974. This excellent 16-page booklet outlines methods of tying down mobile homes and other means of protection such as positioning and windbreaks. Out of print, but may still be available at major libraries. See also *Wind Load Provisions of the Manufactured Home Construction and Safety Standards: A Review and Recommendations for Improvement,* 1993, which contains the results of a Department of

Housing and Urban Development (HUD)–supported study performed by the National Institute of Standards and Technology (NIST). Wind load design criteria for manufactured homes were studied based on the effects of Hurricane Andrew (1992). Concludes that manufactured homes built after the Manufactured Home and Construction and Safety Standards and accompanying HUD labels were issued experienced less damage than did units constructed prior to these standards. In general, conventional residential homes fared better than manufactured homes, including those with HUD labels. The report concludes that ASCE standard 7-95 is the most logical reference to provide a basis for wind load design criteria. This report was authored by R. D. Marshall and is available from National Technical Information Service, NISTIR 5189.

Other Publications and Newsletters

Publications List, Coastal Engineering Research Center and Beach Erosion Board, by the U.S. Army Corps of Engineers, is a list (updated periodically) of published research by the U.S. Army Corps of Engineers. Free from the USACE. Lists of earlier publications are available from the same library.

FEMA Publications Catalog, by FEMA, 2000, is a booklet listing more than 300 publications available from FEMA to assist everyone from individual property owners to emergency managers. This list is updated periodically, so ask for the most recent catalog. Request publication FEMA-20 from the FEMA Publications Distribution Center at (800) 480-2520. Publications can be ordered online. Many popular FEMA publications and reports are available online in Adobe Acrobat (.pdf) format. Check the online FEMA library (www.fema.gov/library) and the regular FEMA publication list (www.fema.gov/pubs), or call the FEMA Publications Distribution Center at (800) 480-2520.

Publications of the Natural Hazards Research and Applications Information Center, Boulder, Colorado. The center is a national clearinghouse of research and public policy on hazards. Visit the website at http://www.colorado.edu/hazards. Hundreds of publications are available covering all aspects of natural hazard preparedness, response, mitigation, and planning. A monthly magazine, *Natural Hazards Observer,* has a wealth of information, and the *Natural Hazards Informer* contains peer-reviewed reports. Contact the NHRAIC Publications Clerk, Campus Box 482, University of Colorado, Boulder, CO 80309-0482, (303) 492-6818.

Videos and CD-ROMs

Living on the Edge, a one-hour VHS video, is a consumer's guide to the special problems inherent in buying and owning property on the shoreline and includes a coastal risk assessment field guide. Produced by Environmental Media in association with the Duke University Department of Geology. *The Beaches Are Moving* is a one-hour VHS video providing an introductory course in barrier island geology by Professor Orrin Pilkey, the director of the Program for the Study of Developed Shorelines at Duke University. To order either video, contact Environmental Media, P.O. Box 99, Beaufort, SC 29901, (800) 368-3382 or (803) 986-9034; http://www.envmedia.com.

A House Built on Sand: Common Sense Rules for Buying and Building in Florida's Coastal High-Hazard Area, 1997, and *Against the Tide: When Permanent Structures Encounter a Moving Shoreline,* 1997, are available from the Florida Department of Community Affairs, Florida Coastal Management Program.

Andrew! Savagery from the Sea! by the staff of the *Fort Lauderdale Sun-Sentinel,* 1992, is available for $9.99 from Tribune Publishing, P.O. Box 1100, Orlando, FL 32802-1100, ISBN 0-941263-71-1.

Hurricane Andrew, August 24, 1993, as It Happened. Contact WTVJ-4 News, Miami. Bryan Norcross (800) 551-1010.

Coastal Vulnerability to Sea-Level Rise: A Preliminary Database for the U.S. Atlantic, Pacific, and Gulf of Mexico Coasts (U.S. Geological Survey Digital Data Series DDS-68), by Erika Hammar-Klose and E. Robert Thieler, 2001, is a CD-ROM produced by and available from the USGS.

The Coastal Services Center of NOAA in Charleston, SC, has several CD-ROMs dealing with coastal hazards, assessment, and vulnerability. See especially: *Community Vulnerability Assessment Tool: New Hanover County, North Carolina,* NOAA/CSC/99044-CD. Available from the Coastal Services Center (http://www.csc.noaa.gov/) or by calling (843) 740-1200.

Hurricanes, How to Prepare and Recover: A Permanent Guide to Make Your Home Safe, 1993, is an informative compilation of stories, photographs, and illustrations by the staff of the *Miami Herald.* Published by Andrews McMeel Publishing, Kansas City, MO, 125 pages.

Index

Key Biscayne Inlet, 7
Key Colony Beach, 236, 239
Key Largo, 232, 236, 239, 242. *See also* Florida
  Keys
Key Largo Limestone, 234. *See also* Coquina
Key West, 2, 3, 20, 22, 43, 232, 233, 236, 241,
  244, 245. *See also* Florida Keys
Key West Lighthouse, 22
Kings Bay, 229

Lake Mable, 8
Lake Okeechobee, 191
Lake Rogers, 215
Lake Worth, 8, 50, 134, 212
Lake Worth Inlet, 50, 79, 113, 207, 208, 211, 212
Lake Worth Sand Transfer Plant, 112
Land-use planning, 279
Lauderdale-by-the-Sea, 216
Lighthouse Point Park, 174
Lighthouses, 21, 22, 45; relocated, 85
Limestone, 8, 12, 50; bedrock, 101; island, 232;
  platform, 236
Little Talbot Island, 7, 52, 147
Long Key, 232, 236
Longshore current, 45, 62–64, 76, 77
Longshore sand transport, 49, 50, 58, 77, 79
Lower Keys, 232, 234, 236. *See also* Florida
  Keys
Lower Matecumbe Key, 236. *See also* Florida
  Keys
Loxahatchee River, 212

Magnuson Stevens Fishery Conservation and
  Management Act (MSFCMA), 289
Main Beach, 145
Maine, 36
Mangrove, 16, 17, 137, 193, 236, 237; black, 236;
  coast, 50; red, 236; shorelines, 127; white,
  236
Manhattan Beach, 151
Manufactured homes, 255, 274. *See also* Con-
  struction
Marathon, 238
Marineland, 165
Maritime forest, 17, 127, 132, 141
Marquesas Keys, 233. *See also* Florida Keys
Marsh grasses, 129. *See also* Salt marsh
Martin County, 14, 49, 108, 195, 199, 204, 205
Masonry-walled houses, 256, 269, 270. *See*
  also Construction

Matanzas Inlet, 7, 153, 156, 164
Matanzas River, 134, 165
Matecumbes (Upper and Lower), 232. *See*
  also Florida Keys
Mayport, 147, 150, 152
Mayport Naval Station, 152
McLarty State Museum, 179
Melbourne, 52, 181
Melbourne Beach, 8, 177, 182, 183
Melbourne Causeway, 183
Merritt Causeway, 183
Menendez de Aviles, Pedro, 19
Merritt Island, 52
Miami, 19, 20, 21, 24, 38, 50, 54, 108, 112, 138,
  229, 231, 232
Miami Beach, 3, 8, 19, 20, 50, 65, 73, 77, 88, 97,
  101, 107, 108, 116, 222, 224, 226, 227, 232
Miami Oolite Formation, 234
Mickler Landing, 153
Middens, 18
Middle Keys, 232, 236. *See also* Florida
  Keys
Minimum base elevation, 281
Missiling, 45, 255
Missouri Buyout Program, 98
Mitigation of storm damage, 123, 140–141,
  282
Mobile homes, 255, 274. *See also* Construc-
  tion
Modular units, 276. *See also* Construction
Monroe County, 50, 126, 142, 232
Mosquito Inlet lighthouse, 22
Mosquito Lagoon, 57, 134, 177
Myrtle Beach, 84

Nassau County, 49, 142, 146, 147
Nassau Sound, 142, 147, 150
Nassau Sound Inlet, 7
National Climate Data Center, 40
National Environmental Policy Act of 1969,
  229, 288
National Flood Insurance Act of 1968, 279
National Flood Insurance Program, 126, 251,
  255, 264, 266, 279, 281, 282
National Flood Insurance Reform Act of
  1994, 282
National Flood Mitigation Fund, 282
National Hurricane Center, 37, 39, 41, 126, 253
National Marine Fisheries Service, 284, 290
National Oceanic and Atmospheric Admin-

South Florida Building Code, 251, 253
South Hutchinson Island, 60
South Lake Worth, 113
South Lake Worth Inlet, 211, 212
South Palm Beach, 205, 211, 215
South Ponte Vedra, 155
South Ponte Vedra Beach, 153, 160
South Roosevelt Boulevard, 236
Southwesters, 43. *See also* Northeasters;
    Storm(s)
Spanish Harbor, 235
Spartina, 129. *See also* Marsh grasses; Salt
    marsh
Spits, 52, 53, 121
Standard Building Code, 251, 272
State Minimum Building Codes, 251
St. Augustine, 19, 41, 100, 156, 160, 164, 173
St. Augustine Beach, 153–156, 160, 162, 164
St. Augustine Inlet, 1, 150, 153, 156, 162
St. Augustine lighthouse, 22
St. Johns County, 49, 150, 153, 155, 156, 159,
    160, 162, 165, 169, 173
St. Johns Inlet jetty, 152
St. Johns River, 147; jetty, 150; 152; lighthouse,
    22
St. Lucie County, 49, 193, 195, 196, 199
St. Lucie Inlet, 49, 110, 199, 203, 204
St. Lucie Inlet State Park, 199
St. Lucie Locks hurricane (1947), 204
St. Lucie River, 204
St. Marys River, 1, 142, 146, 147
Storm(s), 67; construction, 249; currents, 45;
    frequency, 66; 100-year storm, 287; over-
    wash, 57; processes, 45; protection, 86, 92,
    257, 271; surge, 46, 47, 61, 69, 83, 90, 92, 120,
    126, 131, 133, 134; surge flooding, 126, 127,
    133, 134; surge scour, 141; waves, 65
Storm (by date or name): 1947 (October),
    173; 1956 (October), 159; 1962 (November),
    159, 180; 1974 (October), 180; 1981, 146, 180,
    196, 215; 1983, 146, 180; Ash Wednesday
    storm (March 1962), 146, 150, 152, 153, 159,
    162, 173, 180, 196; Lincoln's Birthday storm
    (February 1973), 146, 160, 180, 191; Storm of
    the Century (March 1993), 43, 249;
    Thanksgiving storm (November 1984),
    146, 160, 165, 174, 191; Yankee storm (1935),
    218. *See also* Northeasters; Winter storms
Storm-surge ebb, 45, 47, 69, 70, 95; currents,
    134
Straits of Florida, 229, 236

Stronge, W. B., 16
Stuart Beach, 60, 204
Structure, building: discontinuities, 258;
    engineering design, 251; integrity, 253, 271.
    See also Construction
Stuart Beach, 60, 204
Sugarloaf Key, 238
Summer Haven, 154, 159, 160, 162, 164; revet-
    ment, 153
Summerland Key, 238, 242
Sunny Isles, 222
Surf zone, 64, 69, 90; processes, 73
Surfside, 108, 222
Sustainable Fishery Acts, 118
Suwannee Channel, 4

Talbot Island, 3
Tallahassee, 232
Ten Thousand Islands, 41
Texas, 36, 56, 293
T-groins, 77. *See also* Shoreline: engineering,
    hard stabilization
Tidal delta, 15, 56, 57, 65
Tidal inlet, 50
Tie-downs, 255, 262, 263, 272, 274. *See also*
    Construction
Titusville, 179
Tolomato River, 153
Tombolo, 76
Torch Keys, 238
Trail Ridge, 59
Tropical storm, 30, 34; Alberto (1992), 249;
    Beryl (1992), 249; Gilda (October 1973),
    173, 174, 191. *See also* Northeasters;
    Storm(s); Winter storms
Turbidity, 90, 102, 109, 111, 113, 119, 291; aver-
    age, 115; chronic, 117, 119; clouds, 108, 110,
    111; elevated, 114, 115; plumes, 112
Turtles. *See* Sea turtles

Upper Keys, 232, 234, 236, 238. *See also*
    Florida Keys
Upper Matecumbe Key, 238
Upton-Jones Amendment, 281, 282
U.S. Army Corps of Engineers (USACE), 88,
    90, 91, 103, 107, 113, 118, 126, 134, 152, 162,
    174, 181, 196, 204, 212, 216, 284, 289; *Coast of
    Florida* study, 110; evacuation study, 229
U.S. Department of the Interior, 282
U.S. Fish and Wildlife Service, 14, 283, 284,
    289, 290

U.S. Geological Survey, 283
Usinas, 160
Usinas Beach, 153

Vaca Key, 232, 238, 244
Vegetation, 58, 120
Vero Beach, 41, 102, 189, 191, 193
Vilano, 160
Vilano Beach, 153, 162, 164
Virginia Key, 101, 224, 227, 229
Virginia Beach, Virginia, 91, 92
Volusia County, 19, 49, 164, 165, 169, 172, 173, 175–177
Vulnerability, 120, 127, 137, 140, 249
v zone, 141, 266, 280, 287. *See also* Flood Insurance Rate Maps; National Flood Insurance Program

Wabasso Beach, 189, 193
Water: pollution, 100; quality, 116, 117, 119
Waterspouts, 44
Waves: attack, 70, 95, 127, 141; cause of ero-sion, 120, 133; energy, 50, 61; height, 49, 50; refraction, 88
West Palm Beach, 21
Wilbur-by-the-Sea, 169, 175
Wind, 45, 120; force, 252, 258; load, 257; pressure, 252; storm, 44; velocities, 252. *See also* Storm(s)
Windley Key, 232
Windows, 257, 271. *See also* Construction
Winter storms, 43, 115. *See also* Northeasters; Storm(s)

x500 zone, 280. *See also* Flood Insurance Rate Maps; National Flood Insurance Program
x zone, 141, 280. *See also* Flood Insurance Rate Maps; National Flood Insurance Program

Zoning, 67, 68; A zone, 141, 266; B zone, 280; C zone, 280; V zone, 141, 266, 280, 287; x zone, 141, 280

Library of Congress Cataloging-in-Publication Data
Bush, David M.
Living with Florida's Atlantic Beaches : coastal hazards from
Amelia Island to Key West / by David M. Bush . . . [et al.].
p. cm.—(Living with the shore)
Includes bibliographical references and index.
ISBN 0-8223-3251-5 (cloth : alk. paper)
ISBN 0-8223-3289-2 (pbk. : alk. paper)
1. Shore protection—Florida—Atlantic Coast. 2. Coastal zone
management—Florida—Atlantic Coast. 3. Coast changes—
Florida—Atlantic Coast. 4. Beach erosion—Florida—Atlantic
Coast. 5. Storms—Florida—Atlantic Coast. 6. Atlantic Coast
(Fla.)—Environmental conditions. I. Title. II. Series.
TC224.F6B87 2004   333.91'7'09759—dc22   2003021428